Living & Working in
SPAIN

● A Survival Handbook ●

David Hampshire

Survival Books ● London ● England

First published 1995
Second Edition 1998
Third Edition 2000
Fourth Edition 2003
Fifth Edition 2004
Sixth Edition 2006
Seventh Edition 2007
Eighth Edition 2009

Copyright © Survival Books 1995, 1998, 2000, 2003, 2004, 2006, 2007, 2009
Cover photograph: Canteras Beach, Las Palmas,
Gran Canaria © spanishalex (🖥 www.dreamstime.com)
Illustrations and maps © Jim Watson

Survival Books Limited
26 York Street, London W1U 6PZ, United Kingdom
☎ +44 (0)20-7788 7644, 🖶 +44 (0)870-762 3212
✉ info@survivalbooks.net
🖥 www.survivalbooks.net

British Library Cataloguing in Publication Data
A CIP record for this book is available
from the British Library.
ISBN: 978-1-905303-65-6

Printed and bound in India by Ajanta Offset

Acknowledgements

M y sincere thanks to all those who contributed to the successful publication of this eighth edition of *Living and Working in Spain* and previous editions of this book. I would particularly like to thank Joanna Styles (research and updating), Joe and Kerry Laredo (editing and proofreading) and Di Tolland (desktop publishing). I would also like to thank Catherine Wakelin, Charles Peard Clarke, Ron and Pat Scarborough, Pam Miller, Charles King, John Knight, Veronica Orchard, Adèle Kelham and everyone else who contributed to this and previous editions. Also a special thank you to Jim Watson for the superb illustrations, maps and cover design, and to the many photographers (listed on page 374), whose beautiful images add colour and bring Spain to life.

What readers & reviewers have said about Survival Books:

'If you need to find out how France works then this book is indispensable. Native French people probably have a less thorough understanding of how their country functions.'

Living France

'It's everything you always wanted to ask but didn't for fear of the contemptuous put down. The best English-language guide. Its pages are stuffed with practical information on everyday subjects and are designed to compliment the traditional guidebook.'

Swiss News

'Rarely has a 'survival guide' contained such useful advice – This book dispels doubts for first-time travellers, yet is also useful for seasoned globetrotters – In a word, if you're planning to move to the US or go there for a long-term stay, then buy this book both for general reading and as a ready-reference.'

American Citizens Abroad

'Let's say it at once. David Hampshire's Living and Working in France is the best handbook ever produced for visitors and foreign residents in this country; indeed, my discussion with locals showed that it has much to teach even those born and bred in l'Hexagone – It is Hampshire's meticulous detail which lifts his work way beyond the range of other books with similar titles. Often you think of a supplementary question and search for the answer in vain. With Hampshire this is rarely the case. – He writes with great clarity (and gives French equivalents of all key terms), a touch of humour and a ready eye for the odd (and often illuminating) fact. – This book is absolutely indispensable.'

The Riviera Reporter

'A must for all future expats. I invested in several books but this is the only one you need. Every issue and concern is covered, every daft question you have but are frightened to ask is answered honestly without pulling any punches. Highly recommended.'

Reader

'In answer to the desert island question about the one how-to book on France, this book would be it.'

The Recorder

'The ultimate reference book. Every subject imaginable is exhaustively explained in simple terms. An excellent introduction to fully enjoy all that this fine country has to offer and save time and money in the process.'

American Club of Zurich

'The amount of information covered is not short of incredible. I thought I knew enough about my birth country. This book has proved me wrong. Don't go to France without it. Big mistake if you do. Absolutely priceless!'

Reader

'When you buy a model plane for your child, a video recorder, or some new computer gizmo, you get with it a leaflet or booklet pleading 'Read Me First', or bearing large friendly letters or bold type saying 'IMPORTANT - follow the instructions carefully'. This book should be similarly supplied to all those entering France with anything more durable than a 5-day return ticket. – It is worth reading even if you are just visiting briefly, or if you have lived here for years and feel totally knowledgeable and secure. But if you need to find out how France works then it is indispensable. Native French people probably have a less thorough understanding of how their country functions. – Where it is most essential, the book is most up to the minute.

Living France

A comprehensive guide to all things French, written in a highly readable and amusing style, for anyone planning to live, work or retire in France.

The Times

Covers every conceivable question that might be asked concerning everyday life – I know of no other book that could take the place of this one.

France in Print

A concise, thorough account of the Do's and DONT's for a foreigner in Switzerland – Crammed with useful information and lightened with humorous quips which make the facts more readable.

American Citizens Abroad

'I found this a wonderful book crammed with facts and figures, with a straightforward approach to the problems and pitfalls you are likely to encounter. The whole laced with humour and a thorough understanding of what's involved. Gets my vote!'

Reader

'A vital tool in the war against real estate sharks; don't even think of buying without reading this book first!'

Everything Spain

'We would like to congratulate you on this work: it is really super! We hand it out to our expatriates and they read it with great interest and pleasure.'

ICI (Switzerland) AG

Important Note

S pain is a large country with myriad faces and many ethnic groups, religions and customs. Although ostensibly the same throughout the country, many rules and regulations are open to local interpretation, and are occasionally even formulated on the spot. Laws and regulations have also been changing at a considerable rate in recent years. I cannot recommend too strongly that you check with an official and reliable source (not always the same) before making any major decisions or undertaking an irreversible course of action. However, don't believe everything you're told or read, even, dare I say it, herein!

Useful addresses and references to other sources of information have been included in all chapters and **Appendices A, B** and **C** to help you obtain further information and verify data with official sources. Important points have been emphasised, some of which it would be expensive or even dangerous to disregard. **Ignore them at your peril or cost!**

Note

Unless specifically stated, the reference to any company, organisation or product in this book doesn't constitute an endorsement or recommendation. None of the businesses, products or individuals mentioned in this book have paid to be mentioned.

Contents

Authors Notes

◆ Frequent references are made in this book to the European Union (EU) which comprises Austria, Belgium, Bulgaria, Cyprus, the Czech Republic, Denmark, Estonia, Finland, France, Germany, Greece, Hungary, Ireland, Italy, Latvia, Lithuania, Luxembourg, Malta, the Netherlands, Poland, Portugal, Rumania, Slovakia, Slovenia, Spain, Sweden and the UK. The EU countries plus Iceland, Liechtenstein and Norway comprise the European Economic Area (EEA).

◆ References to the Spanish language mean Castilian, spoken as a first or second language throughout Spain, unless otherwise stated (see **Language** on page 117).

◆ Spanish place names (shown in brackets below) are often written differently in English, as in this book, e.g. Andalusia (*Andalucía*), Alicante (*Alacant*), Cadiz (*Cádiz*), Cordoba (*Córdoba*), Malaga (*Málaga*), Majorca (*Mallorca*), San Sebastian (*San Sebastián*), Seville (*Sevilla*) and Zaragossa (*Zaragoza*).

◆ Times are shown using am (Latin: ante meridiem) for before noon and pm (post meridiem) for after noon, e.g. 10am and 10pm.

◆ Prices quoted should be taken only as estimates, although they were mostly correct when going to print and fortunately don't usually change significantly overnight. Most prices in Spain are quoted inclusive of value added tax (IVA incluido), which is the method used in this book unless otherwise indicated (e.g. más IVA).

◆ His/he/him/man/men, etc. also mean her/she/her/woman/women, etc. This is done simply to make life easier for both the reader and the author, and **isn't** intended to be sexist.

◆ The Spanish translation of key words and phrases is shown in brackets in italics, and warnings and important points are shown in **bold** type.

◆ The following symbols are used in this book: ☎ (telephone), 📄 (fax), 🖥 (Internet) and ✉ (email).

◆ Lists of **Useful Addresses**, **Further Reading** and **Useful Websites** are contained in **Appendices A**, **B** and **C** respectively.

◆ For those unfamiliar with the Spanish system of **Weights and Measures**, conversion tables (Imperial/metric) are included in **Appendix D**.

◆ A physical map of Spain is shown inside the front cover and a map showing the regions and provinces is inside the back cover.

Platja d'Aro beach, Costa Brava

Introduction

Whether you're already living or working in Spain or just thinking about it – this is **THE BOOK** for you. *Living and Working in Spain* is designed to meet the needs of anyone wishing to know the essentials of Spanish life – however long your intended stay, you'll find the information contained in this book invaluable. Since the first edition was published in 1995, *Living and Working in Spain* has been the most comprehensive and up-to-date book available to people planning a new life in Spain and it's the only one revised annually or biennially. Furthermore, this updated and fully revised 8th edition is printed in full colour.

Since Spain joined the European Union in 1986, the country has altered beyond recognition and each year brings further changes as Spain catches up with its more advanced fellow members. These are the changes nepwcomers need to know about and this is the book that informs you about them! Inside you'll find the latest information on taxes, residence and work procedures; regional health services, prices and procedures, as well as a wealth of other essential information to help you make a success of your time in Spain.

You may have visited Spain as a tourist, but living and working there is another matter altogether. Adjusting to a different environment and culture and making a home in any foreign country can be a traumatic and stressful experience, and Spain is no exception. You need to adapt to new customs and traditions and discover the Spanish way of doing things, for example finding a home, paying bills and obtaining insurance. As anyone who has lived in Spain knows only too well, accurate, up-to-date information for newcomers is difficult to find, particularly in the English language. My aim in writing this book was to help fill this void and provide the comprehensive practical information necessary for a relatively trouble-free life.

Living and Working in Spain is designed to help reduce your 'beginner's' phase and minimise the frustrations, and will help you make informed decisions and calculated judgements, rather than uneducated guesses and costly mistakes. Most important of all, it will help you save time, trouble and money, and will repay your investment many times over.

Although you may find some of the information a bit daunting, don't be discouraged. Most problems occur once only and fade into insignificance after a short time (as you face the next half a dozen!). The majority of foreigners in Spain would agree that, all things considered, they relish living there. A period spent in Spain is a wonderful way to enrich your life, broaden your horizons and hopefully please your bank manager. I trust that this book will help you avoid the pitfalls of life in Spain and smooth your way to a happy and rewarding future in your new home.

¡Mucha suerte!

David Hampshire

September 2008

1.

FINDING A JOB

F inding a job in Spain isn't easy, particularly outside the major cities, where unemployment is high in many regions. Furthermore, if you don't qualify to live and work in Spain by birthright or as a national of a European Union (EU) country, obtaining a residence permit (see page 54) can be more difficult than finding work. Americans and other foreigners without the automatic right to work in Spain must have their employment approved by the Spanish Ministry of Labour (Ministerio de Trabajo) and obtain a visa before entering Spain. All EU nationals have the same employment rights as Spanish citizens, with the exception of nationals from Bulgaria and Romania, who require a work permit.

Spain attracts few migrants compared with the UK, France and Germany, although the number of foreign residents has been increasing considerably every year since 2001 and over 11 per cent of the Spanish population is now foreign. There's also a large 'floating' population of unregistered foreigners. Just under 40 per cent of foreign residents in Spain come from the EU, the vast majority of these from the UK, Germany and Romania; in some provinces (particularly Malaga and Alicante) over 60 per cent of foreign residents are from the EU.

Many Spaniards also work abroad, notably in France, Germany and Switzerland, and Spain imports low-paid workers from Morocco (the largest group of foreign residents), Colombia, Ecuador and Eastern Europe (mainly Ukraine). Spain (particularly the Canaries and coastal Andalusia) is a key entry point for North African immigrants into Europe, many of whom enter the country illegally.

ECONOMY

Spain has experienced an economic 'miracle' in the last few decades, during which it has been transformed from a basically agricultural country into a modern industrial nation. However, its economic fortunes have been somewhat up and down, with two massive booms – during the '80s and from 1998 to 2006 – and two slumps. The first slump, during the '90s, was severe, as it was in much of the developed world; the second began in late 2007 and was forecast to last at least until late 2009. After three years of the strongest growth rate among the original 15 members of the EU (3.8 per cent in 2007), Spain entered economic decline mainly due a slowdown in the building industry and the effects of the global recession triggered by the US 'sub-prime' mortgage crisis.

The Organisation for Economic Co-operation and Development (OECD) forecasts 1.6 per cent growth for 2008 and 1.1 per cent for 2009. Government predictions are (not surprisingly) more optimistic, the Ministry of the Economy forecasting growth of just over 2 per cent in 2008. However, many experts believe that there won't be another recession and that Spain's economy will start to recover in late 2009 or early 2010.

Unemployment

The recent strength of the Spanish economy had a dramatic impact on its unemployment rate, which fell from over 20 per cent in the '80s to under 9 per cent in 2007. However, the current economic slump has affected the unemployment rate, which reached 9.6 per cent in June 2008, the second highest in the EU. Unemployment is high and rising in the construction and service industries, the 'engines' of growth in Spain, and is expected to near 11 per cent during 2009. Unemployment is high among those aged 20 to 29 (who represent over 40 per cent of the unemployed) and foreigners, almost 14 per cent of whom are registered as unemployed.

The unemployed are often unskilled or even illiterate, although a significant percentage of university graduates are also unemployed. Unemployment in some areas is much higher than the national average. Andalusia, Extremadura and the Canaries are the regions with the highest unemployment rates (between 14 and 15 per cent), while Aragón, Navarra and the Basque Country have the lowest rates (between 5.6 and 6 per cent).

Unemployment has a particularly debilitating effect on the Spanish economy on account of the high social security benefits claimed by those out of work. Reducing unemployment continues to be one of the government's main priorities.

Workforce

Spanish workers have an affluent lifestyle compared with just a decade ago, and employees (particularly executives and senior managers) enjoy high salaries and good working conditions. Spain has a reasonably self-sufficient labour market and doesn't require a large number of skilled or unskilled foreign workers. Women have professional and salary equality with men, although they still fill most low-paid jobs. However, workers' security has been seriously eroded in recent years with an increasing number of workers employed on short-term rather than indefinite contracts. Many Spaniards (particularly low-paid civil servants) hold down two jobs and work overtime and extra shifts in order to pay their bills.

Industrial Relations

Spain has traditionally had more strikes (*huelgas*) and lost more production days due to strikes in the last few decades than any country in the EU, but industrial relations have improved dramatically in recent years, during

which the number of working hours lost to strikes has been reduced by over 20 per cent. Despite the squeeze on pay rises to meet the European Monetary Union (EMU) criteria and qualify for the single currency (in 2002), there has been little industrial unrest in the last few years and in 2007 there were around 750 strikes (down 4 per cent on 2006).

In June 2008, the country almost came to a standstill when lorry drivers and fishermen went on strike in protest against rising fuel prices. Factories and building sites were forced to shut down due to lack of supplies, and panic buying by consumers led to empty petrol stations and supermarket shelves. The situation was brought under control after massive intervention by the police, who escorted non-striking lorry drivers to their destinations.

EMPLOYMENT PROSPECTS

You shouldn't plan on obtaining employment in Spain unless you have a firm job offer, exceptional qualifications or experience for which there's a strong demand. If you want a good job, you must usually be well qualified and speak fluent Spanish. If you intend to arrive in Spain without a job, you should have a detailed plan for finding employment and try to make some contacts before your arrival. Being attracted to Spain by its weather and lifestyle is understandable but doesn't rate highly as an employment qualification! It's almost impossible to find work in rural areas (apart from low-paid farm work) and it isn't easy in cities and large towns, particularly if your Spanish isn't fluent.

Many people turn to self-employment or starting a business to make a living, although this path is strewn with pitfalls for the unwary.

Many foreigners don't do sufficient homework before moving to Spain. The secret to successful relocation is research, research and more research!

While hoping for the best, you should prepare for the worst and ensure that you have a contingency plan and sufficient funds to last until you're established. Before arriving in Spain, you should dispassionately examine your motives and credentials. What kind of work can you realistically expect to do? What are your qualifications and experience? Are they recognised in Spain? How good is your Spanish (or other languages)? Unless your Spanish is fluent, you won't be competing on equal terms with the Spanish (you won't anyway, but that's a different matter!).

Spanish employers aren't usually interested in employing anyone without, at the very least, an adequate working knowledge of Spanish. Are there any jobs in your profession or trade in the area where you wish to live? Could you be self-employed or start your own business?

The answers to these and other key questions can be disheartening, but it's better to ask them **before** moving to Spain than afterwards. Comprehensive information about employment prospects in Spain can be found in this book's sister publication *Making a Living in Spain*.

Women

The number of working women in Spain has increased considerably in the last 20 years and nearly 50 per cent of Spanish women now work full or part time (nearly 80 per cent of part-time workers are women). The number of women in the professions has steadily increased over the years in line with the increase in the number of women graduates (which now exceeds that of men). Women represent nearly half of the working population but well over half of Spain's unemployed.

Nowadays, professional women are common in Spain, particularly doctors and lawyers, and there's less sexism in the professions than in other Latin countries. The government has done much to boost professional women's position by appointing a woman (Teresa Fernández de la Vega) to the vice-presidency and women to over half the cabinet posts. Career women are common in many fields that were previously closed to them, although they still have difficulty reaching senior management positions, only 2 per cent of which are filled by women, *macho* Spanish men often feel threatened by female bosses, and Spanish employers are often reluctant to hire women for responsible positions, particularly if they think they're planning a family.

Women are protected by law against discrimination on the grounds of their sex. A woman doing the same or broadly similar work to a man and employed by the same employer is legally entitled to the same salary and other terms of employment. Women's average salary is around 20 per cent lower than men's, although this is partly due to the fact that most women work in lower-paid industries and hold lower-paid positions than men, rather than to discrimination. Most women are employed in distribution and transport, nursing and healthcare, education, secretarial professions, and service industries such as retailing.

Although there's no official discrimination, in practice it's often otherwise, and it's estimated that women earn up to a third less than men in similar posts. The fact that 'the best man for the job may be a woman' isn't often acknowledged by Spanish employers (or employers anywhere) and women must generally be twice as qualified as men to compete on equal terms. The situation has improved considerably in recent years, however, and women are exploited less in Spain than in some other western European countries.

Under recent legislation promoting sexual equality and regulating positive discrimination, companies whose workforce is less than 50 per cent female may hire only women for new posts.

Spain celebrates a 'day of the working woman' (8th March) and there are associations of business women in many provinces.

Sexual harassment is quite common in Spain but women are now encouraged to report any advances that go beyond complimentary remarks, which are an accepted part of Spanish life and not to be taken seriously. If you receive a sexual advance from your boss, you should report it to your union representative or another superior. Under the sexual equality law, cases of sexual harassment are given priority in courts and resolved urgently.

SPAIN & THE EUROPEAN UNION

On 1st January 1986, Spain became a full member of the European Union (EU), which now consists of 27 states. The European Economic Area (EEA) was formed on the 1st January 1994 and comprises the EU member countries plus Iceland, Liechtenstein and Norway. The Single European Act, which came into effect on 1st January 1993, created a more favourable environment for enterprise, competition and trade, and made it easier for EU nationals to work in other EU countries.

Today, nationals of all EU states (except Bulgaria and Romania) have the right to work in Spain or any other member state without a work permit, provided they have a valid passport or national identity card and comply with the member state's laws and regulations on employment. All EU nationals are entitled

to the same treatment as Spanish citizens in matters of pay, working conditions, access to housing, vocational training, social security and trade union rights, and families and immediate dependants are entitled to join them and enjoy the same rights.

There are, however, still some barriers to the freedom of movement of EU workers. For example, some jobs require applicants to have specific skills or vocational qualifications in certain countries, qualifications obtained in some member states aren't recognised in others, and there are restrictions on employment in the civil service, e.g. on the grounds of public policy, health or security. Nevertheless, mutual acceptance of EU educational and professional qualifications by member states has made it easier to study, train and work abroad, and all equivalent professional and trade qualifications are recognised throughout the EU (although local examinations may be necessary).

QUALIFICATIONS

The most important qualification for working in Spain is the ability to speak Spanish fluently (see **Language** on page 35 and **Learning Spanish** on page 126). Once you've overcome this hurdle, you should establish whether your trade or professional qualifications and experience are recognised in Spain. Theoretically, all qualifications recognised by professional and trade bodies in any EU country are recognised in Spain. However, recognition varies from country to country and in certain cases foreign qualifications aren't recognised by Spanish employers, professional or trade associations. All academic qualifications should also be recognised, although they may be given less 'value' than equivalent Spanish qualifications, depending on the country and the educational establishment that awarded them.

A ruling by the European Court in 1992 declared that where EU examinations are of a similar standard, with limited areas of difference, individuals should be required to take exams only in those areas. EU citizens may become public employees, e.g. teachers and postal workers, and fill other civil service positions in Spain.

Foreigners may take any job in Spain except in the armed forces and the police, which are open to Spanish nationals only.

Professionals whose training was compulsory (regulated by statute, statutory instrument or a professional college) and consisted of at least three years' degree-level training plus job-based training can have their qualifications recognised automatically in member states. These are, however, subject to any professional codes and limitations in force. For example, in Spain a medical practitioner must have his qualifications accepted by the medical college of the province where he intends to practise and by any controlling specialist bodies. He must also show that he is in good standing with the professional authorities in his country of origin. However, professional colleges (*colegios*) in Spain can no longer obstruct the practice of professions by EU citizens holding recognised qualifications earned in another EU country.

All EU member states issue occupation information sheets containing a common job description with a table of qualifications. Intended to help someone with the relevant qualifications look for employment in another EU country, these cover a large number of trades, including agriculture, chemicals, clerical work and administration, commerce, construction, electrical trades and electronics, food, hotel and catering, metalworking, motor vehicle repair and maintenance, textiles, tourism, transport and public works.

In order to have your qualifications recognised in Spain, you must go to the provincial office of the Ministry for Education, Social Policy and Sport (Delegación Provincial del Ministerio de Educación, Política Social y Deporte) in your provincial capital and apply for a *Homologación*, for which you must pay a fee: currently €88.32 for a degree or €44.17 for a lower qualification. You're expected to supply translations of your certificates and a 'transcript', which is a summary of all the examinations, projects and/or course work included in the course(s) you've followed. A transcript is usually obtainable from the university, school or college that awarded the certificate. The recognition process can take up to 18 months for a degree (six to eight months for lower qualifications), so you should apply for recognition well in advance of your Spanish job hunt.

Further details are available from the Ministry for Education website (☎ 902 218 500, ⌨ www.mepsyd.es in Spain; ☎ 020-7727 2462, ⌨ www.mepsyd.es/exterior/uk in the UK; and ⌨ www.mepsyd.es/exterior/usa in the US). Those with British medical or architectural qualifications can use a faster recognition system: go to the National Academic Recognition Information Centre/NARIC website (⌨ www.naric.co.uk) for details or contact NARIC in Spain (☎ 915 065 593).

Information regarding the official validation of qualifications and the addresses of Spanish professional bodies is obtainable from the education department of Spanish embassies. A direct comparison between foreign qualifications and those recognised in Spain can be obtained from any Spanish regional employment office (*oficina de empleo* – see below) where there's a representative of the National Reference Point for Academic Qualifications (Punto Nacional de Referencia sobre Cualificaciones Español/PNR). In the UK, information can be obtained from the National Reference Point for Vocational Qualifications, UK NARIC, Oriel House, Oriel Road, Cheltenham, Gloucestershire GL50 1XP (☎ 0870-990 4088, ⌨ www.uknrp.org.uk).

REGIONAL EMPLOYMENT SERVICES

All regions run their own employment agencies under the 'umbrella' of the National Employment Institute (Instituto Nacional de Empleo/INEM). Some regions provide a more comprehensive service than others, but all are striving to give a more personalised and helpful service. Jobs in the local province are sometimes advertised on a bulletin board, as are perhaps a few national positions requiring specialised experience, training or qualifications. Regional employment offices may also provide a comprehensive career resource library, including lists of Spanish companies, trade publications and a wide range of reference books. If you have a residence permit (*residencia*) – without which you may receive no further help – a personal counsellor may be assigned to your case.

In addition to offering a job placement service, employment offices provide assistance to those wishing to start a business or be self-employed. The INEM website (💻 www.inem.es) provides good basic information, as well as links to regional employment offices.

The INEM publishes a useful guide, *Working in Spain*, downloadable in PDF in English, French, German and Spanish (💻 www.inem.es – go to *Publicaciones* and then *Guías para trabajar en el EEE*).

INEM services are available to all EU nationals and foreign residents in Spain. Unemployed foreigners must register as job seekers (*demandantes de empleo*), after which they receive a document permitting them to legally remain in Spain for six months while seeking employment. However, INEM offices are usually unhelpful to foreign job seekers unless they speak fluent Spanish (or even Catalan in certain parts of Spain!), have already been employed in Spain or are unemployed and receiving unemployment benefit. The INEM isn't service-oriented and the quality of service and co-operation varies with the region, the office and the person handling your case, although the regional services are trying to change this. Most Spanish employers advertise in daily newspapers for personnel.

There's also a European Employment Service (EURES) network, which includes all EU countries. Member states exchange information on job vacancies on a regular basis and you can also have your personal details circulated to the employment service in selected countries, e.g. to the INEM in Spain. Details are available in local employment service offices in each member country. Advice on how to apply for jobs is also provided from ☎ 00-800 4080 4080 (freephone in most EU countries, including the UK and Spain) and 💻 http://europa.eu.int/eures. Note, however, that it isn't a reliable or quick way of finding a job in Spain and an application through EURES can be protracted. If you're intending to apply through EURES, you should obtain a *Número de Identificación de Extranjero* (*NIE*) in advance (see **Foreigner's Identification Number** on page 210).

Private Employment Agencies

Most private employment agencies in Spain operate as temporary employment bureaux (*empresas de trabajo temporal*) only. Most agencies are based in the major cities and deal with enquiries from within Spain only, although you can consult lists of vacancies via the internet. As well as general agencies handling vacancies in a range of industries and professions, there are agencies specialising in particular fields, such as accounting, banking, computing, construction, engineering and technical businesses, hotel and catering, industry, insurance, nannying and nursing, sales, and secretarial and clerical work. Multinational agencies such as Adecco, Flexiplan and Manpower are common in cities and large towns, and generally hire office staff and unskilled and semi-skilled labour. Many secretarial jobs are for bilingual or trilingual secretaries with word processing experience (an agency usually tests your written language and word processing skills).

To be employed by a temporary agency, you must be eligible to work in Spain and have a social security card. You must usually register, which entails completing a registration form and providing a curriculum vitae and references (you can register with any number of agencies). **Always ensure you know exactly how much, when and how you will be paid.** Your salary should include a payment in lieu of holidays and a deduction for unemployment insurance. Due to the long annual holidays in Spain and maternity leave, companies often require temporary staff, and a temporary job can frequently be used as a stepping stone to a permanent position. Agencies are listed in the yellow pages under *Trabajo Temporal: Empresas* or *Selección de Personal* and most have websites where you can search for jobs (e.g. ⌨ www.adecco.es, ⌨ www.flexiplan.es, ⌨ www.interempleo.com, ⌨ www.manpower.es and ⌨ www.temps.es).

Several agencies specialise in finding employment for foreigners fluent in at least English and Spanish, mainly on the Costa del Sol and in Gibraltar. These include Exposure Career Network (⌨ www.exposure-eu.com), offering a comprehensive list of vacancies throughout the country and Gibraltar; JobtoasterSpain (☎ 952 587 453, ⌨ www.jobtoasterspain.com), offering vacancies in several locations, including the Costa del Sol, Barcelona, Cadiz and Granada; Recruit Spain (☎ 952 667 986, ⌨ www.recruitspain.com), with job opportunities on the Costa Blanca and Costa del Sol and in Gibraltar; and Wemploy (☎ 956 785 320, ⌨ www.wemploy.com), with vacancies on the Costa del Sol and in Gibraltar. All websites also offer comprehensive information about working in Spain.

Executive recruitment companies ('headhunters') are common in cities and large towns and have traditionally been used by large Spanish companies to help recruit staff, particularly executives, managers and professionals. Agents place advertisements in daily and weekly newspapers and trade magazines but don't usually mention the client's name (not least to prevent applicants from approaching the company directly, thus depriving the agency of its fat fee). Unless you're an outstanding candidate with half a dozen degrees, six languages and years of experience (but still under 30), sending an unsolicited CV to a headhunter is usually a waste of time.

> There are recruitment agencies in many other European countries which recruit executives, managers and professionals for employers in Spain.

TEACHING & TRANSLATING

English teachers are in huge demand in Spain, where learning English (and other languages) has become extremely popular in the last decade. There are over 20,000 English-language teachers in Spain and, due to the constant demand and high turnover, some schools don't insist on formal teaching qualifications and a graduate native English speaker can often get a job without other qualifications. Nevertheless, anyone with a Teaching English as a Foreign Language (TEFL) or English as a Second Language (ESL) certificate is at a distinct advantage.

Other teaching jobs are few and far between in Spain, and Spanish or equivalent EU qualifications are usually required to teach in state schools. Jobs are also available in international and foreign schools teaching American, British and other foreign children. Teaching jobs in Spain are advertised in the *Times Educational Supplement* (Fridays) and through the European Council of International Schools (ECIS), 21B Lavant Street, Petersfield, Hampshire GU32 3EL (☎ 01730-268244, ⌨ www.ecis.org). For more information about teaching English, obtain a copy of the monthly *EL Gazette* (UK ☎ 020-7481 6700, ⌨ www.elgazette.com) – one of the best resources for English teachers.

Private Language Schools

There are numerous private language schools in Spain (which has the largest number of language schools of any country in Europe) offering English classes for adults and children. The quality of schools and rates of pay vary considerably, and contracts should be carefully examined before committing yourself. Salaries are low – usually between €800 and €1,200 a month or around €8 an hour, although board and lodging may be subsidised by the school (and you can supplement your earnings by giving private lessons). Hours are long and anti-social and schools occasionally exploit teachers.

Teachers are usually employed on short-term contracts, which may run parallel with school terms (September to June). Many jobs, particularly those in smaller schools, are advertised locally only and those advertised abroad tend to be for the larger schools, international agencies and government institutions. Several recognised international language schools have branches in Spain, including Berlitz, International House and Linguarama, although they often require applicants to attend their own teacher-training courses.

Information about language schools is provided by Spanish consulates or you can write to the Association of Language Teaching Institutions in the region you wish to teach in (e.g. in Andalusia, the Asociación de Centros de Enseñanza de Idiomas de Andalucía, C/Asunción, 52, 41011 Sevilla (☎ 954 274 517, 💻 www.aceia.es). The organisation TESOL-Spain also offers information about English-language teaching in Spain, including schools, contracts and teaching resources (💻 www.tesol-spain.org). Language schools are listed in yellow pages under *Idiomas* or *Escuelas de Idiomas*.

The British Council

The British Council (💻 www.britishcouncil. org) recruits English-language teachers and supervisory staff for two-year placements in its language centres in Barcelona, Bilbao, Madrid, Palma de Mallorca, Segovia and Valencia. It's necessary to have an RSA diploma or PGCE in TEFL and two years' experience for most positions. For managerial posts, a postgraduate qualification and a minimum of five years' experience are required. For further information contact the British Council by phone (UK ☎ 0161-957 7755) or online (💻 www.britishcouncil.org) – the website includes vacancies and allows online applications. The British Council in Spain

(☎ 932 419 977, 💻 www.britishcouncil.org/spain) can also provide a list of major English-language schools in Spain.

Private Tuition

There's high demand for private English teachers in Spain and many teachers employed in language schools supplement their income by giving private lessons. You can advertise in local schools, universities and retail outlets and, once you're established, additional students can usually be found through word of mouth. You could also try placing an advertisement in a Spanish newspaper or magazine. The rate for private lessons varies considerably with the city or area and the competition – between €10 and €30 an hour.

> ☑ SURVIVAL TIP
>
> The demand for private lessons is particularly strong during the summer months, from parents of children who failed their end-of-term English examination.

Language Assistants

The language assistants' scheme enables students from the UK and over 30 other countries to spend a year working in a school or college in Spain assisting language teachers. Assistants spend 12 to 15 hours a week in the classroom under the supervision of the English (or other language) teacher, helping students improve their command of English and gain an insight into the Anglophone way of life. Graduates and undergraduates aged 20 to 30 of any discipline with the relevant foreign language qualification, e.g. at least A Level standard in the UK, are eligible to apply. Students aged 18 to 20 with an A Level or equivalent qualification in Spanish can apply for a position as a junior language assistant at secondary schools in Spain from January to June. Comprehensive information for language assistants and a guide to making applications can be found on the British Council website (💻 www.britishcouncil.org).

and representatives, sports instructing (e.g. tennis, golf and watersports), fruit and grape picking, and other agricultural jobs.

If you aren't an EU national, it's essential to check whether you're eligible to work in Spain before your arrival and whether you need a visa (see page 53). Check with a Spanish embassy or consulate in your home country well in advance of your visit.

Although a summer job in Spain may be a working holiday to you, with lots of sunbathing and little work, to your employer it means exactly the opposite. Long hours and low pay are par for the course and you're often required to work ten hours a day with only one day a week free. Due to the large number of unemployed, unskilled workers in Spain, it can be difficult to find work in the construction and farming (e.g. fruit or grape picking) industries and, when found, work is hard and low paid. Unemployment is high in resort areas, although foreigners can often find work in bars, clubs and other tourist-oriented businesses where fluent English (or other foreign language fluency) is an advantage.

Bear in mind that seasonal workers are often employed illegally (i.e. unregistered) and have few rights and little legal job protection in Spain; you can generally be fired without compensation at any time.

See also **Temporary & Casual Work** below.

Translators & Interpreters

Those who are fluent in Spanish and English (and other languages) may be able to find work as translators and interpreters. The best job prospects for translators are in the major cities, where most translation work involves business correspondence (although it can be low paid). It's also worthwhile contacting major exporters who must translate their technical and other documentation into English and other languages. Translation agencies are listed in yellow pages under *Traductores*.

SEASONAL JOBS

Most seasonal jobs are for the summer tourist season (May to September), although a few are available in the small Spanish winter sports industry (December to April) and some are simply casual or temporary jobs for a few weeks or months only at a particular time of year, e.g. fruit picking. Spanish fluency is required for all but the most menial and worst-paid jobs and is at least as important as experience and qualifications (although fluent Spanish alone won't guarantee you a well paid job).

There are seasonal jobs in hotels and restaurants; holiday camps and campsites; ski resorts; bars, clubs and discos (particularly on the *costas* and in the Balearic and Canary Islands); and the construction industry. Jobs include couriers

Hotels & Restaurants

Hotels and restaurants are by far the largest employers of seasonal workers, and jobs are available year round, from hotel managers to kitchen hands. Experience, qualifications and fluent Spanish are required for all the better and higher paid positions, although a variety of jobs are available for the untrained and inexperienced. Note that, if accommodation with cooking facilities or full board isn't provided with a job, it can be expensive and difficult to find. Ensure that your salary is sufficient to pay for accommodation, food and other living expenses, and hopefully leave some money for you to save (see **Cost of Living** on page 244).

Couriers & Representatives

One of the best seasonal jobs or foreigners is as a courier or representative with a foreign package holiday company. There are also various jobs at holiday camps and campsites in Spain. Competition for jobs is fierce, however, and Spanish fluency is usually necessary, even for employment with foreign tour operators. Most companies apply age limits, the minimum usually being 21, although many companies prefer employees to be older. Note that most companies recruit from outside Spain, so you should apply before travelling to Spain.

To find out which companies operate in Spain, check the brochures in your local travel agent's or consult a trade travel directory in your local library. Make applications well before the season starts; for example, for summer work you should apply in November or December, as many positions are filled by January or February.

TEMPORARY & CASUAL WORK

Temporary and casual work in Spain is usually for a fixed period, ranging from a few hours to a few months, or it may be intermittent. Casual workers may be employed on a daily, first-come, first-served basis. Work often entails heavy labouring and is therefore intended mostly for males, although if you're tough enough there's usually no discrimination against the 'fairer' sex. However, anyone looking for casual unskilled work in Spain must usually compete with unskilled immigrants, who are usually prepared to work for less money than anyone else, although nobody **should** be paid less than the minimum wage (€600 a month). Many employers illegally pay temporary staff in cash without making deductions for social security (see **Illegal Working** on page 34). The following types of temporary and casual work may be available:

♦ Office work, which is well paid if you're qualified and the easiest work to find in major cities due to the large number of temporary secretarial and office staff agencies. You must be fluent in Spanish.

♦ Work in the construction industry, which can be found by applying at building sites and through industrial recruitment agencies (such as Adecco). However, the building industry is experiencing a recession at the moment with few jobs available.

♦ Jobs in shops at the height of the tourist season and during Christmas and annual sales in major cities.

♦ Promotional work for bars, restaurants and other businesses in the summer season, which usually consists of distributing leaflets to tourists.

♦ Gardening jobs in private gardens and public parks, and for landscape gardeners and garden centres, particularly in spring and summer.

♦ Selling ice cream, cold drinks, food or suntan lotion in summer, e.g. on beaches.

♦ Various jobs in ports, including yacht-minding, crewing, servicing, cleaning and boat delivery. Work as a deck-hand on a yacht pays well and usually also includes tips, although you must have sea legs, as the Mediterranean isn't always calm! You should have private medical insurance.

♦ Market research, which entails asking people personal questions in the street or house to house (an ideal job for nosy parkers with fluent Spanish).

♦ House sitting, which involves caring for a house and garden (possibly including a pet) while the owners are away. Not usually paid, but provides free accommodation.

♦ Modelling at art colleges. Both sexes are usually required and not just the body beautiful.

♦ Nursing and auxiliary nursing in hospitals, clinics and nursing homes (temporary staff are often employed through nursing agencies to replace permanent staff at short notice). The best-paid nursing jobs are in private clinics and hospitals, or working directly for private patients in their own homes.

♦ Newspaper, magazine and leaflet distribution.

♦ Courier work (own transport required – motorcycle, car or van).

♦ Driving jobs, including coach and truck driving, and ferrying cars for manufacturers and car rental companies.

♦ Office cleaning, babysitting, labouring and other 'menial' jobs, which are available from a number of agencies specialising in temporary work.

Temporary jobs are advertised on notice boards in supermarkets, expatriate clubs, churches and organisations, and in expatriate newsletters and newspapers. See also **Recruitment Agencies** on page 28 and **Seasonal Jobs** on page 25.

JOB HUNTING

When looking for a job (or a new job) in Spain, it's advisable not to put all your eggs in one basket, as the more job applications you make, the better your chances of finding the right job. Contact as many prospective employers as possible, by writing, telephoning or calling on them in person. Whatever job you're looking for, it's important to market yourself appropriately, which depends on the type of job or position you're seeking. For example, the recruitment of executives and senior managers is often handled by recruitment consultants, who advertise in the Spanish national press and trade magazines.

At the other end of the scale, unskilled manual jobs requiring no previous experience may be advertised at regional employment offices, in local newspapers and on notice boards, and the first suitable applicant may be offered the job on the spot. When job hunting, you should use all the resources available (detailed below). Before accepting a job offer from an employer, you should also ask yourself the following questions:

♦ What are his prospects?

♦ Does he have a good reputation?

♦ Does he have a high staff turnover?

Newspapers

Obtain copies of Spanish national and regional newspapers, all of which contain 'situations vacant' (*trabajo vacante* or *ofertas de empleo*) sections on certain days, usually Sundays. Most professions and trade associations publish journals containing job offers (see *Benn's Media Directory Europe*). Jobs are also advertised in various English-language publications, such as the *International Herald Tribune* (🖳 www.iht.com) and *Wall Street Journal Europe* (🖳 www.europesubs.wsj.com). The expatriate Spanish press (see **Appendix B**) also contains 'situations vacant' and 'situations wanted' advertisements. You can place an advertisement in 'situations wanted' (*demanda*) columns in most publications. It's best to place an advertisement in the middle of the week and to avoid the summer and other holiday periods.

When writing for jobs, address your letter or email to the personnel director or manager and include your curriculum vitae (in Spanish) and copies of all references and qualifications. If possible, offer to attend an interview and state when you're available. Letters and emails should be tailored to individual employers and be professionally translated if your Spanish isn't perfect.

☑ SURVIVAL TIP

Spanish companies are notoriously bad at answering letters and emails, and you should follow up letters with a telephone call.

Employment Offices

Visit your local employment office in Spain. Jobs on offer are mainly non-professional skilled, semi-skilled and unskilled jobs, particularly in industry, retailing and catering.

Recruitment Agencies

Apply to international recruitment agencies acting for Spanish companies. These companies mainly recruit executives and key personnel, and many have offices in major Spanish cities as well as worldwide. Contact recruitment agencies in Spain for temporary positions. Note that many Spanish agencies find positions only for EU nationals and non-EU foreigners with a residence permit.

Internet

There are hundreds of websites for jobseekers, including corporate and recruitment company sites and newspaper and magazine sites (you can use a search engine to find them). Job hunting via the internet is extremely popular. Most job vacancy websites also offer advice and the opportunity to post your CV online. The most popular sites include the following:

- 💻 www.computrabajo.es – general;
- 💻 www.eurojobs.com – jobs throughout Europe;
- 💻 www.financialwebjob.com – finance;
- 💻 www.infoagro.com – agriculture and farming;
- 💻 www.infoempleo.com – general;
- 💻 www.jobpilot.es – an international site in English which includes job vacancies in Spain;
- 💻 www.laboris.net – general;
- 💻 www.monster.es – general;
- 💻 www.novanotio.es – IT and technology job vacancies;
- 💻 www.primerempleo.com – jobs for those who have never worked before or with no experience;
- 💻 www.tecnoempleo.com – IT and telecommunications jobs;
- 💻 www.trabajos.com – general;
- 💻 www.turiempleo – jobs in tourism and the leisure industry.

SALARY

It's often difficult to determine the salary (*sueldo*) you should command in Spain, as salaries aren't generally quoted in job advertisements, except in the public sector, where employees are paid according to fixed grades and salaries are public knowledge. Salaries vary considerably for the same job in different parts of Spain. Those working in major cities, particularly Madrid and Barcelona, are generally the highest paid, primarily due to the high cost of living, especially accommodation.

If you're able to negotiate your own salary, you should ensure that you receive the salary and benefits commensurate with your qualifications and experience (or as much as you can get!). If you have friends or acquaintances working in Spain or who have worked there, ask them what an average or good salary would be for your trade or profession.

> ### ☑ SURVIVAL TIP
>
> When comparing salaries, you must take into account compulsory deductions such as tax and social security, and also consider the cost of living.

Salaries for managers and professionals compare favourably with those in other developed countries and are among the highest in Europe. Directors usually earn between €70,000 and €180,000 a year depending on the size of the company and middle managers between €40,000 and €70,000. Salaried professionals earn around €40,000 to €60,000. Blue-collar workers, on the other hand, earn an average of €20,340 a year compared with the European average of €34,400 (only Greek and Portuguese workers earn less) and over 50 per cent less than German workers.

Typical salaries start at around €3,300 a month for an IT professional (one of the highest-paid professions), around €1,200 a month in nursing and around €1,000 a month in administration. A surprisingly high number of jobs (even skilled) offer a maximum salary of €1,000 per month and in some areas of Spain (e.g. the Costa del Sol), it's difficult to earn more. As a result, thousands of employees are known as *mileuristas* (€1,000-earners). However, most employees in Spain receive a month's extra salary (*paga extraordinaria*) twice a year, at Christmas and before the August summer holiday.

For many employees, particularly executives and senior managers, remuneration is much more than what they receive in their monthly pay packets. Many companies offer benefits for executives and managers, including a company car (rarer in Spain than in some other European countries); private health insurance and health screening; paid holidays; private school fees; inexpensive or interest-free home and other loans; rent-free accommodation; free public transport tickets; a free or subsidised company restaurant; sports or country club membership; non-contributory company pension scheme membership; stock options; bonuses and profit-sharing schemes; complementary tickets for sports events and shows and 'business' conferences in exotic places.

Minimum Wage

Spain has a statutory minimum wage (*salario mínimo interprofesional*), which was €600 per month (€3.75 per hour) in 2008 for an unskilled worker aged from 16 to 59, one of the lowest rates in the EU. Minimum salaries are set for all workers under collective labour agreements, however, and most workers receive more than the minimum; fewer than 600,000 employees are directly affected by minimum wage rates (although an increase in the minimum wage usually serves as a benchmark for wage demands). Unskilled workers (particularly women) are usually employed at or near the minimum wage, while semi-skilled and skilled workers receive a premium of up to 100 per cent.

SELF-EMPLOYMENT

If you're an EU national or a permanent resident, you can be self-employed (*trabajador autónomo*) or work as a sole trader (*empresa individual*) in Spain. Under Spanish law every self-employed person must have an official status and it's illegal simply to hang out a sign and start business.

If you want to be self-employed in a profession or trade, you must meet certain legal requirements and register with the appropriate organisation, e.g. a professional must become a member of the relevant professional college (*colegio*). Members of some professions and trades must possess professional qualifications (see page 20) and certificates recognised in Spain, and are usually required to sit a written examination in Spanish. You're subject to any professional codes and limitations in force, e.g. a medical practitioner must have his qualifications accepted by the medical college of the province where he intends to practise and any other controlling specialist

bodies. You must also show that you're in good standing with the professional authorities in your own country. In certain professions, such as the legal profession, it's unusual to be permitted to practise in Spain without Spanish qualifications.

As a self-employed person you don't have the protection of a limited company should your business fail, although there are certain tax advantages. It may be advantageous to operate as a limited company, for example. However, you should obtain professional advice before deciding whether to operate as a sole trader or form a company in Spain, as it has far-reaching social security, tax and other consequences./

All self-employed people must register for income tax, social security and value added tax (VAT/*IVA*), and anyone with an income in Spain requires a fiscal identification number (*número de identificación fiscal/NIF*), obtainable from your local national police station (*comisaría de policía nacional*). For foreigners this number is called a *número de identificación de extranjeros/NIE* (see page 208). You may also need an opening licence (*licencia de apertura*) from the local council; for information refer to *Making a Living in Spain* (Survival Books – see page 373).

Whatever people may tell you, working for yourself isn't easy but requires a lot of hard work (self-employed people generally work much longer hours and earn less than employees), a considerable investment and sufficient operating funds (under-funding is the major cause of business failures), good organisation (e.g. budgeting and planning), excellent customer relations, and a measure of luck (although generally the harder you work, the more 'luck' you will have). Don't be seduced by the apparently relaxed way of life in Spain – if you want to be a success in business, you cannot play at it.

Social Security

There's a 'special' social security scheme for self-employed workers (*régimen especial de autónomos*). Social security contributions for the self-employed are higher than for salaried employees and you receive fewer benefits (which encourages illegal working). For example, you aren't entitled to unemployment benefit should your business fail. Furthermore, if you have two unconnected part-time jobs, you officially require two sets of papers and must pay social security twice! In 2008, contributions were a minimum of €244.35 a month irrespective of income. You receive a book of payment slips from your social security office or payments can be made directly by your bank by direct debit.

If you're self-employed and employ others, you must register your business in the general social security scheme and must affiliate all your employees and comply with the requirements of the *Inspección Provincial de Trabajo*.

Business Tax

Business tax on economic activities (*impuesto sobre actividades económicas (IAE)*, is levied only on businesses with profits of over €600,000 a year. Anyone conducting a business, however, must still register as a self-employed worker or professional with the tax

office, who give you the tax code designated for your profession. This code must be quoted in your annual tax return.

Value Added Tax

Most self-employed people must register for value added tax (VAT), irrespective of income, and levy VAT (*impuesto sobre el valor añadido/IVA*) at 16 per cent on all services or goods. VAT must be declared and paid quarterly. For details, see **Value Added Tax** on page 225.

STARTING A BUSINESS

Most foreigners find Spain a frustrating country in which to do business. The bureaucracy associated with starting a business there is staggering and ranks among the most pernicious in the developed world: the process takes an average of over seven months and there are more than 70 documents and procedures to be completed. Not surprisingly, only some 15 per cent of those who start manage to finish! Nevertheless, Spain is traditionally a country of small companies and sole traders, and there are some 1.5m family-run businesses (of all sizes) employing over 80 per cent of the working population.

In an attempt to facilitate the process and encourage self-employment, the government has recently introduced new measures. Every province in Spain now has a 'one-stop' office (*ventanilla única*) for businesses, where all information and documents are available and where you can present everything related to your application. Information (in Spanish only), including the addresses of provincial offices, is available from ☎ 902 100 096 or 🖥 www.ventanillaempresarial.org. Nevertheless, foreigners can still find the red tape impenetrable, especially if they don't speak Spanish; you're inundated with official documents and must be able to understand them.

Only when you're setting up a business and come up against the full force of Spanish bureaucracy do you understand what it **really** means to be a foreigner in Spain!

One way to get round the red tape is to employ a *gestor* (a licensed professional, expert in administrative and tax affairs – see page 320) to do the paperwork for you. His fee depends on the amount of work involved but is usually good value – many Spaniards use the services of a *gestor*! If you decide to 'go it alone', among the best sources of help and information are your local chamber of commerce (*cámara de comercio*) and town hall (*ayuntamiento*).

Starting a business is one of the quickest routes to bankruptcy known to mankind. In fact, the majority of foreigners who open businesses in Spain would be better off investing in lottery tickets! Many would-be foreign entrepreneurs leave Spain with literally only their shirts on their backs, having learnt the facts of Spanish business life the hard way.

Most people are far too optimistic about the prospects for a new business and over-estimate income levels (it can sometimes take years to make a profit). Be realistic or even pessimistic when estimating your income: overestimate the costs and underestimate the revenue (then reduce it by another 50 per cent!). While hoping for the best, you should plan for the worst; new projects are rarely completed on time or within budget.

However, although there are numerous failures for every success story, many foreigners **do** run successful businesses in Spain. Those who make a go of it do so as a result of extensive market research, wise investment, excellent customer relations and, most important of all, a lot of hard work.

For further information about self-employment and starting a business in Spain, see our sister publication, *Making a Living in Spain*.

TRAINEES & WORK EXPERIENCE

Spain is a participant in an international trainee (*aprendiz*) programme designed to give young people the opportunity for further education and occupational training, and to enlarge their professional experience and knowledge of languages. The programme has exchange agreements with different countries depending on the scheme, although Austria, Belgium, Canada, Denmark, Finland, Germany, Ireland,

Luxembourg, the Netherlands, New Zealand, Norway, Sweden, Switzerland, the UK and the US are generally included.

If you're aged between 18 and 30 (US 21 to 30) and have completed your vocational training (minimum of two years), you may be eligible for a position as a trainee in Spain. The trainee agreement covers most occupations, and employment must be in the occupation in which you were trained. Positions are usually granted for one year and in exceptional circumstances can be extended for a further six months. Information about the trainee programme can be obtained from INEM offices (see page 31) in Spain and government employment offices abroad.

Technical and commercial students who wish to gain experience by working in industry and commerce in Spain during their holidays can apply to the International Association for the Exchange of Students for Technical Experience (IAESTE – www.iaeste.org), which has representation in over 60 countries. Applicants must possess a working knowledge of Spanish and be full-time students of agriculture, architecture, applied arts, engineering or

science and aged between 19 and 30. Most foreign trainees in Spain are sponsored by employers or colleges under exchange arrangements. For information about trainee and work experience schemes in Spain, contact IAESTE in Spain (☎ 963 699 480), your country's national employment services agency or the national trade association for the industry in which you wish to train, who may be able to put you in contact with a suitable Spanish employer.

General details about training and apprenticeship programmes in all EU countries are available via the EU Ploteus portal (🖳 http://europa.eu.int/ploteus).

Leonardo da Vinci Programme

The Leonardo da Vinci Programme is an EU-sponsored programme providing support for young people wishing to undertake vocational training and work experience in another EEA or Eastern European country. Placements are for between three weeks and 12 months and are targeted at young people already in vocational training, young workers and jobseekers, and those taking part in an advanced training programme after starting work. Applications must be submitted through relevant training organisations or colleges or regional employment offices.

AU PAIRS

Single males and females aged between 18 and 30 (ages vary with the agency or employer) are eligible for a job as an au pair. The au pair system provides young people with an excellent opportunity to travel, improve their Spanish and generally broaden their education by living and working in Spain. Au pairs in Spain are accepted from most countries.

If you're an EU national, you need only a valid passport and it's unnecessary to arrange an au pair position before arriving in Spain. In fact it's often better not to do so. Some agents allow you to meet families in Spain, before making a decision. This is advisable, as you can interrogate the family, inspect their home and your accommodation, and meet the children who will make your life heaven or hell! If you arrive in Spain without a position, you can usually find one within a few weeks.

Applicants from non-EU countries must obtain a visa (See Chapter 3) before arriving in Spain and require an offer of a position from a Spanish family. This must be presented to your local Spanish embassy or consulate (with your passport) in order to obtain a visa.

> Au pairs are usually contracted to work for a minimum of six months and a maximum of a year.

Most families require an au pair for at least the whole school year, from September to June. The best time to look for an au pair position is therefore before the beginning of the school year in September. You should apply as early as possible and not later than a month before your preferred start date – at least two months if you need a visa. There are also summer au pair programmes of two to three months, for which enrolment must usually be made before 31st March. Au pairs employed for the summer only aren't required to attend Spanish lessons. In addition to regular au pair positions, some agencies offer positions where a room is provided in exchange for around ten hours' work a week (e.g. for full-time students). Agencies usually charge a registration fee of around €60, although some offer free registration.

Au pairs are generally placed with Spanish-speaking families with children, although in areas popular with expatriates, families may be of other nationalities. Duties consist of light housework, including simple cooking for children; clothes washing (with a machine) and ironing (children's clothes only); washing up and drying dishes (if the family doesn't have a dishwasher); making beds; dusting; vacuum cleaning and other such jobs around the home. To enjoy life as an au pair you should be used to helping around the house and enjoy working with children. An au pair isn't a general servant or cook (although you may possibly be treated as one) and you aren't expected to look after physically or mentally disabled children.

As an au pair you receive free meals and accommodation and have your own room. Usually you're housed with the family, although this may not always be possible. Working hours are officially limited to 30 a week, five hours a day (morning or afternoon), six days a week, plus a maximum of three evenings' babysitting. You should have at least one full day (usually Sunday) and three evenings free each week, and should be free to attend religious services. In some families, au pairs are expected to holiday with the family, although you may be free to take Christmas or Easter holidays at home. Choose a wealthy family and you may be taken on exotic holidays.

For your labours you're paid the princely (princessly?) sum of between €70 and (in cities) €100 per week 'pocket money'. You're required to pay your own fare to Spain (and back). A family employing an au pair must make a declaration to the Spanish social security administration and make monthly contributions. If you're ill or have an accident during your stay in Spain, you can obtain treatment under the Spanish health system (see Chapter 12).

An au pair position can be arranged privately with a family or through an agency, in Spain or abroad. Au pair positions can also be found through magazines (such as The Lady in the UK – 🖥 www.lady.co.uk) and newspapers, but you're usually better off using an agency. The best agencies vet families, make periodic checks on your welfare, help you to overcome problems (personal or with your family), and may organise cultural activities (particularly in major cities). Agencies send you an application form (questionnaire) and usually ask you to provide character (moral) references, a medical certificate, school references and a number of passport-size photographs.

Au pairs must usually have had secondary (high) school education (or equivalent) and have a good basic knowledge of Spanish. Au pairs must attend Spanish language classes organised for foreign students. An application form can sometimes be completed in your own language, although it's better to complete it in Spanish, even if it means obtaining help (forms are often printed only in Spanish).

Your experience as an au pair will depend entirely on your family. If you're fortunate enough to work for a warm and friendly host family, you will have a wonderful experience and lots of free time, and may even be treated to wonderful holidays in Spain or abroad. Many au pairs grow to love their children and families and form lifelong friendships. On the other hand, abuses of the au pair system are common in all countries and you could be treated as a servant or slave rather than a member of the family, and be expected to work long hours and spend most evenings babysitting. Many families employ an au pair simply because he costs much less than the lowest-paid nanny. If you have any questions or complaints about your duties, you should refer them to the agency that found you your position (if applicable). There are many families to choose from and you should never remain with a family you're unhappy with. You're usually required to give notice if you wish to go home before the end of your agreement, although this won't apply if the family has abused the contract.

Au pair agencies in the UK are listed in the Au Pair and Nanny's Guide to Working Abroad by Susan Griffith and Sharon Legg (Vacation Work). Several websites (e.g. 🖥 www.aupairs.co.uk and 🖥 www.findaupair. com) also provide lists of agencies and useful general information. You should contact a number of agencies and compare registration fees and pocket money, both of which may vary considerably (although the terms of employment should be the same).

It's possible for responsible Spanish-speaking young women, even without experience or training, to obtain employment as a nanny in Spain (and in many other countries). Duties are basically the same as an au pair, except that a position as a nanny is a real job with a real salary!

ILLEGAL WORKING

Illegal working (*trabajo ilegal*) thrives in Spain, where it has been estimated that the turnover of the 'black economy' (*economía sumergida*) equals between 20 and 25 per cent of the official gross national product, and that real unemployment is much less than the official figure. After Italy, Spain has the largest black economy in the developed world (it's reckoned to be most widespread in Andalusia, Galicia and Valencia). Official estimates put the number of illegal workers at over a million, although the real figure is probably at least double this.

In recent years, there has been a clampdown on illegal labour and there are large fines for employers and workers, and even imprisonment for the most serious offenders. Companies employing illegal foreign labour can be fined for each illegal employee, and illegal workers can be deported and barred from entering Spain for up to three years. A foreigner has the right to a hearing before a court when an expulsion order is made. Occasionally amnesties are declared, during which illegal immigrants are given the opportunity to become legal without reprisals or penalties. One such amnesty in 2005 allowed some 690,000 immigrants to legalise their situation in Spain.

If you work illegally and don't pay tax or social security contributions, you have no entitlement to state insurance against work injuries, health care, unemployment benefits or a state pension. If you use illegal labour or avoid paying *IVA*, you have no official redress if goods or services are substandard.

It's strictly illegal for non-EU nationals to work in Spain without a work permit.

LANGUAGE

Although English is the *lingua franca* of international commerce and may help you to secure a job in Spain, the most important qualification for anyone seeking employment there is the ability to speak good Spanish (or the local regional language). Spanish is the official language of 19 countries and is spoken worldwide by some 285m people. It's the world's second most important commercial language after English and the third most widely spoken after Chinese and English.

What most foreigners refer to as Spanish is actually Castilian (*castellano*), which developed into classical Spanish. Castilian is the most spoken Spanish language, particularly among the educated classes; it's spoken by 65 per cent of Spaniards as their first or only language and is understood by most Spaniards. All references to Spanish in this section (and elsewhere in this book) are to Castilian.

The remaining 35 per cent of the population include the inhabitants of the autonomous regions of the Basque Country, Catalonia and Galicia, where Basque, Catalan and Galician (respectively) are joint-official languages with Castilian (see below). However, even in these regions most people speak or understand Castilian (although they may be reluctant to do so). See also **Learning Spanish** on page 126.

Regional Languages

Regional languages were banned under Franco, schools were forbidden to teach them and regional language books weren't allowed to be published (many existing books were destroyed). Since the death of Franco in 1975 – and with the large degree of autonomy subsequently ceded to the regions – regional languages have made a strong comeback and are now taught in schools alongside Castilian. Basque, Catalan and Galician have also been revived by regional television and radio broadcasters and local film industries.

There are, however, also several dialects of Spanish, Catalan and Galician. For example, in the Balearics there are *Mallorquín* (Majorca), *Menorquín* (Menorca) and *Ibicenco* (Ibiza). All three are related to Catalan and similar in vocabulary, many words having their origin in Arabic, French, Italian or Portuguese. Many Spanish gypsies, who arrived with the Moors from North Africa, speak *caló*, a language that includes Spanish and elements borrowed from Sanskrit and other European languages.

In the Basque Country, Catalonia and Galicia, many street and buildings names, road signs, notices and official documents are in Spanish and the relevant regional language. The dominance of regional languages in the autonomous regions is causing increasing problems for foreigners and even for Spaniards from other regions of Spain. It's an important consideration if you're planning to live in Catalonia, Galicia or the Basque Country (particularly if you have school age children), where Spanish is a 'minor' language. In these regions, all communications from the authorities may be in the local language only and officials may refuse to speak any other language. This practice is especially widespread in Catalonia, where many people are obsessive about speaking Catalan and public notices and even restaurant menus are printed only in Catalan. Do you wish to learn Catalan or Basque, particularly if you already speak Spanish? Do you want your children to grow up speaking a 'foreign' and minority language?

Catalan

Catalan (*catalán*) is spoken by some 6.5m people in Catalonia, the Balearics, Valencia, the principality of Andorra and parts of the French Pyrenees. Catalan is by far the predominant language in Catalonia, where Spanish speakers feel linguistically oppressed in much the same way that Catalan speakers were under Franco. This is particularly noticeable in schools, where all lessons apart from Spanish are conducted in Catalan. However, in Barcelona almost everyone speaks Spanish, while less than half are fluent in Catalan. Most Catalans readily speak Spanish, particularly to non-Catalans, although some refuse to speak it or pretend not to understand it.

Galician

Galician (*gallego*) is the language of the north-west province of Galicia. Some 2.5m Galicians (80 per cent) speak Galician, and half of them (mostly in rural areas) don't speak Spanish. To make matters even more complicated, three dialects of Galician are spoken.

Basque

Basque (*euskera*) is spoken by around 500,000 inhabitants of the Basque Country, mostly in rural areas. Although some words are borrowed from Spanish and French, the basic vocabulary and structure of Basque are unique. It's an ancient tongue of unknown origin and bears no relation to any other modern European language; it's thought by some scholars to be the only remaining representative of a pre-Indo-European language (a possible link has recently been found between Basque and the ancient Etruscan tongues). It's cluttered with consonants, particularly Ks, Xs and Zs, and unfathomable by anyone but native speakers.

English

Unlike those in many other European countries, the majority of Spanish businesses don't use English as a working language (although the ability to speak and write good English is required for most jobs in business!) and the vast majority of Spaniards don't speak any foreign languages, particularly older Spaniards and people in rural areas. The amount of English spoken varies hugely with the area or city and the individual (professionals are more likely to speak English than shop assistants, for example). In resort areas, such as the *costas* and the Balearic and Canary Islands, English is widely spoken and understood, as is German. It's also understood by many people in Barcelona and Madrid, but don't count on it!

Cuchia, Cantabria

2.

EMPLOYMENT CONDITIONS

Employment conditions in Spain are largely dependent on the 1980 Workers' Statute (*Estatuto de los Trabajadores*). Other governing factors include collective agreements (*convenios colectivos*), an employee's individual employment contract (*contrato de trabajo*) and an employer's in-house regulations. Salaried foreigners are employed under the same conditions as Spanish citizens, although there are different rules for different categories of employee, e.g. directors, managers and factory workers.

As in many countries, part-time, seasonal and temporary workers often aren't protected by employment laws and have few rights. Consequently, an increasing number of employers are engaging staff on a temporary basis, on short-term contracts, and it's estimated that over 30 per cent of workers (the highest in the European Union/EU) are in temporary or short-term employment.

There has traditionally been a link between a labour contract and a job for life in Spain. However, the situation has changed dramatically in recent years, during which Spain's economic problems have been exacerbated by the unions' uncompromising defence of high wages and rigid employment terms, which has become outdated in today's increasingly competitive world.

Spain has one of the most rigid and costly labour markets in Europe and critics claim that the requirements of the Workers' Statute are a major disincentive to investors and employers, and restrict employment due to the high cost of hiring and firing employees. In spite of a historic agreement reached between the employers and unions in 1997, whereby unions reduced their entitlement to redundancy payments in return for permanent jobs, many employers hire most new employees on short-term contracts, rather than permanent ones.

The government provides incentives for employers offering permanent contracts to new employees; for example, employers receive between €500 and €3,200 per employee annually for four years from the government and there are discounts on social security payments. However, in spite of the financial incentives, many employers prefer temporary contracts.

Those fortunate enough to be permanent employees enjoy excellent employment conditions and social security benefits, and extensive rights under Spanish law. The Workers' Statute details the minimum conditions of employment, including labour contracts, terms of hiring and dismissal, working conditions, employee representation and trade union rights. Spain has a statutory minimum wage (see page 29) and pay and employment conditions in many industries are governed by collective agreements, which are negotiated nationally or regionally for each industry and stipulate the rights and obligations of employees and employers in a particular industry or occupation.

Employees are protected by the Workers' Statute prohibiting discrimination on the grounds of sex, marital status, age, race, language (i.e. between Spain's various official languages – see page 35), social status, religious belief, political opinion or trade union membership. Discrimination is also illegal with respect to mental or physical disability, provided a disabled person is able to perform the work required. Children under 16 cannot be employed, and certain restrictions apply to under 18s, e.g. a prohibition on working overtime, night work, and certain dangerous and unhealthy jobs.

EMPLOYMENT CONTRACTS

Employees usually have an employment contract (*contrato de trabajo*), stating such particulars as job title, position, salary, working hours, benefits, duties and responsibilities, and the duration of employment. Note that the legally binding minimum terms of employment and minimum wages are usually decided by agreement between employers and trade unions and also apply to employees with individual contracts.

All contracts must be written in Spanish. (Note that the relationship between employer and employee constitutes a legally binding contract, even if there's no written contract, although you're strongly recommended to obtain one.) All contracts are subject to Spanish labour law, although references may be made to other applicable regulations, such as collective agreements. Anything in contracts contrary to statutory provisions may be deemed null and void.

There are usually no hidden surprises or traps for the unwary in a Spanish employment contract. Nevertheless, as with any contract, you should know exactly what it contains before signing it.

> ☑ **SURVIVAL TIP**
>
> If your Spanish isn't fluent, you should obtain an English translation of your contract (your Spanish must be excellent to understand the legal jargon in some contracts) or at least have it translated verbally so that you don't get any nasty surprises later.

Employment contracts usually contain a paragraph stating the date from which they take effect and to whom they apply.

There are two main types of employment contract in Spain: an indefinite-term contract (*contrato por tiempo indefinido*) and a defined-term contract (*contrato por tiempo definido* – see below), which will be referred to respectively here as permanent and short-term contracts. Note that where a short-term contract covers another employee's period of sickness or maternity leave, for example, or when there's a temporary increase in business, this should be specified.

In addition to a contract, you should receive a copy of your employer's standard conditions, containing general rules and regulations regarding behaviour and benefits that are applicable to all employees (unless stated otherwise in your employment contract).

Short-term Contracts

Short-term contracts are usually for a minimum of a year and up to three years, after which an employer must either terminate your employment or employ you permanently. Under Spanish law, employers cannot renew more than two short-term contracts per employee within two years. At the end of the three-year period, an employer can fire an employee and it costs him nothing; if he does so one day later, it can cost him hundreds of euros!

The salary of an employee hired on a short-term contract mustn't be less than that paid to a similarly qualified person employed in a permanent job, and a short-term contract can be terminated before the end of its period in specific circumstances only, for example, when the employer or employee has committed a serious offence, in the case of an event beyond the control of both parties, or with the agreement of both parties. Short-term contracts don't usually cover seasonal workers, who have few rights.

SALARY & BENEFITS

Salaries in most industries in Spain are decided by collective bargaining between employers and unions. Salary increases are usually in line with inflation, including those of public employees. (Government attempts to freeze public employees' salaries have been overruled by the Spanish Supreme Court.) Salary increases usually take effect from 1st January.

linked to profits, equal to around 10 to 20 per cent of their annual salary.

Your salary (*sueldo*) is stated in your employment contract, where details of salary reviews, planned increases and cost of living rises may also be given. Salaries may be stated in gross or net terms. Salaries are paid weekly, fortnightly or monthly, depending on the employer. If a bonus is paid, such as a 13th or 14th month's salary (see below), this should be stated in your employment contract. General points, such as the payment of your salary into a bank account and the date of salary payments, may be included in your standard employment terms and conditions. Each time you're paid, you should receive a pay slip (*nómina de sueldo*) itemising your salary and deductions. See also **Salary** on page 28.

Extra Months' Salary & Bonuses

Most employers pay their employees a number of extra months' salary (*pagas extraordinarias*), usually two: one in July before the annual summer holiday and the other in December. Some companies pay as many as four months' extra salary, although this is exceptional. Extra months' salary isn't mandatory unless part of a collective agreement, when it should be stated in your employment contract; in practice, however, it's universal and taken for granted by most employees.

In your first and last years of employment, your extra months' salary and other bonuses should be paid pro rata if you don't work a full calendar year. Where applicable, extra months' salary are guaranteed bonuses and aren't pegged to a company's performance (such as with profit-sharing). Senior and middle managers may receive extra bonuses, perhaps

Expenses

Expenses (*gastos*) paidby your employer are usually listed in your employment conditions. These may include travel costs from your home to your place of work, which may consist of a rail season ticket or the equivalent amount in cash (paid monthly with your salary). Travelling expenses to and from your place of work are tax deductible. Companies without an employee restaurant or canteen may pay a lunch allowance or provide luncheon vouchers. Expenses paid for travel on company business or for training or education may be detailed in your terms and conditions or listed in a separate document.

Relocation Expenses

Relocation expenses to Spain depend on your agreement with your employer and are usually included in your employment contract or terms and conditions. If you're hired from outside Spain, your air ticket and other travel costs to Spain are usually paid for by your employer or his representative. In addition, you can usually claim any extra travel costs, for example the cost of transport to and from airports. If you travel by car to Spain, you can usually claim a mileage rate or the equivalent air fare cost.

An employer may pay a fixed relocation allowance based on your salary, position and size of family, or he may pay the total cost of removal. The allowance should be sufficient to move the contents of an average house (*castillos* aren't usually catered for!) and you must normally pay any excess costs yourself. If you don't want to bring your furniture to Spain or have only a few belongings to ship, it may be possible to purchase furniture locally up to the limit of your allowance (check with your employer). When it's liable for the total cost, a company may ask you to obtain two or three removal estimates.

Generally, you're required to organise and pay for the removal in advance. Your employer usually reimburses the equivalent amount in euros after you've paid the bill, although it may must elapse between the end of one working day or shift and the start of the next.

Salaried employees, particularly executives and managers, aren't generally paid overtime, although this depends on their employment contracts. Managers and executives generally work long hours, even allowing for their often long lunch breaks. Weekends are sacrosanct, however, and few people in Spain work on Saturdays and Sundays.

It may come as a nasty surprise to some foreigners to discover that many Spanish employers (including most large companies) require all employees to clock in and out of work. Employees caught cheating the clock are liable to instant dismissal.

Checklist

◆ What are your weekly working hours?

◆ Are you required to clock in and out of work?

◆ Can you choose to take time off in lieu of overtime or be paid for it?

HOLIDAYS & LEAVE

Spanish workers have generous public and annual holiday allowances, detailed below.

Annual Holidays

Under Spanish labour law, a full-time employee is entitled to one month's (20 working days') paid annual holiday (*vacaciones*). Employers cannot count official Spanish public holidays (see below) as annual holiday. Some collective agreements grant extra holiday for long service.

Most employees take three or four weeks' summer holiday between July and August and perhaps a week in winter (often around the Christmas and New Year holiday period) or at Easter. August is traditionally the month for summer holidays, many businesses closing for the whole month or operating on a skeleton staff. When a company closes during the summer, all employees are obliged to take their holiday at the same time. Some businesses also close for two weeks over Christmas and the New Year.

Before starting a new job, check that any planned holidays will be honoured by your new employer. This is particularly important if they fall within your trial period (usually the first three months), when holidays may not be permitted.

Public Holidays

The central government allows for 14 national holidays (*días de fiestas*) per year – more than any other country in Europe – but only nine are celebrated in all parts of Spain. Of the remaining five, regional authorities may choose up to four and add regional or local holidays (not listed below) to make up the total of 14.

Public Holidays	
Date	**Holiday**
1st January	New Year's Day (Día del Año Nuevo)
6th January	Epiphany or Three Kings Day (Día de los Reyes Magos)
March/April	Good Friday (Viernes Santo)
1st May	Labour Day (Día del Trabajador)
15th August	Assumption of the Virgin (Asunción)
12th October	Virgin of Pilar/National Day (Día de Virgen del Pilar)
1st November	All Saints' Day (Día de Todos los Santos)
6th December	Constitution Day (Día de la Constitución)
8th Decembe	Immaculate Conception (Inmaculada Concepción)
25th December	Christmas Day (Día de Navidad)

When a holiday falls on a Saturday or Sunday, another day isn't usually granted as a holiday. However, when a public holiday falls on a Tuesday or Thursday, the Monday or Friday is usually declared a holiday as well, although this depends on the employer. This practice is called making a bridge (*hacer un puente*). If a holiday falls on a Wednesday, employees may take the two preceding or succeeding days off, a practice known as making a viaduct (*viaductos*). When there are two to a maximum of 12 months' salary), unless otherwise agreed by contract. Although the minimum compensation for executives is less than that for 'ordinary' employees, it's common practice for contracts to allow for higher compensation than the minimum.

If you run a small business and are planning to employ a part-time or temporary employee, you should get him to sign a written statement agreeing to terms of termination, or you could be sued for unfair dismissal.

Medical Examination

Apart from a few large companies, Spanish businesses don't usually require employees to undergo a pre-employment medical examination, although some must pass a psychological examination. However, a medical examination may be required where good health is of paramount importance for safety reasons, in which case an examination may be necessary periodically (e.g. every one or two years) or when requested by the employer. Where applicable, an offer of employment is subject to a prospective employee being given a clean bill of health.

Medical examinations may also be required as a condition of membership of a company health, pension or life insurance scheme.

In any case, some companies insist that key employees undergo regular health screening,

particularly executives and senior managers – which is as much to their benefit as the company's.

Part-time Job Restrictions

Restrictions on part-time employment (*media jornada* or *trabajo a tiempo parcial*) may be detailed in your employment conditions. Most Spanish companies don't allow full-time employees to work part-time (i.e. 'moonlight') for another employer – particularly one in the same line of business. You may, however, be permitted to take a part-time job in a completely different line; for example, you could write a book!

Trial & Notice Periods

For most jobs in Spain there's a trial period (*período de prueba*) of between 15 days and six months, depending on the type of work and the employer. It's usually 15 working days for unqualified workers, six months for university graduates and three months for other employees. The length of a trial period is usually stated in collective agreements, which impose restrictions on the maximum period. During the trial period, either party may terminate the employment contract without notice or any financial penalty, unless otherwise stated in a collective agreement.

Notice periods vary according to your position and length of service. Generally, the higher the position, the longer the notice period. Although many employees prefer to leave immediately after giving notice, they have the right to work their notice period. However, both parties can agree that an employee receives payment in lieu of notice. Compensation must also be made for any outstanding paid annual holidays up to the end of the notice period. See also **Dismissal & Redundancy** above.

Checklist

♦ If a dispute arises over your salary or working conditions, under the law of which country will your employment contract be interpreted?

♦ What is the required notice period?

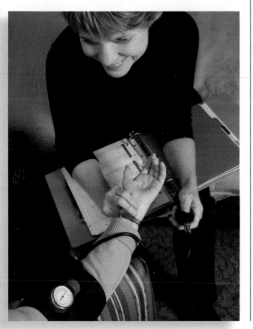

3.
PERMITS & VISAS

Before making any plans to live or work in Spain, you must ensure that you have a valid passport (with a visa if necessary) and the appropriate documentation to obtain a residence or work permit.

The European Union (EU) allows the free movement of goods, services, capital and people between member states, and any EU citizen has the right to live, study, work or start a business in Spain, although Bulgarian and Romanian nationals require a residence permit.

Nationals of Iceland, Liechtenstein, Norway and Switzerland who are employees, self-employed or full-time students in Spain don't require a residence permit, though employees must have a legal contract of employment and pay monthly social security contributions and taxes, and the self-employed must be registered with the local authorities, as well as with the tax office and pay monthly social security contributions. However, EEA nationals must apply for a registration certificate (*certificado de registro* – see page 54.

Non-working and retired European Economic Area (EEA) nationals must apply for a residence permit, and **all** foreigners require an identification number.

Citizens of non-EU countries must also obtain a visa from a Spanish consulate in their home country before coming to Spain to work, study or live (see below).

When in Spain you should always carry your foreign identity card, passport or Spanish residence permit (or a copy certified by a national police station) and produce it on demand to the authorities; if you don't have it, you can be fined.

Permit infringements are taken seriously by the Spanish authorities and there are penalties for breaches of regulations, including large fines, deportation and even imprisonment for flagrant abuses.

Spain has been criticised in recent years for its strong-arm, repressive tactics with regard to the deportation of illegal African immigrants, of whom there are many. On the other hand, thousands of illegal immigrants are granted residence permits under periodic amnesties and under a foreigners' law (*Ley de Extranjería*) passed in 2000. The latest (and, according to the government last) amnesty, in spring 2005, allowed around 690,000 immigrants who were working (illegally) and had been in the country since August 2004 to legalise their situation and obtain residence permits.

In mid-2008, rising unemployment among Spain´s immigrant population led the government to introduce an incentive programme for immigrants to return to their home countries. Immigrants receive their unemployment benefit in two lump sums (40 per cent when they leave Spain and 60 per cent when they arrive in their home country) on the condition that they don't return to Spain for at least three years. Those returning to a permanent job in Spain after three years automatically qualify for permanent residence. It's expected that over 1m immigrants will take advantage of this programme.

Immigration is a complex subject and the information in this chapter is intended only as a general guide. You shouldn't base any decisions or actions on the information contained herein without confirming it with an official and (hopefully) reliable source, such as a Spanish consulate.

4.

ARRIVAL

Spain is a signatory to the Schengen agreement, an open-border policy between member countries, which are Austria, the Baltic States, Belgium, the Czech Republic, Denmark, Finland, France, Germany, Greece, Hungary, Iceland, Italy, Luxembourg, Malta, the Netherlands, Norway, Poland, Portugal, Slovakia, Slovenia, Spain and Sweden. Under the agreement, immigration checks and passport controls take place when you first arrive in a member country, after which you can travel freely between member countries.

If you cross into Spain by road, you may drive through the border post without stopping, unless asked to do so. Customs officials are entitled to stop anyone for a spot check, e.g. for drugs or illegal immigrants, and any goods and pets that you're carrying mustn't be subject to any prohibitions or restrictions (see page 63).

> ☑ **SURVIVAL TIP**
>
> Not all border posts are open 24 hours a day; some smaller posts open only from early morning until some time in the evening and times may vary with the season. If you plan to enter Spain via a minor border post, check the opening times in advance – or you may be spending the night in your car.

If you arrive at a seaport by private boat, you must produce the boat's registration papers on request. A vessel registered outside the European Union (EU) may remain in Spain for a maximum of six months in any calendar year, after which it must be exported or imported (when duty and tax must be paid). However, you can get the local customs authorities to seal (*precintar*) a foreign-registered boat while you're absent from Spain and unseal it when you wish to use it, thus allowing you to keep it in Spain all year round, provided you use it for no more than six months of the year. Foreign-registered vehicles and boats mustn't be lent or hired to anyone while in Spain.

In addition to information regarding immigration and customs, this chapter contains a list of tasks that must be completed before (or soon after) arrival in Spain, and includes suggestions for finding local help and information. Note that in Spain you should always carry your foreign identity card, passport or Spanish residence permit (or a copy certified by a Spanish police station).

IMMIGRATION

If you arrive in Spain from another country party to the Schengen agreement (see above), there are usually no immigration checks or passport controls (see above). EU nationals arriving in Spain from a non-Schengen EU country, e.g. the UK, must go through passport control.

If you're a non-EU national and arrive in Spain by air or sea from outside the EU, you must go through immigration (*imigración*) for non-EU citizens. This involves completing a registration card, which is usually provided on the aircraft or ship, and having your visa checked. If you have a single-entry visa, it will be cancelled by the immigration official. You may wish to get a stamp in your passport as confirmation of your date of entry into Spain.

in particular to animal products; plants (see below); wild fauna and flora and products derived from them; live animals; medicines and medical products (except for prescribed medicines); firearms and ammunition (see below); certain goods and technologies with a dual civil/military purpose; and works of art and collectors' items.

☑ SURVIVAL TIP

If you're unsure whether any goods you're importing fall into the above categories, you should check with Spanish customs.

To import some types of plant (e.g. rooted trees from outside Europe), you must obtain a plant health certificate from the export authorities in your home country. If you're importing house plants, flower seeds or vegetables in your personal effects, they aren't usually subject to controls, but check with customs beforehand.

If you're planning to import sporting guns into Spain, you must obtain a certificate from a Spanish consulate abroad, which is issued on production of a valid gun (firearms) licence. The certificate must be presented to customs on entry into Spain and can be used to exchange a foreign gun licence for a Spanish licence when taking up residence.

EMBASSY REGISTRATION

Nationals of some countries are required to register with their local embassy or consulate after taking up residence in Spain. For example, non-EU residents may require a certificate (or consular inscription) from their country's consulate in Spain declaring that they're registered with them in order to obtain a residence permit. In any case, most embassies like to keep a record of their country's citizens resident in Spain, and registration can be in your interest if there's a national emergency or natural disaster, for example. Many countries (particularly European countries with a lot of residents in Spain) maintain consulates throughout Spain, which are an important source of local information for residents and can often provide valuable contacts (see **Appendix A** for a list of addresses).

US nationals can register with the US embassy in Spain online before they leave the US (🖳 https://travelregistration.state.gov/ibrs).

FINDING HELP

One of the major problems facing new arrivals is how and where to get help with matters such as finding accommodation and enrolling children in school. In addition to the comprehensive general information provided by this book, you will need detailed local information. How easily you find it will depend on your employer, the town or area where you live (e.g. residents of resort areas are far better served than those in rural areas), your nationality, your Spanish proficiency (there's an abundance of information available in Spanish, but little in English and other foreign languages) and your sex (women are generally better catered for through women's groups).

An additional problem is that much of the available information isn't intended for foreigners and their particular needs. You may find that expatriate acquaintances and colleagues offer advice based on their own experiences and mistakes. But, well meant though it invariably is, such information may not apply to your particular situation.

Your local town hall (*ayuntamiento*) may be a good source of information, but you usually need to speak Spanish to benefit and may be sent on a wild goose chase from department to department. However, town halls in areas where there are many foreign residents often have a foreigners' department (*departamento de extranjeros*) where staff speak English, and possibly other languages, such as Danish, French, German, Norwegian and Swedish (an advantage of living somewhere where there are many other foreigners). Some foreigners' departments also publish useful booklets in English and other languages. A foreigners' department can save you having to engage a legal professional such as a *gestor* or lawyer.

Some companies employ staff to help new arrivals or contract this job out to a relocation consultant, particularly multinationals. Most Spanish employers, however, are totally unaware of (or uninterested in) the problems and difficulties faced by foreign employees and their families.

In major cities and resort towns, a wealth of valuable information is provided by English-speaking clubs and expatriate organisations. Most consulates provide their nationals with local information, including details of lawyers, translators, doctors, dentists, schools, and social and expatriate organisations. Contacts can also be found through many expatriate magazines and newspapers (see **Appendix B**).

CHECKLISTS

Before Arrival

The following checklist contains a summary of the tasks that should (if possible) be completed before your arrival in Spain:

◆ Obtain a visa, if necessary, for you and all your family members. Obviously this **must** be done before arrival in Spain.

◆ Visit Spain in advance of your move to organise schooling for your children.

◆ Find temporary or permanent accommodation.

◆ Buy a car, register it and arrange insurance.

◆ Obtain an international driving permit, if necessary.

◆ Arrange the shipment of your personal effects to Spain.

◆ Arrange health insurance for yourself and your family. This is essential if you won't be covered by Spanish social security.

◆ Open a bank account in Spain, transfer funds and give the details to your employer (you can open an account with many Spanish banks from abroad). It's also wise to obtain some euros before your arrival in Spain, as this saves you having to change money on arrival.

◆ Obtain an international credit or charge card, which will be invaluable during your first few months in Spain.

◆ Collect all your family's official documents, including birth certificates, driving licences, marriage certificate, divorce papers or death certificate (if a widow or widower), educational diplomas, professional certificates and job references, school records and student identity cards, employment references, medical and dental records, bank account

and credit card details, insurance policies and receipts for any valuables that you have.

◆ You will also need the documents necessary to obtain a residence permit plus certified copies, official translations and numerous passport-size photographs (students should take at least a dozen).

After Arrival

The following checklist contains a summary of tasks to be completed after arrival in Spain (if not done before):

◆ On arrival at a Spanish airport or port, have your visa cancelled and your passport stamped, as applicable.

◆ If you don't own a car and need one, rent one for a week or two until you buy one. It's practically impossible to get around in rural areas without a car.

◆ Apply for a residence permit at your local town hall within 15 days of your arrival (see page 54).

◆ Register with your local embassy or consulate).

◆ Register with your local social security office .

◆ Find a local doctor and dentist (see **Chapter 12**).

◆ Arrange whatever insurance is necessary (see **Chapter 13**).

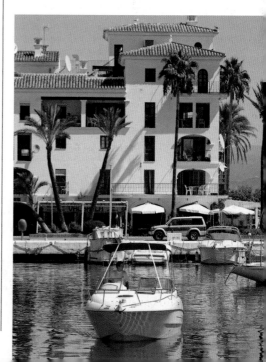

5.
ACCOMMODATION

Most Spaniards live with their parents until well into their 20s, and some 50 per cent of those aged between 25 and 30 still live in their parents' house, often because high property and rental prices mean they cannot afford to live away from home. However, nearly 90 per cent of Spaniards own their own homes, compared with some 75 per cent in the UK and Italy, 55 per cent in France and 45 per cent in Germany. Around 10 per cent of Spanish families also own a second home in Spain and the proportion is increasing annually.

There are more than 2m foreign property owners in Spain, which is Europe's favourite country for second homes, particularly among buyers from the Benelux countries, Germany, Ireland, Scandinavia and the UK. British and German property owners account for some 70 per cent of the total. Most foreigners are concentrated on the Mediterranean coast (the *costas*) and in the Balearic and Canary Islands. Officially, some 20 per cent of foreign property owners in Spain are residents, the majority of whom are retired, although the real figure is much higher, as many foreigners fail to register as residents.

You've probably heard a number of horror stories concerning property transactions in Spain, many of which are unfortunately true, although some stories are hugely exaggerated by the press. Nevertheless, buying property in Spain isn't the lottery it once was and most problems in recent years have been due to bankruptcies rather than fraud and a surprisingly high percentage have been caused by foolish buyers who are seemingly prepared to confide in complete strangers, hand over huge amounts of money or commit themselves to buying property they don't want or cannot afford!

It's vital to obtain expert, independent legal advice and beware of fraudsters when buying and selling property in Spain. Make your maxim for all property transactions: 'If you wouldn't do it in your home country, don't do it in Spain'.

PROPERTY MARKET

In most areas of Spain, finding accommodation to rent or buy isn't difficult, provided that your requirements aren't too unusual. In cities and large towns, for example, apartments are much more common than detached houses, which are rare and prohibitively expensive. There are, however, a few exceptions. In the major cities in particular, rented accommodation is in high demand and short supply, and rents can be astronomical. Accommodation, which normally accounts for around 25 per cent of the average Spanish family's budget, can be up to 50 per cent in the big cities. For example, the type of apartment that rents for €500 per month in Almería will cost at least €1,200 a month in Madrid or Barcelona, and at least €600 a month in most northern cities.

The most expensive cities to buy a property in are Madrid (average €3,005 per m^2), Barcelona (€2,761 per m^2), the Balearics (€2,408 per m^2) and Malaga (€2,348 per m^2). In contrast, prices in the provinces of Cáceres and Badajoz (both in Extremadura) average around €1,020 per m^2.

Since the last property recession, in 1997, property prices have risen at a steady rate

annually and from 2000 to 2004 soared throughout the country with yearly increases of over 20 per cent in many areas. Since 2004 the property market has slowed down considerably and annual rises in 2006 and 2007 were 10.4 per cent and 5.8 per cent respectively.

The property boom has brought with it a massive increase in construction with over 800,000 new homes started in 2006, as the skyline of cranes in many areas testified. In resort areas, rising prices were fuelled by the seemingly endless demand for holiday homes, particularly from foreigners (especially British), and nearly one in three homes in Spain are second or holiday homes. However, higher property prices and interest rates meant that non-resident investment in property fell sharply during 2006 and 2007, and this tendency is expected to continue during 2008-9.

The knock-on effect of the US sub-prime crisis together with a rise in interest rates (in June 2008 the Euribor interest rate rose above 5 per cent, its highest level since 2002) has led to a slow-down in the Spanish property market. In the first quarter of 2008, Spain's largest developers reported a massive 75 per cent drop in sales and it's estimated that there are some 2m properties (off-plan and resale) currently on the market. Experts are divided on whether the current situation is short or long term, but most agree that prices won't outstrip inflation during at least 2008 and 2009.

TEMPORARY ACCOMMODATION

On arrival in Spain, you may find it necessary to stay in temporary accommodation for a few weeks or months, e.g. before moving into permanent accommodation or while waiting for your furniture to arrive. Some employers provide rooms or self-contained apartments for employees and their families, although this is rare and is often only for a limited period. Many hotels and hostels (see pages 248 and 249) cater for long-term guests and offer reduced weekly and monthly rates – though usually only outside the tourist season. In most areas, particularly in Madrid and other large cities, serviced apartments are widely available, with private bathrooms and kitchens. These are cheaper and more convenient than hotels, particularly for families, and are usually let on a weekly basis.

In cities and resorts, self-catering holiday accommodation (see page 250) is widely available, although it's prohibitively expensive during the main holiday season (June to mid-September).

RELOCATION CONSULTANTS

If you're fortunate enough to have your move to Spain paid for by your employer, it's likely that he will engage a relocation consultant to handle the details. There are an increasing number of relocation consultants in Spain and many deal with corporate clients and/or individuals. Fees are usually around €250 per day or you can choose a package of services for a set fee, e.g. €2,500. The main service provided by relocation consultants is finding accommodation to rent or buy and arranging viewing.

Other housing services include conducting negotiations, drawing up contracts, arranging mortgages, organising surveys and insurance, and handling the house move. Relocation consultants also provide reports on local schools, health services, public transport, sports and social facilities, and other amenities and services. Some companies provide daily advice and assistance, e.g. assisting clients in their dealings with local officials and businesses.

Finding rental accommodation for single people or couples without children can usually be accomplished in a few weeks, while housing families may take longer, depending on the location and your requirements. You should usually allow at least two months between engaging a consultant and moving into a purchased property in Spain.

BUYING PROPERTY

Buying property in Spain is usually a good long-term investment and is preferable to renting. However, if you're staying less than two or three years, you may be better off renting. The Spanish don't generally regard property as an investment and you shouldn't expect to make a quick profit when buying property; you need to own a house for up to three years simply to recover the fees associated with buying (around 10 per cent of the price), and prices aren't rising as fast as in recent years (if at all). Capital gains tax (see page 237) can also take a large chunk out of a profit made on the sale of a second home, particularly for non-residents.

As when buying property anywhere, it's never advisable to be in too much of a hurry. Have a good look around your preferred area(s) and make sure that you have a clear picture of the types of properties available and their relative prices. There's a huge variety of properties in Spain, ranging from

derelict farmhouses requiring complete restoration to new luxury apartments and villas with all modern conveniences; some are vastly overpriced and others, which seem to be a bargain, will end up costing you even more.

Some people set themselves impossible deadlines in which to buy a property or business (e.g. a few days or a week) and often end up bitterly regretting their impulsive decision. Although it's a common practice, mixing a holiday with a property purchase isn't advisable, as most people are inclined to make poor business decisions when their mind is on play rather than work.

It's a wise or lucky person who gets his choice absolutely right first time, which is why most experts recommend that you rent before buying unless you're absolutely sure what you want, how much you wish to pay and where you want to live. To reduce the chance of making an expensive error when buying in an unfamiliar region, it's often prudent to rent for 6 to 12 months, taking in the worst part of the year (weather-wise). This allows you to become familiar with the region and the weather, and gives you plenty of time to look around for a permanent home at your leisure. There's no shortage of properties for sale in Spain and whatever kind of property you're looking for, you will have an abundance to choose from. Wait until you find your 'dream' home and then think about it for another week or two before signing a contract.

For comprehensive information on all aspects of buying a property in Spain, see our sister publication, *Buying a Home in Spain*.

RENTED ACCOMMODATION

If you're planning to stay in Spain for only two or three years, renting is usually a better solution than buying. Long-term rental is also the answer for those who don't want the trouble, expense and restrictions associated with buying a property. It saves you tying up your capital and can be surprisingly inexpensive in many regions (some people let out their family homes abroad and rent one in Spain, and sometimes make a profit). Renting also affords you maximum flexibility should you wish to move to another region in Spain, return home or even move to another country. In today's uncertain financial climate, there are considerable risks associated with buying property, particularly if you're unsure of your long-term plans.

Even if you're looking for a permanent home in Spain, it's wise to rent for a period until you know exactly what you want, how much you wish to pay and where you want to live. This is particularly important for those who don't know Spain well. Renting allows you to become familiar with an area, its weather and amenities and the local people; to meet other foreigners who have made their homes in Spain and share their experiences; and, not least, to discover the cost of living at first hand. 'Short-term' rentals (i.e. for between around a month and a year) are considered here; for information about holiday rentals see **Self-catering** on page 250.

In most resort areas, however, there's a shortage of short-term rental accommodation, particularly in the summer, because property owners prefer the higher returns from holiday lets. You may be able to rent a property from October to May but have to vacate it for the summer. The majority of properties in major cities are rented apartments, but they're mostly small (one- or two-roomed); large apartments and houses are difficult to find and prohibitively expensive.

☑ SURVIVAL TIP

Although they're common in resort areas, particularly for short-term rentals, furnished (*amueblado*) properties can be difficult to find in cities.

Many long-term rental properties in Spain are let unfurnished. Note that 'unfurnished' doesn't simply mean 'without furniture' in Spain. An unfurnished property, particularly in major cities, is usually an empty 'shell' with no light fixtures, curtain rods or even a television aerial. There's also no cooker, refrigerator or dishwasher and

there may even be no kitchen units or kitchen sink! Always ask before viewing what fixtures and fittings are included, as you may save yourself a wasted trip. If the previous tenant has fitted items such as carpets and kitchen cupboards, he may ask you to reimburse him for the cost. You should be prepared to negotiate the price accordingly.

In an attempt to alleviate the saturated rental market, the government is allocating grants of up to €6,000 to landlords, whose income is tax free if they're under 35. And tenants aged between 22 and 30 earning less than €22,000 a year are entitled to €210 a month towards their rent, a loan of €600 for the deposit and €120 towards a bank guarantee; for details go to 🖥 www.alquilerjoven. es (in Spanish only).

Finding a Rental Property

Your success or failure in finding a suitable rental property depends on many factors, not least the type of rental you're looking for, how much you want to pay and the area where you wish to live. There are a number of ways of finding a property to rent, including the following:

♦ Ask friends, relatives and acquaintances to help spread the word, particularly if you're looking in the area where you already live. A lot of rental properties, particularly in major cities, are found by word of mouth. You can also look out for 'to rent' (*se alquila*) signs in windows. If you're looking for an apartment in a block in Madrid or Barcelona, ask the concierge (*portero*) if there are any vacancies in a building or if anything will be vacant soon.

♦ Check the advertisements in local Spanish newspapers and magazines under *Alquiler*. In major cities, there are property newspapers and magazines. There's little jargon or abbreviations in Spanish rental advertisements and most can be deciphered without too much trouble. However, if you cannot speak Spanish, you may prefer to respond to advertisements in expatriate newspapers and magazines (see **Appendix B**), where advertisers are likely to speak English or other foreign languages.

♦ Use the internet. There are numerous sites, including 🖥 www.fotocasa.es and 🖥 www. idealista.com (two of the largest), 🖥 www. easypiso.com (for shared accommodation) and 🖥 www.enalquiler.com (advice as well as lets).

straight away. You must be available to inspect properties immediately or at any time. Even if you start phoning at the crack of dawn, you're still likely to find a queue when you arrive to view a choice property in Madrid or Barcelona. The best days for advertisements are usually Fridays and Saturdays. You can insert a 'rental wanted' advertisement in many newspapers and on notice boards, but don't count on success using this method.

Young people aged between 18 and 35 in the regions of Aragon, Baleares, Canaries, Cantabria, Castilla-La Mancha, Castilla y León, Catalonia, the Comunidad Valenciana, Galicia, Madrid and Navarra have access to a regional 'Young Person's Accommodation Centre' (*Bolsa de Vivienda Joven*), where general information about accommodation, legal advice and accommodation lists are available. Further information about these centres is provided by the Youth Services department (*Servicios de Juventud*) at regional government offices.

Rental Costs

Rental costs vary considerably with the size, quality and age of a property, and the facilities provided. However, the most significant factor affecting rents is the region, the city and the neighbourhood. In major cities, particularly Madrid and Barcelona, where rental accommodation is in high demand and short supply, rents are high. A two-bedroom unfurnished apartment (e.g. 75m^2) rents for around €1,000 a month in Madrid or Barcelona – around twice as much as in most smaller cities and rural or resort areas. However, rents have risen considerably on the Costa del Sol and in other resort areas. Rents are lowest in small towns and rural areas, although good rented accommodation is often difficult to find.

Many Spanish families live in communal property developments called *urbanizaciones* (which surround Spanish cities), where rents may be lower than in city centres. In an apartment block, generally, the higher the apartment, the more expensive it is. However,

◆ Visit accommodation and letting agents. Most cities and large towns have estate agents (*agentes de propiedad inmobiliaria*) who also act as letting agents for owners. It's often better to deal with an agent than directly with owners, particularly concerning contracts and legal matters. Some agents advertise abroad in property publications and many companies handling holiday rentals also offer longer term rentals, particularly during the winter. **Agents usually charge commission equal to a half or one month's rent for long-term rentals.** If you wish to avoid agency fees ask before viewing, as advertisers who appear to be private individuals are often agencies.

◆ Check the advertisements in shop windows and on notice boards in shopping centres, supermarkets, universities and colleges, and company offices.

◆ Obtain copies of newsletters published by churches, clubs and expatriate organisations, and also check their notice boards.

To find accommodation through advertisements in local newspapers you must usually be quick off the mark. Buy the newspaper as soon as it's published and start phoning

you, they will direct you to the office where you can make a formal complaint.

Inventory

When renting a property you may be required to complete and sign an inventory (*inventario*) of the fixtures, fittings and furnishings, and make a report of its general condition and that of fixtures and fittings, furniture and carpets, etc. (if furnished), the cleanliness and state of the decoration, and anything missing or in need of repair.

Don't sign the inventory until after you've moved in. If you find a serious fault after signing the inventory, send a registered letter to your landlord asking for it to be attached to the inventory.

An inventory document should be provided by your landlord or letting agent and normally includes every single item in a furnished property. Note, however, that many rental companies in resort areas in Spain are negligent when it comes to providing an inventory. This is to your advantage, as the landlord or agent can hardly charge you for breakages or missing items when no inventory was provided. However, if an inventory isn't provided, you can ask for one to be prepared and annexed to the lease. Where applicable, an inventory should be drawn up when you move in and when when you vacate a property. If the two inventories don't correspond, you must make good any damage or deficiencies or the landlord can do so and deduct the cost from your deposit.

Although Spanish landlords are no worse than landlords in most other countries, some use any excuse to prevent repaying a deposit. When leaving rented accommodation you may be required to pay for cleaning, unless you leave it in a spotless condition. Check that you aren't overcharged; the going rate in most areas is from €8 to €14 an hour, although some landlords may try to charge you €15 or more an hour.

MOVING HOUSE

After finding a home in Spain it usually takes only a week or two to have your belongings shipped from within continental Europe, around four weeks from the east coast of the US, six weeks from the US west coast and the Far East, and around eight weeks from Australasia. Customs clearance is no longer necessary when shipping your household effects between

European Union (EU) countries (see **Chapter 4**). However, when shipping your effects from a non-EU country to Spain, you should enquire about customs formalities in advance. If you fail to follow the specified procedure you can encounter problems and delays, and may be erroneously charged duty or fined. The relevant forms to be completed by non-EU citizens depend on whether your Spanish home is your main residence or a second home. Removal companies usually take care of the paperwork and ensure that the correct documents are provided and properly completed.

It's advisable to use a major shipping company with a good reputation. For international moves it's best to use a company that's a member of the International Federation of Furniture Removers (FIDI, 🖳 www.fidi.com) or the Overseas Moving Network International (OMNI, 🖳 www.omnimoving.com), with experience of delivering to Spain. Members of FIDI and OMNI usually subscribe to an advance payment scheme providing a guarantee, whereby, if a member company fails to fulfil its commitments to a client, the removal is completed at the agreed cost by another company or your money is refunded. Some removal companies have subsidiaries or affiliates in Spain, which may be more convenient if you encounter problems or need to make an insurance claim.

If you engage a shipping company in Spain, it's wise to avoid unregistered companies ('a man with a van'), as some have been known to disappear with their client's worldly possessions. A Spanish shipping company should have a Spanish business address, a licence number and a value added tax (VAT/IVA) number.

You should obtain at least three written quotations before choosing a company, as rates vary considerably. Removal companies should send a representative to provide a detailed quotation. Most companies will pack your belongings and provide packing cases and other containers, although this is naturally more expensive than packing them yourself. Ask a company how they pack fragile and valuable items, and whether the cost of packing material and insurance (see below) is included in a quotation. If you decide to do your own packing, most shipping companies will provide packing crates and boxes. Shipments are charged by volume, e.g. the square metre (m2) in Europe and the square foot (ft2) in the US.

You should expect to pay from €4,000 to €10,000 to move the contents of a three- to four-bedroom house within western Europe, e.g. from London to the south of Spain. If you're flexible about the delivery date, shipping companies will usually quote a lower fee based on a 'part load', where the cost is shared with other deliveries. This can result in savings of 50 per cent or more compared with a bespoke delivery, but it usually involves a delay. Whether you have an individual or shared delivery, obtain the maximum transit period in writing; otherwise you may have to wait months for delivery!

Insurance premiums are usually 1 to 2 per cent of the declared value of your goods, depending on the type of cover chosen. It's prudent to make a photographic or video record of valuables for insurance purposes. Most insurance policies cover for 'all risks' on a replacement value basis. Note, however, that china, glass and other breakables can usually be included in an all-risks policy only when they're packed by the removal company. Insurance usually covers total loss or loss of a particular crate only, rather than individual items (unless they were packed by the shipping company).

If there are any breakages or damaged items, they must in theory be noted before you sign the delivery bill, although it may be possible to report these within a certain period after delivery. Be sure to read the small print, as some companies require clients to make a claim within a few days, although seven is usual. If you need to make a claim, send it by registered post. Some insurance companies apply an 'excess' of around 1 per cent of the total shipment value when assessing claims. This means that if your shipment is valued at €25,000 and you make a claim for less than €250, you won't receive anything.

If you're unable to ship your belongings directly to Spain, most shipping companies will put them into storage and some offer a limited free storage period before shipment, e.g. 14 days. **If you need to put your household effects into storage, it's important to have them fully insured, as warehouses have been known to burn down!** Make a list of everything to be moved and give a copy to the removal company. Don't include anything illegal (e.g. guns, drugs or pornography) with your belongings, as customs checks can be rigorous and penalties severe. Provide the shipping company with detailed instructions how to find your Spanish address from the nearest motorway (or main road) and a telephone number where you can be contacted.

If your Spanish home has poor or impossible access for a large truck you must inform the shipping company (the ground must also be firm enough to support a heavy vehicle). Note also that if large items of furniture need to be taken in through an upstairs window or balcony, you may need to pay extra.

☑ SURVIVAL TIP

Be sure to fully insure your belongings during removal with a well established insurance company. Don't insure with a shipping company that carries its own insurance, as they will usually fight every euro of a claim.

After considering the shipping costs, you may decide to ship only selected items of furniture and personal effects, and buy new furniture in Spain. If you're importing household goods from another European country, it's possible to rent a self-drive van or truck, although if you rent a vehicle outside Spain you must usually return it to the country where it was hired.

If you plan to transport your belongings to Spain personally, check the customs requirements in the countries you must pass through. Most people find it isn't advisable to do their own move unless it's a simple job, e.g. a few items of furniture and personal effects only. It's no fun heaving beds and wardrobes up stairs and squeezing them into impossible spaces! If you're taking pets with you, you may need to get your vet to tranquillise them, as many pets are frightened (even more than people) by the chaos and stress of moving house. See also **Pets** on page 323.

Bear in mind when moving home that everything that can go wrong often does, so allow plenty of time and try not to arrange your move to your new home on the same day as the previous owner is moving out. That's just asking for fate to intervene! See also **Checklists** in chapter 20.

Inventory

When moving into a property that you've purchased, you should make an inventory of the fixtures and fittings, and check that the previous owner hasn't absconded with anything which was included in the contract or paid for separately, e.g. carpets, light fittings, curtains, fitted cupboards, kitchen appliances or doors.

ELECTRICITY

In January 2003, the energy market was liberalised and clients can now theoretically choose which company provides their electricity; in practice, however, unless you live in a large city, you usually have no choice, as there's only one provider, as follows:

♦ Endesa (☎ 902 509 509, 🖥 www.endesaonline.com) –

covers Andalusia, the Balearics (where it's known as Enesa Gesa), the Canaries and Catalonia;

♦ Gas Natural (☎ 900 700 365, 🖥 www. gasnatural.com) – supplies most of Spain except the islands;

♦ Hidrocantábrico (☎ 902 860 860, 🖥 www. h-c.es) – covers Asturias and Madrid;

♦ Iberdrola (☎ 901 202 020, 🖥 www. iberdrola.es) – Asturias, the Basque Country, Cantabria, Catalonia (including the Costa Brava), Comunidad Valenciana, Galicia and Madrid;

♦ Unión Fenosa – central Spain, including Madrid (☎ 901 404 040, 🖥 www.union fenosa.es).

Spain's main electricity companies are Endesa (the largest, with 44.5 per cent of the market), Gas Natural, Hidrocantábrico, Iberdrola and Unión Fenosa.

Power Supply

The electricity supply in most of Spain is 220 volts AC with a frequency of 50 hertz (cycles). However, some areas still have a 110-volt supply and it's even possible to find dual voltage 110 and 220-volt systems in the same house or the same room! All new buildings have a 220-volt supply and the authorities have mounted a campaign to encourage homeowners with 110-volt systems to switch to 220 volts. Note that most appliances, e.g. televisions (TV), designed to operate on 240 volts will function with a power supply of 220 volts.

Power cuts are frequent in many areas of Spain, although the situation improved greatly in 2007 in all areas except Barcelona (where one cut saw the city without electricity for more than two days). Saturation of power lines is a serious problem in Spain (demand has far outstripped supply) and the Andalusian coastlines, the Costa Blanca and Barcelona are among the worst affected areas. When it rains heavily, the electricity supply can become very unstable, with frequent power cuts lasting from a few micro seconds (just long enough to crash a computer) to a few hours (or days). If you use a computer, it's advisable to fit an uninterrupted power supply (UPS) with a battery backup (costing around €150), which allows you time to save your work and shut down your computer safely after a power failure.

☑ **SURVIVAL TIP**

If you live in an area where cuts are frequent and you rely on electricity for your livelihood, e.g. for operating a computer and other equipment, you may need to install a back-up generator. Even more important than a battery back-up is a power surge protector for appliances such as TVs, computers and fax machines, which prevents equipment being damaged or destroyed.

If you buy a remote rural property (*finca rústica*), you may be obliged to pay for the installation of electricity lines or transformers plus the connection to your property if the mains services don't run near your home, although in most areas there are public guarantees of the supply of electricity (and water, sewerage and telephone) and you must pay only for the connection to your property. In many remote areas, there's no mains electricity at all and you must install a generator, solar panels or a large windmill if you want electricity, although some people make do with gas and oil lamps. Note that in some urbanisations, water is provided by electric pump and, therefore, if your electricity supply is cut off, so is your water supply.

If the power keeps tripping off when you attempt to use a number of high-power appliances simultaneously, e.g. an electric kettle, a dishwasher and a heater, it means that the power supply (*potencia*) to your property is too low. This is a common problem in Spain. If this is the case, you may need to contact your electricity company and ask them to upgrade the power supply in your property (it can also be downgraded if it's more than you require). The power supply increases in increments of 1.1KW, which is the minimum, e.g. 2.2KW, 3.3KW, 4.4KW, 5.5KW. Note, however, that it can take some time to get your power supply changed. The power supply is usually shown on your meter. Your standing charge depends on the supply, which is why owners tend to keep it as low as possible and most holiday homes have a power rating of just 3.3KW.

Make sure your power supply is high enough for your needs. If you install air-conditioning, you will probably need to increase your power supply. Electrical fires caused by overloaded domestic power supplies are common.

Registration

Immediately after buying or renting a property (unless utilities are included in the rent), you must sign a contract with the local electricity company. This usually entails a visit to the company's office, although most companies now offer the possibility of registering by telephone or online (provided you can find a power supply to run your computer!). Some electricity companies have service lines where foreign customers can obtain information in English and German, in addition to Spanish.

If you're visiting a company's offices, you must take identification with you (e.g. your passport or residence permit) and, if possible, copies of the previous owner's contract and bills (and a good book, as queues can be long). In order to register for electricity via the internet or telephone, you will need to give some identification (your name and your passport or identity card number), as well as the reference number for the electricity supply (usually found in the top left-hand corner of a bill under *Contrato de Suministro Nº*).

Make sure all bills have been paid by the previous owner; you're liable only for

purchased from a distributor (though treatment for a hernia incurred by lifting it into and out of your car can cost a lot more). You can buy only 'camping-size' bottles at petrol stations and supermarkets, and in some areas you may buy only from a local distributor.

Bear in mind that gas bottles have a habit of running out at the most inconvenient times, so keep a spare bottle handy and make sure you know how to change them (get the previous owner or a neighbour to show you). A bottle used just for cooking can last an average family up to three months. If a gas boiler is installed outside, e.g. on a balcony, it must be protected from the wind; otherwise you will continually be re-lighting the pilot light.

You must have your gas appliances serviced and inspected at least every five years. If you have a contract with Repsol Butano, they will do this for you or it will be done by your local authorised distributor. Some distributors will try to sell you a package which includes third-party insurance and free parts should they be required, although it isn't necessary to have this insurance and it may be a waste of money.

Beware of 'bogus' Repsol Butano representatives calling unannounced to inspect gas appliances; even if they represent legitimate companies, their charges will be extortionate and they will give you a large bill for changing tubing and regulators (which usually don't need changing at all), and demand payment in cash on the spot. If you wish, you can let them make an inspection and give you an estimate (*presupuesto*) for any work that needs doing, but don't let them do any work or pay any money before checking with your local Repsol Butano distributor. Incidentally, plastic tubes have an expiry date printed on them and you can buy them from a hardware store (*ferretería*) and change them yourself.

HEATING

Central heating (*calefacción*) is essential in winter in northern and central Spain. If you're used to central heating and like a warm house in winter, you will almost certainly miss central heating at some time everywhere in Spain except the Canaries. Central heating systems may be powered by

oil, gas, electricity, solid fuel (usually wood) or even solar power. Oil-fired central heating isn't common in Spain due to the high cost of heating oil and the problems associated with storage. Many modern houses now include under-floor heating operated by electricity. In rural areas, many houses have open, wood-burning fireplaces and stoves, which may be combined with a central heating system.

Whatever form of heating you use, it's important to have good insulation, without which up to 60 per cent of the heat generated is lost through walls and roof. Many homes, particularly older and cheaper properties, don't have good insulation, and even in a new home you may find that the builder hasn't observed the regulations regarding insulation. In cities, apartment blocks may have a communal central heating system providing heating for all apartments, the cost of which is divided among the tenants.

If you're a non-resident or absent from Spain for long periods, you should choose an apartment with a separate heating system; otherwise you will be contributing towards your neighbours' heating bills.

AIR-CONDITIONING

In some regions of Spain, summer temperatures can reach over 40 °C (104 °F) and although properties are built to withstand the heat, you may wish to install air-conditioning (*aire acondicionado*). Note, however, that there can be negative effects if you suffer from asthma or respiratory problems. You can choose between a huge variety of air-conditioners – fixed or moveable, indoor or outdoor, and high or low power. Air-conditioning units cost from around €600 (plus installation) for a 2,000 BTU (*frigorías*) unit, which is sufficient to cool an average-size room. Some air-conditioners are noisy, so check the noise level before buying one. Although slightly more expensive, it's advisable to buy an inverter air-conditioner, which maintains a low electric current once the desired temperature has been reached and is up to 30 per cent cheaper to run than a standard model.

An air-conditioning system with a heat pump provides cooling in summer and economical heating in winter. A system with an outside compressor providing radiant heating and cooling costs around €1,200 per room. Many people fit ceiling fans (costing from around €65) for cheaper cooling in the summer, and these are standard fixtures in some new homes.

WASTE DISPOSAL

The amount of waste produced per head in Spain is one of the lowest in the EU, and there are TV, radio and school campaigns encouraging recycling. Most municipalities now recycle glass (green bins), paper and cardboard (blue bins), aluminium, cans and plastic (yellow bins), batteries and other materials, although few collection points are sometimes few and far between. Many municipalities also recycle garden waste, which is then sold as compost. Some municipalities publish leaflets detailing where and when to dump your household rubbish.

> Most non-recyclable rubbish goes into landfill sites, although more municipalities are now incinerating it (which creates smoke pollution).

The problem of landfill sites, some of which pollute ground water used for household consumption, is serious and growing and many municipalities have a shortage of available sites. When buying a property in Spain, make sure that you aren't within 'smelling' distance of the local rubbish dump (or that one isn't planned close by), as they're sometimes located close to residential areas (although this is illegal).

Rubbish collection is efficient in most towns and cities, although in some rural areas residents are required to take their rubbish to a collection point, which may be located some kilometres away. However, most community properties have communal skips or rubbish bins where residents are required to deposit their rubbish in sealed plastic bags. Bins are usually emptied daily (at night) except on Sundays. In some areas, residents have personal bins. If this is the case, ask your neighbours when you should put out your rubbish for collection, as some municipalities levy fines if rubbish is put out for collection too early, e.g. before 9pm.

By the year 2002, residents in municipalities with over 5,000 inhabitants were supposed to have been required to deposit different types of rubbish in separate containers, although the implementation of this measure has been repeatedly postponed. Most areas now have separate containers for glass, paper and plastics, but relatively few have containers for organic waste (*basura orgánica*).

Most municipalities charge an annual fee for rubbish collection, which varies according to whether you live in a town or a rural area, e.g. from €30 to €200 a year. Costs are usually reduced for the elderly on low incomes. Check with your town hall and have the bill sent to your bank and paid directly by them, as (like all municipal bills) if you don't pay it on time it's increased by 20 per cent.

WATER

Water, or rather the lack of it, is a major concern in Spain and the price paid for all those sunny days. Like some other countries that experience regional water shortages, Spain as a whole has sufficient water, but it isn't distributed evenly. There's (usually) surplus rainfall in the north-west and centre and a deficiency along most of the Mediterranean coast and in the Balearic and Canary islands. In the Canaries, there's a permanent water shortage and most drinking water is provided by desalination plants, while in the Balearics, 20,000 wells are employed to pump water to the surface (there are also desalination plants in Majorca and Ibiza).

There are three large desalination plants on the mainland located at Carboneras (Almería), Marbella and San Pedro del Pinatar (Murcia) and a further 17 plants are under construction along the Mediterranean and expected to be working by 2008-9. On the Costa del Sol, purification plants recycle waste water from urban areas to irrigate crops and water golf courses.

Shortages are exacerbated in resort areas, where the local population swells five to tenfold during the summer tourist season, the hottest and driest period of the year. Politicians from all regions and political parties are frequently divided over solutions to Spain's desperate shortage of water. In April 2008, there was widespread controversy over a government decision to pipe water from the river Ebro in southern Catalonia north to Barcelona, which was suffering from severe water restrictions. Protesting farmers were joined by politicians in the Comunidad Valenciana and Murcia who want water from the river Ebro to be permanently piped to their regions. Much to many politicians' relief, heavy rain in Catalonia filled the reservoirs and the pipe plan was shelved, but Spain's regions continue to fight over the distribution of water, particularly for crop irrigation (intensive and often wasteful agricultural irrigation accounts for around 80 per cent of all water used).

There's also relatively little emphasis on water conservation in Spain, particularly considering the frequent droughts, although consumption has reduced considerably in the last decade in many areas. The Costa del Sol uses double the national average per person for its numerous swimming pools, lawns, gardens and golf courses. Inhabitants of towns and cities consume more water per person, per day than any other Europeans. At the same time, hundreds of rural towns and villages have water on tap for just a few hours a day during the summer months and farmers regularly face ruin due to the lack of water for irrigation.

Storage Tanks

If you have a detached house or villa, you can reduce your water costs by collecting and storing rainwater (e.g. for car washing and plant watering). It's also possible (and desirable) to have a mains storage tank, which fills automatically and will give you a supply of water for up to a week if there's a shortage. Mains storage tanks can be roof-mounted or installed underground; the latter are cheaper and can be any size but require an electric pump. Check whether a property has a storage tank or whether you can install one. Most modern properties have them. It's also possible to use recycled water from baths, showers, kitchens and apparatus such as washing machines and dish washers, to flush toilets or water a garden.

Rates

The cost of water has risen dramatically in Spain in recent years, and in some towns water bills have increased by over 100 per cent per year, although the price of water is still lower than in most other European countries. The cost is usually between around €1 to €1.20 per cubic metre (m^3), but water costs considerably more in some areas.

According to a survey carried out by *Consumer* magazine (✉ *www.consumer.es*), Alicante, Barcelona, Cadiz and Murcia have the most expensive water, while A Coruña, Castellón and Pamplona enjoy some of the cheapest (and plenty of it).

Most municipalities levy a standing charge, which usually 'includes' a certain amount of water per quarter or month, e.g. 45m^3 a quarter or 15m^3 a month. However, like all standing charges this charge is payable whether any water is used or not (which hits non-residents hardest). Standing charges range from €7 to €25 a quarter.

Some municipalities levy a quarterly 'service' charge (*canon de servicio*) and regional governments may also levy a charge for water purification. Sometimes a higher water rate is charged for holiday homeowners or owners in community developments where the water supply isn't controlled by the local municipality. Water bills usually include sewerage and may also include rubbish collection, e.g. when a city provides all services, in which case the cost of rubbish collection may be calculated according to how much water you use! Some municipalities arbitrarily levy higher tariffs on certain urbanisations, although this is illegal. There's also a rental charge for a water meter, e.g. around €4 per quarter. Always check your water bill carefully, as overcharging (accidental or otherwise) is widespread.

To reduce your water costs, you can buy a 'water saver' that mixes air with water, thus reducing the amount of water used. The cost of fitting an apartment with a water saver is only around €40, which can reportedly be recouped in six months through lower water bills. Water savers can be purchased from El Corte Inglés and Hipercor stores, hypermarkets and DIY stores (see **Chapter 17**).

Hot Water

Water heating in apartments may be provided by a central heating source for the whole building, or apartments may have their own water heaters. If you install your own water heater, it should have a capacity of at least 75 litres. Many holiday homes have quite small water boilers, which are often inadequate for more than two people. If you need to install a water heater (or fit a larger one), you should consider the merits of electric and bottled gas heaters.

An electric water heater with a capacity of 75 litres (sufficient for two people) costs from €140 to €300 and usually takes between 60 and 90 minutes to heat water to 40 °C in winter. A gas flow-through water heater is more expensive to purchase (from €150 to €325, although there's little difference in quality between the cheaper and more expensive heaters) and install than an electric water heater, but you get unlimited hot water immediately whenever you want it. Make sure that a gas heater has a capacity of 10 to 16 litres per minute if you want it for a shower.

A gas water heater with a permanent pilot light may use up to 50 per cent more gas than one without a self-igniting flame.

Puerto Duquesa, Costa del Sol

6.
POSTAL SERVICES

There's a post office (*oficina de correos*) in most towns and at major railway stations, airports and ports in Spain, a total of over 6,000. These generally provide only a limited range of non-postal services, such as telegram, fax and telex transmission, and domestic and international giro money orders. All Spanish post offices also operate as agents for Deutsche Bank and offer a full range of banking services. Telephones aren't available in most Spanish post offices.

Unlike almost all other European post offices, the Spanish post office produces few leaflets and brochures. Postal and telegraphic tariffs are listed in a free booklet, *Tarifas Postales y Telegráficas*, theoretically obtainable from post offices but seldom seen on counters. However, tariffs can also be consulted online (🖳 www.correos.es – click on *Tarifas*).

You shouldn't expect post office staff to speak English or other foreign languages, although main post offices may have an information desk with multilingual staff.

The identifying colour used by the Spanish post office (and most European countries) is yellow, which is the colour of Spanish post boxes (*buzones*), post office signs and post vans. Postmen (*carteros*) usually wear yellow and navy uniforms.

There are usually long, slow-moving queues at post offices, although service has improved in recent years (queues used to be even longer and even slower-moving). In main post offices there are usually several windows dealing with all services (*admisión polivalente*), including stamps, registration of letters, giros, telegraphs, telegrams and telex, though there may be a spearate window for the collection

of parcels (*entrega*). In smaller post offices there may be one window for stamps (*venta de sellos*), another to register a letter or send an express letter (*certificados – postal exprés*) and yet another to prepare and post a parcel (*prep. paquete*).

Some larger post offices have a queuing system, whereby customers take a numbered ticket for the service they require (e.g. A for most transactions, B for collection of parcels and registered post and C for giros and telegrams) from a machine (usually by the door) and wait for their number to be displayed over the corresponding desk. The system is designed to save people queuing for hours for a simple operation, but at peak times you can still expect to wait at least 30 minutes for a stamp. If you just want to buy stamps, it's quicker to buy them from a tobacconist's (*estanco* or *estancos*), although they don't always have scales and therefore may be unable to tell you the postage required for a particular item.

Most European post offices are models of efficiency compared with the Spanish post office, which handles around 5.2m items of postage a year, of which it manages to lose over 100,000 (though even this, it must be said, is a better record than that of the Italian post office!). Spanish business is badly let down by the failings of the country's postal system and many businesses routinely send important post by courier.

Complaints (*reclamaciones*) about the postal service can be made at any post office and don't need to be made at the post office where the problem occurred or originated (if applicable). In the case of loss of post, the person sending the post must make the complaint. If you don't receive satisfaction, you can take your complaint to the Jefatura Provincial de Correos or the Inspección General de Correos, Plaza de la Cibeles s/n, 28014 Madrid. There's also a phone service (☎ 902 197 197) from Mondays to Fridays between 8am and 9pm and on Saturdays between 9am and 1pm; alternatively you can make your complaint online (💻 www.correos. es – look under *Quejas y Reclamaciones*). Complaint forms (*hojas de reclamaciones*) are available in post offices. If you have a complaint about bad service, the service **may** be improved, but no compensation will be paid.

More information about postal services is available via the telephone (☎ 902 197 197) or you can consult the comprehensive post office website (💻 www.correos.es – in Spanish only), which provides contact details and business hours for all post offices in Spain. Go to 'Oficinas', enter the name of the place (*localidad*) and province (*provincia*) and click on 'ver oficinas'.

GENERAL INFORMATION

Business Hours

Business hours (*horas de oficina*) at main post offices in cities and large towns are usually from around 8am until around 9.30pm, Mondays to Fridays, and from 9am to 2pm on Saturdays. Main post offices in major towns don't close for lunch and may also provide limited services outside normal business hours. Some post offices in major cities also open for a period on Sundays, although the range of services may be limited.

In small towns and villages, post offices usually open from 8.30 or 9am until between noon and 2.30pm, Mondays to Fridays, and from 9.30am to 1pm on Saturdays. Note also that some services may be available at post offices for a limited number of hours only each day, including sending telegrams and faxes; the preparation, posting and collection of parcels and poste restante (*lista de correos*). There are also post offices at international airports, generally only open in the morning, and mobile post offices in some areas usually operating from around 10am to 1pm.

Telecor

Under an agreement with Spain's flagship department store, El Corté Inglés, the post office runs Telecor shops, a kind of 'one-stop' shop for telephone (fixed and mobile), television and utility services. The shops, available in main post offices and in provincial capitals, offer clients the chance to sign up for these services with various companies.

Postage Stamps

Stamps can be bought at tobacconists' (shown by a sign of a yellow letter 'T' on dark red background), hotels and some shops as well as at post offices. Shops selling postcards don't usually sell stamps, however. Stamps are always sold at face value and no surcharge may be added. 'Stamps' sold at main post offices are usually self-adhesive. Main post offices also have vending machines that print postage labels (*estampillas*) for the amount required. Official fiscal stamps (*papeles del estado*), used to legalise documents and pay government taxes are sold exclusively by tobacconists.

Collectors' Stamps

The Spanish post office provides a service for stamp collectors and publishes leaflets for new editions (in English, French, German and Spanish). For information contact Correos y Telégrafos, Servicio Filatélico (☎ 902 197 197, ✉ Atcliente.filatelia@correos.es). The post office website also offers extensive information and services, including a shop for stamp collectors where you can buy online.

Post Boxes

Post boxes (*buzones*) are bright yellow with red stripes circling the base and are usually free standing. In cities, post boxes often have two slots, one for local post (*ciudad* or *localidad*) and the other for post to other provinces (*provincias*) and international post (*provincias y extranjero*). However, there may be separate boxes for Madrid (*Madrid Capital*), local post, the rest of Spain (*resto España*) and international (*extranjero*) post. There are also red post boxes at main post offices in cities for express (*urgente*) post. (You may also see green post boxes, which are reserved for the use of postal staff.)

Post boxes are scarce in some areas and can be difficult to locate, although there's always one outside a post office or railway station. It's best to post letters at main post offices or railway stations, as collections are more frequent and delivery may be expedited. During the winter in resort areas, some post boxes may be emptied infrequently, irrespective of the collection times (*horas de recogida*) listed on them, which may be hand written and illegible (if a post box looks abandoned, don't use it). Some urbanisations have an 'unofficial' post box, which may be marked *Sólo Para Recogida de Correo para su Despacho*.

Post Codes & Addresses

The international identification letter for Spanish addresses is 'E', which should precede the postcode (as shown below), although its use isn't mandatory or widespread. Spain uses five-digit post codes (*distrito* or *código postal*), where the first two digits indicate the province and the last three the town. Small villages often use the post code of a nearby town, in which case the village name should be included in the address before the post code. Freepost (*franqueo en destino*), where the addressee pays the cost of postage, is available to large companies only in Spain and isn't as widely used as in many other countries.

The Spanish post office publishes a guide to post codes (*guía de códigos postales*), listing

each street in cities and individual houses in small villages. You can also look up post codes on the post office website (💻 www.correos.es).

Spanish addresses (*dirección*) often include a number of abbreviations, for example 'C/ España, 33, 3º A dcha'. This means España street (C/ is short for *calle* meaning street) number 33, third floor (3º), apartment A on the right (*derecha* or *dcha*). An apartment on the left (when facing the front of an apartment block) is indicated as *izda* (*izquierda*) and one in the centre is *cto* (*centro*).

Often a house has no street number, which is indicated by s/n (*sin número*). On many roads (*carretera* or *ctra*), the address includes a kilometre marker, e.g. N-340, km 148 or N-V, km 64. '*Ctra* town 1-town 2, km 25' means 25km along the road between town 1 and town 2, while '*Ctra de* town, km 7' means 7km along the road from the town specified. Confusion may arise over the use of regional languages (Basque, Catalan or Gallego) in street and town names, which replace or are written alongside their Castilian (Spanish) counterparts.

> A typical Spanish address is shown below:
>
> Sr. Don Pulpo
> C/Pescado, 16
> E-12345 Fruta del Mar
> Spain/España

If a letter cannot be delivered due to being wrongly addressed or the addressee having moved, it will be stamped 'return' (*devuelto*) or 'return to sender' (*a su procedencia*). A box headed *devuelto* may be stamped on the reverse of a letter stating the reason for non-delivery. You should write your name and address on the back of all letters and parcels and mark them 'sender' (*remitente/rte*), as the Spanish post office won't usually open post to obtain a return address. If you send post with insufficient postage (*insuficiencia de franqueo*), the addressee must pay double the amount that's underpaid for national post or double the underpaid amount plus €0.60 for international post.

Domestic Delivery

If you live in an apartment block in a town or city, your post is put in your post box (make sure that it has a lock), which is located in a central area such as the foyer. Often post boxes aren't big enough for magazines and large packets, which are left in a common storage area. If you prefer, you can arrange to have a post office box and collect your post from there. Postmen aren't required to deliver parcels weighing over 500g, which must usually be collected from a post office (however, parcels up to 10kg will be delivered if a surcharge is paid).

If you live in a house, your letter box must be directly accessible from a public road (i.e. postmen won't open your gate and walk up your drive to deliver your post as they do in the UK, for example). If you live in a private road, you must install a box at the end of the road, where it meets a public road.

Letters are supposedly delivered once a day, but in many areas (even within large towns) you may receive a delivery only a couple of times a week. In some rural areas, there isn't a home delivery service (*reparto*) at all, and post must be collected from a local post office, a postal 'depot' or even a shop which functions as a post collection point. Post for rural urbanisations is usually deposited in numbered post boxes, which may be several kilometres away (this may be something you wish to take into account before buying or renting a home in Spain).

Delivery Periods

The Spanish post (*correo*) delivery service has a reputation for being one of the slowest and most unreliable in Europe, with deliveries sometimes taking weeks or months (or post disappearing altogether). Delivery periods are well below the European Union (EU) average and while deliveries within and between major cities are adequate, deliveries to (and between) small towns and rural areas in different provinces can be very (very) slow. In some areas, deliveries are delayed or stop altogether when the local postman goes on holiday! It's

advisable to send all international post by airmail (*por correo aéreo*).

There's a cheaper surface post (*por barco* or *correo ordinario*) service outside Europe, but it takes aeons, e.g. six weeks or more to North America. Delivery periods in Europe vary according to the country of destination and where letters are posted in Spain (possibly even the post box used). Letters may arrive more quickly when posted at a main post office – but don't count on it!

Although letters posted in Spain often arrive at European destinations in two to four days, it's advisable to allow at least seven days. Airmail letters between Spain and North America usually take five to ten days, although you should allow up to two weeks. Sending letters by express (*exprés/urgente*) post isn't the answer, as there's no guarantee they will arrive earlier than ordinary post. Although international post delivery can be fairly fast, delivery times cannot be relied upon. The only guaranteed way to send something urgently, within Spain or internationally, is by courier (*mensajería* or *transportes*), e.g. the post office's *EMS postal exprés* service or by private couriers (or to send correspondence by fax or email).

Redirected Post

If you want your post to be redirected (*reenvío postal*), you should fill in the official form at your local post office, where you must give your name, your old address and your new address. The cost (which includes 20 pre-stamped cards for you to send out your new address) is around €26 for one month, €40 for two months and €55 for six months within Spain. International costs are around €40 for one month, €60 for two months and €80 for six months.

Always carefully check your post and don't throw anything away unless you're certain it's junk mail (unsolicited post, circulars, newspapers, etc.). It isn't unknown for foreigners to throw away important bills and correspondence during their first few weeks in Spain. Look between the pages of the junk post for 'real' post.

LETTER POST

There's one set of rates for all standard domestic (*interurbana*) letter post, whereas international letter rates depend on the destination. It costs the same to send letters (*cartas*) and postcards (*tarjetas postales* or *postales*), irrespective of the destination, the maximum weight for domestic and international letters being 2kg. The table below shows the cost of posting a letter up to 100g in Spain (for letters or parcels over 100g see **Parcel Post** opposite):

Letter Post Prices			
Weight	**Spain**	**Zone 1***	**Zone 2****
Up to 20g	€0.31	€0.60	€0.78
21 to 50g	€0.43	€1.29	€1.66
51 to 100g	€0.73	€1.55	€2.50

* Europe
** rest of the world

You should affix an airmail (*por avión*) label or use airmail envelopes for post destined for outside Europe, although this isn't necessary for post to European countries, as European post is automatically sent by air.

According to post office rules, you aren't supposed to send coloured envelopes by post, but many people do and the envelopes

reportedly arrive at their destinations – sooner or later.

Express Post

A domestic and international express service (*urgente*) is available for urgent post, which can be deposited in special red post boxes at main post offices in major cities. Express post guarantees 24-hour delivery within Spain and three days in Europe, although international post can take up to ten days to European destinations (or the same as ordinary post). The express post surcharge (payable in addition to ordinary postage) for a letter weighing up to 20g is €2.60 for destinations within Spain, €3.10 for Europe and, oddly, €3 for other international destinations. The post office offers a 'tracking' facility for express letters whose progress can be followed via the internet (⌨ www.correos.es) or by phone (☎ 902 197 197).

Digital Post

The Spanish post office runs a digital postal service (*Correo Digital*) whereby you can send a letter electronically. You have to register (free of charge) on the website before you can use this service. Once you've entered the site, you choose the format you wish to give your letter, including logos and pictures, fill in the recipient's name and address, and write your letter. The letter is then printed and 'posted' by the post office. Letters sent via this service are **supposed** to arrive quicker than conventional post. The cost of sending a digital letter is €0.52 to an address within Spain, €0.81 for Europe and €0.99 for the rest of the world.

PARCEL POST

The Spanish post office provides a range of services for sending parcels (*paquete* or, if small, *pequeño paquete*), both domestic and international. Sample rates are given below. Domestic and international parcels containing printed matter (*impresos*), e.g. books and magazines, are limited to 5kg and take 'for ever' to be delivered). Otherwise, there's no weight limit, although items over 20kg attract heavy surcharges.

Parcels (*paquetes*) are usually dealt with at a separate window in main post offices,

marked *entrega paquetes, reembolso.*
Parcels to non-EU addresses must have an
international customs label (*impreso para la
aduana*) affixed to them (these are no longer
required for parcels sent within the EU).

☑ SURVIVAL TIP

When sending parcels to or from Spain,
always ensure that they're securely sealed
or wrapped; otherwise they may arrive in
tatters.

When sending anything heavy, use strong
cloth envelopes (e.g. Tyvek), which even
Spanish postal workers have a problem tearing
to shreds (and ask your correspondents to
use them when sending post to you). The post
office sells a selection of good value stationery,
including padded envelopes in three sizes (200
x 265mm for €0.80, 250 x 326mm for €1.00 and
333 x 450mm for €1.75); reinforced envelopes
in three sizes: small (€0.65), medium (€0.90)
and large (€1.10); boxes in four sizes costing
from €1.65 to €2.60; special packs for sending
bottles (€2.45 for one bottle and €4.55 for
three) and normal envelopes in two sizes
priced at €0.10 for the small size and €0.20 for
the medium.

Domestic Parcel Rates

The standard surface domestic parcel service
(*paquete azul*) costs around €6 for parcels up
to 2kg, €7 between 2 and 5kg, €8 between 5
and 10kg, €10.50 between 10 and 15kg, and
€12.75 between 15 and 20kg. There's also a
fast domestic service (*postal exprés*), the cost
of which varies according to the destination,
e.g. parcels sent to an address within the same
province cost around €7 up to 1kg and €7.50
between 1 and 2kg; parcels sent outside the
province cost €12.25 up to 1kg and €13.50
between 1 and 2kg.

International Parcel Rates

Several international parcel services are
available. The cheapest is the *paquete
internacional económico* costing around €3 per
kg within Europe and €4.50 per kg elsewhere.
A *paquete internacional prioritario* (delivery

takes between three and six days within
Europe) costs €3.50 per kg within Europe and
€9 per kg elsewhere.

Express Parcels

The fastest and most convenient way to send
domestic or international parcels (or letters)
is via the post office's *postal exprés/EMS*
service (serving around 160 countries).
Within Spain, *EMS* packages up to 20kg
are guaranteed to arrive at their destination
within 24 hours and post sent to EU countries
is usually guaranteed delivery within 48
hours, depending on the country. The
maximum time for delivery to any country is
three or four days. Although it's expensive,
it can be much cheaper than some private
courier services. For example, an item
weighing from 500g to 1kg costs €37.50 to
zone A (Europe, including the UK, France
and Germany), €55 to North America (zone
C) or €62 to the rest of the world (zone D).
Items can be insured for up to €3,000. *EMS*
is one of the few reliable services provided
by the Spanish post office!

Spanish railways also operate an express
package and parcel service within Spain (24
hours) and to most European countries (a
little longer). Charges vary according to the
speed of despatch required, the distance,
and whether the package is to be collected
or delivered. Many private courier and
transport companies also provide an express
parcel delivery service, nationally and
internationally, and some companies (such
as DHL and Seur) have branches in most
cities and large towns.

REGISTERED & RECORDED POST

Registration is common in Spain when
sending official documents and important
communications. You can send important
letters and parcels by registered post
(*certificado*), with or without proof of delivery
(*aviso recibo*), and send items that need to
be paid for (e.g. if you're running a mail-order
business) by cash on delivery (*reembolso*)
nationally or internationally. Important letters
can also be sent by *burofax*. The sender
(*remitente*) is required to complete a form,

which includes his name and address, and the name and address of the recipient (*destinario*). The registration fee, which must be paid in addition to the standard postage charge (see above) is €2.44 for domestic letters and parcels, €2.84 for post to Europe and €3.02 for post to the rest of the world. You will receive a receipt.

Proof of delivery (*aviso recibo*) costs an additional €0.57 for domestic post and €1.22 for international post. Payment on delivery (*pago contra reembolso*) costs an extra €1.40 for national post and €1.80 for international post, which must also be registered. Note that the payment-on-delivery service isn't available to some countries, including the UK. Pre-paid envelopes for registered postage up to 1kg can be purchased.

Registered letters require a signature and proof of identity on delivery. If the addressee is absent when a delivery is made, a notice is left and the letter must be collected from the local post office (see **Post Collection** below).

If registered post isn't delivered or the contents damaged, you can make a claim (*reclamaciones reglamentarias*) and obtain compensation. Compensation (*indemnización*) is paid for the loss or damage of registered post (*pérdida o sustracción de certificado*), e.g. €1.77 per €50 declared for domestic post and €2.15 per €50 declared for international post, up to a maximum of €2,400. This means in effect that the maximum compensation is €84.96 (domestic) or €103.30 (international). If this is inadequate to cover your potential loss, you can insure (*asegurar*) registered domestic and international post. The cost for domestic post is 1 per cent of the declared value up to a maximum of €3,000.

POST COLLECTION

If the postman calls with post requiring a signature or payment when nobody is at home, he will leave a collection form (*aviso*). This also applies to post weighing over 500g, which must usually be collected from a post office (although parcels up to 10kg will be delivered on payment of a surcharge).

Normal post is kept at the post office for one month, after which it's returned to the sender, so if you're going to be away from home for longer than this you should ask the post office to hold your post. There's no charge for this service. Note, however, that proof of delivery and registered post are kept for only three and seven days respectively.

To collect post, you must present the collection form at your local post office or postal 'depot', the address of which is written on the form. In large post offices there may be a separate window for collection (marked *lista, poste restante*). You need some form of identification, e.g. your passport, residence permit or Spanish driving licence. A post office may refuse to give letters to a spouse addressed to his or her partner, or to give letters to a house owner addressed to his tenants or guests. You can give someone authorisation to collect a letter or parcel on your behalf by entering the details on the back of the collection form in the box marked *autorización*, for which the addressee's **and** collector's identification is required.

Poste Restante

You can receive post at any post office in Spain via the international poste restante (*lista de correos*) service. If you live in a large town or city, make sure your post is addressed to a specific post office, or it may be sent to the central post office (*Correo Central*). Sometimes a post office displays a list of people for whom they have *poste restante* post. Letters should be addressed as follows:

Blenkinsop-Smith, Marmaduke Cecil
Lista de Correos
Correos Central [or name of post office]
Postcode, City Name (Province)
Spain/España

Post sent to a *poste restante* address is returned to the sender if it remains unclaimed after 30 days. Identification (e.g. a passport) is necessary for collection and there's no fee. Post can be forwarded from one main post office to another.

Private Post-holding Services

If you have an American Express card or use American Express travellers' cheques, you can have post sent to an American Express office in Spain. Standard letters are held free of charge (registered letters and packages aren't accepted). Post, which should be marked 'client mail service', is kept for 30 to 90 days before being returned to the sender. Post can be forwarded to another office or address, for which there's a charge. Other companies that also provide post-holding services for customers include Thomas Cook and Western Union.

Boxes & Post Forwarding

You can obtain a post office box (*apartado de correos*) at most post offices for a fee of €59.50 for the first year and €49.50 for subsequent years. If you have a post office box, all your post will be stored there and the postman will no longer deliver to your home. Boxes are allocated on a first come, first served basis and may be unavailable. You can arrange to be informed when registered or express post arrives.

If you need post held or forwarded for only a month or two, there's a window in a post office where you can register to receive all types of correspondence, packages and money orders (*giro postal*), which can also be forwarded to another post office in the same city for no charge. The latter service is called *reenvío postal* and costs €26.70 for one month and €40 for two. Proof of identity must be provided to collect post.

FINANCIAL SERVICES
Banking

The Spanish post office acts as an agent for Deutsche Bank, which provides the usual range of banking services, including cheque and savings accounts, house purchase, savings and retirement plans. These accounts provide the same services as bank accounts, including international money transfers (by post and telegraph to many countries), payment of bills, and cheque, cash and debit cards. Post offices don't, however, operate cash machines (ATMs).

Postal Giros

Cash transfers can be made within Spain and to Algeria, Morocco and Tunisia, with a postal giro (*giro postal*), by completing a form at any post office. Domestic postal giros are useful for sending money to someone in Spain when you don't have a Spanish bank account or when sending money to someone without a Spanish bank account. Some companies insist on payment by postal giro, as the cost of processing bank cheques is prohibitive.

You can choose between an ordinary giro (*giro ordinario*), which takes around two to three days to reach its destination, whether in Spain or abroad, and an urgent giro (*giro urgente*), which takes between 4 and 24 hours for Spanish and international destinations. You're required to complete a form and pay the amount to be transferred plus the fee in cash. Fees for national giro payments depend on whether the recipient has a post office giro account and whether the payment is sent by post or made by telephone. There are set fees plus 0.77 per cent of the amount being transferred.

There are usually various giro windows at main post offices, e.g. for sending ordinary giros (*giro ordinario admisión*), sending urgent and international giros (*giro urgente e internacional admisión*), paying for ordinary giros (*giro ordinario pago*) and paying for urgent and international giros (*giro urgente y internacional pago*). Note that it isn't possible to make giro transfers to some countries and some countries accept only ordinary giro payments.

Western Union Transfers

The Spanish post office also has an agreement known as 'Money in minutes' (*Dinero en minutos*) with Western Union by which you can send money fast to anywhere in the world from Spain up to a maximum amount of €3,000. The examples of rates given on the Post Office website (and presumably 'translated' from pesetas) are €33.50 for €610 and €69 for €2,030.

Picos de Europa,Cantabrian Mountains

7.

TELEPHONE

Spain has one of the lowest numbers of fixed-line telephones per head in the European Union (EU), around 38 per 100 people, with a total of around 16m lines in service. The Spanish aren't habitual telephone users and don't usually spend hours on the telephone (many business men prefer to meet in person or exchange letters). However, the last few years has seen the cost of mobile phones fall considerably and Spain now has around 51m users, with greater consumer spending on mobile phone calls than on fixed-line services.

The main telephone service company is Telefónica, which is the only one that can install telephone lines, but there are numerous others providing line rental and telephone call and internet access services, although even in these areas Telefónica has a huge market share. In 2008, the main telecommunication providers for private customers were:

- Jazztel (☎ 1565, 🖥 www.jazztel.com);
- ONO (☎ 902 929 000, 🖥 www.ono.es);
- Orange (☎ 902 012 220, 🖥 www.orange.es);
- Spantel (☎ 902 020 202, 🖥 www.spantel.es);
- Tele2 (☎ 800 760 790, 🖥 www.tele2.es);
- Telefónica (☎ 1004, 🖥 www.telefonica.es);
- Ya.com (☎ 902 903 633, 🖥 www.ya.com).

In recent years, telephone services in Spain have improved significantly in terms of quality as well as value, fewer than 1 per cent of calls having problems and most faults being fixed within 24 hours. The waiting time for new telephone installations has also fallen dramatically and is now similar to other EU countries. Telefónica has made a huge investment in advanced technology (such as fibre optics), and standards in Spain now compare favourably with those in North America and the most advanced European countries.

Costs listed in this chapter are exclusive of value added tax (VAT/*IVA*) at 16 per cent, where applicable, unless otherwise stated.

EMERGENCY NUMBERS

The main national emergency numbers (*servicios de urgencia*) are as follows;

Number	Service
112	All-purpose emergency number (if you dial this number you're then connected to the emergency service you require).
061	Ambulance service (*ambulancia*)
062	Civil Guard (*guardia civil*)
080	Fire service (*bomberos*)
092	Local/Municipal police (*policía local/municipal*)
900-202-202	Maritime rescue and security (*salvamento y seguridad marítimo*).
091	National police (*Policía*)

These and other emergency numbers are listed at the front of all telephone directories (white and yellow pages), including numbers to call for civil protection (*protección civil*), poison information (*información toxicológica*) and help with drug addiction (*fundación de Ayuda contra la Drogadicción*); crisis lines such as the Samaritans (*Teléfono de la Esperanza*); and the numbers of first aid posts (*casas de socorro*), the Red Cross (*Cruz Roja*), social security (*seguridad social*) and urgent health services (*servicio de salud – urgencias*).

You should dial ☎ 1002 to report a telephone breakdown or line problem. (For other service numbers see below.)

Make a note of the above numbers and those of your doctor and insurance company, etc. and keep it by your phone. When reporting a medical emergency, you should state the type of emergency, e.g. accident (*accidente*), serious illness (*enfermedad grave*) or heart attack (*ataque cardiaco* or *infarto*), and whether an ambulance or doctor (*médico*) is required. See also **Emergencies** on page 179.

From a private telephone, calls to ☎ 112 are free but other emergency calls cost €0.04 to €0.09 depending on the telephone company. From a phone box, all emergency numbers are free, but you must insert at least €0.10 or a telephone card to make a call (your money is returned when the emergency service answers). There are free 'SOS' telephones on motorways and main roads.

SERVICE NUMBERS

Useful service numbers are listed in the information pages (*páginas informativas*) at the front of all telephone directories, under the heading 'other services of interest' (*otros servicios de interés*). They include numbers for regional government information (*información ciudadana*); water (*agua*), electricity (*electricidad*) and gas problems; airports (*aeropuertos*), post offices (*oficinas de correos*), rail (RENFE) bus services (*estaciones de autobús*); telegrams (*telegramas*) and road information (*ayuda en carretera*).

Useful local telephone numbers (*teléfonos útiles*), usually including emergency and hospital numbers, are listed in English-language and other expatriate newspapers and magazines, generally by town.

The following service and information numbers can be dialled throughout Spain:

Service Numbers	
Number	**Service**
096**	Automatic alarm call
095**	News (*Radio Nacional de España/NE*)
1008	Operator-assisted calls to Europe, Algeria, Libya, Morocco, Tunisia and Turkey
1005	Operator-assisted calls to the rest of the world
1009	Operator-assisted calls within Spain
097**	Sports information
1002	Technical assistance
1004	Telefónica commercial enquiries
093*	Time

*   Calls to this number cost €0.50.
** Calls to these numbers cost €0.75.

INSTALLATION & REGISTRATION

When moving into a new home in Spain with a telephone line, you must have the account transferred to your name. If you're planning to move into a property without a telephone line and want to have one installed, this costs around €80, although there are frequent offers, e.g. installation was free in July 2008. To have a telephone installed or reconnected, you can visit your local Telefónica office. Telefónica has an *Oficina Comercial* or an *Oficina de Atención al Usuario* in each province. You must take your passport or residence permit (*permiso de residencia* – see page 54), proof of your address such as a recent electricity bill, and a copy of your property deed (*escritura*) or rental contract.

Alternatively, you can phone Telefónica (☎ 1004 – in Spanish only) or fill out a form online (🖥 www.telefonica.es in Spanish or

⌨ www.telefonicainenglish.com in English). If you're renting and don't have a residence permit, you must pay a deposit of around €200.

If you're taking over a property from the previous occupants, you should arrange for the telephone account to be transferred to your name from the day you take possession. Before buying or renting a property, check that all the previous bills have been paid; otherwise you may find yourself liable for them.

You aren't required to rent or buy a telephone from Telefónica and renting doesn't work out cost effective in the long term. A cordless (*inalámbrico*) telephone can be bought from Telefónica for around €25 and other retailers have similar offers. Cordless digital phones are also available, and at the top end of the scale there's a wide range of all-singing, all-dancing models to choose from.

Note that if you're using a callback service, you should buy a phone with a memory facility – unless you like the idea of dialling around 20 digits every time you make a call!

All telephones must be approved (*aprobado*) by Telefónica, which means that you cannot officially buy a telephone abroad

and use it in Spain. In any case, any telephone purchased abroad may not work in Spain.

Registering with Other Companies

Registering with telephone companies other than Telefónica is usually straightforward and can be done by phone or online. You must provide your personal details, including passport or residence permit number and a bank account number. If you choose to use the company's pre-set dialling service (to avoid having to dial the company's prefix every time you make a call), you must sign a form provided by the company.

Problems & Complaints

Telephone and internet services account for one of the main sources of consumer complaints (there were a record number of over 47,000 in 2007 alone, an increase of 30 per cent on the previous year's total) and most complaints involved bills and the difficulty of terminating a contract. In fact, the Ministry of Industry runs an entire office for telephone service complaints from consumers and guarantees that all complaints will be resolved within six months. The office (☎ 901 336 699) is open from 9am to 7pm Mondays to Fridays and 9am to 2pm on Saturdays. Complaints can also be made online (⌨ www.usuariosteleco. es); the website has downloadable complaint forms.

Temporary Disconnection

If you're non-resident or plan to leave your Spanish home for at least three months per year, you can arrange for Telefónica to temporarily disconnect your line, a service known as *Linea Vacaciones*. You must specify the exact dates for disconnection and reconnection by telephone using a code (obtained when the line is installed). The service is free and you pay the monthly line rental (€13.97) only for the months when the line is connected.

USING THE TELEPHONE

Each province in Spain has an area code (*prefijo* or *código territorial*), all of which are listed overleaf. All telephone numbers consist of nine digits and include the area code, which

Area Codes

A Coruña	981	Córdoba	957	Ourense	988
Alava	945	Cuenca	969	Palencia	986
Albacete	967	Girona	972	Pontevedra	986
Alicante	96	Granada	958	La Rioja	941
Almería	950	Guadalajara	949	Salamanca	923
Asturias	98	Guipúzcoa	943	Sta Cruz Tenerife	922
Avila	920	Huelva	959	Segovia	921
Badajoz	924	Jaén	953	Seville	95
Baleares	971	Las Palmas	928	Soria	975
Barcelona	93	León	987	Tarragona	977
Burgos	947	Lleida	973	Teruel	978
Cáceres	927	Lugo	982	Toledo	925
Cadiz	956	Madrid	91	Valencia	96
Cantabria	942	Malaga	95	Valladolid	983
Castellón	964	Melilla	95	Vizcaya	94
Ceuta	956	Murcia	968	Zamora	980
Ciudad Real	926	Navarra	948	Zaragoza	976

Note: The code for Andorra is 376 and for Gibraltar it's 350.

must be dialled whether you're making a local call or calling Spain from abroad. Area codes are shown on a map in telephone directories (the provinces are shown on the map in **Appendix E**).

When making a domestic call within the same province, i.e. to a number with the same provincial code, you must still dial the code. When calling from outside Spain you must add the international dialling code (e.g. 00 from the UK) followed by 34 for Spain. So to call the Ceuta 123 456 you must dial 00-34 956 123 456. (Note that for convenience all Spanish telephone numbers are written in groups of three in this book, although in some cases the code has only two digits.) For information on making international calls from Spain see page opposite.

Note that if you're using a service provider other than Telefónica, you must dial the company's prefix, e.g. 1073 for Tele2, before making a call. So to call 956-123 456 with Tele2, you would dial 1073-956 123 456. However, most telephone companies offer a pre-set dialling service where the company's prefix is automatically set on your telephone line and precedes all numbers you dial, although if you wish to use another company, including Telefónica, for certain calls you must then dial **that** company's prefix.

Numbers beginning 900 are free, although they aren't widely advertised in Spain. Numbers beginning 901 and 902 are charged at reduced (e.g. local) call rates. Numbers beginning 80 (e.g. 803, 806 and 807), on the other hand, are expensive – from €0.35 a minute (reduced rate) to a massive €3.40 a minute (peak rate), plus VAT – and generally used by companies providing services such as weather forecasts, financial and health information and 'leisure' services such as horoscopes. 80 numbers are the most common source of complaints from consumers, and the government has introduced legislation designed to reduce the incidence of fraud. You can ask Telefónica to make it impossible to dial 80 numbers from your phone.

All mobile phone numbers in Spain begin with the digit 6, and these numbers are generally more expensive to call than fixed-line numbers.

The tones used in Spain are similar to those in other European countries, e.g. the dialling tone (señal para marcar) is a continuous low sound (as in the UK and the US), a ringing tone is a repeated long tone, and the engaged (busy) signal is a series of rapid pips. If you get a recorded message immediately after dialling, it may be telling you that all lines are engaged and to try again later. The message may also be telling you that the number you've dialled doesn't exist (e.g. *el número marcado no existe*). If this happens, check that the number is correct and redial; if you're dialling an international number, make sure you haven't dialled the first zero of the area code.

To make a reverse charge/collect call (*cobro revertido*) dial 1009 for numbers within Spain, 1008 for countries in Europe, Algeria, Libya, Morocco, Tunisia and Turkey, and 1005 for all other countries. Person-to-person (*persona a persona*) calls can be made via the operator (*operadora*). A surcharge is made for reverse charge and person-to-person calls, which can also be made to certain countries via the home direct service. As with anything that requires interaction with the operator, this can be a very slow process and it may be easier to make a short direct call and ask the party to call you back.

The usual Spanish response when answering the telephone is 'speak' (*diga*) or 'speak to me' (*dígame*). The caller may begin what he has to say with 'listen' (*oiga*). 'I'm trying to connect you' is *le pongo/paso con* and 'go ahead' may be simply *adelante*. A call is *una llamada* and to call is *llamar*. Other useful words and phrases include *coger* (to answer the telephone), *colgar* (to hang up), *marcar* (to dial), *póngame con* (connect me) and *número equivocado* (wrong number).

In Spain, telephone numbers are usually dictated on the telephone two digits at a time. If someone asks you to spell (*deletrear*) something on the telephone, such as your name, you should use the telephone alphabet. Obviously, to use it you must be able to pronounce the alphabet in Spanish and the words listed below; the pronunciation of each letter is given in brackets. For example if your name's Smith you say, '*essay para Sábado, emay para Madrid, ee para Inés, tay para Tarragona y achay para Historia*'.

International Calls

It's possible to make international direct dialling (IDD) calls from Spain to most countries, from private and public telephones. To make an international call from Spain, first dial 00 to obtain an international line, then dial the country code, e.g. 44 for the UK, the area code **without** the first zero and the telephone number of the person you're calling. So to call the London number 020-8123 4567 you must dial 00-44 20 8123 4567. To make a call to a country where there isn't IDD you must dial 1008 for European countries plus Algeria, Libya, Morocco, Tunisia or Turkey, and 1005 for all other countries.

A full list of IDD country codes, plus codes for main cities, is shown in the information pages (*páginas informativas*) of your local directory.

To obtain an operator with one of the three major US telephone companies, call ☎ 1-800 -247 7246 (AT&T), ☎ 1-800-676 4003 (Sprint) or ☎ 1-800-937 7262 (Verizon). You're connected directly and can make calls with a domestic US telephone card or make a collect (reverse charge) call.

Phonetic Alphabet			
A (ah)	Antonio	N (enay)	Navarra
B (bay)	Barcelona	Ñ (enyay)	Ñoño
C (thay)	Carmen	O (oh)	Oviedo
CH (chay)	Chocolate	P (pay)	Paris
D (day)	Dolores	Q (ku)	Querido
E (ay)	Enrique	R (eray)	Ramón
F (efay)	Francia	S (essay)	Sábado
G (zhay)	Gerona	T (tay)	Tarragona
H (achay)	Historia	U (oo)	Ulises
I (ee)	Inés	V (oo-bay)	Valencia
J (hota)	José	W (oo-bay-doblay)	Washington
K (kah)	Kilo	X (ekiss)	Xiquina
L (elay)	Lorenzo	Y (ee greeyay ga)	Yegua
LL (elyay)	Llobregat	Z (thayta)	Zaragoza

International calls can also be made from Telefónica telephone booths (*locutorios públicos*) in major towns and cities (see page 102), where you can pay for calls costing over €3 with a credit card. There are also numerous private telephone offices in resort towns.

Internet Telephone Services

If you have correspondents or friends who are connected to the internet, you can make international calls for the price of a local telephone call. Once on the internet there are no other charges, no matter how much distance is covered or time spent online. Internet users can buy software from companies such as Quarterdeck and Vodaltec that effectively turns their personal computer into a voice-based telephone (both parties must have compatible computer software). You also need a sound card, speakers, a microphone and a modem, and access to a local internet provider (which may be free or cost a fixed monthly fee plus connection costs).

Users of the MSN Messenger service can speak to fellow users when online – you just need a microphone (from €7) – and companies such as Skype (🖳 www.skype.com), have revolutionised the internet telephone service, are another alternative. You can download the software from the website and speak to any other Skype user free. While the quality of communication isn't always as good as using a telephone (it's similar to using a CB radio) and you must arrange call times in advance (Messenger and Skype users can automatically see if fellow users are available when they go online – but they don't know whether they're actually listening), international calls cost virtually nothing.

CHARGES

Line rental and call charges in Spain are among the highest in Europe, although they've reduced considerably in recent years with increased competition. If you have a private line (*línea individual*) and use Telefónica, the standard monthly line rental or service charge (*cuota de abono*) is around €14 (levied monthly). Monthly line rental with other companies was cheaper at the time of writing (July 2008) and some companies offer free line rental. People who are disabled or over 65 who have an income below the Spanish minimum pension pay a reduced tariff on monthly rental and call charges.

There's intense competition for business among the numerous companies and tariffs change continuously. Shop around and choose a company with the lowest rates for the type of calls you wish to make. Be aware that rates for calls may not be consistently low in the same company and that some companies have aggressive marketing campaigns with cheap offers which often expire once you've signed up.

There are essentially three tariffs in Spain: local/metropolitan calls (*metropolitana*), calls within your province (*provincial*), calls outside your province (*nacional/interprovincial*) and international calls. However, in recent months, all telephone companies have introduced packages which conceal the cost of individual calls; you pay a fixed monthly charge for, for example, your telephone line rental and all calls within Spain and/or broadband connection, which makes it difficult to compare costs. A typical package, including line rental and all calls to landlines within Spain, costs from €18 to €28 per month.

Competition for 'long-distance' customers is fierce and in the last few years a price war has been waged by telephone companies. For example, most companies have now waived their 'connection' fees, although Telefónica is among those that haven't. Most companies have a flat rate at all times for calls to western

Europe and the US, ranging from around €0.06 per minute (Ya.com) to €0.10 per minute (ONO and Telefónica). Calls to Australia are considerably more expensive, e.g. €0.55 per minute (Telefónica) and €0.64 per minute (ONO).

Note that tariffs are constantly being reduced and you should consult companies to find the cheapest rate for countries you call frequently. Calls to Gibraltar are charged at the same rate as national calls. There's a high surcharge for operator-connected international calls.

BILLS

Bills (*facturas*) are sent at varying intervals depending on the company, although they're usually monthly and you're given 20 days to pay. VAT at 16 per cent is levied on all charges. Itemised bills (*factura detallada*) are provided, listing all numbers called with the date and time, duration and the charge. Bills can be paid in cash at most banks or at the service provider's office; cheques aren't normally accepted. Simply present the bill with your payment and you will be given a receipt. You can also have your telephone bill paid by direct debit (*domiciliación bancaria*) from a bank account, which is advisable for holiday-home owners, as it ensures that you aren't disconnected for non-payment.

If your bill isn't paid within 20 days, your line may be cut without further warning, although a new system has been introduced where lines with unpaid bills are reduced for ten days to incoming calls only, before the service is cut completely. If your line is cut, there's a reconnection fee (which depends on the amount owing and the elapsed period), on payment of which you should be reconnected within two working days. All companies offer the possibility of checking your bills and telephone usage online.

If you complain about your bill being too high, Telefónica may install a counter on your telephone for a number of days to check for a malfunction. If the test fails to discover any line problems, Telefónica won't reduce your bill.

You must pay your telephone bill, even if you contest the amount; otherwise Telefónica may cut your line. If you're unable to pay the whole amount of a contested bill, you should pay your usual amount and contest the rest.

Telefónica's bills include the following details (reading from top to bottom):

Understanding Your Phone Bill	
Item	Description
Datos del cliente	Name and address of subscriber plus your fiscal number, the phone number the bill is for, details of the bank account (if paid by direct debit), including the date the bill will be paid. The last four digits of your bank account are obscured by asterisks for security reasons.
Conceptos de la factura	A break-down of charges for each part of your bill
Cuotas de abono (date)	Standing charges
Cuotas otros servicios	Charges for other services (e.g. packages or call transfers)
Consumos	Charges
Descuentos	Discounts
Total (base imponible)	Total (before VAT)
IVA 16%	16% VAT
Total a pagar (euros)	Total payable (in euros)
Importe medio de consumo diario	Average daily cost of phone use

DIRECTORIES

Telephone directories (*guías telefónicas*) are published by province, each province having its own telephone book. In some provinces the telephone book is in more than one volume, e.g. the Madrid white pages (*páginas blancas*) and yellow pages (*páginas amarillas*) each have two volumes. The directories for the province where you live or have your business are provided free of charge. If you want other directories they're available from provincial Telefónica offices but you must pay.

The white pages directory begins with a number of information pages, including emergency and useful local numbers, Telefónica service numbers, national and international codes, instructions on how to use the telephone (in English, French, German and Italian) and possibly tourist information. The second section in the white pages is the alphabetical list of subscribers. White pages information can also be accessed via the internet (💻 www.paginasblancas.es). The yellow pages directory contains useful local numbers at the front, a list of towns covered by the directory and local information. Yellow pages information is also available by phone (☎ 11888) or via the internet (💻 www. paginasamarillas.es). Blue pages directories (*páginas azules*) are also published and contain an alphabetical index of streets and subscribers by street number. New directories are published annually.

Euro pages is a European business directory containing some 150,000 suppliers (💻 www. europages.es for information). In some areas, there are English-language directories, e.g. the English Speaker's Telephone Directory (ESTD) for the Costa del Sol and Gibraltar (☎ 956 776 958, 💻 www.esp.gi/publishing.htm), in others free local directories (e.g. Tu Distrito (💻 www. tudistrito.com) and QDQ (💻 www.qdq.com).

> When you have a telephone installed, your name and number is automatically included in the next edition of your local white pages directory (published annually). You can choose to have an unlisted number (*no registrado*), for which there's no charge.

Subscribers are listed in the white pages under their town or village (*ciudad*) and not alphabetically for the whole of a province. When looking for a subscriber's number, you must therefore know the town, not just the province, where they live. If you don't know this, don't bother to ring directory enquiries (*servicio de información*), as you will be asked for the name of the town!

PUBLIC TELEPHONES

Public telephones (*cabinas telefónicas* or *teléfonos públicos*) are located in bus depots, railway stations and airports, bars, cafés and restaurants, motorway rest areas and various business premises, and on streets in towns and villages. Public telephones aren't found in post offices with the exception of a few main post offices in major cities. All payphones allow IDD, but international calls can also be made via the operator. Most old-style call boxes have been replaced by new 'vandal-proof' telephones (both are blue and green). Virtually all public telephones accept coins and many also accept telephone cards (credit cards aren't accepted in public telephone boxes). Some public telephones accept only telephone cards, although they're usually placed immediately next to a coin public telephone.

Telephone cards (*tarjetas telefónicas*), costing €5, €10 or €15 and available from post offices, newsagents' (*papelerías*), tobacconists' (*estancos*) and some other retailers, save you having to find change or carry lots of coins.

Telephone Booths

You can also make calls from booths (*locutorios públicos*) in Telefónica offices. Office opening hours vary and may be from 8 or 9am until 10pm on work days (*días laborables*), including Saturdays, and from 9am until 9pm on Sundays and public holidays (*domingos y festivos*). However, Sunday hours vary considerably and many offices are open only for a few hours. Telephone cards and most credit cards are accepted for calls costing over €3. Reverse charge (collect) calls can also be made. You can make an unlimited number of calls and receive an itemised receipt which includes the surcharge and VAT. In smaller towns, these offices are often franchised businesses, where you pay a 35 per cent surcharge on all calls.

There are also booths which are leased from Telefónica by private companies (they're usually blue and green and are advertised as *centros telefónicos* or *cabinas*). *Centros telefónicos* have shorter business hours than Telefónica offices, e.g. 10am to 2pm and 5 to 10pm daily. They charge a high commission on all calls and don't handle reverse charge calls, as they make no profit on them.

Many businesses in resort areas (such as restaurants) have telephone booths and may also offer a fax service. Note that (according to the Spanish Consumers' Union/UCE) some operators charge excessive rates, which can be over ten times higher than Telefónica rates. However, in recent years new companies, such as Call Box and Call Home, have entered the market in resort areas, offering calls at **much** lower rates than other public phones, as well as fax and mailbox services.

Most booths have a full set of telephone directories.

MOBILE PHONES

Mobile phones (*telefonía móvil*) were relatively slow to take off in Spain, but in the last few years prices have fallen dramatically and sales have rocketed, making Spain the fastest-expanding country in the European Union for mobile phones, currently with around 51m users. All the major population areas (some 98 per cent of the population) are covered by analogue and digital networks, although sparsely populated areas aren't served or reception is difficult. Spain has three main digital networks – Movistar, Orange and Vodafone – plus numerous smaller networks such as Carrefour Móvil, Simyo and Yoigo. All providers offer pre-paid ('pay as you talk') and contract arrangements. All mobile telephone numbers start with the number 6.

Mobile phones start at around €40, which usually includes at least €20-worth of calls. Many people have a mobile phone rather than a fixed-line phone (landline) because connection is cheaper and instantaneous, you can move house and retain the same number, and you can use the phone almost anywhere, in Spain and internationally.

Tariffs have fallen dramatically due to the price war that has been raging between the three service providers in the last few years, and packages are constantly changing, as are the times of peak and reduced rates. Tariffs can be found on the mobile telephone company websites (e.g. 🖳 www.orange.es, 🖳 www.movistar.com and 🖳 www.vodafone.es).

For a comparison of mobile phone call charges (in Spanish only), consult the ADSLZone website (🖳 www.adslzone.net – go to 'Comparativa Móvil').

If you have a pre-paid phone, you can top it up (*recargar*) in many shops and supermarkets or at ATM cash machines at many banks (simply key in the telephone number and the amount and it's debited directly from your account).

If you arrive from the UK or another European country, you can usually use your 'home' mobile telephone in Spain, which operates on the GSM network. However, calls are routed via your home country and are therefore expensive, so it's advisable to buy a Spanish mobile telephone as soon as you can, or have a Spanish SIM card fitted to your existing telephone. The latter system works well if you're travelling frequently between Spain and your home country, as you can simply change the SIM card whenever you're in a different country.

As in many other countries, text messaging is extremely popular in Spain and all providers offer competitive rates for sending text messages. Much to linguists' and teachers' dismay, the use of text messaging has brought with it many new spellings for Spanish, such as the widespread use of 'k' instead of 'qu'. Some messages are almost impossible to read unless you're *au fait* with text message spelling!

There are numerous mobile phone scams, including many which leave you a message asking you to phone a number urgently for important news regarding your family or a prize. The number you must ring is invariably a high charge number (e.g. beginning 806) and you're deliberately kept on the line by an answering machine or telephonists for as long as possible, resulting in a very expensive phone call. Needless to say, the important news or prize doesn't exist. The Consumers' Association advises mobile phone users to ignore all such messages. You should also be aware that mobile phone theft is big business. Keep your mobile phone in a secure place and never leave it visible in your car.

⚠ Caution

The use of hand-held mobile phones while driving is prohibited, and fines start at €300 with a three-point deduction from your licence. You should install a 'hands free' unit in your car if you wish to use your mobile phone while driving but note that it must not require headphones or earpieces, which are also illegal.

INTERNET

Like mobile phones, the internet (*internet*) got off to a slow start in Spain due to the high cost of local calls and the lack of home computers, but there has recently been a spectacular increase in use. Around a third of households are online, compared to just 23 per cent in 2002 and a mere 0.7 per cent in 1996, but Spain still lags behind in the broadband stakes, with an 18 per cent take-up (the UK

has nearly 26 per cent and Denmark has over 35 per cent). However, all state primary and secondary schools are online and it's now unusual to find a medium-size or large company without a website.

Connecting to the internet costs the same as a local call, although most companies offer packages, which generally comprise a fixed number of discounted access hours per month (though you don't benefit from the discount if you don't use them all!). Telefónica offers several such packages, e.g. the '*Bono Navega 10*' package offering ten hours per month at any time and costing €3.50. Most companies also offer the possibility of combining local calls and internet access under the same discount scheme. Note that any unused time in a month isn't refundable and if you go over your contracted number of hours the excess time is charged at the normal rate.

Broadband

Broadband (ADSL) internet connection is now available in most of Spain's urban areas, although you should check with Telefónica. Rural areas are less well served and some remote areas don't have ADSL facilities at all, although the government plans to rectify this in the near future. Advantages of ADSL include fast internet access, unlimited connection time and simultaneous access to a phone line. On the other hand, monthly charges are high (at least €15) and your computer is more vulnerable to viruses if connected to broadband. Unless you use the internet for several hours a day, it's probably cheaper (though slower) to use a conventional internet connection with a discount package.

Some 50 companies provide ADSL access and the top four are Telefónica (☎ 1004, 🖳 www.telefonicaonline.com), ONO (☎ 902 929 000, 🖳 www.ono.es), Orange (☎ 902 012 220, 🖳 www.orange.es) and Ya.com (☎ 902 903 633, 🖳 www.ya.com). Competition for clients is fierce and there are occasional good deals (e.g. free installation). Speed on ADSL connections varies; most companies now offer 1Mb/sec as the minimum speed.

A 2007 Organisation for Economic and Co-operative Development (OECD) survey found that Spain had the most expensive broadband (in comparison with GDP) of all member countries.

All companies use the same broadband infrastructure, which is controlled and maintained by Telefónica. ADSL is, as yet, unregulated in Spain and subject to numerous consumer complaints, particularly with regard to speed of connection and customer service. Before committing yourself to an ADSL line, read the terms and conditions carefully, and check the minimum duration of the contract (usually at least six months, although several companies now have no minimum contract length requirement).

If a cabled broadband connection isn't available where you live in Spain, it may be worth considering the following options.

Satellite Internet Services

A satellite connection offers the same speed of transmission as conventional ADSL, but installation costs are much higher (around €500) with monthly charges starting at around €75, and you must install a satellite dish. The other disadvantage of satellite internet connection is that European satellite broadband capacity is shared, so if you have a lot of material to transfer the process can be slow at peak times. Some companies offer a monthly 'priority traffic' allocation, but above this you must share the service with other users. However, satellite internet connection may be better than none at all.

Satellite internet providers covering Spain include Avonline (🖥 www.avonlinebroadband. co.uk), BusinessCom (🖥 www.bcsatellite.net) and Global Telephone and Telecommunication (🖥 www.globaltt.com).

Mobile Phone Internet Services

Another alternative is a connection via a mobile phone with 3G (Third Generation) technology. Advantages include high-speed connection (often faster than conventional broadband) and availability anywhere with mobile phone reception, making 3G technology ideal for homeowners in areas where telephone lines aren't available.

To access high-speed internet using 3G technology you need a 3G mobile phone or a mobile phone and a 3G card, and a laptop computer or PDA to connect to your phone. 3G internet access software is available from most mobile phone companies (some offer free downloads from their website). Monthly costs vary greatly according to the amount of connection time and whether your mobile phone service is pay-as-you-go or on a contract arrangement; packages start at €19 a month for contracts and at €60 a month for pay-as-you-go. As with other aspects of telecommunications, it's expected that prices will fall over the next few years as competition increases and technology improves.

8.
TELEVISION

T he Spanish are avid TV viewers (over 90 per cent of Spanish homes have a TV) and according to surveys rate around fourth in Europe (after Portugal, the UK and Italy) in average viewing time per day, per head. Some 90 per cent of Spaniards over the age of 14 watch TV every day and most get their news from the TV (only some 40 per cent of Spaniards read a newspaper every day).

A 2007 survey showed that Spaniards spend an average of 223 minutes a day – over three-and-a-half hours – watching TV.

Spanish television (TV) isn't renowned for its quality, although it has improved in recent years and is probably no worse than the fare dished up in many other European countries. Nevertheless, much of its output is termed 'junk TV' (*telebasura*) by its critics, with sex and violence prominent, even during children's viewing times, although under recent legislation television officially deemed unsuitable for children may be broadcast only after 10pm. The consolation is that there's no TV (or radio) licence in Spain – so at least the rubbish is 'free'!

Satellite TV reception is excellent in most areas of Spain (as is terrestrial TV reception) and it's particularly popular among the expatriate community (not that much of its output is any better than Spanish TV). Cable TV isn't as common as it is in northern European countries and is subscribed to by just 6 per cent of the population. Digital TV is available and offered by various companies. Spanish radio (including many expatriate stations) is generally excellent and the equal of most other European countries' services.

The principal TV broadcaster, Televisión Española (TVE), has for years been controlled by the government, its news and current affairs programmes consequently being heavily in favour of the ruling party. In an attempt to rectify this bias, legislation was passed in 2006 under which TVE became an independent body subject to parliamentary (not cabinet) control. The director is nominated by TVE's governing body (rather than the cabinet). Less popularly, the state absorbed the company's monumental debt (over €7bn at the end of 2005). Two years later, TVE's programmes are generally more objective and the company announced profits of €18.4m at the end of 2007.

TELEVISION

Standard

TV sets and video recorders operating on the British (PAL-I), French (SECAM) or North American (NTSC) systems won't function in Spain, which, along with most other continental European countries, uses the PAL-BG standard. It's possible to buy a multi-standard European TV (and VCR) containing automatic circuitry that switches between different systems. Some multi-standard TVs also offer the North American NTSC standard and have an NTSC-in jack plug connection allowing you to play back American videos. A standard British, French or US TV won't work in Spain, although British TVs can be modified. The same applies to a 'foreign' video or DVD recorder, which won't operate with a Spanish TV unless dual-standard. Some expatriates opt for two TVs, one to receive Spanish TV programmes and another (e.g. SECAM or NTSC) to play back their favourite videos or DVDs.

Buying & Renting

If you decide to buy a TV in Spain, you will find it advantageous to buy one with teletext (*teletexto*), which, apart from allowing you to display programme schedules, also provides a wealth of useful and interesting information. A 36cm (14-inch) portable colour TV with remote control can be purchased in Spain for around €75. A 55cm (21-inch) set costs from around €130 and a 62.5cm (25-inch) model from around €200. Many TVs feature Nicam stereo sound, a high-quality digital TV sound signal available in most areas of Spain. Digital widescreen TVs are available and, although still relatively high, prices continue to fall and now start at around €600. Home cinemas (prices start at around €1,000) are widely available and increasingly popular.

It's now difficult to rent a TV in Spain, even in resort areas, and most furnished rental property comes equipped with a TV. In any case, it's usually cheaper to buy one in the long run.

Programmes & Channels

Spanish TV consists of a surfeit of moronic game shows, chat shows, football, basketball and bullfighting, although there are also excellent news programmes, documentaries, wildlife and history programmes. Football reigns supreme in Spain, where TV companies pay a staggering sum to televise live football matches, which has had a significant effect on the restaurant trade (live matches are screened at least two nights a week). One thing you can be sure of: whatever is showing on one of the three main channels, a similar programme will be showing on the others (called counter-programming). The introduction of commercial TV has provided much-needed competition for the state-run channels and has helped improve the choice, if not always the quality.

Dramas and sitcoms such as *Hospital Central*, *Los Serrano* and *Aída* are hugely popular and regularly top the audience ratings. Other popular programmes include *Cuéntame cómo pasó* ('Tell Me How It Happened', a drama recounting events in recent Spanish history since the '60s), *Operación Triunfo* (Spain's 'Pop Idol', now into its seventh series), *CSI* and *Mira Quién Baila* (a celebrity dancing competition). *Gran Hermano* ('Big Brother') continues to appear annually and is still hugely popular. South-American soap operas have made a comeback and are many Spaniards' staple TV diet. Gossip programmes such as *Corazón Corazón*, *Gente* and *La Noria* are also widely followed, reflecting the Spaniards' seemingly insatiable interest in other people's lives.

US-produced dramas are very popular in Spain and the Spanish are avid viewers of *CSI*, *Desperate Housewives*, *Grey's Anatomy* and *House*. All programmes are dubbed into Spanish so don't be surprised when you hear Hugh Laurie and Eva Longoria speaking perfect Spanish!

Popular current affairs programmes include *Informe Semanal* (La1) and *Los Reporteros* (Canal Sur). Chat shows with a magazine-type format such as *Sabor a ti* (Antena 3) and *A Tu Lado* (Tele 5) are also popular and have largely replaced children's programmes in the afternoon. Political satire has found a niche among the Spanish, who regularly watch programmes such as *El Guiñol* and *Caiga quien caiga*. TV news, both domestic and international, is comprehensive and upbeat and contains regular items about the arts, e.g. ballet or opera. There's generally no censorship on Spanish TV and 'sexy' and risqué programmes are commonplace, particularly on the autonomous channels.

The main Spanish TV stations are listed below. Most areas of Spain can receive six of them (TVE's two, Antena 3, Cuatro, Tele 5 and La Sexta) with a standard external aerial.

◆ **TVE** – TVE (💻 www.rtve.es) is the former state television company, which, despite increased competition, remains Spain's largest and most popular TV network with its two channels, La1 and La2, between them claiming around 28 per cent of viewers, although La1 rarely tops audience ratings. La1 places emphasis on light entertainment such as game and chat shows, music shows, comedy, soap operas, children's shows, news and films, while La2 puts focuses on sport, live cultural broadcasts, regional shows, serials, documentaries and films. Not surprisingly, La1 attracts around triple the audience of La2. Both TVE channels broadcast 24 hours a day.

◆ **Antena 3** – Antena 3 (💻 www.antena3. com) went on air in January 1990 and is now mainly owned by Telefónica. Its output consists of fairly conservative programmes such as game shows and 'home-made soaps' aimed at a family audience. Antena 3 regularly attracts around 18 per cent of the TV audience (usually ahead of La1).

◆ **Cuatro** – Cuatro (💻 www.cuatro.com) was Spain's first new national private channel for several years when it started broadcasting in November 2005. Cuatro's output consists mainly of game shows, foreign soaps such as *House*, films and general entertainment. Cuatro also broadcasts major sporting events (it screened the 2008 football European Cup). Cuatro attracts around 8 per cent of TV viewers.

◆ **Tele 5** – Tele 5 (💻 www.telecinco.es) claims to be Spain's 'entertainment channel' (as if the others offered some kind of torture ...) and broadcasts popular children's programmes, even more popular 'home-made' soaps, blockbuster films and political satire. Since May 2004, Tele 5 has topped the audience ratings almost every week and broadcasts at least five of the top ten weekly programmes.

◆ **La Sexta** – La Sexta (💻 www.lasexta.es) is Spain's newest television channel and started broadcasting in spring 2006. The channel isn't available nationwide and it currently broadcasts to around 80 per cent of the population in analogue and 85 per cent in digital. La Sexta's programming consists of light entertainment, foreign soaps, films and documentaries, although the channel's strong point is sport. La Sexta attracts audience ratings of around 8 per cent.

◆ **Localia TV** – Localia TV (💻 www.localia.es), launched in 2004, broadcasts in main towns and cities throughout the country with an emphasis on local events and news with films, current affairs and culture.

◆ **Regional stations** – There are several regional channels broadcast in the local language in the Basque Country (two), Catalonia (two) and Galicia, and others in Andalusia (two), Aragon, Asturias, the Balearics, Castilla La Mancha, the Canaries, Madrid (two) and Valencia. Most are controlled and sponsored by regional governments and serve as supplements to the national network – and most are deep in debt. Despite this apparent drawback, Extremadura and Murcia plan to start broadcasting in the near future. Regional channels attract around 14 per cent of audience ratings. Around 1,000 municipalities have their own TV stations (usually embarrassingly amateurish!), which usually serve as little more than a platform for the ruling political party.

◆ **Canal+** – Canal+ (💻 www.plus.es) is Spain's only scrambled national television channel and offers films, sports and documentaries. Many films are fairly recent and are often screened with the original soundtrack and Spanish subtitles. It also shows National Geographic documentaries and live sports events, including Spanish first division and US NBA basketball matches. It offers decoders to subscribers for a refundable deposit of around €100 (periodic offers waive this charge), a connection fee of €30 and a monthly subscription ranging from around €20 to €62.

There are no stations aimed at foreigners in Spain and the only option for English-speakers is the Gibraltar TV channel GBC (showing BBC programmes), which can be received in southern Spain, for which a decoder is necessary.

☑ **SURVIVAL TIP**

There have been numerous complaints about poor reception and if you want English-language programmes you're better off with satellite TV.

TV scheduling can be extremely 'flexible', programmes often being shown half an hour earlier or later than advertised and sometimes not at all.

All Spanish TV channels carry advertising and there's a continuous battle for advertising revenue, broadcasters offering ever more time for ever less money. The result is that advertising is pervasive (currently 12 minutes an hour, although this will be reduced to nine in 2010) and there's even advertising during live sports events such as football matches (at the bottom of the screen) whenever the ball goes out of play (football coverage is also constantly interrupted by replays, which are often shown while play is in progress).

TV programmes are listed in on the television channels' websites (see above), on the Teletexto website (🖳 www.teletexto. com), in all Spanish newspapers and in TV guides such as *TelePrograma*. Some Spanish TV programmes are also listed in English-language newspapers and magazines, along with satellite TV programmes.

Digital TV

Digital TV, offering better sound and image quality as well as many more channels than analogue TV, has been slow to take off in Spain. However, analogue broadcasting is due to disappear on 3rd April 2010, so the change-over is gathering pace. Until then, the main TV channels (see above) broadcast in analogue and digital (known as *simulcast*). TVE broadcasts seven digital channels, private stations four and regional stations eight. Most regional stations have four channels, though there are eight in Barcelona, Bilbao, Madrid, Seville and Valencia.

To watch digital TV you require no special aerial or dish, only a digital decoder (*terminal digital terrestre/TDT*), often known as a Digibox, costing from €30 – and, of course, a digital TV (costing at least €600!).

Telephone companies offer their own digital TV products broadcast via broadband internet connections (ADSL). For example, Telefónica offers *Imagenio*, currently available in large cities only and costing a €40 subscription fee plus €17 to €25 a month depending on the number of channels you want to receive.

Satellite TV

There are a number of satellites positioned over Europe, carrying over 200 stations broadcasting in a variety of languages. Satellite TV has been growing apace in Spain in recent years, although mostly among the foreign population.

Astra

The Astra satellites offer a huge choice of English and foreign-language channels – at least 100 (or over 500 with digital TV) – most of which can be received throughout Spain with a 60 or 85cm dish. Among the many English-language channels available via Astra are Channel 5, The Discovery Channels, The Disney Channel, Eurosport, Film Four, Plus, Sky Cinema 1 & 2, Sky Movies 1–9, Sky News, Sky One, Sky Sports (three channels), TCM, UK Gold and UKTV Gold. Other channels are broadcast in Dutch, German, Japanese, Swedish and various Indian languages. The signal for many channels is scrambled (the decoder is usually built into the receiver) and viewers must pay a monthly subscription to receive programmes. The best served by unscrambled (clear) channels are German-speakers. Further information can be found on Astra's website (⌨ www.astra.lu).

A bonus of Astra is the availability of radio stations, including all the national BBC stations (see **Cable & Satellite Radio** on page 113).

Sky Television

In order to receive Sky television you need a Sky digital receiver (digibox) and a dish. There are two ways to obtain the equipment and the necessary Sky 'smart' card. You can subscribe in the UK or Ireland (personally, if you have an address there, or via a friend) and then take the Sky receiver and card to Spain, although for the first year of your contract the digibox must be connected to a telephone line (so that Sky can sell you interactive services); if you export it during this period and connect it to a foreign telephone line, Sky will terminate your contract (Sky's call centre can tell what country a call/connection is being made from). After the first year, the digibox no longer needs to be connected to a telephone line and so can (although strictly should not) be exported. Similarly, a Sky card shouldn't be used outside the UK.

Alternatively, you can buy a digibox and obtain a Sky card 'privately' in Spain (a number of satellite companies supply Sky cards); however, you're subject to the same restrictions as noted above. Moreover, boxes and cards are much more expensive in Spain: around €400 plus the monthly subscription, while the card on its own costs around €200 (plus the subscription). To receive Sky TV in Spain, a dish must be at least 1.2m in diameter (costing from around €200).

Store Satellite website (⌨ http://storesatellite. com) has a useful map of Spain showing the size of dish necessary to receive Sky in different areas. According to the map, sizes range from 0.8m in the north of Spain to 3m in parts of the Canaries.

You must subscribe to Sky to receive most English-language channels (other than Sky News, which isn't scrambled). If you subscribe to the basic package, costing around GB£16, you will have access to around 100 channels, including BBC1, BBC2, ITV1, CH4 and CH5, though some of these are now available free. Various other packages are available costing up to around GB£45, for which you have access to the Movie and Sports channels, along with many interactive services such as Sky News Active.

Further information about Sky installation (in the UK) and programme packages can be found on Sky's website (⌨ www.sky.com).

Eutelsat

Eutelsat was the first company to introduce satellite TV to Europe and it now runs a fleet of communications satellites carrying TV stations to over 50m homes. The English-language stations available via Eutelsat include Eurosport, BBC World and CNBC Superchannel. Other stations are broadcast in Arabic, French, German, Hungarian, Italian, Polish, Portuguese, Spanish and Turkish. Further information can be found on Eutelsat's website (⌨ www.eutelsat.org).

BBC

The BBC's commercial subsidiary, BBC Worldwide Television, broadcasts two 24-hour channels: BBC Prime (general entertainment) and BBC World (24-hour news and information). BBC World is free-to-air, while BBC Prime is encrypted and requires a D2-MAC decoder and a smartcard, available on subscription from BBC Prime, PO Box 5054, London W12 0ZY, UK (☎ 020-8433 2221, ⌨ www.bbcprime.com). For more information and a programming guide contact BBC Worldwide Television, Woodlands, 80 Wood Lane W12 0TT, UK (☎ 020-8433 2000, (⌨ www.bbcworldwide.com).

A programme guide is also available on the internet (⌨ www.bbc.co.uk/schedules) and both BBC World and BBC Prime have websites (⌨ www.bbcworld.com and ⌨ www.bbcprime. com). When accessing them, you need to enter the name of the country (e.g. Spain) so that schedules appear in local time.

Equipment

A satellite receiver should have a built-in Videocrypt decoder (and others such as

Eurocrypt, Syster or SECAM, if required) and be capable of receiving satellite stereo radio. A system with an 85cm dish (to receive Astra stations) costs from around €300; installation may be included in the price. Shop around, as prices vary hugely. With a 1.2 or 1.5m motorised dish, you can receive hundreds of stations in a multitude of languages from around the world. If you wish to receive satellite TV on two or more TVs, you can buy a satellite system with two or more receivers.

To receive stations from two or more satellites simultaneously, you need a motorised dish or a dish with a double feed antenna (dual LNBs). There are many satellite sales and installation companies in Spain, most of which advertise in the expatriate press. Shop around and compare prices. Alternatively, you can import your own satellite dish and receiver and install it yourself. Before buying a system, ensure that it can receive programmes from all existing and planned satellites.

Location

To receive programmes from any satellite, there must be no obstacles between the satellite and your dish, i.e. no trees, buildings or mountains. Dishes can usually be mounted in a variety of unobtrusive positions and can also be painted or patterned to blend in with the background.

☑ SURVIVAL TIP

Before buying or erecting a satellite dish, check whether you need permission from your landlord, community or the local municipality. Some towns and buildings (such as apartment blocks) have strict laws concerning the positioning of antennae, although generally owners can mount a dish almost anywhere without receiving any complaints.

Communities

When an apartment or townhouse is advertised as having satellite TV, it often means that stations are received via a communal satellite dish (or a number) and transmitted via cable to all properties in an urbanisation. Only a limited number of programmes are usually available and no scrambled programmes may be included. Only two English-language stations are currently unscrambled on Astra, Sky News and Eurosport, although some urbanisations pay to receive more.

Programme Guides

Many satellite stations provide teletext information and most broadcast in stereo. Sky satellite programme listings are provided in a number of British publications such as *What Satellite, Satellite Times* and *Satellite TV Europe*, which are available on subscription and from newsagents' in Spain. Satellite TV programmes are also listed in expatriate newspapers and magazines in Spain. The annual *The Directory of Global Broadcasting* (available from WRTH – ☏ UK 01865-514405, 🖥 www.wrth.com) contains over 600 pages of information and the frequencies of all radio and TV stations worldwide.

RADIO

The Spanish are avid radio listeners and spend more time listening to the radio than they do watching TV (which is saying something). Spain has an estimated 37m radios (for 46m people) and radio has a regular average daily audience of 17m people (much higher per capita than in most other European countries).

There are numerous high-quality radio stations – public and private, local, regional, national and foreign. Among the most popular national radio stations are SER (consistently top of audience ratings), Radio Nacional de España (RNE), COPE (owned by the church and the second-largest network of private stations), Onda Cero and Punto Radio. In the autonomous regions, many stations broadcast in the regional language. Most stations and networks broadcast on FM, rather than medium wave (there are no long-wave stations in Spain).

There's a wealth of excellent FM stations in the major cities and resort areas, although in remote rural areas you may be lucky to receive one or two FM stations clearly. Spain has many excellent music stations playing mainly

American and British pop songs, although classical or 'easy listening' music is rare. RNE 2 is one of the few stations to play classical music around the clock. As in all countries, Spanish radio stations plumb the depths to unearth their DJs, who babble on (and on) at a zillion words a minute in a secret language intelligible only to other DJs and teenagers. (When you can understand Spanish DJs, you know you've really mastered the language!)

English & Other Expatriate Stations

There are English and other foreign-language commercial radio stations in major cities and resort areas (there are around eight stations on the Costa del Sol and around five on the Costa Blanca), where the emphasis is on music and chat with some news. Some expatriate stations broadcast in a variety of languages, including English, Dutch, German and various Scandinavian languages at different times of the day. Unfortunately (or inevitably), expatriate radio tries to be all things to everyone and not surprisingly falls short, particularly with regard to music, where it tries to cater for all tastes. However, it generally does a good job and is popular among expatriates.

The main English-language radio stations in Spain include Bay Radio, Holiday FM, OCI, REM and Spectrum on the Costa Blanca; REM and Spectrum on the Costa de Almería; Central FM, Coastline Radio, Global Radio, OCI, REM and Spectrum on the Costa del Sol; and Oasisfm and Power FM on Tenerife. Some English-language radio programme schedules are published in the local expatriate press in Spain.

BBC

The BBC World Service is broadcast on short wave on several frequencies (e.g. short wave 12095, 9760, 9410, 7325, 6195, 5975 and 3955Khz) simultaneously and you can usually receive a good signal on one of them. The signal strength varies according to where you live in Spain, the time of day and year, the power and positioning of your receiver, and atmospheric conditions. The BBC World Service plus BBC Radio 1, 2, 3, 4 and 5 are also available via the Astra (Sky) satellite. For a free BBC World Service programme guide and frequency information contact the BBC World Service (BBC Worldwide, Woodlands, 80 Wood Lane, London W12 0TT, UK, ☎ 020-8433 2000).

Cable & Satellite Radio

If you have cable or satellite TV, you will also be able to receive many radio stations via your cable or satellite link. For example, BBC Radio 1, 2, 3, 4 and 5, BBC World Service, Sky Radio, Virgin 1215 and many foreign-language stations are broadcast via the Astra satellites. Ask a satellite expert for advice regarding equipment and installation. Radio stations broadcast via satellite are listed in British magazines such as the *Satellite Times*. If you're interested in receiving radio stations from further afield, obtain a copy of *The Directory of Global Broadcasting* (available from WRTH – UK ☎ 01865-514405, 🖳 www.wrth.com), published annually.

9.

EDUCATION

Although Spain's state schools aren't among the best in Europe, the Spanish education system has improved dramatically in the last few decades. Until the '80s, there were insufficient places in state schools in many areas and many parents had to choose between sending them to a private school and keeping them at home. However, since those dark days, the education budget has increased considerably (although at 4.3 per cent of gross domestic product/GDP it's still one of the lowest in the European Union/ EU) and Spain's educational system had undergone profound (and long overdue) reforms. Most changes were necessary, although some have been controversial and haven't met with universal support from parents and teaching staff.

The educational system is still in a state of flux. The latest reform, known as the *Ley Orgánica de Calidad* (*LOE*), came into effect during the 2006-07 academic year (its principal effects are detailed in this chapter), and several more are pending. Nevertheless, the Organisation for Economic Co-operation and Development (OECD) education report released in late 2007 rated Spanish education among the worst of all member countries and highlighted the fact that Spain has the highest percentage of unqualified school leavers in OECD countries.

Spain's results in the Programme for International Student Assessment (PISA) study in 2006 also highlighted the country's poor academic performance. PISA assessed students in some 57 countries in three areas: language comprehension, mathematics and science. Reading comprehension is by far Spain's weakest point – Spanish students came 35th, behind Portugal and Slovakia. In mathematics and science, Spanish students achieved average positions, but even these were lower than its previous PISA results, in 2003. However, as the Minister for Education was keen to point out, testing for the latest PISA report took place before the latest education reforms had taken effect. On the other hand, the PISA report placed Spain eighth in terms of equal access to education, well ahead of the UK and the US.

In the light of these reports, the government promised a huge injection of public funds into the education system.

Education is compulsory for all children aged between 6 and 16.

The Spanish take education very seriously and have a deep respect and a great thirst for learning that aren't found in many other countries. In the current highly competitive labour market, parents and students are acutely aware that academic qualifications and training are of vital importance in obtaining a good job. Critics of the Spanish education system complain that its teaching methods are too traditional and unimaginative, with the emphasis on learning by rote. It has also been plagued by poor teacher training, badly motivated and poorly paid teachers, and a high student failure rate, although all have improved in the last decade.

Spain's state-funded school system (*escuelas públicas*) is supported by a comprehensive network of private schools (*escuelas privadas*), including many foreign and international schools. Around one-third of Spain's schoolchildren attend private schools, most of which are mixed (co-educational) day schools. State education in Spain is almost exclusively mixed and is entirely free, from nursery school through to university (including the children of foreign residents).

Over 90 per cent of children aged three to five attend nursery school and over 55 per cent of students remain in full-time education until they're 18, around 25 per cent going on to vocational training and 30 per cent to university. Education standards at Spain's finest universities are comparable with the best in Europe, although they're generally overcrowded and courses tend to be long and inflexible.

Generally, the younger a foreign child is when he enters the Spanish system, the better he copes. Conversely the older he is, the more problems he has adjusting. Foreign teenagers often have considerable problems learning Spanish and adjusting to Spanish school life. Many foreign parents prefer to educate younger children in Spanish nursery and primary schools, where they quickly learn Spanish, and to send children of secondary school age to an international school.

Despite the difficulties, however, for many children, the experience of schooling and living in a foreign country is a stimulating challenge, and it offers invaluable cultural and educational experiences. Children become 'world' citizens and are less likely to be prejudiced against foreigners and foreign ideas. This is particularly true when they attend an international school with pupils from different countries, although many state schools also have students from a number of countries and backgrounds, especially in Barcelona, Madrid and resort towns on the *costas*.

Information about Spanish schools, state and private, can be obtained from Spanish embassies and consulates abroad, and from foreign embassies,

educational organisations and government departments in Spain. Information about local schools can be obtained from town halls (*ayuntamientos*). The Ministry of Education, Social Politics and Sport (Ministerio de Educación, Política Social y Deporte) provides a general information service at its central office (Servicio de Información, C/Alcalá, 36, 28071 Madrid, ☎ 902 218 500, 🖥 www.mepsyd.es), open Mondays to Fridays from 9am to 5.30pm and Saturdays 9am to 2pm. The autonomous regions have their own education offices in regional capitals.

In addition to a detailed look at the Spanish state and private school system, this chapter contains information about higher education and language schools in Spain.

STATE SCHOOLS

Although state-funded schools are called public schools (*colegios públicos*) in Spain, the term 'state' has been used in preference to 'public' in this book to prevent confusion with the British term 'public school', which refers to a private, fee-paying school. The state school system in Spain differs considerably from the school systems in, for example, the UK and US, particularly at secondary level.

State education is ultimately the responsibility of the Ministry of Education, Social Politics and Sport (Ministerio de Educación, Política Social y Deporte) although the 17 autonomous regions now have considerable responsibility for their own education system (including higher education). State education is free, but in some regions parents must pay for school books, which are expensive; they're provided free in Andalusia, Aragon, the Basque Country, the Canaries, Cantabria, Castilla La Mancha, Catalonia, Galicia and La Rioja. Many town councils partially or completely subsidise other school supplies and extra-curricular activities such as sports and arts and crafts for low-income families.

For most Spanish children, school starts with nursery or pre-school (*preescolar*), from around the age of three or four (places for three-year olds are available in many regions). Compulsory education (*escolaridad obligatoria*), termed the basic general education (*educación general básica/EGB*), begins at six years of age in a primary school (*escuela primaria*) and lasts for six years. At the age of 12 (equivalent to Year 8 in the UK and sixth grade in the US), pupils move on to secondary education (*educación secundaria obligatoria/ESO*) for the next four years.

When they're 16, and if they've completed the four years, students are awarded a *graduado en educación secundaria* certificate and may attend a higher secondary school (or the same school in some cases) to study for their baccalaureate leading to university entrance. Pupils who haven't successfully completed four years' secondary education are awarded a school certificate (*certificado de escolaridad*) and may attend a vocational school (*formación profesional*) providing specialised training for a specific career.

A general criticism of Spanish state schools made by many foreigners is the lack of extra-curricular activities such as sport, music, drama, and arts and crafts. State schools don't have clubs or sports teams and if children want to do team sports they must usually join a private club. However, sports and other activities are often organised through parents' and sports associations; fees are low and activities usually take place directly after school.

Attending a state school helps children integrate into the local community and learn the local language, and is highly recommended if you plan to remain in Spain indefinitely. Note that while it's fairly easy to switch from a state school to a private school, the reverse isn't true. If you must move a child from a private school to a state school (e.g. for financial reasons), it can also be difficult for the child to adjust, particularly if he is a teenager.

Having made the decision to send a child to a state school, you should stick to it for at least a year to give it a fair trial, as it can take a child this long (or longer) to fully adapt to a new language, the change of environment and the different curriculum. If you choose to send your child to a Spanish school you should learn to speak Spanish well enough to communicate with your child's teachers – few Spanish teachers speak English.

There are state schools for pupils with particular education needs, e.g. learning difficulties due to psychological, emotional or behavioural problems, but children are sent to such schools only in exceptional circumstances.

Pupils usually go to local village (*pueblo*) nursery and primary schools, but attending secondary school can entail travelling long distances, though subsidised or free buses are usually provided. Normally, children must attend a state school (primary or secondary) within a certain distance of their home, so if you have a preference for a particular school, it's important to buy or rent a home within that school's catchment area.

Town halls and provincial Ministry of Education offices can provide a list of local schools. In some rural areas, there's little or no choice of schools, while in Madrid and other cities there are usually a number of possibilities. Naturally, the schools with the best reputations and exam results are the most popular, and therefore the most difficult to gain acceptance to. You should plan well ahead, particularly if you wish your child(ren) to be accepted at a superior school.

Language

There are many considerations to be made when choosing an appropriate school in Spain, not least the language of study. The only schools in Spain using English as the main teaching language are private foreign and international schools, although several state schools (e.g. in Andalusia and Madrid) teach some subjects in English or French. (A number of international schools teach pupils in English and Spanish.) If your children attend any other school, they must study all subjects in Spanish.

For most children, studying in Spanish isn't such a handicap as it may at first appear, particularly for those aged below ten.

The majority of children adapt quickly to a new language and most become reasonably fluent within three to six months. However, not all children adapt equally well to a change of language and culture, particularly those aged ten or over, many of whom have great difficulties during their first year. Children who are already bilingual usually have little problem learning Spanish, while American and British children tend to find it more difficult.

> Spanish children are generally friendly towards foreign children, who often acquire 'celebrity' status (particularly in rural schools), which helps their integration.

Some state schools provide intensive Spanish lessons ('bridging classes') for foreign children, although this is more common in certain provinces or regions (e.g. the regional government of Andalusia operates a scheme for non-Spanish primary pupils, some 6,000 children from 122 countries, although the scheme is at present implemented only in Malaga and Almería). It may be worthwhile enquiring about the availability of extra Spanish classes before choosing where to live. Foreign children are tested and put into a class suited to their level of Spanish, even if this means being taught with younger children. Children who don't read and write Spanish are often set back a year to compensate for their lack of Spanish and different academic background. Once a child has acquired a sufficient knowledge of spoken and written Spanish, he's assigned to a class appropriate to his age.

If your local school doesn't provide extra Spanish classes, your only choice will be to pay for private lessons or send your children to another (possibly private) school, where extra Spanish tuition is provided. Some parents send children to an English-speaking school for a year and then to a bilingual or Spanish school, while other parents believe it's better to throw their children in at the deep end. It all depends on the character, ability and wishes of the child. Whatever you decide, it will help your children **enormously** if they have intensive Spanish lessons before arriving in Spain.

An added problem in some regions is that state schools teach most lessons in a regional language such as Basque, Catalan and Galician, although parents may be offered a choice of teaching language. For example, in Catalonia and Valencia (including the Costa Blanca) children aged between 3 and 12 are generally taught most subjects in Catalan – except Spanish, which is taught for a few hours a week. Learning a regional language can be a huge problem, not only for foreign children, but also for Spanish-speaking children. However, immersion courses in the local language are usually offered to Spanish-speaking children. If you live in an area where education is dominated by a regional language, you should consider educating your child at a private school.

Enrolment

State schools have an annual quota for pupils and places are allocated on a first-come, first-served basis. The enrolment period usually lasts for one month early in the year e.g. March or April, although it varies from region to region. Individual schools will provide exact dates. The process of enrolment depends on the age of your child but may require an interview and in rare cases an examination. To enrol a child in a Spanish state school you must provide the following documents:

◆ your child's birth certificate or passport (the original and a photocopy), with an official Spanish translation (if necessary) and the parents' passports (originals and photocopies);

◆ proof of immunisation (Spanish immunisation requirements are similar to those in the UK – ask at a local health centre for details);

◆ proof of residence (*empadronamiento*) from your town hall (*ayuntamiento*);

◆ proof of verification, if applicable (see below);

◆ two passport-size photographs (for a studnt identity card and school records).

Verification

If your child is going to start a Spanish secondary school in the third year of *ESO* (around the age of 14) or later, you must have his education record verified by the Spanish Ministry of Education. The process is known as *homologación* or *convalidación*. You must complete the official form provided by the Ministry, which is available from Spanish consulates and embassies abroad, from regional departments of education or directly from the Ministerio de Educación, Política Social y Deporte, C/Alcalá 36, 28071 Madrid (☎ 902 218 500, 🖳 www.mepsyd.es). The form is downloadable from the website in the section on *Títulos Oficiales* and *Homologación* (the form is referred to as the *modelo oficial*). You should also submit your child's school record book and/or exam qualifications, plus his birth certificate.

If possible, this process should be completed before arriving in Spain, as a child may not be accepted at a school until the official papers confirming verification have been stamped by the Spanish Department of Education. The process takes around three months, although if you show a school proof of the Ministry's receipt of the verification documents, your child should have no problems being accepted.

School Hours

Hours vary from school to school but are usually from 9am until 4pm with a one-hour break for lunch, although an increasing number of schools don't have a lunch break and finish classes at 2pm. Lessons are usually divided into teaching periods of 45 minutes. Some schools offer school lunches, although many children bring a packed lunch or go home for lunch if they live nearby. Some schools are now opening early (e.g. at 8am) and providing activities after school until 5 or 6pm in an attempt to make childcare provision easier for working parents.

School Holidays

The academic year in Spain runs from mid-September to mid-June, the main holidays being Christmas, Easter and the long summer break. Spanish schoolchildren have very long school holidays (*vacaciones escolares*) compared with those in many other countries. The school year is made up of three terms, each averaging around 11 weeks. Terms are fixed and are generally the same throughout the country, although they may be modified to take account of local circumstances (such as *fiestas*). The following table shows the main school holidays for the 2008-09 school year (all dates inclusive):

School Holidays	
Holiday	Dates
Christmas (*Navidad*)	23rd December to 7th January
Easter (*Semana Santa*)	4th to 13th April
Summer (*Verano*)	24th June to 7th or 14th September

Some provinces (e.g. Malaga) also give pupils a week's holiday in the middle of the spring term (usually in February), known as 'white week' (*semana blanca*), as many people use it to go skiing. Pupils transferring from primary to secondary school are sometimes given an additional two weeks' summer holiday, which usually includes an 'end of school' trip (*viaje de estudios*) with fellow pupils. Schools are also closed on public holidays when they fall within term time.

School holiday dates are published by schools and local communities well in advance, thus allowing parents plenty of time to schedule family holidays. Normally, you aren't permitted to withdraw a child from classes during the school term, except for visits to a doctor or dentist, when the teacher should be informed in advance.

Pre-school

The term pre-school embraces nursery school (*guardería*), kindergarten (*jardín de la infancia*) and infant school (*escuela infantil*). Spain has a long tradition of state-funded pre-school (*educación infantil*), over 90 per cent of children aged three to five attending for at least a year before starting compulsory schooling. Note, however, that the provision of public and private pre-school facilities varies considerably with the town and the region, particularly regarding state schools.

State pre-school education is divided into two cycles, imaginatively called First Cycle (*primer ciclo/1° ciclo*) for children aged one to three and Second Cycle (*segundo ciclo/2° ciclo*) for ages three to six. Attendance is free in public centres in many areas.

There are also many private, fee-paying nursery schools, usually taking children aged from two to six, some of which are part of a primary school. Arrangements are generally flexible and parents can choose attendance during mornings or afternoons, all day, or only on selected days. Many schools provide transport to and from homes. Fees are generally low and schools are popular, well organised and good value.

Note that some nursery schools are more nurseries than schools, and simply an inexpensive way for parents to obtain supervised childcare. The best pre-schools are designed to introduce children to the social environment of school and concentrate on basic co-ordination skills, encourage the development of self-awareness and provide an introduction to group activities. Activities include arts and crafts (e.g. drawing, painting and pottery), music, dancing, educational games, perceptual and motor exercises, and listening skills.

During the final years of nursery school, the rudiments of reading, writing and arithmetic are taught in preparation for primary school. There are plans to teach English from the age of three or four in state schools throughout Spain. Children are also taken on outings and it's common to see groups of small children 'roped' together (for their own protection), being shepherded by a teacher.

☑ SURVIVAL TIP

Nursery school is highly recommended, particularly if your children are going to continue with a state education. After one or two years of nursery school they will be integrated into the local community and will have learnt Spanish in preparation for primary school. Research (in many countries) has shown that children who don't attend pre-school are at a distinct disadvantage when they start primary school.

Primary School

Compulsory education (*escolaridad obligatoria*), also called 'basic general education' (*educacion general básica/EGB*), begins at the age of six in a primary school (*escuela primaria*) and lasts for six years. Primary school is split into three cycles, called (you've guessed it) First Cycle (*primer ciclo/1° ciclo*), years 1 to 2; Second Cycle (*segundo ciclo/2° ciclo*), years 3 to 4; and Third Cycle (*tercer ciclo/3° ciclo*), years 5 to 6.

The primary curriculum includes natural and social sciences (*conocimiento del medio*), Spanish (*lengua*) and a regional language (if applicable), literature, mathematics, arts (*dibujo y plástica*), physical education and a foreign language (usually English or French), which is compulsory from the second cycle, although many state schools now offer English from the age of six. Catholic religion is optional and when your child starts school you're asked whether you want your child to attend religious classes. Alternatives may include extra reading, ethics or theatre studies. Under the new education reforms, all pupils have daily reading time and pupils in the Third Cycle (years 5 and 6) also study *Educación para la Ciudadanía* (Education for Citizens), covering

moral and social values such as sexual equality and care of the environment.

In most schools, pupils have three evaluations (*evaluaciones*) each year. If a child fails to achieve the required standard set for a particular cycle, he may be required to repeat the previous year unless he can show considerable improvement in the autumn (many private and state schools offer 'recovery' classes during the summer holidays to help pupils catch up). The opinions of teachers, tutors, parents and the sector's psychological and pedagogical team are taken into account when deciding whether a pupil must repeat a year. Pupils cannot be required to repeat more than one year during their primary education.

Secondary School

Compulsory secondary education (*enseñanza secundaria obligatoria/ESO*) was instituted in 1990 for pupils aged 12 to 16 and completes their compulsory education. It provides pupils with more specialised training than their previous education and prepares them for the baccalaureate (see below) or vocational training. The four years of compulsory secondary school (*Instituto de Educación Secundaria/IES*) are divided into two, two-year cycles (no prizes for guessing their names), the curriculum containing compulsory and optional subjects.

Oddly, the subjects change halfway through the Second Cycle. For the first three years students follow a common curriculum of six subjects (seven in regions with their own language). Compulsory subjects are natural sciences, Spanish language and literature, geography and history, mathematics, physical education and a foreign language.

The options for the remaining two subjects are moral and social studies (*educación para la ciudadanía*), art, music, IT and a second foreign language. In the fourth year, six subjects – Spanish language and literature, mathematics, social sciences, a foreign language, physical education and ethics and civic education

(*educación ético-cívica*) – are compulsory and students must choose three of the following subjects: biology and geology; fine and visual arts; physics and chemistry; IT; Latin; music; a second foreign language; and technology. Students in regions with a regional language must also study the regional language and literature. The Catholic religion is an optional subject in all four years.

As with primary education, a pupil can be required to repeat a year if he hasn't passed the end-of-term exams or the autumn repeats (pupils who fail three or more subjects in the end-of-term exams must repeat the year), and pupils can be required to repeat two years in secondary education. A planned reform is to make provision for small groups to help pupils who struggle academically – all pupils currently study the same topics at the same level.

Upon completion of *ESO*, pupils who have achieved the set standards are awarded a 'graduate of secondary education' (*graduado en educación secundaria*) certificate enabling them to study for the baccalaureate or undergo specialised vocational training. This certificate is a basic requirement for most jobs in Spain. All pupils, whether or not they've achieved the course objectives, receive a document stating the school years completed, the marks obtained in each subject, and recommendations regarding their academic and vocational future.

Under the *LOE*, pupils aged 16 to 21 who have repeated two years of *ESO* study and failed to pass a further year are eligible for the Professional Qualification Programme (*Programa de Cualificación Profesional*), whose aim is to provide these pupils with a further opportunity to gain their 'graduate of secondary education' certificate or the chance to gain other qualifications.

BACCALAUREATE

The Spanish baccalaureate (*bachillerato* or *bachiller*) programme consists of two years' academic training to prepare pupils for higher education or high-grade vocational training (see above) or to start a career. The baccalaureate is studied for at an *ES* (see above); there's no Spanish equivalent of the French *lycée* or the British sixth form college, for example. Under the *LOE* reforms, all baccalaureate students are required to study Spanish language and literature, philosophy and citizenship (*filosofía y ciudadanía*), a foreign language, a regional language (if applicable), the history of philosophy, the history of Spain, 'science for the modern world' (*ciencias para el mundo contemporáneo* – covering topics such as genetics, the origin of the universe and the latest scientific advances) – and physical education.

In addition to these seven (or eight) compulsory subjects, students must choose one of three specialities – art (fine art, technical drawing, history of art, and design); science and technology (maths, biology, chemistry, physics, geology, mechanics and technical drawing); or humanities and social sciences (Greek, Latin, economics and history).

At the end of the second year, pupils take an examination known as the *prueba general de bachillerato/PGB*. If they pass this exam and have also passed the exams during the two-year course, they're awarded the *título de bachiller* (called simply *bachiller*), which includes the average mark obtained. The *bachiller*, together with an oral exam in a foreign language (usually English), allows pupils to study at Spanish universities and is recognised as an entrance qualification by universities throughout the world, provided the student's proficiency in the language of study is up to the required standard. Pupils who fail the *PGB* are awarded a certificate of attendance and can proceed to vocational training (see below). Pupils who fail three subjects in their first year of the baccalaureate are required to repeat the year.

PRIVATE SCHOOLS

There's a wide range of private schools (*escuelas privadas*) in Spain, including parochial schools, bilingual schools, international schools and a variety of foreign schools (e.g. American and British). Around a third of children in Spain are educated at private school. Most private schools are mixed (co-educational), Catholic day schools, although a number of schools (including some American and British schools) take weekly or term boarders.

Your choice of foreign schools depends on where you live in Spain. There's a good choice of English-speaking schools (accepting children from 3 to 18) in Barcelona, Madrid, Palma de Mallorca and Tenerife and on the *costas*. For example, there are British schools in Alicante, Barcelona, Cadiz, Fuengirola, Madrid, Las Palmas, Palma de Mallorca, Marbella, Torremolinos and Valencia, and on the islands of Ibiza, Lanzarote, Minorca and Tenerife. In other cities and areas, there may be only one English-speaking school or none at all. There are also French, German, Swedish and other foreign-language schools in Spain. Under Spanish law, all foreign schools must be approved by their country's embassy in Spain. Like state schools, most private schools operate a Monday-to-Friday timetable, with no Saturday morning classes.

Private schools teach a variety of syllabi, including the British GCSE and A Level examinations, the American High School Diploma and college entrance examinations (e.g. ACT, SAT, achievement tests and AP exams), the International Baccalaureate (IB) and the Spanish *bachillerato*. However, most Spanish private schools, i.e. schools teaching

wholly in Spanish, are state-subsidised and follow the Spanish state-school curriculum. Some international schools are also subsidised and follow a totally bilingual (English/Spanish) curriculum and are authorised to accept Spanish pupils. They must teach the Spanish curriculum, including primary and secondary education, and the *bachillerato*. They provide the opportunity for children to become bilingual and to choose between a Spanish and foreign-language university or career.

To receive state subsidies, a school must have at least 25 per cent Spanish pupils (and at least 20 per cent in each class) and be subject to inspection by the Spanish school authorities. Many international private schools have mixed Spanish and foreign student bodies, e.g. one-third American or British students, one-third Spanish and one-third other nationalities, although they may be called American or British.

Private school fees vary considerably according to whether they're subsidised and, among other things, their quality, reputation and location, but are generally low compared with those in northern Europe and North America. Not surprisingly, schools in Madrid and Barcelona are among the most expensive. Fees at subsidised Spanish schools are around €700 a year, whereas fees at independent foreign schools range from around €4,000 a year to well over €10,000 a year (for boarders) at senior level. Fees don't usually include registration, books, materials, laundry, insurance, extra-curricular activities, excursions, meals and transport (most private schools provide school buses), for which you should allow around €800 per term. Most private schools subscribe to insurance schemes covering accidents, in school and during school-sponsored activities. Some schools award scholarships or offer grants to parents with low incomes.

Private foreign and international schools usually have a more relaxed, less rigid regime and curriculum than Spanish state schools. They provide a more varied and international approach to sport, culture and art, and a wider choice of academic subjects. Many also provide English-language summer school programmes combining academic lessons with sports, arts and crafts, and other extra-curricular activities. Their aim is the development of a child as an individual and the encouragement of his unique talents, rather than teaching on a production-line system. This is made possible by small classes, which allow teachers to provide pupils with individually-tailored lessons and tuition.

The results are self-evident and many private secondary schools have a near 100 per cent university placement rate. On the other hand, one of the major problems of private foreign-language education in Spain is that children can grow up in cultural 'ghettos' and be 'illiterate' as far as the Spanish language and culture are concerned. Although attending a private school may be advantageous from an academic viewpoint, integration into Spanish society can be severely restricted.

You should make applications to private schools as far in advance as possible, as many international schools have waiting lists for places. You're usually requested to send school reports, exam results and other records. Before enrolling your child in a private school, make sure that you understand the withdrawal conditions in the school contract.

☑ **SURVIVAL TIP**

Check whether a school is recognised by the Spanish education authorities and whether it belongs to an accredited organisation. Most British schools in Spain belong to the National Association of British Schools in Spain (NABSS, 💻 www.nabss.org), whose members are visited and approved by British school inspectors. Advice about international schools in Spain can be obtained from the British Council (💻 www.britishcouncil.org/spain) and the European Council of International Schools (ECIS, 💻 www.ecis.org).

VOCATIONAL TRAINING

Vocational training (*formación profesional/FP*) was traditionally taken by pupils who failed to achieve the standards required to study for the baccalaureate (*bachillerato*) and long discredited as only for those who weren't bright enough to pursue an academic career. These days, as in other countries, vocational training is regarded as equally important as academic training and there has recently been increasing interaction between educational establishments and the labour market, which is of vital importance to Spain's economic future. In particular, new vocational training courses have been introduced, enabling successful pupils to take specialist baccalaureate courses and proceed to higher education.

Vocational training consists of cycles of between 1,300 and 2,000 teaching hours depending on the profession. The first phase of *FP* (*grado medio*) is open to pupils who have been awarded a *graduado en educación secundaria* certificate (see **Secondary School** on page 121) and opt for vocational training rather than studying for the baccalaureate. The second phase (*grado superior*) is open to pupils who have passed the baccalaureate or the *examen de prueba de acceso a formación profesional*, which includes subjects from the baccalaureate.

FP pupils divide their time between study (around 75 per cent) and on-the-job training in commerce or industry (25 per cent). Vocational training is free for most pupils, whether it takes place in a public centre or a private institution, as the latter are financed by the state (but employ their own teachers and have different rules from state centres). In recent years, emphasis has been placed on IT and telecommunications skills and EU languages, particularly English and German.

Pupils who complete a *grado medio* course receive a 'technical specialist' (*técnico especialista*) certificate and those who complete a *grado superior* course receive a 'superior technical' (*técnico superior*) certificate. Holders of the latter certificate may continue their studies at university.

HIGHER EDUCATION

Spain has 70 universities (*universidades*), 48 of them state-run (and attended by 90 per cent of higher education students) and 22 run by private enterprises or by the Catholic church. There are a number of other higher education institutes specialising in physical education, tourism, dramatic arts, dance and music, as well as a number of highly rated business schools (mostly American).

There are a number of US universities with faculties in Madrid, including the Schiller International University (🖳 www.schillermadrid. edu), the St Louis University (🖳 http://spain. slu.edu) and Suffolk University (🖳 www.suffolk. es). All classes at American universities are taught in English. The European university has a branch in Barcelona.

Although few Spanish universities are world-renowned, Spain has a long history of university education, the university system dating back to the middle ages. Spain's oldest university (Salamanca) was founded in 1218 and even before this the Moors had 'universities' in Spain (long before anyone else had even thought of them). The largest and most highly regarded Spanish universities are Complutense in Madrid and Central in Barcelona, with student bodies of around 86,000 and 55,000 respectively. Granada and Seville universities each have over 56,000 students.

There are some 1.4m university students in Spain, a figure generally considered to be too high for a country with a population of 46m.

Overcrowding is a huge problem, particularly in first-year classes (you must usually arrive early to get a seat at a lecture). However, many students drop out after the tough exams set at the end of the first year. The number of female students has increased by around 40 per cent in the last decade and they now outnumber male students (61 per cent of students who complete their courses and obtain degrees are women). The number of foreign students has also increased greatly over the last few years and foreigners now account for over 8 per cent of students, a third coming from EU countries.

Courses

Studies at Spanish universities are divided into three cycles. The first cycle, lasting four years (five for medicine and architecture), leads to a *grado*. The second cycle, lasting one or two years, leads to a *máster*, which is equivalent to an American or British MA or MSc. The third cycle is a PhD (doctorate) programme, which results in the academic title of *doctor* or *Doctor en Filosofía y Letras*.

The Spanish university system is rigidly structured: students must follow a fixed curriculum and aren't usually permitted to change universities during their studies (except for family or health reasons).

University courses are currently being revised as Spain starts to bring them into line with EU regulations due to be in place by 2010 and designed to make university studies across the EU as homogeneous as possible. Under the changes (to be adopted in the 2008-09 academic year) the number of available courses is to be reduced from around 140 to fewer than 80 and their duration from five to four years, except architecture and medicine; it will no longer be possible to study one foreign language only; and degree awards will include a certificate (*Suplemento al Título*) with a detailed description of the student's completed studies in an attempt to make recognition of qualifications within the EU easier.

Applications

In general, the academic year runs from October to June and applications should be made as soon as possible (e.g. on receipt of final school exam results). Applications must be submitted to universities and addressed to the student secretariat (*vice-rectorado de alumnos*).

Competition for places at Spanish universities is high, as there are generally too few places for all the students wishing to attend, although in 2006 and 2007 supply exceeded demand in some subjects for the first time in 20 years. Applicants must pass the *prueba general de bachillerato* (*PGB*) examination (see **Baccalaureate** on page 121) and acceptance depends on the result obtained in this exam, as well as the average mark gained during the two years of study for the baccalaureate. Those who pass the *PGB* with a high mark are generally awarded a university place in July, while others may have to wait until August to find out whether they've been accepted.

Suitably qualified EU nationals are entitled to compete for places at Spanish universities on equal terms with Spanish nationals. In addition, a small number of places at most universities, e.g. 5 per cent, is allocated to non-EU students. In general, qualifications that are accepted as entry requirements in a student's home country are accepted in Spain. Spanish universities accept British A Levels as an entrance qualification, but an American high school diploma isn't usually accepted; American students must usually have spent two years at college or hold a BA, BBA or BSc degree.

For information about the recognition of EU diplomas in Spain, contact the Ministerio de Educación, Política Social y Deporte, C/Alcalá, 36, 28071 Madrid (☎ 902 218 500, 🖳 www.mepsyd.es). As with school enrolment, foreign qualifications must be verified via a process known as *homologación* by the Spanish Department of Education and Culture in Spain.

Many foreign university students (and Spanish students abroad) can study in Spain under EU exchange programmes for periods ranging from a few weeks to several months. However, all foreign students require a thorough knowledge of Spanish, although preparatory courses are provided. **Note that in regions where there's a second official language (e.g. the Basque Country,**

Catalonia and Galicia), courses may be conducted in the local language.

Costs

In most regions, university fees (*tasas*) are set by the Spanish Ministry of Education, Social Politics and Sport. In regions with responsibility for their own education, fees are set annually by the university council and the local regional government. Private universities under the auspices of the Catholic church set their own fees. Spanish university fees are low for residents and EU nationals, e.g. from €300 to €1,200 a year, depending on the faculty and location, but considerably higher for non-resident non-EU nationals. Grants and scholarships are available to Spanish and foreign students and around one in seven students receives a grant. (Note that a disadvantage of moving to Spain is that foreign children resident in Spain may be classified as overseas students by their home countries, making them no longer eligible for grants and possibly liable to pay fees or higher fees.)

In addition to course fees, students should expect to pay €400 to €1,500 a month for meals and accommodation. There's a huge difference in the cost of living between cities and regions, Madrid and Barcelona being the most expensive. Finding a part-time job to help pay your living expenses is difficult and shouldn't be relied upon. Some universities have their own student halls of residence (*colegios mayores*), although places are in high demand and short supply. The availability and cost of private rented accommodation (see page 69) varies with the location.

Spanish students under the age of 28 and registered at a Spanish institute of higher education are covered for health insurance by a students' insurance fund. This fund also covers many foreign students under reciprocal agreements, including those from EU countries. Students over the age of 28 and others who aren't covered must have private health insurance.

Many Spanish students attend the nearest university to their home and treat university as an extension of school, particularly in Madrid and other large cities where accommodation is expensive. Spanish students don't usually work during their studies or during holidays and most go home at weekends. Therefore few university facilities are open at weekends. Note that, like Spanish state schools, universities offer few extra-curricular sporting or social activities.

Further information about higher education in Spain can be obtained from the cultural sections of Spanish embassies abroad and from the Secretaría General del Consejo de Coordinación Universitaria, C/ Albacete, 5, 28027 Madrid (☎ 916 037 000, 🖳 www.micinn.es/univ/ccuniv). The Spain Exchange website (🖳 www.spainexchange.com) includes a wealth of useful information about studying in Spain, as well as a detailed description of all universities and higher education establishments in the country.

LEARNING SPANISH

If you don't speak Spanish, it's advisable to enrol in a course at a language school, preferably before arriving in Spain. If you're planning to work in Spain, you may wish to obtain a formal qualification for non-native speakers (*diploma de español como lengua extranjera*), administered by the Spanish Ministry of Education, the Instituto Cervantes (see **Further Information** below) and the University of Salamanca (☎ 923 294 400, 🖳 http://corintio.usal.es). Information is also available from Spanish embassies. Courses are held worldwide and diplomas are awarded at three levels (beginner, intermediate and advanced). Diplomas are particularly useful when formal evidence of Spanish proficiency is required, e.g. for employment or study in Spain.

Most people can teach themselves a great deal through the use of books, tapes, videos, CDs and DVDs. However, even the most able and dedicated students require some help. Spanish classes are offered by language schools (see below), Spanish and foreign colleges and universities, private and international schools, foreign and international organisations, local associations and clubs, chambers of commerce and town halls, and private teachers (see below). Classes range from beginners' courses through specialised business or cultural courses to university-level courses leading to higher diplomas.

Most Spanish universities offer language courses all year round, including summer courses. These are generally cheaper than those provided by language schools, although classes may be much larger. Free or heavily subsidised courses are organised for resident foreigners in some provinces, e.g. Alicante and Malaga, by the Spanish department of the Escuela Oficial de Idiomas. If you already speak some Spanish, but need conversational practice, you may wish to enrol in an art or craft course at a local institute or club.

Language Schools

Spain has around 3,000 language schools (*escuelas de idiomas*), the highest number in Europe, and there are schools in all Spanish cities and large towns. Most offer a range of classes; which one you choose will depend on your current language ability, how many hours you wish to study a week, how much money you want to spend and how quickly you need to learn. Courses are graded according to ability, e.g. beginner, intermediate or advanced, and usually last from 2 to 16 weeks. Courses are usually open to anyone over the age of 18 and some also accept students aged from 14. All schools offer free tests to assess your level and a free introductory lesson. You may wish to check that a school is a member of a professional association such as the Asociación para la Enseñanza del Español como Lengua Extranjera (ASELE).

Courses generally fall into the following categories: extensive (4 to 15 hours per week); intensive (15 to 30 hours) and total immersion (30 to 40 hours). The most common are intensive courses, providing four hours' tuition a day from Mondays to Fridays (20 hours a week). The cost of an intensive course is usually between €250 and €400 for a two-week course, €300 to €450 for three weeks or €350 to €500 for four weeks. The highest fees are charged in the summer months, particularly during July and August. Commercial courses are generally more expensive, but include more tuition, e.g. €600 for two weeks and a total of 60 hours' tuition. Courses that include accommodation are often excellent value and many schools arrange home stays with a Spanish family (full or half board), or provide apartment or hotel accommodation. Accommodation with a host family typically costs €300 to €400 per week half board.

Some schools offer combined courses where language study is combined with classes in Spanish art and culture, reading, conversation or Spanish history, traditions and folklore. Many schools combine language courses with a range of social or sporting activities such as horse riding, tennis, windsurfing, golf, skiing, hang-gliding and scuba-diving.

Don't expect to become fluent in a short time unless you have a particular flair for learning languages or already have a good command of Spanish. Unless you desperately need to learn quickly, it's usually better to arrange your lessons over a long period. However, don't commit yourself to a long course of study, particularly an expensive one, before ensuring that it's the right course for you. Whichever type of course you choose, you should shop around, as tuition fees vary considerably.

Private Lessons

You may prefer to have private lessons, which are a quicker (although more expensive) way of learning Spanish. The main advantage of private lessons

is that you learn at your own speed and aren't held back by slow learners or left floundering in the wake of the class genius. Don't forget to ask your friends, neighbours and colleagues if they can recommend a private teacher. Private Spanish teachers often advertise in English-language publications in Spain (see **Appendix A**). Private lessons cost from €15 per hour with an experienced tutor.

One way to get to know the Spanish and improve your language ability is to find a Spanish partner wishing to learn English (or your mother tongue), called a 'language exchange' (*intercambio*). Partners get together on a regular basis and half the time is spent speaking English (or another foreign language) and half speaking Spanish. You can advertise for a private teacher or partner in local newspapers, on bulletin and notice boards (in shopping centres, supermarkets, universities, clubs, etc.), and through your or your partner's employers.

Further Information

Information about Spanish language schools can be obtained from the Departamento de Español para Extranjeros, Escuela Oficial de Idiomas, Jesús Maestro s/n, 28003 Madrid (☎ 915 335 802, ⌨ www.eoidiomas. com). A list of Spanish language schools in Spain (as well as of organisations arranging courses, exchange visits and home stays in Spain for children and adults) can be obtained from the Instituto Cervantes (⌨ www.cervantes.es), which has offices in many countries, including the UK (Leeds, Manchester and London – 102 Eaton Square, London SW1 W9AN, ☎ 020-7235 0353, ⌨ http://londres.cervantes.es) and the US (211–215 East 49th Street, NY 10017, New York, ☎ 212-308 7720, ⌨ http:// nyork.cervantes.es). The Instituto also runs Spanish classes in some 30 countries.

A good source for Spanish language-learning books and materials in the UK is European Schoolbooks (5 Warwick Street, London W1B 5LU, ☎ 020-7734 5269, ⌨ www.eurobooks.co.uk).

For further information about Spanish languages, see **Language** on pages 35 and 117.

MO-M1-M2-M3 ↓

Sortida
Way out
Salida

Recollida d'equipatges
Baggage claim
Recogida equipajes

B

↓ ✈ MO-M1-M2-M ↓ ✈

Sortida
↓ Way out
Salida

↓ ✈
Info
Trans
Info

Recollida d'equipatges
↓ Baggage claim
Recogida equipajes

B

↓ ✈ MO-M1-M2-M3 ↓ ✈ | Portes
Puertas **01:39**

Sortida
Way out
Salida

Informació Trànsits
Transit information
Información Trànsitos

↓ ✈ Recollida d'equipatges
Baggage claim
Recogida equipajes

B

10.
PUBLIC TRANSPORT

Public transport (*transporte público*) **is generally excellent in Spanish cities, most of which have efficient urban bus and train services, some supplemented by underground railways** (*metros*) **and, occasionally, trams** (*tranvía*). **Spanish railway services are efficient and reasonably fast, particularly between cities served by high-speed trains (see below). Spain has comprehensive inter-city bus and domestic airline services and is also served by frequent international coach, train and airline services. On the down side, trains are non-existent in many areas and buses are sometimes infrequent in coastal resorts and rural areas, where it's generally essential to have your own transport.**

Transport within major cities is inexpensive and efficient, and most cities have extensive suburban rail networks. Systems are totally integrated and the same ticket (sold at tobacconists') can be used for all services. A range of commuter and visitor tickets are also available. There are travel agencies such as Viajes Marsans, Halcón Viajes and Viajes Meliá in major cities and large towns, and several specialist online agencies, such as Last Minute (🖳 www.lastminute.com) and Viajar (🖳 www. viajar.com).

Students with an International Student Identity Card (ISIC) receive discounts on some Iberia flights and some buses. The agency Viajes TIVE specialises in travel for young people. People aged 65 or over also receive discounts on most forms of public transport (if you aren't offered a discount, don't forget to ask).

RAIL

The Spanish rail network is run by the state-owned company RENFE, which operates some 15,000km (over 9,000mi) of track and 2,500 stations (*estaciones*). The RENFE network takes in all major cities, although it doesn't run to many small towns, and is supplemented by a few suburban networks, such as the *Ferrocarrils de la Generalitat de Catalunya* (*FFCC*, but commonly referred to as the *Generalitat*) in Barcelona, and private narrow-gauge railways.

Little freight is transported by train within Spain or to other European Union (EU) countries, compared with the tens of thousands of tonnes shipped by road. Like most state-owned businesses in Spain, the railways were grossly under-funded under Franco and RENFE remains western Europe's most idiosyncratic railway (many lines are still single track), despite huge investment in new rolling stock. Occasional accidents occur on Spain's rail network, but travelling by train is usually very safe and considerably safer than travelling by car.

The network is centred on Madrid, from where three main lines radiate to other parts of the country (two extend to the French border and the other to Andalusia and the Levante). Consequently, there are good links between Madrid and other cities, although to travel long-distance without going via Madrid often requires a circuitous journey. Madrid has two main stations, both in the city centre:

♦ **Chamartín** – serves A Coruña, Albacete, Alicante, Bilbao, Cartagena, Irún, León, Lugo, Ourense, Oviedo, Salamanca, Santander, Soria, Vallodolid and Zamora, as well as destinations in France and the local area;

♦ **Puerta de Atocha** – serves Castilla La Mancha, Andalusia and Extremadura, including Almería, Badajoz, Cadiz, Ciudad Real, Cordoba, Cuenca, Granada, Malaga, Mérida, Salamanca, Seville, Toledo and Valencia, as well as all *AVE* routes and destinations in Portugal and the local area.

The main stations in Barcelona are França and Sants (the more important and the *AVE* arrival and departure point), which has a link to Barcelona airport. Trains to all major Spanish cities and to France (via Gerona) leave from Sants, while França has daily international trains to Geneva, Milan, Paris and Zurich. Note that in smaller towns, stations are often located a few kilometres from the town centre and there may be no bus service.

Spain's railway network is well below average by European standards, particularly regarding speed and punctuality, although it's also one of the continent's cheapest. However, RENFE has undergone a comprehensive modernisation programme in the last decade, during which journey times have been reduced by up to 50 per cent.

TRAINS

International Trains

Spain has many international services, although they're slow and expensive compared with air travel. There are direct trains to many western European cities (e.g. Geneva, Milan, Montpellier, Paris and Zurich), a 'Train-hotel' (*Trenhotel*) service running from Madrid to Paris (*Francisco de Goya*) and from Barcelona to Milan (*Salvador Dalí*), to Paris (*Joan Miró*) and to Zurich (*Pau Casals*), and there's even a train from Madrid to Moscow taking around three days.

International trains usually have two classes, first (*gran clase*) and second/tourist (*turista*), plus sleeping cars (*coches camas*) with a choice of individual compartments or couchettes. At border stops it may be necessary to change trains due to the fact that Spain uses a wider gauge than the rest of Europe, except for *Talgo* trains, which have adjustable axles.

Further information is available from the RENFE website (🖳 www.renfe.es) or from the telephone helpline for international enquiries (☎ 902 243 402), open from 7am to 11pm.

High-speed Trains

Spain's domestic high-speed trains (known as *AVE* and travelling at speeds of up to 300kph/185mph) operate from Madrid to Andalusia (Cordoba, Malaga and Seville), to Toledo, to Aragon (Zaragoza and Huesca), Catalonia (Barcelona and Lleida) and to Segovia and Valladolid, both north of Madrid.

> Refunds are offered if an *AVE* is significantly late arriving at its destination, e.g. 25 per cent if the delay is between 20 and 40 minutes, or a full refund if it's more than an hour late.

The *AVE* service is currently being extended countrywide and, when the network is finished, all provincial capitals will be under four hours from Madrid and all provinces under six and a half hours from Barcelona. The stretches that are currently under construction are Madrid-Galicia (due to be completed in 2012), Madrid-Extremadura (2012) and Madrid-Valencia (2010). By 2020 Spain will have over 10,000km of high-speed train network, the largest in Europe, and this will eventually comprise part of a Europe-wide, high-speed rail network connecting with the French and Portuguese networks.

There are three classes of *AVE*: first (*club*), business (*preferente*) and tourist (*turista*), plus sleeping accommodation for international travel. *AVE*s are air-conditioned and equipped with reclining seats, televisions (films are shown), a restaurant and cafeteria, a drinks/refreshment trolley service and, in first class, free newspapers and the *AVE* magazine (*Revista Paisajes*).

Other Trains

RENFE operates a variety of other trains, which can be grouped into three types of service: long-distance (*largo recorrido*), medium-distance (*medio recorrido*) and local or suburban (*cercanías*).

A variety of trains operate on the long- and medium-distance routes, and vary greatly in speed. Long-distance (*largo recorrido*) trains include the *Talgo* and the *Talgo 200*, which has first- and tourist-class sections and is similarly equipped to *AVEs*. *Talgo* trains are generally slower than *AVEs*; the fastest run at speeds of between 160 and 200kph. The main *Talgo* routes are from Barcelona along the Mediterranean coast.

In general, fast trains stop only at main stations, while slow trains stop at all stations. Long- and medium-distance trains usually have first and second class carriages, although there's a bewildering variety of fares within each class and for different train types. Local and suburban trains are second/tourist class (*turista*) only and stop at all stations.

Despite their names, an *exprés* is a slow night train, usually with sleeping cars, and a *rápido* is a daytime version of the *exprés*. Night trains have various types of couchette (*literas*) and bed.

Fares

Spanish rail fares are low by European standards. Fares are graded according to a train's speed and comfort and there are surcharges (*suplementos*) on fast trains, including *TER*, *Talgo*, *Intercity* and *ELT* trains, which can increase fares by up to 80 per cent. A first-class ticket costs around 50 per cent more than second/tourist class (*turista*). If you aren't in a hurry, it's advisable to compare the cost of slow trains with fast trains, as the savings are considerable on slow trains (and they allow plenty of time to enjoy the sights).

RENFE tickets can be bought by telephone (☎ 902 240 202) or online (💻 www.renfe.es). If you purchase by telephone, you're given an eight-digit code (this can also be sent to you by text message or email), which must be presented when you collect your tickets.

General Information

♦ All *AVE* and long-distance trains have a bar-buffet and/ or a restaurant car (*wagón restaurante*) with waiter service. Medium-distance trains have a refreshment trolley (*carrito de restauración*) offering drinks and snacks at your seat. Note that catering on trains is expensive and isn't good quality by Spanish standards (many passengers take a picnic).

♦ Main railway stations provide a variety of services, including an information booth; tourist office; post office; accommodation service; luggage lockers and storage; wash, shower and brush-up facilities; car rental; telephones; cafeterias and restaurants; bank with ATMs; currency exchange; photocopiers; instant passport photograph machines and assorted shops and kiosks.

♦ Smoking is forbidden on all trains, including sleeping cars and in stations and on platforms.

♦ Public telephones are available on *AVE* and other fast trains, and accept domestic and international calls. They must be used with a Telefónica phone card available from train cafeterias.

♦ Platforms (*andenes*) aren't always clearly numbered, so make sure you're waiting at the right one. Lines often have different numbers from platforms, which can be confusing. The destination of trains is usually written or displayed on the outside of carriages.

♦ Car parks are often provided close to railway stations, where long-term parking costs around €12 per day (monthly season tickets are available).

♦ You can hire (rent) a car from many main railway stations and leave it at another major station. Cars can be reserved at travel agencies.

Barcelona station

♦ Beware of thieves when travelling on trains and try to store your bags in an overhead rack where you can keep an eye on them.

♦ Self-service luggage lockers (*consignas*) and left-luggage offices are usually available at major railway stations, but for security reasons (particularly since the train bombings in March 2004) they may be closed. Where available, lockers large enough for large suitcases or backpacks cost around €2 to €4 per day. Main stations also have left luggage offices open from around 8am until 10pm. Luggage forwarding up to 20kg is free for long-distance rail passengers.

Further information is available from the RENFE website (💻 www.renfe.es) or from the telephone helpline (☎ 902 240 202), open from 0.15am to 11.50pm (weekends from 2.30am to 11.50pm).

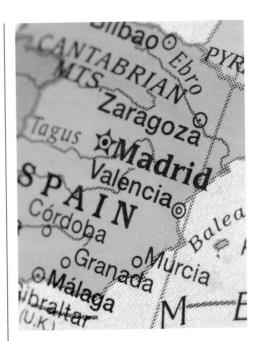

UNDERGROUND RAILWAYS

There are underground railway systems (*metros*) in Madrid, Barcelona, Bilbao and Valencia, where a single public transport ticket or pass permits travel on all modes of transport, including *metro*, bus and suburban train services. *Metros* offer the quickest way to get around these cities, although they're crowded during rush hours. No smoking is permitted on *metro* trains or in stations, which are clean and fairly safe. Crime is generally rare on Spanish *metros*, although you should watch out for pickpockets, especially on the Madrid system. *Metro* systems are also under construction in Malaga and Seville.

Madrid

Madrid has the largest and oldest *metro* system in Spain with 16 lines and 190 stations covering most of the city, operating from 6am until 2am. Apart from Sundays and late at night, trains run around every five to eight minutes (more frequently during rush hour). The system is used by over 620m people a year. The fare is €1 per journey or €6.70 for a ten-journey ticket. Monthly or annual season tickets are available for people aged under 21 (*abono joven*), commuters (*abono normal*) and for those over 64 (*abono tercera edad*). Season tickets offer exceptionally good savings for unlimited travel on public transport, including the underground, city buses and local trains (*cercanías*). Pensioners, who pay only €10.50 a month for unlimited travel, get a particularly good deal.

A free map (*plano del metro*) showing the lines in different colours is available from ticket offices. Tickets are sold at station ticket booths and from machines. The *metro* is easy to navigate; simply note the end station of the line you want and follow the signs. When entering or leaving a train, you must open the doors by pressing a button.

Madrid has invested heavily in its *metro* system and the *Nuevos Ministerios* station in the city centre is now connected by underground to Barajas airport (Terminals 1 and 2), which can be reached in just 15 minutes; flight check-in facilities are available at the station. An extension to the south of the city has recently been finished, the new *MetroSur* line connecting many suburbs, including Alcorcón and Fuenlabrada, to the central underground lines. Comprehensive information is available from ☎ 902 444 403 and 💻 www.metromadrid.es.

Barcelona

Barcelona's *metro* is one of the world's most modern systems, although it has just six lines (large areas of the city aren't covered by it the *metro*) and most connections require long walks between platforms. Stations are indicated at street level by a large red 'M' within a diamond.

A map (*xarxa de metro* in Catalan) is available from tourist offices and at ticket windows in stations (there's also a *metro* map on the back of the free tourist office city map). Lines are marked in colours, and connections between lines (*correspondencia*) and between *metro* and train systems (*enlace*) are clearly indicated. Stops are announced over an intercom and illuminated panels show where the train has come from, the station you're approaching and, as the train departs after stopping, the next station (an excellent idea which should be adopted by all *metro* systems).

A single journey costs €1.30. A *tarjeta multiviaje* (*T-10*) pass costs €7.20 and is valid for ten journeys on the *metro*, city buses, the blue tramway (*Tibidabo*), the Montjuic funicular railway and Catalan railways *Generalitat* (*FFCC*) city lines. Numerous other passes are available, costing from €46.25 to €131 depending on the zones and the period covered (e.g. one, three or five days).

> The Barcelona *metro* is open from 5am until midnight on Mondays to Thursdays, Sundays and public holidays, and until 2am on Fridays, Saturdays and the day before public holidays.

Comprehensive information on all Barcelona's public transport systems is available on the Transports Metropolitans Barcelona website (🖥 www.tmb.net), which includes a useful guide to public transport arranged by street name; when you type in the name of a street the public transport operating in the area is shown.

Bilbao

Bilbao's *metro* system consists of two lines and 32 stations, and transports over 73m passengers a year. A one-journey ticket costs €1.30 and monthly discount passes are available (€28.70 to €40 depending on the number of zones covered). Trains generally run from 6am to 11pm during the week and until 2am at weekends, when a night service runs between certain stations. Information is available from ☎ 944 254 025 and on 🖥 www.metrobilbao.net.

Valencia

The *metro* system in Valencia consists of four lines. Single-journey tickets cost €1.30 and a ten-journey ticket (*bonometro*) costs €6.10. Other discounts and passes are also available. Trains generally run from 5am to midnight (2am at weekends). Further information is available from ☎ 900 461 046 and 🖥 www.metrovalencia.com, which includes details of other public transport in Valencia.

BUSES & TRAMS

There are excellent bus (*autobús*) services in all major cities and towns and comprehensive long-distance coach (*autocar*) services between major cities. Buses are the cheapest and most common form of public transport in Spain and most coastal towns and rural villages are accessible only by bus. The buses vary considerably in quality and age, from luxurious modern vehicles (in most cities) to ramshackle relics (in some rural areas). Private bus services are often confusing and uncoordinated, and buses may leave from different locations rather than a central bus station (*estación de autobuses*), e.g. Madrid has eight bus stations and most cities have two or more (possibly located on the outskirts of town). There are left luggage offices (*consignas*) at central bus stations. **Smoking isn't permitted on buses.**

Before boarding a bus at a bus terminal, you must usually buy a ticket from the ticket office or a machine. When boarding anywhere else, you can buy a single ticket from the driver or conductor as you enter the bus (they usually give change for small banknotes). Passengers usually enter a bus via the front door (marked *entrada*) and dismount from a central or side exit (*salida*). Most buses are driver-only operated, although on some city buses (e.g. blue buses in Madrid) there's also a conductor, who sits by the rear (entrance) door. You must usually signal before the stop (*parada*) where you wish to get off by pressing a button (which activates a bell in the driver's cab).

City Buses

Most full bus services run from around 6am until between 11pm and midnight, when a reduced night service normally comes into operation (which is usually more expensive). There's usually a ten-minute service on the most popular routes during peak hours and an hourly night service, although services are considerably reduced on Sundays and public holidays.

Note also the following with regard to city buses:

♦ They're generally very slow and, although there are bus and taxi lanes in some cities (e.g. Madrid), there are still frequent traffic jams.

♦ They're often very crowded and buses that aren't air-conditioned can be uncomfortable in the summer.

♦ Most have few seats, so as to accommodate the maximum number of passengers (hold on tight when standing!).

♦ There are numerous bus routes in major cities and it can be difficult to find your way around. Routes are numbered and terminal points are shown on buses and displayed on signs at stops in most cities.

♦ Timetables and route maps are available from bus company offices, bus stations and tourist offices.

♦ Tourist buses are provided in major cities, most of which follow a circular route.

♦ Tickets are available from bus offices and tobacconists'.

Fares

Bus and *metro* fares are the same in Madrid and tickets can be used on both systems. A single bus trip costs €1 and a ten-trip ticket (*metrobús*) is available for €6.70. Fares are similar in other cities. In Barcelona, a ten-ride *T-10* pass can be used on all urban public transport, including the *metro* (see page 134). In Madrid and Barcelona (and some other cities), tickets are valid for an entire bus route, but not for transfers to other buses.

In most cities, there are reductions for pensioners, and those aged between 15 and 21 can buy a youth card (*carnet joven*) providing discounts on public transport and other discounts (e.g. entrance fees to museums). Day and multi-day passes offering unlimited travel are also available, plus a range of season tickets (*abono*), e.g. for a week, month or year.

☑ SURVIVAL TIP

Multi-ride tickets and passes must be stamped in a machine upon boarding a bus and there are on-the-spot fines for anyone found travelling without a valid ticket.

Rural Buses

In rural and resort areas, bus services are often operated by the local municipality and services are usually infrequent, e.g. four to six buses a day on most routes, although some have an hourly service (there may be no service during the lunch break, e.g. 1.30 to 3pm). The first bus departs at any time between 6.30 and 9am, and the last bus may depart as early as 4 or 5pm on some routes (most last buses depart before 9pm). However, services are usually reliable and buses run on time.

Small towns can often be reached only via their provincial capital and in the centre of Spain it's difficult to get from one major city to another without going via Madrid. Local bus timetables may be published in free newspapers and magazines.

Long-distance Buses

There are many long-distance bus companies, mostly privately owned, including Alsa (☎ 902 422 242, 🖥 www.alsa.es), the largest and part of the National Express group, and Auto Res (☎ 902 020 999, 🖥 www.auto-res.net). Inter-city buses are usually faster than trains and cost less. Fares on long-distance routes are reasonable, for example Madrid-Alicante return around €45 and Madrid-Barcelona around €65. The most luxurious buses are comfortable and offer air-conditioning, films and sometimes free soft drinks. All the main companies have telephone and internet information and booking services.

Bus companies offer excursions throughout Spain (packages may include meals, sightseeing and ferry travel.

International Coaches

There are regular international coach services between Spain's major cities and many European cities. For example, Eurolines (part of the National Express group) runs coach services from the UK to some 45 destinations in Spain. Journeys are very long, e.g. from London it's 25 hours to Barcelona and 29 hours to Madrid, and often little cheaper than flying (it's worth comparing bus fares with budget flight fares) – although much 'cheaper' in terms of carbon emissions per capita. Coaches are, however, comfortable and air-conditioned, have toilets and show films.

Most services operate daily during the summer holiday season and two or three times a week out of season. Discounts are provided for students and youths on some routes. Bookings can be made at travel agencies in Spain and abroad. Typical single fares with Eurolines are Barcelona-London around €90 and Madrid-London around €100. Returns booked well in advance are much better value.

Trams

Few Spanish cities have retained their tram systems (*tranvía*), although trams have been reintroduced in Bilbao, Seville and Valencia. Barcelona also has a city-centre tramline, called '*Combino*'. Trams are integrated with other public transport services, using a 'univseral' ticket.

TAXIS

Madrid has more than 16,000 licensed taxis (one of the highest densities in the world), which are black or white with a horizontal red stripe on the side and the city's coat of arms on their doors.

Taxi ranks (*paradas de taxi*) are located outside railway stations, at airports, and at main junctions in towns and cities. In major cities you can hail a taxi in the street, but in small towns they're available only at taxi ranks. You can also call a radio-taxi in most towns and

cities, but you must pay for the taxi's journey to the pick-up point (taxi ranks also have phones). It's advisable to book on the day you want a taxi, preferably close to the time required (if you book too far in advance a taxi may not appear at the desired time). In cities and many towns, you can also rent luxury chauffeur-driven cars (*grandes turismos*), by the hour or for a fixed fee for a particular journey.

Spanish taxis are among the cheapest in Europe and many people routinely use them when shopping. Tariffs are controlled and the fares for the most popular destinations may be displayed on a board at taxi ranks. All taxis levy a standing charge (flagfall), a charge per kilometre, a surcharge and/or higher kilometre rates at night and on Sundays, and various surcharges. In Madrid the fare is €1.90–2.95 (standing charge) plus €0.92 per km in the city centre and €1.10 per km outside. If you go outside a city's limits (shown by a *limite taxi* sign), you may be required to pay double the fare shown on the meter (e.g. in Madrid).

In all cities and major urban areas, taxis are fitted with meters (make sure that the meter is switched on). Beware of unlicensed and unmetered 'taxis' operating (illegally) in main cities and preying on foreign visitors. If you must use a taxi without a meter, agree the

fare before commencing your journey. If you aren't fluent in Spanish, it's advisable to write down your destination and get the driver to write down the fare, so that there's no misunderstanding.

Taxis usually have a maximum capacity of four passengers. There are special taxis for disabled passengers in many towns which carry wheelchairs (ask when booking). Taxis usually carry luggage free of charge, and most taxis won't take dogs.

Licensed taxi drivers are usually honest and, unlike those in some countries, generally take passengers by the most direct route and don't overcharge. If you think you've been cheated, ask for an official receipt (recibo oficial) showing the taxi licence number, start and finish points of the journey, the date and time, and the driver's signature. Send it to the local licensing authority with your complaint. Contrary to the practice in most other countries, it isn't usual to tip taxi drivers in Spain.

A recent consumer survey found that the most expensive taxis were in Lugo, Murcia and Tarragona, and the cheapest in Almería and Santa Cruz de Tenerife.

You should only hail a taxi that's travelling in the direction you wish to go, as they won't usually do U-turns. A free (libre) sign or a green light at night indicates that a taxi is for hire. If a taxi is displaying a red sign with the name of a local neighbourhood, it means the taxi driver is on his way home and isn't obliged to pick up passengers unless their destination is on his route.

FERRIES

International Services

Regular car and international ferry services operate all year round between Spain and the UK and Morocco, and domestic ferries run between the mainland and the Balearics, the Canaries and Spain's North African enclaves of Ceuta and Melilla. Spain's most important ports include Algeciras, Almería, Barcelona, Bilbao, Cadiz, Las Palmas (Gran Canaria), Palma de Mallorca, Santander, Santa Cruz (Tenerife) and Valencia.

Two companies – Brittany Ferries and P&O – operate ferry services between the UK and Spain (Santander and Bilbao respectively). There's little to choose between them for comfort, services and fares. Ships provide a variety of facilities and services, including a choice of bars and restaurants, swimming pool, Jacuzzi, sauna, cinema, shops, hairdressing salon, photographic studio, medical service, children's playroom and evening entertainment, including a nightclub with live music, a casino and a discotheque.

There are various tariffs (depending on the time of year) and a choice of single fares, mini-cruises (spending around five hours in Spain or the UK), mini-breaks (five days abroad) and ten-day returns, as well as standard return fares. Children under four travel free and those between 4 and 15 travel for half fare. It's advisable to book well ahead when travelling during peak periods and at any time when you require a luxury cabin. If possible, it's best to avoid travelling at peak times, when ships can be uncomfortably crowded.

Travelling between the UK and Spain by ferry will save you around 1,200km (750mi) of driving compared with travelling via France. Ferries can also work out cheaper than driving or flying. Travelling from the UK to southern Spain by road (via France) entails spending three full days driving and making two overnight stops, with accommodation, meals and petrol costs to be taken into account, although it usually works out cheaper than the ferry if you use budget accommodation and don't splash out on gourmet meals.

 Caution

The sea is often rough between Spain and the UK (the Bay of Biscay is notorious for its swell) and travelling isn't advisable during bad weather if you don't travel well. Check the weather report and be prepared to travel via France or fly. If you do travel by ferry, keep a good supply of seasickness pills handy!

Brittany Ferries

Brittany Ferries operates a year-round, twice-weekly service between Plymouth in the UK and the Spanish port of Santander. The days and times of sailings vary according to the time of year. Always check the departure times carefully. The journey time is just over 20 hours and one night is spent on board ship.

To book call UK ☎ 0871-244 0744 or Spain ☎ 942 360 611 or visit the British or Spanish website (🖳 www.brittanyferries.co.uk or 🖳 www.brittanyferries.es). Brittany Ferries runs a Property Owners' Travel Club for frequent travellers, offering savings of up to 30 per cent off single and standard return fares.

P&O Ferries

P&O Ferries operates a year-round service leaving every three days between Portsmouth in the UK and the Spanish port of Bilbao (the ferry port is actually at Santurtzi, around 13km/8mi northwest of the city centre). The journey takes 35 hours from Portsmouth and 28 hours from Bilbao (which is downhill). Ferries operate for most of the year. Like Brittany Ferries, P&O offers luxury cabins with a double bed, writing desk, television (TV), shower, toilet, washbasin, two easy chairs, two large windows and room service.

To book call UK ☎ 0871-664 5645 or Spain ☎ 902 020 461 or visit the website (🖳 www.poferries.com).

Other International Services

There are hourly car ferry services from Algeciras to Tangier and Ceuta and an additional hourly service from Algeciras to Tangier in summer (when there are usually long delays as thousands of Moroccan migrant workers are returning home). There's also a ferry service from Gibraltar to Tangier, a year-round hydrofoil service from Tarifa to Tangier, and ferry services to Melilla from Almería and Malaga.

Domestic Services

Domestic ferry services operate from mainland ports to the main Balearic and Canary islands, and inter-island ferries serve the smaller islands. The main Balearics services are Barcelona to Palma, Ibiza and Mahon; Dénia to Ibiza and Palma; Gandía to Ibiza and Formentera and Valencia to Palma, Ibiza and Mahon. Canaries services operate from Cadiz on the mainland to Tenerife, Las Palmas, Lanzarote and Fuerteventura.

Tickets should be purchased well in advance, particularly in summer; they can also be bought on board, but a surcharge is payable. Ferries are very crowded in summer, with erratic schedules. There are various tariffs depending on the time of year, the type of ferry and the type of seat required (couchettes are available on night trips). The fare from Barcelona to the Balearics is from €50 single (reclining seat), from €90 for a (shared) cabin and from €125 for a car. Tickets for high-speed ferries are often twice the price.

Ferries carry cars, trailers, buses and trucks, and are equipped with restaurants and coffee shops, bar-lounges, TVs, discotheques and shops.

There are regular inter-island ferries in the Balearics and Canaries, including a two-hour 'hydrojet' service between Palma de Mallorca and Ibiza, and an ordinary ferry service from Ibiza to Formentera. Frequent inter-island ferry services also operate in the Canaries, including a hydrofoil service between all the islands.

Most domestic routes to and from the mainland and the Balearic and Canary islands are operated by Compañía Trasmediterránea/ TRAS) (for reservations ☎ 902 454 645, 🖳 www.trasmediterranea.es). Trasmediterránea offers youths and retirees over 59 a 20 per cent discount outside the high season to the Canaries and Africa, and residents of the

Balearics or Canaries (you must present proof of this when you book your ticket) a 38 per cent discount.

For the Balearics, ferry services are operated by the following companies:

◆ **Balearia** (☎ 902 160 180, 🖳 www.balearia. net) – from Barcelona to the three main islands, from Dénia (Costa Blanca) and Valencia to Ibiza and Majorca, and inter-island services;

◆ **Iscomar** (☎ 902 119 128, 🖳 www.iscomar. com) – ferries from Barcelona and Valencia to Majorca, from Dénia to Ibiza, and inter-island services;

◆ **Trasmediterránea** (☎ 902 454 645, 🖳 www.trasmediterranea.es) – from Barcelona and Valencia to the three main islands.

For the Canaries, ferry operators include:

◆ **Fred Olsen** (☎ 902 100 107, 🖳 www. fredolsen.es) – services from Tenerife to La Gomera, Gran Canaria, El Hierro and La Palma;

◆ **Naviera Armas** (☎ 902 456 500, 🖳 www. navieraarmas.com) – from Tenerife to the western islands and from Gran Canaria to the eastern islands;

◆ **Trasmediterránea** (see above) – between Cadiz and Gran Canaria, Tenerife and La Palma, and inter-island services from Las Palmas to Santa Cruz, Fuerteventura and Lanzarote.

AIRLINE SERVICES

Most major international airlines provide scheduled services to Madrid and many also fly to Barcelona and other major cities. Inexpensive charter and budget flights to Spain are common from many European countries, particularly the UK and Germany. In recent years, the number of budget airlines has increased greatly and competition is fierce – in 2007 over 32 per cent of passengers arriving at Spanish airports did so on budget airlines.

Most transatlantic flights from North America travel via Madrid. If you're unable to get a direct intercontinental flight to Spain, it's usually advisable to fly via London, from where there are inexpensive daily flights to airports throughout Spain.

Fares

In general, the earlier you book a seat with any airline the cheaper it is. If you're able to book more than six months in advance, bargains are available and many scheduled airlines (particularly budget airlines) have ticket 'sales' at certain times of the year. Cheap seats are also available if you book literally at the last minute, but you run the risk of not getting a seat at all.

The cheapest Spanish destinations from the UK are Malaga, Alicante and Palma de Mallorca, one-way fares with operators such as Air Berlin, Easyjet and Ryanair starting as low as £10 (€12) in the low season and rising to between £100 and £300 (€125 to €375) in the peak season (mid-June to mid-September). However, budget airlines' advertised prices usually don't include airport taxes, which can be high (e.g. €20 one-way), and they normally make a 'fuel surcharge' (as if an aeroplane could fly without it!) and at least £3.50 (€5) for booking with a credit card. In addition, they charge (e.g. £30/€40) for any changes to flight details and further charges are levied for bulky items such as skis and golf clubs. Luggage allowances are generally low, and some budget airlines (e.g. Ryanair) have even started charging for each item of luggage. Shop around and don't assume that travelling to Spain is cheaper by budget airline, particularly if you can take advantage of the periodic offers of the major airlines.

Major airlines, including Aer Lingus, British Airways and Iberia, often allow changes in your flight details (e.g. dates or destination) free of charge, although you must usually pay for last-minute changes and cancellations. Major airlines also tend to have higher weight allowances for luggage and will transport large items, e.g. golf clubs, free of charge.

Flights from other European countries are generally more expensive than those from the UK, Ireland and Germany – up to 50 per cent more – although several budget airlines now offer cheaper inter-European flights (e.g. Air Berlin and Vueling).

Charter flights from New York to Madrid cost around $350 (€250). It may be cheaper

for North Americans, and others travelling on intercontinental flights, to fly to London and get a charter or budget flight from there, particularly outside the summer season.

If you're buying a seat online, before you confirm your booking, make sure the quoted price includes everything; on some airline websites the final price isn't quoted until the end of the booking process, making it difficult to compare prices between companies.

All airlines now operate a 'no-ticket' policy and when you check in you simply give a code (provided when you book) and/or your name, showing identification (e.g. passport or driving licence). Make sure the name you give matches the name on your identification. There's no airport departure tax in Spain.

British Airways & Iberia

Iberia and British Airways (BA) operate daily flights to the main Spanish airports from several destinations in the UK. BA and Iberia are both members of the One World Alliance (www.oneworldalliance.com) along with several other major airlines such as American Airlines, Cathay Pacific and Qantas. This allows them to offer flights to most destinations in the world via other airlines in the alliance at competitive fares. Travel agents are the best source of information for the cheapest seats on One World flights.

The Spanish national privatised airline, Iberia, is Spain's major international carrier. Although it isn't rated as one of the world's best airlines, it has an excellent safety record and its standard of service has improved considerably

in recent years. Iberia's fares have become more competitive and the company has been in the black for the last few years (Iberia saw record profits of €327.6m in 2007). In early 2007 Iberia launched its low-cost airline, ClickAir (www.clickair.com), which offers budget flights to most European capital cities from many Spanish airports.

Iberia provides good connections to Central and South America and throughout Europe, but few connections to North America (New York and Miami only) and the rest of the world apart from Tel Aviv and a number of destinations in North and West Africa.

Charter Flights

Since the advent of budget airlines, seat-only bookings on charter flights to Spain have become less common, at least from the UK. Among the largest charter companies operating from the UK are Avro, Cosmos, First Choice, Monarch and Thomson Fly, which nevertheless offer good flight deals to Spain from a wide range of UK airports, particularly if you book well in advance.

Charter flights are available to most Spanish resorts but tend to run from April to October only (longer to the Canaries). Charter flights from New York to Madrid cost from $350, but it may be cheaper for North Americans and others travelling on intercontinental flights to fly to London, Amsterdam or Frankfurt and get a charter or budget flight from there, particularly outside the summer season.

Tickets for flights (and package holiday deals) can be purchased from travel agents, by telephone or online. As a general rule, the further in advance you buy your ticket, the cheaper it is (and the greater the penalty for cancelling), although late bookings can also be good value. The main disadvantage of charter flights is that they usually have fixed return dates and a maximum of four weeks between the outward and return flights. Most charter flights restrict stays to 7, 14, 21 or 28 days, although you can always throw away the return ticket (it may still be cheaper than a single fare on a scheduled flight). Charter tickets aren't transferable and it's illegal to use a ticket issued in someone else's name; tickets are checked against passports and if the names don't match you're refused boarding (and you can be prosecuted). It's advisable to take out insurance against missing your flight, as there are no refunds for charter flights.

Domestic Flights

A number of airlines offer domestic services in Spain, including Air Europa (☎ 902 410 501, 🖥 www.air-europa.com – tickets can also be purchased at Halcón Viajes travel agencies), Iberia (☎ 902 400 500, 🖥 www.iberia.com), Spanair (☎ 902 131 415, 🖥 www.spanair. com) and various small airlines such as Air Nostrum (☎ 902 400 500, 🖥 www.airnostrum. es) and Binter Canarias (☎ 902 391 392, 🖥 www.bintercanarias.es) – both subsidiaries of Iberia. Air Europa and Spanair cover most of the same routes as Iberia and are generally cheaper.

There are frequent flights between Spain's international airports and regional airports (Iberia operates from Barcelona and Madrid to around 20 domestic airports), but many domestic flights are routed via Madrid or Barcelona, so it can be difficult to get a direct flight between regional cities.

Single flights are available to most domestic destinations from €60 (from €90 to the Canaries) during the day; cheaper night (nocturno) flights are available to some cities. Youths are entitled to large discounts. Flights to the Balearics from the mainland are only slightly more expensive than ferries, although you must usually book well in advance during the summer season. Residents in the Balearics or Canaries are entitled to discounts of 33 per cent on flights between the islands and the mainland. Tickets for Iberia domestic flights can be purchased from machines at airports (using a credit card).

There's an 'air bridge' (*puente aéreo*) shuttle service between Barcelona and Madrid, operating half-hourly at peak times and hourly at other times, which carries over 2m passengers a year.

Airports

Many Spanish airports have been expanded and modernised in recent years, including Madrid and Barcelona (see below), Malaga and Seville, although you should expect delays at major airports during the summer season (the worst airports for delays in summer include Alicante, Malaga, Palma, Ibiza and Mahon, particularly at weekends). Always carefully check your luggage on collection and report any damage immediately. Most airports have sufficient luggage trolleys, although you usually need a €1 (or £1) coin to use one; porters (who charge a set rate per piece of luggage) are also usually available.

All major Spanish airports have 'duty-free' shops, although some are open only during the main tourist season. Note, however, that it's usually cheaper to buy alcohol in a local off-licence or supermarket. Secure 24-hour parking is provided at most Spanish airports, where parking fees are usually reasonable, e.g. from €8 a day, with discounts for two weeks or longer. There are also parking areas near to airports, but not within the grounds, which cost from around €3 a day.

Information about all airports in Spain, including flight arrival and departure updates in English and Spanish, is available from AENA (🖥 www.aena.es – go to '*elija aeropuerto*' or 'choose airport' on the left and scroll down to the airport you're looking for).

Madrid

Madrid's Barajas airport (*aeropuerto de Barajas*) is Spain's busiest, handling around 52m passengers a year. Barajas is Spain's main airport for intercontinental flights and is also served by direct flights from most European and North and South American cities. It's also the hub of Spanish domestic flights; typical flight times to other major cities are Barcelona (55 minutes), Bilbao (50 minutes), Seville (50 minutes), Valencia (30 minutes), Palma de Mallorca (one hour) and the Canary Islands (2 hours 30 minutes).

Barajas airport is 15km (9.3mi) outside the city on the A-2. It has recently undergone extensive modernisation, including the building of a second runway. The airport has three terminals for international and domestic flights (T1, T2 and T4). T4 is some distance from the other terminals and cannot be reached from outside the airport by public transport, so if your flight is operating from T4 allow extra time for your journey. A free 24-hour bus service running every three minutes connects the three terminals.

There are various ways of getting from the airport to Madrid city centre: by bus (every 12 to 16 minutes from around 6am to around midnight to the Avenida de América costing around €1.50); by *metro* (to Nuevos Ministerios station, where flight check-in facilities are available, open from 6am to 2am, costing €2); by taxi (costing at least €20); and by AeroCity's 24-hour airport shuttle service (€17), which will take you anywhere in the city. AeroCity also offers a booking facility by phone or internet (☎ 917 477 570, 🖥 www. aerocity.com). Flight information is available from ☎ 902 404 704.

Barcelona

Barcelona's airport (*El Prat de Llobregat*) is Spain's second busiest, with around 33m passengers a year. Located 14km (9mi) from the city centre, it's one of the finest airports in the world and currently under expansion. The fastest and cheapest way from the airport to the city is by RENFE train, costing €2.60; services run from 6am till around midnight. There's also a bus service (*aerobús*) running every 7 to 15 minutes from 6am to midnight and costing €4.05. A taxi to the city centre costs from €15. Flight information is available from ☎ 902 404 704.

Other Airports

Palma de Mallorca airport handles around 23m passengers a year (mainly summer charter flights) and Malaga 13.5m.

International and domestic flights are available from many of Spain's 'regional' airports, including Alicante, Almería, Asturias, Bilbao, Fuenteventura, Gerona (Costa Brava), Granada, Gran Canaria, Ibiza, Jerez de la Frontera (Costa de la Luz), La Coruña, Lanzarote, Las Palmas, Malaga, Melilla, Menorca, Murcia, Palma de Mallorca, Reus (Tarragona), San Sebastián, Santander, Santiago de Compostela, Seville, Tenerife, Valencia, Vigo, Vitoria and Zaragossa. Domestic-only airports include Ampurias (Gerona), Badajoz, Burgos, Cáceres, Cordoba, Logroño, Mahón (Menorca), Puigcerdá, Pamplona, Salamanca, Seu d'Urgell and Valladolid.

11.
MOTORING

Motoring in Spain has altered dramatically in the last few decades, during which the number of cars on Spanish roads has vastly increased and the roads have been improved beyond recognition. Traffic has almost tripled since 1980, and there are around 30m cars for 46m people. Not only have new roads and bypasses been built, but existing roads have also been widened, lanes added for heavy traffic, and signs and road markings improved. The road-building programme (and provision of parking spaces) has, however, failed to keep pace with the increasing number of cars and consequently Spain's roads are rapidly becoming saturated in many regions.

Driving long distances is usually cheaper than using public transport, particularly when the costs are shared between a number of people and you avoid motorways. In any case, unless you're travelling between major cities, you will have little choice but to drive, as public transport is generally poor in rural areas. If possible, you will, however, find it quicker and certainly less stressful to take the train or fly, though driving can be enjoyable in rural areas – particularly outside the tourist season, when it's possible to drive for miles without seeing another motorist (or a caravan). Those travelling to Spain from the UK may prefer to take the ferry (see page 138) to northern Spain rather than drive through France.

If you live in a city, particularly Madrid or Barcelona (where public transport services are excellent), a car is a liability and driving is a nightmare to be avoided if at all possible. A recent nationwide survey found that on an average working day it takes eight minutes to travel one kilometre in a large city. In Madrid, the survey found the average traffic speed was below 10kph (6mph)!

As a result of the *siesta*, Spain has four 'rush hours' (*horas puntas*): 8 to 9.30am, 12.30 to 2.30pm, 3.30 to 5pm and 6.30 to 8.30pm; the quietest period is usually between 3 and 5pm. Traffic jams (*atascos*) are particularly bad in cities such as Madrid and Barcelona, where the rush 'hour' lasts all day.

Jams are also common on coastal roads and in resort towns during summer and on roads heading south out of Madrid and Barcelona, particularly at the start and end of holiday periods, when some 12m Spaniards and foreigners take to the roads.

Anyone who has driven in Spain won't be surprised to learn that it has one of the worst accident records in the European Union (EU), although as elsewhere in the EU the annual death toll is gradually being reduced. Spain's 2,700 deaths in 2007 was down 9 per cent on 2006 and a huge improvement on the 4,400 deaths in 2005. The government has made reducing the number of car accident victims one of its top priorities and to this end introduced a licence points system in 2006 (see page 158) and greater police vigilance on the roads. However, Spain still has a long way to go before traffic accidents cease to be the largest cause of death among young Spaniards.

Eccentric and impatient drivers, *machismo*, compulsive speeders (speeds of over 180kph aren't uncommon), drunk drugged motorists and pedestrians (around 40 per cent of drivers in fatal accidents are over the alcohol limit), and stray animals, vehicles without lights, badly maintained and marked roads, and sharp bends without crash barriers, all contribute to the hazards of driving in Spain. The most important thing to bear in mind when driving in Spain is to drive defensively and always expect the unexpected from other road users.

IMPORTING A CAR

Anyone wishing to import a vehicle into Spain must be a permanent resident, own property in Spain or have a rental agreement for a minimum of a year and hold a Spanish driving licence. The regulations and paperwork regarding car importation are now comparatively simple, but many people still find the red tape forbidding and employ a *gestor* (see page 320) to do the paperwork for them. The procedure for the importation of a caravan or motorcycle with an engine capacity over 49cc is the same as for a car, while mopeds with engines below 49cc can be freely imported as part of your personal possessions and require no separate paperwork.

After you've completed the importation procedure (outlined below), you mustn't drive your car until your local provincial traffic department has issued temporary (green) registration plates (see page 151).

These are valid for a limited period (usually ten days) and allow you to drive to the nearest testing station for an *inspección técnica de vehículos* (*ITV*) test (see page 152), which must be passed before you receive a permanent registration number (see **Registration** on page 150).

The exact paperwork required depends on whether the car you wish to import is new or second-hand and from the EU or outside the EU. Personal documentation required by the importer includes proof of residence in Spain (a residence card or a certificate from the local police in Spain stating that you live in the locality), proof of owning or renting a property (the rental contract must be for a minimum of a year) and your driving licence.

Documentation for the vehicle includes the technical inspection certificate; the completed form for vehicle registration (*certificado unico para la matrícula de vehículos*) available from your local provincial traffic department; the invoice for the purchase of the car if you've bought it within the last six months; proof of payment of road tax (*impuesto municipal sobre vehículos de tracción mecánica/IVTM* and proof of payment of the appropriate taxes (see **Taxes** below). Cars imported from outside the EU may need to undergo the homologation process as well (see below). A vehicle imported tax and duty free into Spain mustn't be sold, rented or transferred within a year of its registration.

The importation of right-hand drive (RHD) cars was prohibited in 1991, but this was subsequently reversed (after protests from British residents to the European Commission!). However, only immigrants importing an RHD car may register it in Spain; existing residents aren't permitted to purchase an RHD vehicle abroad and register it in Spain.

☑ SURVIVAL TIP

Importing a right-hand-drive (RHD) car into Spain isn't recommended, as driving an RHD car on the right-hand side of the road is dangerous and your visibility is greatly reduced, particularly when you want to overtake or pull out onto a main road. Numerous accidents occur every year involving RHD cars – usually because they pull out in front of another car they cannot see.

Details for the exact paperwork and documentation required can be found on the Department of Traffic's website (🖥 www.dgt. es – go to *Vehículos*), where you can also download forms.

Taxes

The following taxes and duty must be paid when importing a vehicle into Spain:

♦ VAT (*IVA*) at 16 per cent on cars imported from outside the EU or on a tax-free car (on which VAT hasn't previously been paid) imported from an EU country.

♦ registration tax (*impuesto sobre circulación de vehículos*), which varies according to the vehicle's emissions. See New Cars on page 149 for details. However, residents coming to live permanently in Spain and importing a car on which they've previously paid VAT and which they've owned for at least six months are exempt. An application for exemption must be made within a month of the date of issue of your residence permit, and you must present a certificate of non-residence (*certificado de baja de residencia*) from the country you're leaving.

The government recently changed the registration tax in an attempt to discourage buyers from purchasing high-polluting cars. Cars with emissions below 120g of CO_2 per km – over 40 models meet this criterion (80 per cent of which are diesel) – are exempt from tax. Cars whose emissions are 120g to160g of CO_2 per km pay 4.75 per cent tax. Those emitting 160g to 200g of CO_2 per km attract 9.75 per cent tax and cars with emissions over 200g per km incur 14.75 per cent tax. In May 2008, car dealers reported a significant drop in sales of 4x4 vehicles (the most polluting and therefore attracting the highest tax rate).

♦ import duty of 10 per cent on vehicles imported from outside the EU unless you're a resident (see above).

Each of the above tax rates is applied to the original price of the vehicle, with a reduction for each year of its age up to ten years, e.g. 20 per cent after the first year, 30 per cent after two years, 50 per cent after four years, and 80 per cent after ten years.

Homologation

Homologation (*homologación*) is the procedure whereby vehicles are made to comply with local safety and other requirements before they can be registered. A vehicle imported from a country outside the EU must be certified by the manufacturer or an officially recognised laboratory, undergo homologation and be tested before it can be registered in Spain. This costs between €120 and €400, depending on the make of car. It's a long and complicated process and the information demanded by the authorities often varies with the region of Spain.

Anyone who illegally drives a vehicle on foreign plates can be fined up to €3,000 and the vehicle can be confiscated.

Driving With Foreign Registration Plates

Residents

Vehicles registered outside the EU cannot generally be driven in Spain or any other EU country by EU residents, although there are a few exceptions.

Non-residents

The regulations for non-residents depend on whether you're an EU national or not:

♦ **EU nationals** – Non-residents of Spain resident in another EU country can bring a vehicle registered in another EU country to Spain and can use it (for up to 182 days per year) without paying Spanish taxes. The vehicle must be legal in its country of registration, meaning that it must be inspected (for roadworthiness) as appropriate and taxed there.

♦ **Non-EU nationals** – A person resident outside the EU may temporarily import a vehicle registered outside the EU for a total period of six months (which needn't be continuous) within a calendar year. In certain circumstances, the six-month period can be extended. This applies, for example, to those regularly crossing into EU territory to work, full-time students from outside the EU, and people from outside the EU on a mission for a specified period. The vehicle can be used only by the owner, his spouse, parents and children (who must also be non-residents). Note, however, that it's necessary for non-EU citizens to have a foreign-registered vehicle 'sealed' (*precintado*) by customs during periods of absence from Spain.

CAR HIRE

To hire (rent) a car in Spain, you must usually be at least 22 years old – 25 for certain cars – and most companies also have an upper age limit, e.g. 65. Drivers must produce a valid licence (a copy isn't acceptable) and non-EU licence holders require an international driving permit. All the drivers' names must be entered on the hire agreement.

The major car hire (*alquiler de coches*) companies, such as ATESA, Avis, Budget, EasyCar, Europcar, Helle-Hollis and Hertz, have offices in most cities and at major airports. ATESA are generally cheaper than the international companies, although cheapest of all are small local companies. Car hire companies are listed in yellow pages under *Automóviles Alquiler* and local companies are listed by town. You may be approached at airports by representatives of local companies, most of which are reputable (but check their credentials).

If you're a visitor, it's advisable to reserve a car before arriving in Spain, particularly during peak periods (more visitors hire cars in Spain than in any other European country). When booking, you should specify an automatic model if you're unused to a manual (stick-shift) gearbox, as most hire cars in Spain are manual. Fly-drive deals are available through most airlines and travel agents.

Car hire in Spain is the cheapest in Europe, due mainly to the cut-throat competition, particularly during off-peak periods. The rates of major international companies vary little, although you may get a better deal by booking well in advance. One of the advantages of using a national or international company is that you can hire a car in one town and drop it off in another, although you should check the cost of this service. Although cheaper, some small local companies require you to return the car to the office you got it from or to the local airport.

As an example of prices, ATESA charge around €250 for six days for their cheapest (Group A) cars, such as a Citroën C2 (without air-conditioning), including unlimited kilometres, collision damage waiver (CDW) and VAT. Tariffs for business use are higher. A small company in a resort area might charge €200 per week in winter, e.g. between 15th November until 30th April, for a similar car, rising to around €250 a week in summer. Note, however, that some inexpensive hire companies cut corners on maintenance and repairs, and cars can sometimes be unsafe. Always carefully check a car (e.g. for body damage and to ensure that everything works) and the rental contract before setting out.

Most companies have low rates for weekend hire, e.g. from 4pm on Friday to noon on Monday, and for rentals of 14 days or longer. When comparing rates, check that prices include insurance and taxes (VAT at 16 per cent), that insurance cover (including personal accident) is adequate and that there are no hidden costs. Check the cost of any extras, such as collision damage waiver/CDW (*cobertura de daños por colisión*), theft cover (*cobertura contra robo*), personal accident insurance/PAI (*asistencia por lesiones personales*), airport tax (*cargo de aeropuerto*), roof rack, baby seat, air-conditioning, and additional drivers. Some companies don't offer unlimited kilometres (*kilometraje ilimitado*), which usually works out more expensive unless you plan to drive only a short distance.

☑ SURVIVAL TIP

If planning to take a car out of Spain, e.g. to France or Portugal, check whether you need extra insurance.

If you're touring, you should ensure that you have sufficient power for mountain driving, e.g. at least a 1.6 litre petrol engine or a 2 litre diesel engine for two people and their luggage. If you're going to be doing a lot of driving in summer, air-conditioning is a must.

Unless you're paying by credit card, you must usually pay a high cash deposit; in some cases, the whole hire charge must be paid in advance. When paying by credit card, carefully check your bill and your statement, as unauthorised extra charges aren't unknown.

BUYING A CAR

New cars are more expensive in Spain than in some other EU countries (although cheaper than in the UK) and up to double the cost of cars in the US. However, although cars may be more expensive to buy, they depreciate more slowly than in most other European countries, so the extra you pay when buying a car is usually gained when you sell it. Spanish-made cars are generally cheaper than imported cars, due to import taxes and duty.

Cars may be bought in Spain by residents or by non-residents owning a property in Spain, renting a property for a minimum of a year or registered as an inhabitant of their municipality (*empadronado*).

New Cars

After record sales of cars during 2006 and 2007, the new car market saw a marked slow-down in 2008. By May, sales had decreased by more than 15 per cent on the previous year, so it would seem to be a good time to buy a new car in Spain. Spain is the world's seventh largest car manufacturer and around 80 per cent of new cars are exported to the European market. Nevertheless, new cars are more expensive than in many other European countries owing to taxes, which include registration tax (*impuesto sobre la circulación*) of up to 14.75 per cent and VAT (*IVA*) at 16 per cent. Most new cars are sold at list price, although you should still shop around for the best deal, as dealers compete in offering discounts, guarantees, financing terms and special deals.

Residents can buy cars on a hire purchase agreement (instalment plan), although those who aren't property owners must usually provide a financial guarantee or obtain a guarantor. You also need a certificate from your Spanish bank stating that you pay your bills regularly, a copy of your employment contract and a copy of your previous year's tax return.

The deposit (down payment) varies with the dealer and payments can be spread over one to four years. After making the deposit, you're asked to sign a number of 'bills of exchange' (*letras de cambio*), usually one for each monthly instalment due (a reassuringly antiquated system!). These are like cheques or individual direct debit advices and are addressed directly to your bank for payment. Most car dealers also sell car insurance, although you should shop around, as you will probably get a better deal elsewhere.

It's possible to buy a new car VAT free in another EU country, e.g. from the factory of a European manufacturer or from an exporter in countries such as Belgium, Denmark (usually the cheapest due to high local taxes), Greece and the Netherlands, and personally import it into Spain, paying Spanish VAT on import. In this way, you can save not only on the cost of the car but also on VAT if the rate in the country of purchase is higher than in Spain. In some countries (e.g. the UK) you can buy a VAT-free car up to six months before exporting it.

Personally importing any car from the US is usually much cheaper than buying the same car in Spain or elsewhere in Europe. However, before importing a car from outside the EU, you should ensure that it's manufactured to Spanish specifications, or you will encounter problems getting it through the homologation inspection.

Used Cars

The used or second-hand (*de segunda mano/de ocasión*) car market in Spain is currently booming and more used than new cars have been sold every year since 2005. However, the used car market is also suffering the effects of the recession and sales decreased during the first half of 2008.

Used cars tend to be more expensive in Spain than in many other EU countries, as cars hold their value better. It often pays to buy a used car that's around two years old, as depreciation in the first one or two years is considerable (high mileage cars, particularly ex-rental cars, are good value). Note, however, that older cars in Spain (outside their warranty period) aren't always well maintained.

Used car dealers have the same dreadful (and usually well deserved) reputation in Spain as in most other countries, and caution must be taken when buying from them. There are many 'cowboys' (often foreigners) selling worthless wrecks – the small advertisements in the expatriate press are full of them – and it's generally better to buy from a reputable dealer, even if you pay a bit more, and obtain a warranty.

There are various motoring journals advertising used cars, including the weekly *Auto Semanal* and *Coche Actual* (www. cocheactual.es). Most daily newspapers contain used car sections, as do expatriate newspapers (which include foreign-registered cars), and there are free magazines in most areas devoted to car sales, such as *Mi Coche* (💻 www.micoche.com) and *Don Anuncio* (💻 www.donanuncio.es). There are also numerous websites advertising used cars (e.g. 💻 www. autonetplus.com and 💻 www.supermotor.com). Second-hand car prices vary with the region and are generally higher in remote areas and the islands than they are in Madrid and other major cities.

If you intend to buy a used car in Spain, whether privately or from a garage, check the following:

♦ that it has a current *ITV* test certificate and card, if applicable;

♦ that it hasn't been involved in a major accident and suffered structural damage;

♦ that the chassis number tallies with the registration document (*permiso de circulación*), which should be in the name of the seller when a car is purchased privately (check his identity card or passport);

♦ that it has a genuine service history that confirms the kilometres or miles shown on the clock;

♦ that the service coupons have been completed and stamped and that servicing has been carried out by an authorised dealer;

♦ that you receive a 'transfer of ownership' (*transferencia*) form from the seller. The form is available from the provincial traffic department;

♦ whether a written guarantee is provided; car dealers usually give warranties on used cars up to 12 months old.

When you're buying a used car from a garage, try to negotiate a reduction, particularly when you're paying cash and aren't trading in another vehicle. When you buy a car from a dealer, he will arrange the transfer of ownership, usually for a small fee. Alternatively, you can employ a *gestor* to handle the transfer or do it yourself at the local provincial traffic department.

> ⚠️ **Caution**
>
> Be extremely wary of buying a car with foreign registration plates, as it can be very expensive to register it in Spain if you need to (see below).

When you buy a second-hand car in Spain, the seller must de-register it at the provincial traffic department, after which you receive the registration document (*permiso de circulación*), the *ITV* test certificate and card and photocopies (if applicable), the road tax receipt and a photocopy, and a receipt for the payment of transfer tax. You have ten days to register the vehicle in your name.

REGISTRATION

When you import a car into Spain or buy a new or second-hand car, it must be registered (*matriculación*) at the traffic department in the province where you're resident. If you import a car, you must obtain customs clearance and, if it's imported from a country outside the EU, it may need to undergo a homologation inspection before it can be registered (see page 147). When you buy a car from a dealer

in Spain, he usually arranges for the issue of the registration certificate (*permiso de circulación*) or the transfer of ownership. If you buy a car privately, you can do the registration yourself or you can employ a *gestor* to do it for you.

When you buy a second-hand car, you must apply for a change of registration (*cambio de titularidad*) within ten days of purchase at the *vehículos* counter of the local traffic department, and pay a fee of €44.20. The following documents are required:

♦ a completed application form (*notificación de transferencia de vehículos*), obtainable from the local provincial traffic department;

♦ the current registration document (*permiso de circulación*) with the transfer of ownership listed on the reverse, including the seller's signature;

♦ the road tax (*impuesto municipal sobre vehículos de tracción mecánica/IVTM*) receipt for the current year and a photocopy;

♦ the current *ITV* test certificate and card and photocopies, if applicable;

♦ a receipt for the payment of transfer tax (due on the sale of second-hand cars);

♦ your residence permit (*residencia*) or, if you aren't a Spanish resident, a photocopy or the title deeds (*escritura*) of your Spanish home and your foreigner's identification number (*NIE* – see page 210). It's usually necessary to be a Spanish resident in order to operate a car on Spanish plates, although a certificate confirming that

you've registered with the local municipality (*certificado de empadronamiento*) may be accepted.

♦ a stamped, self-addressed envelope (for the return of the new registration document).

If a person other than the new owner makes the application, he must provide written authorisation from the owner and supply his own residence permit and a copy.

If your car is stolen or scrapped, you should complete a *baja de matrícula* form, available from your provincial traffic department. You require the same documents as for registration (listed above), with the exception of the receipt for payment of transfer tax. If the vehicle has been stolen, a copy of the police report (*denuncia*) is required. If the vehicle is more than 15 years old, no fee is charged; otherwise, you must pay €7.60. The *baja* ensures that you no longer receive road tax bills or traffic fines, even if someone else puts the vehicle back on the road.

Registration Plates

Since 2001, all Spanish registration plates have consisted of four digits followed by three letters, e.g. 1234 ABC, meaning that you cannot tell where a car is from, but there are thousands of cars on the road with old-style registration plates, which consisted of one or two letters denoting the province where the vehicle is registered (e.g. B for Barcelona and M for Madrid), followed by four digits and one or two more letters (e.g. M-1234-A). The original registration normally remains permanently with a car, although it's possible to re-register a vehicle. If you're buying a pre-2001 car and don't want to re-register it, it's best to buy one registered in the province where you live, or you will be permanently identified as a 'stranger' (which could cause you problems in some areas).

Since 1st July 1995, Spanish registration plates have incorporated the EU flag and an 'E' for *España* on the left-hand side of the plate. Tourist plates (see below) have a T followed by numbers and a date of expiry in red. Green plates signify an imported vehicle or one previously on tourist plates awaiting standard plates.

Tourist Plates

It's possible for non-residents to register a vehicle under Spain's 'tourist registration' scheme (*matrícula turística*). It must have been bought outright with foreign currency or, if you paid for it in euros, you must provide proof that it was bought outside Spain. The vehicle will be issued with tourist plates, which cost €70.80 and must be renewed annually for a similar fee. They can be renewed indefinitely provided you don't work in Spain.

If you're a non-EU national, you must make a sworn statement (*declaración jurada*) that you don't reside in Spain for more than six months a year and the vehicle may be used only by you and your immediate family and must be 'sealed' (*precintado*) by customs during periods of absence from Spain.

Most car dealers will handle the registration and renewal of tourist plates, as will a *gestor*, who should charge around €50 to complete the paperwork.

When a non-resident with a vehicle on tourist plates becomes a resident, he has three months from the date of receipt of his residence card to change to standard plates. Anyone who illegally drives a vehicle on tourist plates can be fined up to €3,000 and the vehicle can be confiscated. Spanish road tax (see below) must be paid on all cars kept in Spain on tourist plates.

TECHNICAL INSPECTION

All cars over four years old must have a regular technical inspection (*inspección técnica de*

vehículos/ITV) at an authorised test station. The test must be carried out every two years until the car is ten years old, after which time the test is annual. Motorcycles are first tested after five years, after which the test is due every two years. If a vehicle is involved in a serious accident, it must usually undergo an *ITV* test after repair to establish whether the repair has been carried out correctly.

There are *ITV* test stations in most major towns (listed in yellow pages under *Automóviles Inspección Técnica de Vehículos*). Make an appointment to avoid a long wait or a wasted journey. The test fee varies from province to province and is from €25 to €50, usually payable only in cash.

If you don't speak Spanish, you should get a garage to take your car in for a test or take a Spanish speaker with you so that you understand any instructions given at the test. Most garages will get your car tested for you, although if you ask a garage to take your car in for a test, make sure that you don't pay for unnecessary repairs, either before or after the test. The Real Automóvil Club de España (RACE) will also take members' cars for testing.

When taking a vehicle for a test, make sure it contains a reflective waistcoat, two approved red warning triangles, a full set of spare bulbs and fuses, a spare wheel and the tools for changing a wheel. If it doesn't, it will fail.

If a vehicle fails the test, you receive a blue form listing the faults and you're given 15 days to have it repaired and re-tested. If possible, get the *ITV* examiner to write down the repairs necessary to pass the test, or you could receive a large bill for unnecessary repairs. Tests aren't exhaustive or rigorous, and old wrecks that should have been consigned to the scrap heap decades ago flourish in Spain, particularly in rural areas.

When your car has passed the test, you're given a certificate showing the month and year when the test is next due, which must be displayed in the top right-hand corner of your windscreen. Certificates are a different colour for each year. You also receive an *ITV* card (*tarjeta de inspección técnica de vehículos*), which details the results of each part of the test. You can be fined up to €1,500 for failing to display a valid *ITV* certificate.

Note that the Spanish *ITV* test has no value in other EU countries and, if you operate a car in Spain that's registered in another EU country, it must be tested in accordance with the law of the country where it's registered in order to be legal in Spain. If you import a car into Spain, it must pass the *ITV* test before it can be registered in Spain.

ROAD TAX

All Spanish-registered vehicle owners (including motorcycle owners and owners of vehicles on tourist plates) must pay an annual road tax (*impuesto municipal sobre vehículos de tracción mecánica/IVTM*). Like all Spanish taxes, road tax has increased in the last decade, although it's still lower than in most other EU countries, where it applies. Minimum and maximum limits are established by law, but within these taxes are set by individual municipalities and vary from town to town; rates are higher in municipalities with over 100,000 inhabitants, which may double the minimum tax rate. Among the cheapest cities are Madrid (surprisingly), Valencia and Zaragoza, and among the most expensive

Barcelona (around 20 per cent higher than Madrid), Bilbao and Córdoba.

The amount of tax payable also varies with the 'fiscal horsepower' (*potencia fiscal* or *caballos fiscales*) of your car, which is a nominal amount not necessarily related to the engine power of a vehicle, as follows:

Road Tax	
Fiscal Horsepower	**Tax Range**
0 to 8	€15 to €30
9 to 12	€45 to €70
13 to 16	€90 to €150
17 to 20	€130 to €200
Over 20	€160 to €250

It's advisable to check your bill, as some town halls overcharge by up to 100 per cent by using the wrong formula to calculate the horsepower.

Payment

Road tax must be paid to your local authority, usually some time between March and May. Contact your town hall to find out when and how it must be paid and to obtain a payment form. Announcements are made on municipal notice boards and in local newspapers and banks, and the town hall may send you a reminder (but don't count on it!). Tax can be paid in person at the town hall (where there are usually long queues) or at the tax office (*recaudación* or *oficina municipal de impuestos*), via certain local banks (or by direct debit from your account) or by post.

When a vehicle is purchased, the tax payable is calculated pro rata for the current tax year. If a car is to be unused for a whole calendar year, you can have its registration · temporarily suspended (*baja temporal*) at your provincial traffic department. However, if a vehicle is used for just one day in a year, tax must be paid for the whole year.

There's a late payment surcharge (*recargo*) of 5 per cent in the first month and 20 per cent thereafter, and the unpaid sum is also liable to interest. Some people have been able to avoid paying road tax for many years, although municipalities are now clamping

and can be fined €60 for not having them if you're stopped by the police. Car insurance is available from many Spanish insurance companies and a number of foreign insurance companies in Spain, including direct insurance companies (who don't use agents). Always shop around and obtain a number of quotations. In the summer of 2008, there was intense competition among car insurance companies for customers. See also **Breakdown Insurance** on page 174.

down on non-payers, whose vehicles can be impounded by local police. Note that a Spanish-registered car is automatically logged by your local municipality when you register your ownership with the provincial traffic department.

A Spanish road tax certificate isn't displayed inside your car's windscreen or on your registration plates. However, you should keep the receipt in your car with your other vehicle documents, as the local police may ask to see it.

CAR INSURANCE

All motor vehicles and trailers must be insured when entering Spain, and you can be fined between €600 and €3,000 for failing to have proper insurance. It isn't mandatory for cars insured in most European countries to have an international insurance 'green' card (see below) and motorists insured in an EU country, Hungary, Liechtenstein, Norway and Switzerland are automatically covered for third-party liability in Spain.

There are an estimated 2m drivers without insurance in Spain, where there's also more insurance fraud than in any other EU country. Note, however, that driving without obligatory insurance (*seguro obligatorio*) is a serious offence, for which you can be fined up to €3,000 or even imprisoned. You must carry your insurance documents when driving

Green Cards

All Spanish and most insurance companies in western Europe provide an automatic 'green' card (*certificado internacional de seguro de autómovil*), which extends your insurance cover to other European countries. This doesn't include cars insured in the UK, however, where green cards are expensive and insurance companies usually provide one for limited periods only (e.g. 30 or 45 days) and for a maximum number of days per year, e.g. 90. However, you should shop around, as some companies allow drivers a green card for up to six months a year. Nevertheless, if you're British and have comprehensive insurance, it's wise to have a green card when visiting Spain.

Note that EU rules require all vehicles to be insured in their country of registration. For example, if you keep a British-registered car in Spain, you can insure it through the Spanish branch of a British-based insurance company, but you **cannot** insure it with a Spanish insurance company. If you drive a British-registered car and spend over six months a year on the continent, you must therefore take out a special (i.e. expensive) European insurance policy with a British insurer, insure with a British insurance company with offices in Spain, or obtain insurance with a Spanish company. Similarly, if you have a Spanish-registered car, it must be insured with a Spanish insurance company (or a foreign insurance company with an office in Spain).

Types of Insurance

The following categories of car insurance are available in Spain:

Third-party

Third-party insurance (*responsabilidad civil obligatoria* or *seguro obligatorio*) is the minimum required by law, and you must be insured for claims of €360,000 for personal injury and €100,000 for damage to third-party property, which will cost you from around €300 a year. You can choose to pay an extra premium for additional cover up to a specified or unlimited amount (*ilimitada*), which is highly recommended. Unlimited third-party cover usually costs around €50 extra per year. Note that the driver and passengers don't count as third parties and must be insured separately (see **Driver & Passenger Insurance** and **Premiums** below).

Roadside assistance (*asistencia en viajes*), glass breakage (*rotura de lunas*) and legal expenses (*defensa penal*) in the event of a court case may be included in basic third-party cover or can be added for an additional premium.

Third-party, Fire & Theft

Third-party, fire and theft insurance (*responsabilidad civil obligatoria, incendio y robo*), known in some countries as 'part comprehensive', includes cover against fire (*incendio*), natural hazards (e.g. rocks falling on your car), theft (*robo*), broken glass (e.g. windscreen), legal expenses (*defensa penal*), and possibly damage or theft of contents (although this is rare). Insurance against the theft of a stereo system is usually available only from the manufacturer (it may be included in the purchase price). You may be able to take out fire cover independently, although it's usually combined with theft cover.

Comprehensive

Comprehensive (sometimes called 'fully comprehensive') insurance, known in Spain as 'all risks' (*todo riesgo*), covers all the risks listed under third-party, fire and theft (above) plus all other types of damage to your vehicle irrespective of how it's caused.

> ☑ **SURVIVAL TIP**
>
> Some insurance companies don't provide comprehensive cover for vehicles more than two or three years old (although it's possible to get comprehensive cover on vehicles up to ten years old).

Comprehensive insurance may be compulsory for lease and credit purchase contracts. Note that Spanish insurance doesn't usually pay for a replacement car when your car is being repaired after an accident.

Driver & Passenger Insurance

Driver and passenger insurance (*seguro de ocupantes*) is included in a comprehensive policy but otherwise optional. There are usually various levels of insurance, e.g. from €5,000 for minimal cover to €25,000 for death and permanent disability compensation.

Premiums

Insurance premiums in Spain are among the lowest in the EU, although they vary considerably according to numerous factors, including the following:

- **the type of insurance** – see above;

- **the type of car and its use** – Cars are divided into eight categories, based on their performance (some companies don't insure high-performance vehicles), the cost of repairs, where and how much they're used (some premiums are based on the number of kilometres driven each year), whether they're garaged, and whether they're used for business or pleasure.

- **your age and accident record** – Drivers with less than two or three years' experience usually pay a 'penalty' (*penalización*) and drivers under a certain age, e.g. 25, also pay higher premiums. Some insurance companies refuse to insure drivers under 25. Drivers aged over 70 may also pay a penalty. Some companies offer low-cost policies for experienced older drivers, e.g.

those over 50 or 55, with a good record; others give discounts of 10 to 20 per cent for experienced drivers of any age.

♦ **the area where you live** – Premiums are highest in Madrid and other major cities and lowest in rural areas.

♦ **whether the car is garaged** – Some insurance companies give an additional discount (e.g. 5 per cent) if a vehicle is garaged overnight.

Premiums vary from around €300 a year for basic third-party insurance for a small family saloon to €1,500 or more a year for comprehensive insurance for a high-performance sports saloon. Short-term policies (for periods of less than a year) are available from some companies, although premiums are high, e.g. 50 per cent of the annual rate for three months and 70 per cent for six months. Value added tax (VAT/*IVA*) at 16 per cent is payable on insurance premiums. You can reduce your premium by choosing to pay an excess (*franquicia*), e.g. the first €150, €200, €300, €450 or €600 of a claim. Insurance companies must give two months' notice of an increase in premiums.

⚠ **Caution**

If you're convicted of drunk or dangerous driving, your premium will be increased considerably. In fact, if you're convicted of drunk driving, your insurance company will probably refuse to pay on a claim! Note also that, if you have an accident while breaking the law, e.g. drunk driving or illegal parking, comprehensive insurance may be automatically downgraded to third-party, which means that you must pay for your own repairs and medical expenses.

No-claims Bonus

A foreign no-claims bonus (*bonificación/ sistema bonus-malus*) is usually valid, provided you've had insurance within the last two years, but you must provide written evidence from your present or previous insurance company, not just an insurance renewal notice, and

you may need an official Spanish translation. Always insist on having your no-claims bonus recognised, even if you don't receive the same percentage reduction as you received abroad (shop around).

Most companies offer a 5 per cent discount for each year of no claims up to a maximum discount of 60 per cent, although some offer a maximum of only 50 per cent (or less). Foreign insurance companies may offer a more generous no-claims bonus than Spanish companies.

If you have an accident, you're usually required to pay a penalty (*penalización*) or your bonus is reduced, e.g. one accident may lose you two years' no-claims bonus. You can usually pay an extra premium to protect your no-claims bonus. No-claims bonuses usually also apply to a second family car.

Claims

In the event of an accident, claims are decided on the information provided in accident report forms (*declaración de siniestro de automóvil*) completed by the drivers involved, reports by insurance company experts and police reports. You must notify your insurance company of a claim within a limited period, e.g. two to five days. Many companies have 24-hour helplines for claims, in Spain and abroad. Any damage must usually be inspected and the repair authorised by your insurance company's assessor, although sometimes an independent assessor's report may be permitted and an inspection may be unnecessary for minor damage. Note that when a vehicle is a write-off, Spanish insurance companies usually pay only a percentage of its 'book' value, which is often less than its actual value.

If your car is stolen, you must report it to the local police immediately and submit a copy of the police report with your claim. After reporting your car stolen, 30 days must elapse before an insurance company will consider a claim.

Cancellation

Spanish insurance companies are forbidden by law to cancel third-party cover after a claim, except in the case of drunk driving or when a driver is subsequently disqualified from driving.

A company can, however, refuse to renew your policy at the end of the current period, although they must give you 15 days' notice.

If you wish to cancel your car insurance at the end of the current term, you must notify your insurance company in writing by registered letter and usually give two months' notice. You may cancel your insurance before the term has expired (without penalty) if the premium is increased, the terms are altered, or your car has been declared a write-off or stolen. If you cancel your policy during the term of the insurance, e.g. you sell your car, and don't take out another policy, your insurance company isn't required to give you a refund.

DRIVING LICENCES

The minimum ages for driving in Spain are 14 for a motorcycle (moped) up to 50cc, 16 for a motorcycle with an engine capacity up to 125cc and 18 for a motorcycle over 125cc or for a car. There's also a maximum age of 65 for obtaining your first licence, although this doesn't apply to foreigners aged over 65 who have a foreign licence.

Many foreign driving licences are recognised in Spain under reciprocal agreements, including all EU licences and some US state licences, in which case you can drive on the licence of your home country and aren't required to obtain a Spanish driving licence (permiso de conducción). Nevertheless, you must take your existing licence to your local provincial traffic department to be stamped and

registered. You must also undergo the same medical exams and eye tests as holders of Spanish licences (see below). Note, however, that the above rule isn't always known or recognised by the local police, and there have been cases of EU nationals resident in Spain driving Spanish-registered vehicles and being fined for not having a Spanish licence. For this reason, many people find it's simpler to exchange their foreign licence for a Spanish one!

Holders of licences issued by countries without a reciprocal agreement with Spain must take a Spanish written and/or practical driving test. Previously the written test could be taken in English and other foreign languages, but recent legislation has ruled that the written test must be taken in Spanish. If in doubt, consult a Spanish consulate abroad or your country's embassy or consulate in Spain. All non-resident non-EU licence holders must obtain a Spanish driving licence and are entitled to drive in Spain for a maximum of six months in a calendar year.

An international driving permit (IDP) is obtainable in Spain from the Royal Automobile Club of Spain (Real Automóvil Club de España/ RACE) on presentation of a valid foreign driving licence, a passport and two photographs. Note, however, that if a non-resident obtains an IDP in Spain, it's valid only for driving **outside** Spain.

A Spanish driving licence is a plastic-coated card, the size of a credit card, with personal information (including a photograph) printed on one side and driving information on the other. The card is similar to those issued in Germany, Sweden and the UK. Old-style licences are gradually being replaced by this new type when licences are renewed.

You must carry your foreign or Spanish driving licence at all times when driving in Spain (see **Traffic Police** on page 169.

Validity

The validity period of a Spanish licence depends on your age and the type of licence held, e.g. a motorcycle (A-1/A-2) or car (B-1) licence is valid for ten years if you're under 45 and for five years if you're between 45 and 70. A driver aged over 70 must renew his licence every two years. A commercial, passenger vehicle or heavy goods licence must be renewed every five years up to the age of 45, every three years from 46 to 60 and every two years from 61 to 70.

Points System

In an attempt to reduce the high accident and mortality rate on Spain's roads, the government introduced a points system, similar to that used in France, Germany and Italy. The scheme, widely acclaimed by motoring associations and insurance companies, became law in July 2006, since when there has been a marked decrease (around 20 per cent) in the number of deaths on Spanish roads.

Most drivers receive an initial tally of 12 points with their driving licence, but those with under 30 months' driving experience receive eight points. When a driver commits an offence, a number of points are deducted from the licence depending on the seriousness of the offence, as in the examples below.

- ◆ **Six-point deduction** – drunk driving (over 50mg per 100ml); refusing to take a breath test; driving at more than 150 per cent of the speed limit (e.g. over 75kph in a 50kph zone); dangerous driving;

- ◆ **Four-point deduction** – driving at more than 40kph over the limit (unless this is over 150 per cent of the limit, in which case you incur a six-point deduction); drunk driving (over 25mg per 100ml); ignoring a 'give way' or 'stop' sign or a red light; throwing rubbish out of a car; dangerous overtaking; putting a cyclist in danger when overtaking him;

- ◆ **Three-point deduction** – failing to maintain a safe distance behind the vehicle in front; driving between 30 and 40kph over the limit; driving without lights in poor visibility; using a hand-held mobile phone or wearing headphones while driving; not wearing a seatbelt (or helmet when riding a motorcycle);

- ◆ **Two-point deduction** – stopping on a bend or in a tunnel; driving between 20 and 30kph over the limit.

Drivers who lose all their designated points automatically lose their licence. To regain their licence, drivers must retake the driving test and take a driving course of around 30 hours.

These tests cannot be taken until at least six months after the last driving offence and can be taken only once every two years. Those who have lost points but still have credit on their driving licence regain their points two years after their last offence (e.g. if you lose two points in January 2009, they're due for reinstatement in January 2011, but if you commit another offence in December 2010 you must wait until December 2012 to have those two points reinstated). Good drivers with no points lost receive an additional two points after three years and a further point after four years, giving them a maximum of 15 points. Professional drivers, such as taxi and lorry drivers, have a different system.

Since the system was introduced, numerous drivers have lost all their points (most for drunk driving). Figures released in July 2008 showed that 3 per cent of drivers had lost at least one point and that the vast majority of points (42 per cent) had been deducted for speeding.

> ⚠ **Caution**
>
> Under legislation brought in during 2008, several driving offences are classed as criminal offences and attract a prison sentence of up to two years or a fine and compulsory community work (three to six months). Criminal offences include speeding (e.g. driving at over 200kph on a motorway or over 110kph in an urban area) and drunk driving.

Comprehensive information about the points system and details of your personal points 'score' are available from the Department of Traffic's websites (www.dgt.es and ⌨ www.permisoporpuntos.es).

Applications

To apply for a Spanish driving licence you require the following:

- ◆ a completed application form (*solicitud de carnet del permiso de conducir*), available from the *información-impresos* counter at the local provincial traffic department or downloadable from ⌨ www.dgt.es;

- your Spanish residence permit (*residencia*) and a photocopy;

- your current foreign driving licence and a photocopy;

- a sworn written statement that your licence hasn't been suspended and that you don't own another driving licence in another country (other than the one you wish to change);

- one passport-size photograph. Non-EU citizens require three, one of which must be signed on the back by the doctor performing the medical examination – see below.

- the fee of €18.20, payable at the traffic department.

Holders of non-EU driving licences also require an official translation of their licence and a certificate of equivalence (*certificado de equivalencia*) available from the Royal Automobile Club of Spain (see **Motoring Organisations** on page 175), a medical certificate of fitness to drive (see below) and a stamped self-addressed envelope.

If someone other than the licence owner makes the application, he must provide written authorisation from the owner and supply his own residence card and copy. You can use a *gestor* (see page 320) to obtain a Spanish driving licence or apply through a Spanish motoring organisation such as the Royal Automobile Club of Spain. A *gestor* will charge you €30 to €60 for the work involved.

It usually takes between one and three months to obtain a Spanish licence. You're given an official receipt for your application and a copy of your foreign licence, which is valid until you receive your Spanish licence. When you receive your Spanish licence, your foreign licence is returned to the issuing authority abroad. If you change your address, you must apply to have the address on your licence changed (there's no charge)

Renewals

To renew a Spanish driving licence you require the following:

- a completed application form (see above);

- your current licence;

- your residence permit and a photocopy;

- a medical certificate (see below);

- two or more passport-sized photographs;

- the fee of €18.20 payable at the traffic department (the over 70s are exempt).

If someone other than the licence owner makes the application, he must provide written authorisation from the owner and supply his own residence card and copy.

Medical Certificate

Holders of non-EU driving licences require a medical certificate to obtain a Spanish driving licence and **all** applicants for a renewal of a licence must submit one. The necessary examination is carried out in designated clinics (*centros de reconocimento médico para conductores*), which are open from 10am to 2pm and from 4 to 8pm Mondays to Fridays.

The examination includes eyesight, hearing, pulse and blood pressure tests, and tests for speed of reaction, judgement of the speed of other vehicles and acuteness of visual identification. If you wear glasses or contact lenses, you're tested with them and your licence will be annotated to indicate that you must wear glasses while driving – and carry a spare pair. The examination takes around half an hour and costs around €30. The medical certificate is valid for 90 days, during which time you must make your application for a licence (or a renewal).

Further details of licence application procedures and downloadable forms are available from the Department of Traffic's website (🖳 www.dgt.es).

ROADS

The Spanish road network covers over 300,000km (around 200,000mi), of which around 8,000km (5,000mi) consists of motorways (*autovías/autopistas*). Spain has the second highest density of motorways (in the EU) and further expansion of the network is under way.

Spanish roads have improved considerably in recent years and Spain's best roads are now among the finest in Europe, especially the motorways. Unfortunately, these are also among

the world's most expensive roads and consequently main trunk roads (*carreteras*) are jammed by drivers who are reluctant (or cannot afford) to pay the high motorway tolls.

In contrast to the excellent new motorways and trunk roads, many secondary roads in rural areas and small towns are full of potholes and in a dreadful or even dangerous condition. Some main roads are also in poor condition with surprising undulations and dips, and they aren't often up to the standards of roads in northern Europe. Heavy rain in winter can expose major defects in many roads, including relatively new roads, and some can become treacherous due to inadequate drainage. Heavy rainfall also causes widespread floods, rock falls, landslides and subsidence.

The Spanish Road Association (Asociación Española de la Carretera/AEC) recently published a report on Spanish roads, which found that around a third of them were in poor condition and concluded that €4bn was needed to bring them up to standard. According to the report, Asturias, Castille y León, Catalonia and Murcia have the worst state-maintained roads and Extremadura, La Rioja, Madrid and Murcia the worst regionally maintained.

In major cities, it's usually wise to park your car (if you can find a parking space) and use public transport. Driving in Madrid is the motoring equivalent of hell and should be avoided at all costs. You should also be wary of driving into small towns and villages, where streets are narrow and often come to a dead end (so that you must reverse out). It's better to park on the edge of town.

Types of Road

In 2004, road denominations were changed in order to make them more consistent and easier to understand. Changing all signs (including the kilometre markers on main roads) and maps is still in progress and you can expect to see roads signposted by their new name, old name or both – not to mention plenty of confused motorists! The old and new prefixes are shown in the table opposite. (Note also that the numbering of main roads has been changed from Roman to Arabic numerals; e.g. the old N-II is now the A-2.)

		Spanish Roads	
New Prefix	**Spanish**	**Old Prefix**	**Description**
AP	*Autopista*	A	Motorway – usually marked in blue or red/yellow on maps
E	*Carretera europea*	E	European motorway-standard highway traversing a number of countries, e.g. the E5 running from the French border at Hendaye to Algeciras
A	*Autovía*	N	National trunk road – usually marked in red or yellow on maps
N	*Carretera nacional*	N	Primary road – usually marked in red or yellow on maps
C	*Carretera comarcal*	C	Secondary road – usually marked in green or yellow on maps
Various*	*Carretera autonómica*		Minor road – usually marked in yellow or white on maps

* A two-letter prefix indicates the province, e.g. MA for Malaga. Access roads to main cities are prefixed by the city or province code (e.g. B for Barcelona, M for Madrid and SE for Seville) followed by one or two digits, e.g. M-23 and B-21, shown on a blue background. Some minor roads are unnumbered.

The main trunk roads radiate from Madrid to the coast or the Spanish border, i.e. the A-1 (old N-I) to San Sebastian, the A-2 (old N-II) to Barcelona, the A-3 (old N-III) to Valencia, the A-4 (old N-IV) to Cadiz, the A-5 (old N-V) to Badajoz and the A-6 (old N-VI) to A Coruña.

On the national roads listed above, distances from the Puerta del Sol in Madrid are shown on red and white kilometre stones or markers at the side of the road.

Motorways

Spanish motorways are indicated by blue or green signs and often have an international motorway symbol on them. Most are toll roads (*autopistas de peajes*), which are the most expensive in Europe (Spain has the third-largest network of toll motorways in Europe after France and Italy). Tolls vary, as each motorway operator has its own fee structure, and are generally higher (e.g. 30 per cent) in the summer. Typical low-season toll fees are currently €8.20 from Valencia to Alicante and €6.05 from Malaga to Guadiaro. Not surprisingly, toll roads are avoided by most motorists and are consequently quiet. Partly for this reason, motorways are Spain's safest roads – a relative term!

A ticket is issued automatically at a toll-booth at a motorway entrance (or shortly afterwards); when you reach another toll-booth or leave the motorway, you must normally hand your ticket to an attendant (the toll due is usually shown on a display) and pay (in cash, including major foreign currencies, or by credit card). On some stretches, e.g. around cities, tickets aren't issued and a fixed toll is charged; there may be unmanned toll-booths for those with the correct change, shown by the sign *Automático – importe exacto* (throw the correct amount into the 'basket' and wait for the red light to change to green and the barrier to rise) or booths that accept payment by credit card. Tolls may also be levied at intermediate points.

Regular commuters can buy a season card (*tarjeta de la autopista*) offering savings of 10 to 25 per cent. You insert your card in a machine or, on many motorways, simply drive through the toll gate marked *ViaT* while a machine reads your number plate, which has been previously registered.

All motorways have service areas with a petrol station, cafeteria or coffee shop, toilets, telephones, and possibly a restaurant and shops. Some have repair workshops, bureau de change facilities, information offices and motels.

Motorway exits (*salidas*) are marked on maps, as are service and rest stops (*apartaderos*). Motorway maps and toll information are available from ASETA (💻 www.aseta.es). Most motorway operators provide free maps.

Main Roads

For many Spaniards, driving on motorways is too expensive, so main roads (*carreteras*), many of which run parallel to motorways, are often jammed by cars and trucks. (Even an offer of half price for trucks attracts few takers.) If you must get from A to B in the shortest possible time, there's no alternative to the motorway, apart from taking a plane or train. However, if you aren't in too much of a hurry, want to save money and wish to see more of the country, you should avoid them. The money saved on tolls can pay for a good meal or a hotel room.

Many dual-carriageways (*autovías*), such as the A-4 south of Madrid, have the appearance of motorways and the same maximum speed limit (120kph/75mph). However, they also have left turns and crossings in some places, so take care. The sign '*cambio de sentido*' (change of direction) on a dual-carriageway is an opportunity to reverse your direction by way of an under- or overpass, e.g. when you've missed your exit. On national highways there are 'crawler' lanes on gradients for trucks and other slow-moving vehicles. On single-lane highways you shouldn't expect to cover more than around 70 to 80km per hour.

Secondary Roads

Travelling on secondary roads (particularly mountain roads) invariably takes two or three times longer than travelling on national routes. Mountain passes in Spain are usually open all year, although some are closed intermittently. Most are narrow with hairpin bends, no road

markings and unprotected roadsides with sheer drops, and aren't recommended for timid or nervous drivers, particularly in winter.

EMERGENCIES

Emergency telephones, mounted on orange posts, are sited around every 5km (3mi) on motorways and other main roads. Each telephone is individually numbered and directly connected to the local police station, which will send out a breakdown van or tow truck (*grúa*) with first-aid equipment.

If you've broken down and call from an ordinary telephone, you should ask the operator for the 'rescue service' (*auxilio en carretera*). The *guardia civil* also provides roadside assistance on main roads throughout Spain, as do motoring organisations (see page 175).

> ⚠ **Caution**
>
> If you break down anywhere, you must park your car at the roadside or on the hard shoulder and place emergency triangles 10m behind and in front of your vehicle, visible at a distance of 100m. You must also put on a reflective waistcoat. Never remain in your car when it's parked beside the road or on the hard shoulder, as it's extremely dangerous. Note that you're permitted to stop on the hard shoulder only in an emergency (e.g. not for a 'call of nature').

Information

Road information can be obtained by phone (☎ 900 123 505 – general information only) or via the internet (💻 www.dgt.es). Note that at holiday times and weekends, phone lines and the website are overloaded and it can be impossible to get through.

RULES OF THE ROAD

Spanish road rules were extensively revised in 2004 in an attempt to improve safety and the following is a summary of the most important current regulations. Don't, however, expect

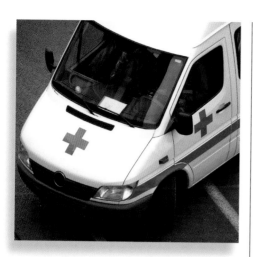

other motorists to adhere to them (many Spanish drivers make up their own 'rules', which are infinitely variable!).

♦ The Spanish drive on the right-hand side of the road (when not driving in the middle). It saves confusion if you do likewise! If you aren't used to driving on the right, take it easy until you're accustomed to it. Be particularly alert when leaving lay-bys, T-junctions, one-way streets and petrol stations, as it's easy to lapse into driving on the left. It's helpful to have a reminder (e.g. a luminous sign saying 'Keep right!') on your car's dashboard.

♦ When driving outside Spain, you must affix the nationality letter (*nacionalidad*) 'E' (*España*) to the rear of a Spanish-registered car unless it has a number plate that incorporates one. Drivers of foreign-registered cars in Spain must have the appropriate nationality plate affixed to the rear of their cars; you can be fined on the spot for not displaying it.

♦ All cars must carry a reflective waistcoat (to be worn if you stop at the side of the road), two approved red warning triangles (to be placed around 10m in front of and behind the vehicle – or both behind on a dual-carriageway – if you must stop at the side of the road), a full set of spare bulbs and fuses, a spare wheel and the tools for changing a wheel. If you don't have the above when your car undergoes its *ITV* inspection, it will fail. It's also advisable (but not

mandatory) to carry a fire extinguisher and a first-aid kit.

♦ Most main roads are designated priority roads (*prioridad de paso*). All secondary roads have a stop sign or a give-way sign, the latter often with the words *ceda el paso* (give way) beneath it. An obligation to give way may also be indicated by a triangle painted on the road. When roads have equal status and no priority is indicated, traffic coming from the right has priority. The priority to the right rule usually also applies in car parks, but never when exiting from car parks or dirt tracks. Failure to observe the priority-to-the-right rule is the cause of many accidents. If you're ever in doubt about who has priority, give way to emergency (ambulance, fire, police) and public utility (electricity, gas, telephone, water) vehicles attending an emergency, trams, buses and all traffic coming from your RIGHT.

♦ Traffic flows anti-clockwise round roundabouts (traffic circles) and not clockwise, as in the UK and other countries where driving is on the left. When approaching a roundabout, you must give way to traffic on the roundabout (coming from your left). There's usually a give-way sign (which may be painted on the road) on all roads approaching the roundabout. Bear in mind that what appears to be a roundabout isn't always one, so check for 'give way' or 'stop' signs.

♦ The wearing of seat belts is compulsory on all roads at all times and includes passengers in rear seats. Children aged under 12 or less than 150cm (5ft) tall must travel in the back seats of cars unless the front seat is fitted with an approved child seat. Failure to wear a seat belt can result in a loss of three points from your licence and an on-the-spot fine of €90, and subsequent offences may mean increased fines or even the loss of your licence. If you have an accident and aren't wearing a seat belt, your insurance company can refuse to pay a claim for personal injury.

♦ A rule introduced in 2002 requires you to leave at least enough space for another car between you and the car in front (barely adequate even at a snail's pace!). If you don't, you may lose three licence points.

- Don't drive in bus, taxi or cycle lanes, identified by a continuous yellow line parallel to the kerb, unless necessary to avoid a stationary vehicle or an obstruction (you can lose three points and be fined for doing so). Be sure to keep clear of tram lines – i.e. outside the restricted area, marked by a line.

- For left-hand turns off a main road with traffic lights, there's often a marked filter lane to the right, from which you cross the main road at right angles.

- The use of horns is forbidden at night in towns, when lights should be flashed to warn other motorists or pedestrians of your presence – and not for any other reason (Spanish drivers sometimes warn other motorists of police radar traps and road blocks by flashing their headlights, although this is illegal). In towns, horns should be used during the day only in emergencies. If you use a horn 'unnecessarily', e.g. to wake the driver in front when the traffic lights change to green, you can be fined up to €60, but judging by the noise of car horns on Spanish streets this penalty is rarely applied!

- Headlamps must be used when driving at night, in poor visibility during daylight and in tunnels at all times (you're reminded by a sign). Be extremely careful when driving in tunnels, some of which have very poor (or no) lighting. Your headlamps must be dipped (luces de cruce) at night when following a vehicle or when a vehicle is approaching from the opposite direction. Failure to dip your lights can result in a fine.

- A vehicle's hazard warning lights must be used to warn other drivers of an obstruction, e.g. an accident or a traffic jam, or if the vehicle is forced to drive at below the minimum speed. Warning triangles and reflective waistcoats must be used as appropriate (see above).

- Most traffic lights are situated on posts at the side of the road, although they may also be suspended above the road. The sequence of Spanish traffic lights (semáforos) is usually red, green, amber (yellow), red. Amber means stop at the stop line, unless doing so may cause an accident, e.g. because another vehicle is a few centimetres from your rear bumper.

Spanish drivers routinely drive through amber – and even red – lights and may be taken by surprise if you stop!

- Flashing amber lights at the side of the road usually indicate that you're approaching traffic lights or a built-up area with a restricted speed limit (e.g. 50kph/30mph). At the entrance to many towns, there are flashing amber traffic lights designed to slow traffic; some have a light mounted above them that changes to red if you approach them too fast, e.g. at more than 50kph. Failure to stop can lead to a loss of four licence points as well as a heavy fine (e.g. from €90 to €600).

- An amber or green filter light, usually flashing and with a direction arrow, may be shown in addition to the main signal. This means that you may drive in the direction shown by the arrow, but, if the light is amber, must give priority to pedestrians or other traffic. In towns, individual lanes sometimes have their own traffic lights showing a green arrow (indicating that you may use that lane) or a red cross (indicating 'no entry'). Flashing amber lights are a warning to proceed with caution and may indicate that you must give way to pedestrians.

You occasionally see a flashing red light, meaning stop or no entry, e.g. at a railway level crossing. Two red lights mounted vertically one above the other indicate 'no entry'.

- Railway (level) crossings are indicated by a sign with a large 'X' or an engine in a triangle. You must take particular care at crossings without barriers, as several people are killed every year by trains at crossings without barriers. Approach a railway level crossing slowly and stop as soon as the barrier or half-barrier starts to fall, as soon as the red warning lights are illuminated or flashing or a warning bell rings, or when you see or hear a train approaching! Your new car may be built 'like a tank', but there won't be much left of it (or you) if it collides with a speeding train.

- White lines are used for traffic lanes. A solid single line or two solid lines means no overtaking (*adelantar*) in either direction. A solid line to the right of the centre line, i.e. on your side of the road, means that overtaking is prohibited in your direction. You may overtake only when there's a single broken line in the middle of the road or double lines with a broken line on your side of the road. No overtaking is also shown by the international sign of two cars side by side (one red and one black). Overtaking is prohibited within 100m of a blind hill and on all roads where visibility is less than 200m. It's illegal to overtake on an inside lane on a multi-lane road unless traffic is being channelled in a different direction.

♦ When overtaking, you must indicate before you pull out and again when returning to your lane. Drivers of trucks, buses and other commercial vehicles often flash their right indicator when it's safe for you to overtake, but don't assume this is the case; they could simply be about to make a right turn! The left indicator means 'don't overtake'. Always check your rear view and wing mirrors carefully before overtaking, as Spanish motorists seem to appear from nowhere and zoom past at a 'zillion' miles an hour, especially on country roads. If you drive a right-hand drive car, take extra care when overtaking (it's advisable to have an overtaking mirror fitted). You're forbidden to overtake a stationary tram when passengers are boarding or alighting. Illegal overtaking can result in a fine of at least €300 and the loss of four licence points or even a suspended licence.

♦ Be wary of mopeds (*ciclomotor*) and bicycles. It isn't always easy to see them, particularly when they're hidden by the blind spots of a car or are riding at night without lights. Many young Spanish moped riders seem to have a death wish and tragically many lose their lives each year. They're constantly pulling out into traffic or turning without looking or signalling. **Follow the example set by Spanish motorists, who, when overtaking mopeds and cyclists, always give them a WIDE berth.** If you knock them off their bikes, you may have a difficult time convincing the police that it wasn't your fault; far better to avoid them (and the police). It's also common to encounter tractors, horses, donkeys and

sheep in rural areas. Keep an eye out for them and give them a wide berth too.

♦ In tunnels and underpasses, vehicles must use dipped headlights and follow any instructions on information panels or loudspeakers. If you must stop, turn off the engine, switch on your hazard lights and place your warning triangles in front of and behind the car. Unless there's a fire, you shouldn't leave your car. Overtaking is prohibited in tunnels unless there are two lanes, and you should keep a minimum distance of 100m or four seconds (whichever is the greater) between you and the vehicle in front.

♦ Three-point turns and reversing into side streets is forbidden in towns. U-turns can be made on main roads where signposted.

♦ Studded tyres and snow chains may be used in winter in mountainous areas. Snow chains are compulsory on some roads in winter, indicated by a sign.

♦ Cars mustn't take more people than they have seats for and it's a serious offence to grossly overload a car. You can lose four points and be fined €300 or more and the police may impound your car. Cars also mustn't be overloaded with luggage, particularly on roof racks, and the luggage weight shouldn't exceed that recommended

in manufacturers' handbooks. Loads on the back of a vehicle (e.g. bicycles) may protrude by up to 10 per cent of the vehicle's length and must display the appropriate sign (white rectangle with diagonal red stripes).

♦ Drivers towing (*con remolque*) a caravan or trailer must display a sign of a yellow triangle on a blue background on the front of their vehicle. Note that towing a another vehicle is prohibited (unless you're driving a tow truck).

♦ A dog must be restrained in a car.

♦ The use of hand-held telephones and the wearing of audio headphones is illegal when driving, and you can be fined up to €300 and lose three points from your licence. 'Hands-free' sets are allowed, although they must be without earphones.

♦ When filling up with petrol, you must turn off the engine, all lights, electrical equipment (including the radio) and your mobile phone.

♦ All motorists in Spain must be familiar with the Spanish highway code (*Código de la Circulación*), available from bookshops throughout Spain.

SPEED LIMITS

The speed limits in the table below (*límites de velocidades*) apply to cars and motorcycles in Spain.

Campervans, cars towing caravans and trailers up to 750kg are restricted to 90kph (56mph) on motorways and dual-carriageways, and 80kph (50mph) on other roads (unless a lower speed limit is in force). Cars towing weights over 750kg are restricted to 80kph on motorways and dual-carriageways, and 70kph

(43mph) on other roads (unless a lower speed limit is in force).

Obligatory speed restrictions are shown on round signs in black figures on a white background with a red rim. Recommended speed limits, e.g. at sharp bends, are shown on square signs in white figures on a blue background.

Most Spanish drivers routinely speed everywhere, particularly on rural roads, and it has been estimated that only some 15 per cent of Spanish drivers observe speed limits. Many drivers are reluctant to slow for 50kph limits in towns, particularly on national highways running through towns, and are often irritated by motorists who do so. Such limits are less likely to be enforced than those in towns, particularly in resort areas, where speeding tourists are among the main contributors to the town halls' coffers. However, radar controls are in use throughout Spain (a large number have been installed recently and many are unmarked), and speed limits are also enforced by motorcycle traffic police operating in pairs. See **Fines** on page 170.

PARKING

Spaniards are parking (*estacionamiento/aparcamiento*) anarchists and are champions at the art of 'creative' parking. They will park on pedestrian crossings, on corners, in front of entrances and exits, in fact almost anywhere it's illegal. Double parking is commonplace, although triple parking or completely blocking the road is generally frowned upon even by the Spanish. Many streets in Spanish villages and towns are very narrow and cars are invariably parked opposite garages, making access even

Speed Limits	
Type of Road	**Speed Limit**
Motorways (*autopistas*)	120kph (75mph)
Dual-carriageways (*autovías*)	100kph (62mph)
Other main roads (*carreteras*)	90kph (56mph)
Built-up areas (*vías urbanas*)	50kph (31mph) or as signposted (e.g. 20kph in some residential areas)

tighter. If someone blocks your car in a town, they will usually be shopping or working locally. You should ask around the local shops and businesses or ask a parking attendant for help before calling the police. Failing that, leaning on your horn (although illegal) may help. Some people leave their cars in neutral and the handbrake off when they double park, so that drivers of other parked cars can move them if necessary.

Parking in most Spanish towns and cities is a nightmare – a recent survey found that it takes an average of eight minutes to find a (legal) parking space in main towns, and nearly twice as long in large cities. Parking is restricted in all cities and towns and prohibited altogether in certain areas, although it isn't usually as expensive as in many other European countries. In major towns and cities, it's wise to park on the outskirts and use public transport. In many small towns and villages, it's advisable to park on the edge of town and walk to the centre, as many towns are difficult to navigate, with narrow and dead-end streets commonplace.

Parking regulations vary with the area of a city, the time of day, the day of the week, and even whether the date is odd or even. In many towns, parking is permitted on one side of the street for the first half of the month (blue and red parking restriction signs marked '1-15') and on the other side for the second half of the month (marked '16-31'). In one-way streets, parking may be permitted on the side with even house numbers on even-numbered days and on the side with odd numbers on odd-numbered days. Parking should be in the same direction as the traffic flow in one-way streets or on the right-hand side of roads with two-way traffic. Some towns have zones where parking is regulated during working hours (*horas laborables*), when you need a permit covering the period you intend to stay.

When buying a property in Spain, it's important to investigate the parking facilities, as few older Spanish apartment and townhouse developments have underground or lock-up garages, or even adequate off-road parking facilities, particularly in towns. Some cities have on-street resident parking areas, marked with black bands on telephone poles and lampposts; residents must buy a parking card from the town hall (proof of residence is required) and display it in their windscreen.

On-street Parking

On-street parking is forbidden in many streets in the centre of main cities. A sign saying '*estacionamiento prohibido*', sometimes accompanied by a sign with a blue background and a red line through it, means that parking is forbidden. Some no parking signs have a large 'E' (for *estacionamiento*) with a diagonal line through it (any sign with a diagonal line means something is prohibited). No parking may also be indicated by yellow, red or white kerb (curb) or road markings. A blue and white kerb stone indicates that you can stop briefly, but cannot park. No parking signs may have an arrow indicating that parking is illegal only to one side of the sign. If parking is illegal in both directions, a sign will have two arrows. A tow-away zone is usually shown by a sign of a hoist on the back of a truck and the words '*retirada grúa*'.

In many towns, private entrances and garage doors have a 'no parking' (*prohibido estacionar* or *vado permanente*) sign accompanied by a police permit number enforcing the parking restriction. Parking in front of this sign may entail a fine or make your car liable to being towed away or clamped.

In most Spanish cities, individual parking meters (*parquímetros*) have been replaced by ticket machines (*expendedor de tickets de estacionamiento*) sited every few dozen metres where parking is restricted. Such areas may be designated as 'blue zones' (*zonas azules*), indicated by blue street markings with blue ticket machines. Parking must usually be paid for from 9 or 9.30am until 2pm and from around 4 until 9pm, Mondays to Fridays, and from 9.30am until 2pm on Saturdays. The charge is from around €0.70 to €1.50 per hour, depending on the town (Barcelona has Spain's most expensive on-street parking). The maximum stay is usually two hours. Buy a ticket for the period required and place it behind your windscreen where it can be seen by a parking attendant.

If you exceed your time and are fined, you can often 'cancel' the fine by paying a penalty (*anulación aviso de sanción*) of around €3 (purchased in ticket form from a ticket machine) and either 'posting' it in a special slot in the ticket machine, displaying it in your car window or giving it to the parking attendant. This must, however, be done within a limited period; otherwise you must pay a fine of up to €40.

In some towns, an *ORA* or *OTA ZONA* system is operated (look out for '*ORA ZONA*' or '*OTA*' signs), whereby parking tickets for 30, 60 and 90 minutes, costing €0.30, €0.60 and €1 respectively, are sold at tobacconists' (*estancos*) and other shops. You punch holes in the ticket indicating the date and time you parked and display it in your car window.

Some towns operate a monthly card system (e.g. *multi-parking* in Malaga), costing around €15 per month. In others, residents qualify for discounted on-street parking in 'blue zones'. You need to register as a resident in the municipality and register your car with the local council. You're given a residents' parking card, which you must display in your windscreen. Cards are usually valid for a one- or three-month period and cost from €10 per month.

In some cities, you may encounter unofficial parking 'attendants' who will demand a fee to 'look after' your car. This may simply be a protection racket and, if you refuse to pay, they may damage your car. However, they usually only want around €1 and, although, there's no guarantee that your car will be safe, it may reduce the risk of having it broken into. Official parking attendants (*guardacoches*) are usually uniformed.

Car Parks

There are off-road car parks in cities and towns, although these are rarely adequate. Rates vary considerably and are usually from around €0.02 per minute or €0.05 for every two minutes. Some car parks also charge an entrance fee, e.g. €1. Spaces available in a multi-storey or underground car park (*aparcamiento subterráneo*) are indicated by a '*libre*' sign at the entrance, while '*completo*' indicates that it's full. If you park in a multi-storey car park, make a note of the level and space number where you leave your car (it can take a long time to find your car if you have no idea where to start looking!).

On entering most car parks, you take a ticket from an automatic dispenser, usually by pressing a button. You must usually pay **before** collecting your car, at a cash desk (*cajero*) or at a machine. You cannot usually pay at the exit. After paying, you usually have around 15 minutes to find your car and the exit, where you insert your ticket in the slot of the exit machine

in the direction shown by the arrow on the ticket. Many multi-storey car parks have video security.

SPANISH DRIVERS

A Spaniard's personality often changes the moment he (or she) gets behind the wheel of a car, when even normally tolerant and patient people turn into suicidal maniacs. Many Spaniards are frustrated racing drivers and they rush around at breakneck speed (totally out of character with their celebrated *mañana* attitude) in their haste to reach their destination (or the next life). To many male Spaniards, driving is like a bullfight and an opportunity to demonstrate their *machismo* to their wives and girlfriends – or any female who happens to be looking. Foreign-registered cars (especially those observing speed limits) are like red rags to a bull to some Spaniards, who **must** overtake them immediately, irrespective of their speed, the speed limit, road markings, weather conditions or oncoming traffic.

Among the many motoring 'idiosyncrasies' you will encounter in Spain are a total lack of lane discipline (lane markings are treated as optional guidelines), overtaking with reckless abandon on blind bends, failure to use mirrors or indicators (especially when exiting from a motorway or dual-carriageway), driving through red lights and the wrong way up one-way streets, and parking anywhere it's illegal. Many drivers routinely park too close to other cars and bang their doors up against them, damaging the paintwork. In Spain, nearly every car has a dent in it.

When driving in Spain, you should regard all drivers as totally unpredictable and drive defensively – although it should be noted that not all Spanish drivers are mad or incompetent. Some Spanish drivers are confused by roundabouts (as are many other Europeans) and they don't always give way to traffic already on roundabouts when entering them (previously traffic on a roundabout had to give way to traffic entering it). When driving at night, watch out for bicycles, motorcycles, donkeys, and horses and carts without lights. Motorists should also keep a wary eye out for pedestrians, particularly older people, who often walk across the road without looking.

Although they aren't among Europe's worst tailgaters, some Spanish drivers sit a few metres (or even centimetres) from your bumper trying to push you along irrespective of traffic density, road and weather conditions, or the speed limit. Always try to leave a large gap between your vehicle and the one in front. This isn't just to give you more time to stop should the vehicles in front decide to come together, but also to give the inevitable tailgater behind you more a chance of stopping before crashing into you.

The most civilised drivers (relatively speaking) are to be found in the north of Spain (e.g. Catalonia), where most people obey at least some of the rules and even stop at red lights. In contrast to most car drivers, Spanish truck drivers are generally competent and courteous, and most use their right indicators to tell you when it's safe to overtake and their left indicators to warn you that there's an oncoming vehicle. Motorists usually use their hazard warning lights when forced to slow rapidly and unexpectedly, e.g. for an accident or road works.

> ⚠ **Caution**
>
> Inexperienced drivers should take extra care, as the accident rate for foreigners is quite high, particularly in Spanish cities, where driving can be absolutely chaotic and is to be avoided if at all possible.

The Germans and the French have the most accidents, being speed-crazy like the Spanish (the sensible British drive more defensively).

TRAFFIC POLICE

In towns, the municipal police (*policía municipal*) are responsible for traffic control, while on Spain's highways the 'civil guard' (*guardia civil de tráfico*) undertake the task, patrolling in cars, motorcycles and helicopters. Motorcycle police usually patrol in pairs (*parejas*), at least one of whom is usually a trained mechanic and the other trained in first-aid; they will stop and help anyone in trouble. Always follow the instructions of traffic police and be prepared to stop. Police in towns blow whistles and wave their arms about a lot – if you don't know what they mean, follow the example of other motorists!

The police often set up check-points and stop motorists at random to ask for their identity and vehicle documents (and also to look for drugs or terrorists). You should always carry your passport or residence permit (*residencia*), driving licence (Spanish, if held), vehicle registration papers (*permiso de circulación*), tax receipt and insurance certificate, although copies are accepted. If a vehicle isn't registered in your name, you also need a letter of authorisation from the owner.

Fines

Police have stepped up their patrols in many areas and may impose fines (*multas*) for the slightest and most obscure infringements.

> Motoring offences are classified as 'minor' (*leve*), 'serious' (*grave*) and 'very serious' (*muy grave*). Minor offences carry fines of up to €90, serious offences (which can include not carrying your driving licence) fines of €91 to €300 with a possible three-month licence suspension, and very serious offences fines of up to €1,500 and an automatic three-month licence suspension.

Speeding fines depend on the degree to which you exceed the speed limit and usually range from €150 to €600; you can also lose your licence and up to six points. There's a 'leeway' of up to 10 per cent above the speed limit to allow for speedometer and radar errors. It's a very serious offence if you're 30 per cent over the limit, e.g. 80kph in a town or 150kph on a dual-carriageway. If you're caught by an unmanned radar, you will be sent a photograph of your number plate, which is deemed to be irrefutable evidence of speeding.

If you're fined, you receive a *boletín de denuncia* specifying the offence and the fine (check that it's the same as the amount demanded). On-the-spot fines of up to €300 can be imposed on non-residents for a range of traffic offences, including speeding, overtaking without indicating, travelling too close to the car in front, not being in possession of your car papers (although you're now permitted to carry a photocopy of your papers in your car) and not wearing a seat belt. If you're unable to pay a fine, your vehicle can be impounded or immobilised, although the police may escort you to a bank or hotel where you can obtain money or change foreign currency to euros. The police can also impound a foreign-registered car if they believe that it's used permanently in Spain (you must prove that you live abroad, which may be difficult).

Unless required to pay on the spot, you can pay a fine at any post office using a post office money order (*giro postal*), some banks (consult ⌨ www.dgt.es for details) or at the local traffic department. Always ensure that you receive a receipt for it.

Fines must be paid within 60 days, but for minor offences residents (and foreigners who pay on-the-spot) receive a 30 per cent discount if they pay within 30 days. The prompt payment discount doesn't apply to serious or very serious offences, although you can attend a training course in lieu of up to 30 per cent of the fine. Some communities offer young traffic offenders the option of doing community service rather than paying a fine, which means that parents no longer have the obligation to pay their children's traffic fines.

If over 60 working days elapse between an offence and your receiving official notification of it, the fine is invalid. If, however, notification of a fine is sent to you in Spain while you're abroad so that you don't see it until much later, your Spanish property can eventually be embargoed for non-payment. Your driving licence may also be suspended without your knowledge and your name listed in the provincial official bulletin (*boletín oficial*).

If a fine seems unreasonably high, you should question it or take legal advice. You can appeal against a fine and there are instructions in English on the back of the *boletín de denuncia* explaining how to do this. A written appeal (in any language) must be made within ten days of an (alleged) offence to the provincial traffic department in the province where the offence took place. The police decide whether to uphold your appeal – and there's no appeal against their decision, so unless you have a cast-iron case it's a waste of time and money. You need the assistance of a notary or a lawyer, which can incur costs of €500 or more. To add insult to injury, if you lose your appeal, you no longer qualify for the 30 per cent prompt payment discount!

In some provinces, the authorities seize cars when road taxes and traffic fines are unpaid. This seizure can be expensive for non-residents, who can have their vehicles towed away and stored (at their expense) for a number of months while they're abroad. Their names are also listed in official bulletins (*boletines oficiales*) displayed at town halls.

In addition to fines, you can lose licence points (see **Points System** on page 156).

MOTORCYCLES

Spain's excellent weather lends itself to motorcycling, and large touring motorcycles (*motocicletas* or *motos*) are increasingly common on Spain's roads. In recent years there has been a marked increase in the number of high-power motorcycles, often driven by inexperienced motorcyclists. The accident rate has risen sharply (27 per cent in 2007) and there are major government campaigns to try to reduce it.

Mopeds (*ciclomotores*), scooters and small motorcycles are a scourge in towns and cities, where their noise may drive you crazy (noise levels are restricted, but restrictions aren't often enforced).

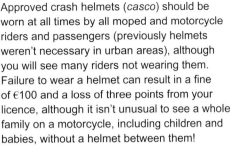

Approved crash helmets (*casco*) should be worn at all times by all moped and motorcycle riders and passengers (previously helmets weren't necessary in urban areas), although you will see many riders not wearing them. Failure to wear a helmet can result in a fine of €100 and a loss of three points from your licence, although it isn't unusual to see a whole family on a motorcycle, including children and babies, without a helmet between them!

Under Spanish law, children must be over seven years of age to ride on a motorcycle with a parent. If a child wishes to ride with an adult other than its parents, written authorisation must be given by the parents. Dipped headlamps must be used at all times by all motorcyclists except moped riders.

When parking a motorcycle in a city, lock it securely (if possible, chain it to an immovable object). Take extra care when parking in a public place overnight, particularly in major cities, where bike theft is rife.

Mopeds and motorcycles of all sizes can be hired (rented) throughout Spain. Note that rental insurance doesn't always include theft. You must usually leave your driving licence as security (it isn't advisable to leave your passport; if the bike breaks down or is stolen, you may have trouble getting it back).

Under 50cc

A 14-year-old can ride a moped (i.e. a motorbike with an engine capacity of up to 50cc). Riders aged under 16 must pass a simple examination on the rules of the road and obtain written parental consent. Riders of mopeds require a provincial licence costing €18.20 and a moped licence (*permiso de conducir de ciclomotores*), if they don't have a regular driving licence. Third-party insurance is also obligatory, but it's expensive (from around €350 per year) and difficult to obtain, as insurance companies have had to pay astronomical amounts in claims for moped accidents in recent years. On the other hand, no registration or road tax are required for mopeds.

Mopeds aren't permitted on motorways and riders must use cycle paths where provided. Nevertheless, many riders are killed each year. Car drivers often cannot see or avoid moped riders, particularly when they speed out of side streets without looking or ride at night without lights.

Over 50cc

A 16-year-old is permitted to ride a motorcycle with an engine capacity of up to 125cc, requiring an A1 licence. At 18, a motorcycle with an engine capacity above 125cc may be ridden, for which an A motorcycle licence (*licencia de conducción de ciclomotores*) is required. Both types of licence are valid for ten years if you're under 45 and for five years if you're between 45 and 70. Riders over 70 must renew their licence every two years.

Speed limits are the same for motorcycles as for cars (see page 166), and motorcycles above 75cc are permitted to use motorways (tolls are lower than for cars).

All motorcycles must be registered with the provincial traffic department. A motorcycle over 500cc must have a manufacturer's certificate, industry certificate, appraiser's certificate and town hall registration.

Motorcycles

must have their first technical inspection (*inspección técnica de vehículos/ITV*) after five years and thereafter annually.

Third-party insurance is obligatory for all bikes, costing around €350 a year.

DRINKING & DRIVING

In Spain, you're no longer considered fit to drive when your body contains more than 50mg of alcohol per 100ml of blood (30mg in the case of drivers with less than two years' experience and professional drivers). Alcohol is a major factor in a high percentage of Spain's road accidents (around a third of drivers in fatal accidents are over the alcohol limit), particularly those that occur at night. The amount you can drink and remain below the limit depends on how much you normally drink, your sex and your weight. A man weighing around 75kg can usually drink around two glasses of wine with a meal and remain below the limit. Your alcohol level rises considerably if you drink on an empty stomach (which is why the Spanish eat lots of bread!).

Breath tests (*alcohol-tests*) can be carried out by the police at any time (they're more widespread during the Christmas and New Year holiday period and in July and August), and motorists who are involved in accidents or who infringe motoring regulations are routinely given alcohol and drug tests.

Drunken driving can result in a fine of up to €1,500, loss of points from your licence, licence suspension or even imprisonment. Drivers who refuse to take a breath test are liable to a prison sentence of 6 to 12 months and a loss of six points. Note that the same penalties (with the exception of the loss of licence points) apply to cyclists!

If you have an accident while under the influence of alcohol, your car and health insurance could be nullified. This means that you must pay your own and any third party's car repairs, medical expenses and other damages, which could run to millions of euros.

CAR CRIME

All European countries have a problem with theft of and from cars, and Spain's is among the worst (particularly thefts from cars). National figures indicate that there's a theft from a car every three minutes in Spain as a whole and even more frequently in Barcelona, Madrid and Valencia. Foreign-registered vehicles, especially campervans and mobile homes, are popular targets. Some 75 per cent of stolen vehicles are taken from outside the owner's home and 10 per cent from garages, but fortunately 70 per cent of stolen vehicles are recovered.

If you drive anything other than a worthless heap, you should have theft insurance, covering your car stereo and belongings. If you drive a new or valuable car, it's wise to have it fitted with an alarm, an engine immobiliser (preferably of the rolling code variety with a transponder arming key) or other anti-theft device, and to also use a visible deterrent such as a steering or gear-stick lock. It's particularly important to protect your car if you own a model that's desirable to professional car thieves, e.g. most new sports and executive models (BMWs, Mercedes and large four-wheel drives are favourites), which are often stolen by crooks to order. In the south of Spain, stolen cars often find their way to Africa and may already be on a ferry by the time their owners report them stolen.

Few cars are fitted with deadlocks (Fords are a notable exception) and most can be broken into in seconds by a competent thief. A good security system won't necessarily prevent someone from breaking into your car or even stop it being stolen, but it makes it more difficult and may persuade a thief to look for an easier target.

Thieves often smash windows (in Spain, BMW stands for 'break my window') to steal stereo systems and other articles from cars – even articles of little worth such as sunglasses or cigarettes. When leaving your car unattended, store any valuables, including clothes, in the boot (trunk). Note, however, that if a car is empty, a thief may be tempted to force open the boot with a crowbar. It isn't advisable to leave your original car papers in your car, which will help a thief dispose of it. When parking overnight or after dark, you should use a secure car park or garage, or at least park in a well-lit area.

Thieves in Spain operate various scams, which include pretending that you have a flat tyre (they may even puncture your tyre in slow-moving or stationary traffic) or that fuel is leaking from beneath your car. While they're pretending to help fix the problem, they steal your belongings (women are popular targets). View any strangers offering to help you with suspicion.

⚠ **Caution**

Some criminals specialise in robbing motorists at motorway toll booths and there has also been an increasing incidence of highway 'piracy', where gangs deliberately bump or ram cars to force drivers to stop (usually late at night when there's little traffic about). **Be on your guard!**

If your car is stolen or anything is stolen from it, report it immediately to the police in the area where it was stolen. You can report it by telephone but must go to the station to complete a report (*denuncia*). Don't, however, expect the police to find it or even take any interest in your loss. Report a theft to your insurance company as soon as possible.

FUEL

Unleaded petrol (*sin plomo*) is available in normal (95 octane) and super (98 octane) grades. Diesel fuel (*gasóleo* or *mezcla*), including 'diesel plus', is available at all petrol stations (*gasolineras*). Leaded petrol (*super*) is no longer available. To prevent errors, petrol pumps and pipes are colour coded: green for unleaded and yellow or black for diesel. Note that there aren't many petrol stations in rural areas off the main highways, so it's advisable to keep your tank topped up when touring. You're permitted to carry a can containing ten litres of petrol.

There are four main fuel companies in Spain: BP, Campsa, Cepsa and Repsol. Prices are no longer fixed by the government and, where there are a number of petrol stations in a town, it's worth shopping around for the lowest price, although the days of cheap petrol are now long gone. Consumer surveys show the cheapest petrol is generally available in Barcelona, Lleida and Valencia. Prices per litre in July 2008 were around €1.25 for diesel, €1.32 for 'diesel plus', €1.22 for unleaded and €1.30 for 'unleaded plus'. Some regions levy a regional tax on vehicle fuel; for example, an extra €0.024 is charged on every litre in Cataluña.

> Information on petrol prices by province is available from ⌨ http://oficinavirtual.mityc.es/carburantes/index.aspx – click on the province and type of fuel.

Most petrol stations are open continuously from around 7am to around 10.30pm, except on *fiesta* days, when opening hours are severely curtailed. In large towns, local petrol stations operate a rota to ensure that at least one station is open 24 hours a day, and many service stations are open 24 hours on motorways and other main highways (although some close overnight).

Self-service (*autoservicio*) stations are now common, although there are still many manned petrol stations, particularly in towns. To have your tank filled at a manned station, say '*Lleno, por favor*'; to ask for '€10/€15/€20 worth' simply say '*deme diez/quince/veinte euros, por favor*'. When paying at self-service petrol stations, simply tell the cashier your pump number. To prevent robberies, some stations don't give change at night and you must fill up to exact cash amounts. In many, you must pay before you can fill up. However, most (but not all) stations accept credit cards such as MasterCard or Visa, and most major chains also provide their own credit cards.

Most petrol stations don't provide any services and it's unnecessary to tip unless an extra service is performed such as checking your oil or tyre pressures, when a tip of around €1 is sufficient. If you need oil (*aceite*) or water (*agua*), ask the attendant. On the other hand, many petrol stations provide services such as car washes, vacuum cleaners and air

(although machines are often out of order), and routine servicing and repairs are also carried out at some stations. Petrol stations usually have toilets or there's a bar/café or restaurant nearby, and many have a shop or vending machines for hot and cold drinks, beer, newspapers, confectionery, snacks and cigarettes.

BREAKDOWN INSURANCE

If you're going to be motoring abroad or you live abroad and are going to be driving in Spain, it's important to have motor breakdown insurance (*seguro de asistencia en carretera*), which may also include holiday and travel insurance, including repatriation for your family and your car in the event of an accident or breakdown.

Motor breakdown insurance covering Spain and other European countries is provided by car insurance companies (see page 154) and Spanish motoring organisations (see below). Insurance companies usually offer an optional accident and breakdown service (*asistencia en viaje*), which is adopted by some 75 per cent of Spanish motorists. The breakdown service normally covers the policy holder, his spouse, single dependent children, and parents and grandparents living under the same roof. The 24-hour telephone number of the breakdown service's head office is shown on a card, which should be kept in your vehicle.

If you have an accident or break down, you simply call the emergency number and give your location, and a recovery vehicle is sent to your aid. Although accidents are covered anywhere in Spain, in the event of a breakdown you must be a certain distance from your home, e.g. 15 or 25km (9 or 15mi). The insurance provides for transportation in the event of a breakdown or illness, although transportation to hospital (if necessary) and medical treatment are covered up to a limited amount, e.g. €350. An interest-free loan and an emergency message service is normally provided in the case of a robbery. The retrieval of your vehicle is also guaranteed from within Spain or abroad. If you're unable to find spare parts locally to repair damage, your insurance company will arrange to have them shipped to you (at your expense).

Most foreign breakdown companies provide 24-hour centres where multilingual staff provide help and advice on motoring, medical, legal and travel matters. Some organisations also provide economical annual motoring policies for those who frequently travel abroad, e.g. owners of holiday homes in Spain.

MOTORING ORGANISATIONS

There are a number of motoring organisations in Spain, although membership of these isn't as large as in many other European countries. There are two national motoring organisations: Real Automóvil Club de España (RACE, ☎ 902 404 545, 🖥 www.race.es), the larger and better known, and Real Automobil Club de Catalunya (RACC, ☎ 902 414 143, 🖥 www.racc.es).

Membership of RACE costs around €30 for registration plus an annual fee of around €120 in mainland Spain; fees are lower in the Balearics (€87) and Canaries (€76).

Membership includes a breakdown service, though to be covered a breakdown must happen at least 25km (15km in the Balearics and Canaries) from your home and there's a limit of three 'free' recoveries each year, after which a fee is charged. RACE transports your vehicle to a garage and makes alternative travel arrangements if you break down while on holiday. Assistance outside Spain is provided only within 60 days of leaving Spain. Other services include assistance in obtaining a driving licence, registration plates and vehicle importation; insurance and financial services; comparative running costs and reliability information for popular cars; tourism (hotel discounts), leisure and sports services; an information service and legal advice.

The RACC offers similar services and fees (registration is €25.60 and there's a €122 annual fee), and both organisations have agreements with foreign organisations such as the AA, AAA, ACI, ADAC, AvD, DTC, RAC and the TCI.

12.
HEALTH

The quality of healthcare and healthcare facilities in Spain is generally good – at their best they're the equal of any country in Europe – and the most recent World Health Organization survey into quality of healthcare ranked Spain seventh in the world (the UK was ranked 17th). Spanish medical staff are highly trained and major hospitals are equipped with the latest high-tech equipment. Healthcare spending per head is, however, below average for the European Union (EU): Spain spends just over 8 per cent of its gross domestic product (GDP) on health, although spending is expected to increase to 12 per cent by 2012. Hospital nursing care and post-hospital assistance are below what northern Europeans and North Americans take for granted, and spending on preventive medicine is low.

Public and private medicine operate alongside each other and complement one another, although public facilities are limited in some areas. An important contribution is also made by voluntary organisations such as the Red Cross (*Cruz Roja*), which is funded totally by voluntary contributions and membership subscriptions.

If you don't qualify for healthcare under the public health system (see **Entitlement** on page 181), it's essential to have private health insurance. You may not be able to get a residence permit without private health insurance. This is often advisable in any case if you can afford it, in order to circumvent the shortage of public health services and waiting lists in some areas. Visitors to Spain should have holiday health insurance (see page 206) if they aren't covered by a reciprocal agreement (see **Medical Treatment Abroad** on page 190).

HEALTH BENEFITS & RISKS

The Spanish are among the world's healthiest people and have an average life expectancy of nearly 84 for women and 77 for men, the highest in the EU. The incidence of heart disease in Spain is among the lowest in the world, a fact partly attributed to their diet (which includes lots of garlic, olive oil and red wine). They do, however, have a high incidence of liver problems and other complaints associated with excessive alcohol consumption. The low infant mortality rate of around 3.5 deaths per 1,000 births (2006 figures) is decreasing.

Nevertheless, for a country with one of the world's healthiest diets, Spain has a shocking obesity problem: over half of the adult population and over a quarter of children are overweight and of these a third are obese – the highest rate in the EU after Italy and Malta. Sedentary lifestyles and changes in diet from traditional balanced menus with plenty of fruit and vegetables in favour of fast food and high calorie snacks are the main causes. The government has introduced a nationwide campaign to improve diet and increase fitness.

Smoking

Smoking-related ailments and deaths are a serious problem; smoking is the leading cause of death among adults in Spain, directly causing some 56,000 deaths a year (Spain rates second highest after Greece in the number of smokers per capita in western Europe). New anti-smoking measures designed to reduce the incidence of smoking and effective from 1st January 2006, include a total ban on tobacco advertising, and no smoking in work places and most public areas. Smoking is banned in all areas that allow access to the under 18s. Legislation for bars and restaurants is different and whether they allow smoking depends on the owner.

Premises larger than 100m^2 may have up to 30 per cent of the space for smoking, but the area must be completely enclosed and with its own ventilation system. In premises under 100m^2 smoking is permitted only if a sign at the entrance clearly states that this is the case. As most customers of premises under 100m^2 smoke, the majority have (not surprisingly) opted to allow smoking; as a result, small bars and cafés are now smokier than ever! However, 2007 saw a record number of smokers attempting to give up and a fall in cigarette sales.

Risks

There are no exceptional health risks in Spain (apart from over-indulgence and falling sick in August, when all the doctors are on holiday) and no immunisations are required. You can safely drink the water, although it sometimes tastes terrible and many people prefer bottled water – when not drinking red wine.

Among expatriates, common health problems include sunburn and sunstroke, stomach and bowel problems (due to the change of diet and more often, water, but also poor hygiene), and various problems caused by excessive alcohol intake, including a high incidence of alcoholism. If you aren't used to Spain's fierce sun, you should limit your exposure and avoid it altogether during the hottest part of the day, wear protective clothing (including a hat) and use a sun block. It's also important to drink sufficient fluids, to replace lost salt and not to over-exert yourself. Too much sun and too little protection dries your skin and causes premature ageing, to say nothing of the risk of skin cancer. Care should also be taken to replace the natural oils lost from too many hours in the sun.

Some health problems are exacerbated by the high level of airborne pollen in spring in many areas, which affects asthma and hay fever sufferers, and noise and traffic pollution (particularly in Spain's major cities).

Climate & Lifestyle

The climate and lifestyle in any country has a marked effect on mental health. With the above provisos, Spain's climate (see page 310) is therapeutic, particularly for sufferers of rheumatism and arthritis, and those who are susceptible to bronchitis, colds and pneumonia. Spain's slow pace of life (outside the cities), including the traditional *siesta*, is also beneficial for those who are prone to stress (it's difficult to remain uptight while lying in a hammock), although it takes most expatriates some time to adjust. When you've had a surfeit of Spain's good life, a variety of health cures are available at spas and health 'farms'.

Retirees

The Costa Blanca and Costa del Sol have one of the highest percentages of retired people in the world, which puts a huge strain on local health services. Health (and health insurance – see page 201) is an important issue for anyone retiring to Spain. Many people are ill-prepared for old age and the possibility of health problems. There's a dearth of welfare and home-nursing services for the elderly in Spain, state or private, and many foreigners who are no longer able to care for themselves are forced to return to their home countries.

There are few state residential nursing homes and hospices (usually funded by private donations) for the terminally ill, although there are a number of private sheltered home developments, particularly in resort areas. There are occasional scandals over unauthorised private nursing homes where the residents live in dreadful and unhygienic conditions. Before you or a relative enters a private home, you should check its credentials carefully.

Spain's provision for disabled travellers is poor, and wheelchair access to buildings and public transport is well below the average for western Europe, although measures are improving.

EMERGENCIES

Keep a record of the telephone numbers of your doctor, local hospitals and clinics, ambulance (*ambulancia*) service, dentist and first aid, poison control and other emergency services (fire, police) next to your telephone.

The action to take in a medical emergency (*urgencias*) depends on the urgency of the treatment required. In a life-threatening emergency such as a heart attack or a serious accident, you should call for an ambulance (see below) and mention the nature of the emergency. The emergency medical services in Spain are excellent.

If the 'emergency' isn't life-threatening and you're physically capable, you can go to a hospital emergency or casualty department (*urgencia*) or a 24-hour public health clinic (*ambulatorio* or *casa de socorro*). Check in advance which local hospitals are equipped to deal with emergencies and the quickest route from your home. This information may be of vital importance in the event of an emergency, when a delay may mean the difference between life and death. In an emergency, a hospital must treat you, irrespective of your ability to pay (although you may be billed afterwards). Most chemists post a list of local clinics and hospitals where emergency medical treatment is available. Note that if you're initially treated at a state medical centre (*centro de salud*) or outpatient clinic (*ambulatorio*), you will usually be referred to a public hospital for treatment (which you may not want if you have private health insurance).

If you're unable to go to casualty or visit your doctor's surgery, your doctor will visit you at home (in Spain, doctors will make house calls at any time of the day or night).

If you need a doctor or some medicine in a non-urgent situation and are unable to contact your doctor, ring the telephone information service (☎ 11818) or your local police station, either of whom will give you the telephone number of a doctor on call or the address of a chemist's (*farmacia*) that's open.

Ambulances

There's no public ambulance service, but private ambulance operators provide a 24-hour service in most towns (listed by town under *Ambulancias* in yellow pages), and most clinics and private hospitals operate their own ambulance services. Ambulance drivers and staff aren't generally highly trained, as paramedics aren't recognised in Spain.

Social security patients don't pay for ambulance services and private patients (who have a private health insurance policy) are usually reimbursed. If you must pay, the cost depends on the type of ambulance required (intensive care ambulances are more expensive) and the distance travelled. Standard ambulances cost from around €90, fully equipped intensive care ambulances from around €120, for a journey of 25 to 30km (15 to 19mi). If your doctor travels with you, the charge is increased by between €35 and €100.

In an emergency, an ambulance will take a patient to the nearest hospital equipped to deal with the particular emergency.

There are various ways of summoning an ambulance, including the following:

♦ Ring the emergency services (*Servicios de Urgencias*) directly on ☎ 112 from anywhere in Spain or, in some cities, using the local three-digit emergency number.

♦ Call the operator (☎ 11818), who will put you through to the emergency services.

♦ Call your local police station, who will tell you who to contact or contact the appropriate service for you.

♦ Call your local social security clinic (*ambulatorio, clínica de salud*) or the Red Cross. (You can become a member of your local Red Cross centre for around €20 a year.)

♦ In resort areas, contact a 24-hour private medical centre (*centro médico*) with ambulance services.

♦ Call a first-aid station (the telephone numbers of first-aid stations are listed at the front of telephone directories), many of which are equipped with ambulances.

Keep all the above numbers next to your telephone. See also **Emergency Numbers** on page 95.

Whoever you call, give the age of the patient and if possible specify the type of emergency, so that the ambulance can bring a doctor if necessary. Some useful words are accident (*accidente*), serious illness (*enfermedad grave*), heart attack (*ataque cardiaco*), ambulance (*ambulancia*) and doctor (*médico*).

Taxis must, by law, transport medical emergencies to hospital when requested to do so. A private car can claim priority when transporting a medical emergency by switching on its hazard warning lights and displaying a piece of white material from a window.

Public Health Service

Spain's public health system provides free or low cost healthcare to those contributing to Spanish social security (see page 195), plus their families, and retirees. The public health service has improved greatly in recent decades. Waiting lists to see specialists and for non-urgent operations have been drastically reduced in most areas, although waiting lists for surgery are still long in many regions – exact statistics are difficult to obtain because each region has its own way of calculating what a waiting list is! Patients can choose any specialist or surgeon in Spain.

In common with many developed countries, the financing of the public health system in Spain is a growing problem – all regions' health services have huge debts (those in Catalonia, Madrid, Murcia and Valencia are particularly high). One of the main contributing factors is that little financial provision has been made for the large recent increases in population (the Balearics' population has grown by 30 per cent in the last ten years). Regions also overspend hugely on prescriptions – a third of Catalonia's health budget goes on doctors' prescriptions (see **Prescriptions & Payment** on page 184). Regions have received vast injections of state funds to help relieve their healthcare debt.

Regions are permitted to increase taxes on petrol to pay for healthcare and six regions (Asturias, Castilla La Mancha, Catalonia, the Comunidad Valenciana, Galicia and Madrid) apply up to 2.4 cents per litre tax. This tax, known as the *céntimo sanitario*, is currently being contested by the EU as illegal.

Spanish health services traditionally placed the emphasis on cure rather than prevention and treated sickness rather than promoted good health, although they've now implemented a comprehensive preventive medicine programme, including regular health checks and an immunisation programme for children. The public health service provides limited resources for outpatient treatment, nursing and post-operative care, geriatric assistance, terminal illnesses and psychiatric treatment, although these are improving.

Perfunctory treatment due to staff shortages, long waiting lists and a general dehumanisation of patients are among the complaints made against Spain's public health system. Many problems are related to crippling bureaucracy, bad management and general disorganisation. However, attempts at reform have had some success, including a huge reduction in waiting times and there are several public hospitals in Spain run as successful profit-making enterprises. Eventually, the health service intends to make all hospitals and general practices self-administering.

Public health benefits include general and specialist medical care, hospitalisation, laboratory services, discounted drugs and medicines, basic dental care, maternity care, appliances and transportation. General and specialist medical treatment is totally free, but you must also pay a percentage of the cost of certain items, including medicines, although these are free to pensioners.

For more information about the public health service and social security, contact the Instituto Nacional de la Seguridad Social (INSS), Servicios Centrales, Padre Damián, 4, 28036 Madrid (☎ 900 166 565, ✉ www.seg-social.es).

Entitlement

If you make Spanish social security (*seguridad social*) contributions, you and your family are entitled to free or subsidised medical and dental treatment on the same terms as Spaniards. Over 90 per cent of the population, including retired EU residents (with a residence permit) in receipt of a state pension, are covered by Spain's public health scheme, which is administered by the regional health authorities.

If you're an EU national of retirement age who **isn't** in receipt of a pension, you may be entitled to public health benefits if you can show that you cannot afford private health insurance. Anyone who has made regular social security contributions in another EU country for two full years before coming to Spain is entitled to public health cover for a limited period from the date of their last social security contribution in their home country. Social security form E-106 must be obtained from the social security authorities in your home country and be presented to the local provincial office of the Instituto Nacional de la Seguridad Social (INSS) in Spain. Legislation in 2000 ruled that illegal immigrants in Spain and their dependants are also entitled to free healthcare.

Similarly, pensioners and those in receipt of invalidity benefits must obtain form E-121 from their home country's social security administration.

If you're receiving an invalidity pension or other social security benefits on the grounds of ill-health, you should establish exactly how living in Spain will affect those benefits. In some countries, there are reciprocal rights regarding invalidity rights, but you must confirm that they apply in your case.

If you're entitled to public healthcare, you're given an electronic card (*tarjeta*), a list of local medical practitioners and hospitals, and general information about services and charges.

If you aren't entitled to public health benefits through payment of Spanish social security or being in receipt of a pension from another EU country, you must usually have private health insurance and must present proof of your insurance when applying for a residence permit.

DOCTORS

When you receive your social security card, you're offered a choice of general doctors (*médicos de cabecera*) in the area where you live. There are excellent doctors throughout

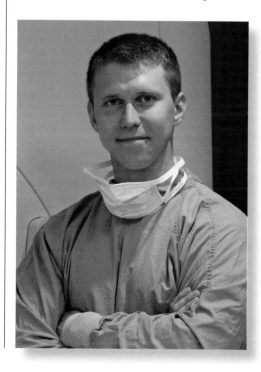

Spain, although finding a doctor who speaks English can be difficult, particularly in rural areas. There are a number of English-speaking Spanish and foreign doctors practising in Spain, including American, British, German and Scandinavian doctors, though mostly in the major cities and resort areas.

Many embassies and consulates in Spain maintain a list of English-speaking doctors and specialists in their area and your employer, colleagues, friends or neighbours may be able to recommend someone. Tourist offices may also keep a list of English-speaking doctors and the names and telephone numbers of English-speaking doctors and dentists are often listed in local English-language newspapers and magazines. If you need the services of a medical auxiliary such as a nurse, physiotherapist or chiropodist, you must usually obtain a referral or prescription from a doctor.

Doctors are permitted to advertise their services and a number advertise in the expatriate press. General practitioners (GPs) or family doctors are listed in yellow pages under *Médicos* and specialists under their speciality, such as obstetricians and gynaecologists (*Médicos Obstetricia y Ginecología*) and heart specialists (*Médicos Cardiología*).

The ratio of doctors to inhabitants in Spain (4.4 per 1,000) is higher than in all other EU countries except Italy, although it varies considerably from town to town and region to region. In most major cities and resort areas, there are more than enough doctors, although in rural areas and some urbanisations surrounding the major cities there's sometimes a shortage of doctors and those who practise there are often over-worked and can spare patients little time (some public health doctors see as many as 40 patients per hour!). This may also apply to some doctors working for Spanish insurance companies, although fees have increased in recent years and doctors are now able to spend more time with patients. Always try to choose a doctor who allocates you sufficient time and who will explain his diagnosis and recommended course of treatment.

Note that if you don't speak Spanish, you should take a translator with you when you visit a Spanish doctor. There have been reports of doctors refusing to treat non-Spanish-speaking patients without an interpreter, though some public health centres in resort areas provide a volunteer interpreter service for foreigners.

☑ SURVIVAL TIP

If you take regular medication, are undergoing a course of treatment, or suffer from a long-term illness or disability, you should ask your present (i.e. overseas) doctor to provide a short statement regarding your medical history and have it translated into Spanish before arriving in Spain.

If you have private health insurance, you can choose to see any doctor at any time and aren't required to register with a doctor or visit a doctor within a certain distance of your home. This also makes it easy to obtain a second opinion, should you wish to do so. Health insurance companies also usually insist on a referral from a family doctor (GP), but if you have a 'free choice' policy you can select your own specialist or other practitioner.

Certain tests requested by a doctor, including ECGs, scans, X-rays, and blood and urine analyses, may be conducted on the premises – especially at a health centre or clinic (public or private). Alternatively, you may be given a form to take to a local hospital or clinic (where you may be given your X-ray images to return to your doctor). Free flu (*gripe*) vaccinations are given each autumn at clinics and medical centres to 'high-risk' groups such as the elderly and young children.

Alternative medical practitioners aren't as common in Spain as they are in some other European countries or North America, although there are a number of expatriates practising in the major cities and resort areas (many advertise in English-language publications). Before choosing an alternative practitioner, you should check whether he is state registered.

Payment

No payment is made by those with a social security card when visiting a public health service doctor and once you've registered with a doctor, you aren't required to produce your card.

For private patients, it's normal practice to pay a doctor (preferably in cash) or other medical practitioner after each visit, although some charge you only after treatment is completed. A routine visit to a doctor's surgery usually costs from €50, a home daytime call from €70 and a home night time call from €80. A consultation with a specialist costs between €50 and €100. If applicable, obtain a receipt for your insurance company.

Hours & Appointments

Surgery hours vary considerably between public health and private doctors and from day to day, e.g. private doctors' surgery hours may be from 9am to 2pm and from 5 until 7pm Mondays to Fridays, while public health doctors in health centres (*centro de salud* or *ambulatorio*) often work from 8am until 6pm without a break.

It's usually necessary to make an appointment (*cita previa*) by phone or in person (in most regions you can book online), although some health centres operate a first-come, first-served system, where patients are given a number and wait until it's called. Appointments with public health doctors can usually be made within 24 or 72 hours, although in some towns it can take a week or more to get an appointment. If your doctor is unavailable, his surgery will give you the name of a standby doctor or you can visit an emergency clinic (*clínica de urgencia*).

Most public health clinics operate a 24-hour service and there are also 24-hour private medical centres (*centros médicos*) in resort areas. If you're unable to attend a surgery, doctors will make house calls, although if you live in a rural area you may have trouble getting a doctor to call on you unless you're an urgent case. If you rely on the public health service, try not to get ill in August, when many doctors and specialists take a month's holiday! This is a serious point, as a number of medical 'disasters' occur in August when doctors are away. See also **Emergencies** on page 179 and **Emergency Numbers** on page 95.

Childcare

There are excellent ante-natal facilities in Spain and arrangements for regular check-ups are made through your family doctor, who then refers you to an ante-natal (or post-natal) organisation or clinic. Children in Spain are

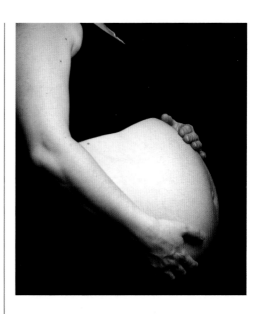

issued with a green vaccination book (*carnet de vacunaciones*), which must be presented when starting school. Once your child is registered at a health centre, you're advised by phone or letter when his vaccinations are due.

MEDICINES

Medicines (*medicamentos* or *medicinas*) prescribed by a doctor are obtained from a chemist's (*farmacia*) denoted by the sign of a green cross. A pharmacist in Spain must own and run his own chemist's (chain chemists are illegal) and their numbers are strictly controlled, although the market is due to be liberalised in the near future.

Pharmacists in Spain are highly trained and provide free medical advice for minor ailments, although you must usually speak Spanish. They're often able to sell you the proper remedy without recourse to a doctor and will also recommend a local doctor, specialist, nurse or dentist where necessary. They can supply a wide range of medicines over the counter without a prescription, though some medicines sold freely in other countries require a prescription in Spain. Homeopathic and herbal medicines are stocked by most chemists', some of which specialise in homeopathy.

Spanish chemists' aren't cluttered with all the non-medical wares found in American and British chemists', although they also sell non-prescription medicines, baby food and essentials, cosmetics, diet foods and toiletries. Chemists' are cheaper than a *perfumería* for cosmetics, but more expensive than a supermarket or hypermarket. Another type of shop is a *droguería*, which sells non-medical items such as toiletries, cosmetics and household cleaning items, but not non-prescription medicines. A *droguería* shouldn't be confused with an American drugstore. A health food shop (*herboristería*) sells health foods, diet foods and eternal-life-virility-youth pills and elixirs.

Hours

Legislation permits unlimited opening hours for chemists'. Most are open from 9.30am to 1.30pm and from 4.30 to 8pm from Mondays to Saturdays. Outside normal opening hours, a notice is posted giving the address of the nearest duty chemist's (*farmacia de guardia*) open after 8pm (a weekly roster may be displayed). There are 24-hour duty chemists' in all towns (usually indicated by a red light), and there may also be chemists' on duty only during the day (e.g. from 9.30am until 10pm) or at night (e.g. from 10pm until 9.30am). In addition to being displayed in chemists' windows, a list of duty chemists is published in local newspapers, and in some towns an annual schedule and map is published (available from tourist offices).

When visiting a chemist's outside normal hours, you must usually ring a bell, speak to the pharmacist (*farmacéutico*), who may be behind a bullet-proof glass door, and be served through a small hatch (this is particularly common in cities, where crime is rife). In some areas, you may even be required to take a policeman with you. A duty chemist's only fills prescriptions (*recetas*) and there may be a surcharge.

Prescriptions & Payment

If you have a social security card, you must pay 40 per cent of the cost of most prescribed medicines (drugs) unless you're a pensioner or disabled, in which case they're free. Many private health insurance schemes also reimburse members fully for medicines. However, there's no refund for some prescribed

medicines or for medicines purchased without a doctor's prescription. In order to reduce the public health prescription bill of nearly €9.5bn a year, the public health service has removed almost 1,000 treatments previously available on social security prescriptions. However, public spending on prescriptions increases annually and further measures such as the introduction of more generic medicines and individual doses are planned in order to reduce Spain's huge pharmaceutical bill.

Prescription medicines in Spain are among the cheapest in the EU. However, chemists have a monopoly on non-prescription medicines (such as painkillers, cough medicine and eye drops), which can be purchased cheaply in supermarkets in other EU countries; for example, 20 paracetamol tablets cost around €1.50. It's therefore a good idea to buy non-prescription medication abroad and stock up before arriving in Spain.

Brand names for the same medicines vary from country to country, so you should ask your doctor for the generic name of any medication you take regularly. If you wish to match medication prescribed abroad, you need a current prescription with the medication's trade name, the manufacturer's name, the chemical name and the dosage. Most foreign medicines have an equivalent in Spain, although particular brands may be difficult or impossible to obtain.

It's possible to have medication sent from abroad free of duty and value added tax (VAT/ *IVA*). If you're visiting Spain for a limited period, you should take sufficient medication to cover the length of your stay. In an emergency, a local doctor will write a prescription that can be filled at a local chemist's or a hospital may fill a prescription from its own pharmacy.

HOSPITALS & CLINICS

All Spanish cities and large towns have at least one hospital (*hospital*) or clinic (*clínica*), many of which are modern establishments with highly trained staff and state of the art, high-tech equipment (most resort areas have a selection of good hospitals and clinics). However, in some areas (particularly poor rural areas) hospitals may not be up to the standard you might expect. There are long waiting lists for beds in some public hospitals (particularly the best ones), although this problem has been alleviated in recent years. Generally, large towns and resort areas have the best hospital facilities.

Hospitals are listed in yellow pages under *Hospitales* and indicated by the international hospital sign of a white 'H' on a blue background. A list of local hospitals and health centres treating social security patients is available from your local social security office.

Types of Hospital

There are many different categories of hospital and clinic in Spain. The principal categorisation is between public hospitals (*hospitales de la seguridad social*) and private hospitals (*hospitales privados*). Then there are general hospitals (*hospitales generales*), district hospitals (*hospitales distritos*), regional hospitals (*hospitales comarcales*), provincial hospitals (*hospitales provinciales*), local hospitals (*hospitales comarcales/locales*), military hospitals (*hospitales militares*), nursing homes (*clínicas de reposo*), private clinics (*clínicas privadas*) and emergency clinics (*clínicas de urgencias*), plus day hospitals performing specialist tests and minor surgery.

Some public hospitals are run by the Red Cross and funded by private donations, although some towns also contribute from public funds, and there are foreign-run private hospitals and clinics in major cities and resort areas.

Not all hospitals have an emergency department (*departamento de urgencias*), and public hospitals with emergency departments are often swamped by patients. Major hospitals have an outpatients department (*consultas externas/departamento de enfermo externo del hospital*) and an emergency clinic. Red Cross posts throughout the country (staffed by volunteers) deal with minor accidents.

Most private hospitals and clinics specialise in inpatient care in particular fields of medicine such as obstetrics and surgery, rather than being full-service hospitals. A number of private clinics advertise in the expatriate press. Many Spaniards and foreign residents have private health insurance (see page 201) and some 40 per cent of Spanish hospitals treat only private patients, including hospitals owned by Spanish health insurance companies, which treat only patients covered by their policies.

Language

In public hospitals in resort areas, up to 40 per cent of patients may be foreigners, many of whom are retirees who don't speak Spanish. Although the reception staff and telephonists at Spanish hospitals in resort areas and major cities often speak English (and other languages), medical staff may speak only Spanish. In hospitals with many foreign patients, local expatriates may organise a team of volunteer interpreters (speaking a number of languages) for patients who are unable to speak Spanish.

Note, however, that if you don't speak Spanish you may be given no information regarding the television (TV), phone, library, interpreting service, meal times and visiting hours, and will be very unlikely to receive any information in English or another foreign language. If your Spanish is poor, you may prefer to be treated at a private hospital or clinic with English-speaking staff.

Facilities

Some public hospitals publish a guide (*guía del usario*) containing a hospital plan, public transport and road connections, department phone numbers, details of services such as cafeteria opening hours, visiting hours and other information. Public hospitals may have a library with books in a number of languages (including English) and may provide a mobile library for bedridden patients.

The facilities provided in public hospitals are often limited compared with private hospitals and there may be no private rooms. If you wish to have a private room, you must pay a supplement, which may be paid by private health insurance (see page 201). You can usually rent a radio, TV or telephone for a small daily fee (if not already included in the room fee) and must usually provide your own pyjamas, robes, towels and toiletries. Public hospitals often have a pay TV and a pay-phone operated by a special key.

If you need crutches or other appliances you may need to obtain them yourself, although a public hospital may provide them.

Procedure

Except for emergency treatment, you're admitted or referred to a hospital or clinic for treatment only after a referral by a doctor or a specialist. If you're a social security patient, you're given a choice of specialists and hospitals offering the treatment you require, usually in your own province. If you wish to be treated in hospital by your personal doctor or specialist, you must check that he is able to treat you at your preferred hospital.

Hospital accommodation in public hospitals is usually basic (in rooms with two to four beds) and can be very noisy with visitors chattering and the TV blaring. Food is variable and at its worst is terrible.

> ### ⚠ Caution
>
> You may find nursing staff cold and impersonal, particularly compared with those in hospitals in northern Europe and North America.

If you have an appointment for treatment or surgery in a public hospital you may have to wait long past your appointment time before you're eventually allocated a bed. Note also that in a hospital with an accident and emergency department, a non-urgent operation may be cancelled a number of times while priority is given to emergency cases. If you need to attend a public hospital outpatient department, bear in mind that it's likely to be totally chaotic. Take a long book (and earplugs) and be prepared to wait a number of hours, even if you have an appointment.

Patients are expected to convalesce at home, not in a hospital, and they're often discharged earlier than would be the case in many other countries. In many areas, back-up and nursing care is provided by the local community or expatriate groups. You can sometimes leave hospital at any time without a doctor's consent by signing a release form, although a doctor's consent is usually required.

Despite the criticisms outlined above, most foreigners are satisfied with their treatment in Spanish hospitals, and expatriate newspapers regularly publish letters from former patients praising their treatment. Many people also report that the difference between the standard of accommodation and treatment varies little between the best public and private hospitals and clinics.

Cost & Payment

The cost of a bed in a private hospital averages around €150 a day in Spain, less than in northern Europe, although specialists' fees may be higher, resulting in comparable overall costs – around €350 a day.

Except in the case of emergencies, you must present your social security card or, if you aren't covered by social security, evidence of your health insurance or the ability to pay (e.g. a briefcase full of euros). If your private insurance company doesn't have an arrangement with a Spanish hospital to pay bills direct, you must pay the bill yourself (credit cards are usually accepted) or seek assurance from your insurance company that they will pay the bill.

DENTISTS

There are excellent dentists (*dentistas*) throughout Spain, although finding a dentist who speaks good English can be a problem, particularly in rural areas (although *Aaargh*! is the same in any language). However, there are many English-speaking foreign and Spanish dentists practising in Spain (particularly in major cities and resort areas), including American, British, German and Scandinavian dentists (although their fees may be higher than those of Spanish dentists). Many embassies and consulates in Spain maintain a list of English-speaking dentists in their area (or dentists speaking their national language) and your employer, colleagues, friends or neighbours may be able to recommend someone. Many tourist offices also maintain a list of English-speaking dentists, and dentists may be listed in local English-language newspapers and magazines.

Dentists are permitted to advertise their services and a number advertise in the expatriate press and are listed in yellow pages under *Dentistas Odontólogos*. Usually, only names, addresses and telephone numbers are listed, and information such as specialities, surgery hours and whether they treat children (some don't) isn't provided. Many 'family' dentists in Spain are qualified to perform treatment, such as endodontics (*endodoncia*) or periodontics (*periodoncia*), which is carried out by specialists in many countries.

Hours

Dentists' surgery hours vary considerably but are typically 9.30 or 10am to 2pm and 5 to 8pm. Some dentists have Saturday morning surgeries, e.g. 9.00am to noon. You must make an appointment. Many dentists provide an emergency out-of-hours service and there are emergency dental services in major cities and resort areas.

Costs & Payment

The cost of dental treatment varies wildly, but as a rough guide you can expect to pay from €40 for an extraction and €40 to €100 for a filling. Before committing yourself to a bill for expensive treatment, it's advisable to obtain a written quotation; if you don't, the final bill may be much higher than 'estimated' (an oral estimate is often much lower than the final bill, even for a simple filling). If you or your family require expensive cosmetic dental treatment, e.g. crowns, bridges, braces or dentures, you may find it cheaper to have treatment abroad. Alternatively, you can ask your dentist if he can reduce the cost by reducing the work involved. See also **Dental Insurance** on page 204.

Dentists expect to be paid in cash or by credit card when treatment is completed, although if you're having expensive treatment such as a crown or a bridge, your dentist may ask for a deposit (e.g. 50 per cent of the cost) in advance. Some dentists operate a membership scheme (e.g. €120 a year) which may include two check-ups, consultations, and a scale and polish. Always obtain an itemised bill if you intend to claim on your health insurance.

Note that only extractions and emergency treatment after an accident are available free under the Spanish public health service (treatment may be performed in a public health clinic or a public hospital), but you must first visit your doctor.

OPTICIANS

As with other medical practitioners in Spain, it isn't necessary to register with an optician or optometrist (*óptico*); simply make an appointment with the optician of your choice. Ask your colleagues, friends or neighbours if they can recommend someone. Opticians are listed in the yellow pages under *Óptica* and ophthalmologists (specialist eye doctors) under *Médicos Oftalmología*.

Eye tests and prescriptions for spectacles are available free under the public health system, and low-income families and pensioners also receive free (basic) spectacles. Public health eye tests are generally performed at a public hospital and patients need a referral from their family doctor. However, many opticians also perform free eye tests.

The optical business is highly competitive in Spain. Prices for spectacles (*lentes*) and contact lenses (*lentillas de contacto*) aren't controlled, so it's wise to shop around and compare costs. You may find that special spectacle lenses and contact lenses are more expensive in Spain than in some other European countries. Always obtain an estimate for lenses and ask about charges for such things as eye tests, fittings, adjustments, lens-care kits and follow-up visits. Note that the cost of tinted and special lenses (e.g. high index) increases the cost of spectacles considerably. Ask about the cost of replacement lenses – if they're expensive it may be worthwhile taking out insurance.

Many opticians and retailers offer insurance against the accidental damage of spectacles for a nominal fee or even free for a limited period. Disposable and extended-wear soft contact lenses are also widely available, although medical experts believe that extended-wear lenses should be treated with caution, as they greatly increase the risk of potentially blinding eye infections. Obtain advice from an ophthalmologist before buying them.

It's advisable to have your eyes tested before arriving in Spain and to bring a spare pair of spectacles and/or contact lenses with you. You should also bring a copy of your prescription in case you need to obtain replacement spectacles or contact lenses urgently.

Many people find it essential to wear sunglasses all year round in Spain. Always buy a good pair that protects your eyes from the sun's harmful ultra-violet rays.

BIRTHS & DEATHS

Births and deaths must be registered at the Civil Registry (*Registro Civil*) at the town hall of the district where they take place. Registration applies to everyone irrespective of their nationality and whether they're residents of Spain or just visitors.

Births

Registration of a birth must be made within eight days at the local civil registry and may be done by the hospital or clinic where the child was born, or by the midwife when a birth takes place at home. Parents are, however, responsible for ensuring that this is done and may have to do it themselves. There are two forms of birth certificate: a full certificate (*certificado literal de nacimiento*) and a short certificate (*extracto de inscripción de nacimiento* or *certificado simple*), showing only the date of birth, the names of the child and parents, and the inscription number. Foreigners should get the full one, which costs only a little more (both are inexpensive). It may also be necessary to register your child at your home country's consulate or embassy in Spain (to obtain a birth certificate and passport from your home country).

A birth certificate must state whether a child is legitimate or illegitimate – a **legitimate** child is one born at least 180 days after its parents' marriage or within 300 days of a divorce, annulment of a marriage or the death of the father. (Note that in cases where paternity is contested, the suspected or claimed father of a child can be compelled to undergo a biological test, at a cost of €275 to €500.)

Abortion is legal in Spain, but it remains a contentious issue, and is fervently opposed by the Catholic Church and right-wing circles. It's currently available during the first 12 weeks of pregnancy in certain circumstances, e.g. when a pregnancy threatens the mother's life, the foetus is severely deformed or the pregnancy was the result of rape, but the current government intends to make abortion legal within the first 14 weeks of pregnancy whatever the circumstances may be.

Deaths

A death must be registered within 24 hours at the town hall of the district where it took place. If the deceased was a foreigner, the town hall needs his passport or residence permit (*residencia*) and the death must also be registered at the deceased's local consulate or embassy in Spain. A death needn't be reported to the police unless it resulted from an accident or crime (or occurred in suspicious circumstances). A death certificate must be prepared and signed by the doctor who attended the death (in a hospital or elsewhere) and be legally certified by a judge. In the case of a foreigner, it must be presented to the deceased person's embassy or consulate in Spain to obtain a certificate valid in the deceased's home country. The certificates are required for insurance claims and to execute a will.

A body can be buried or cremated in Spain or flown to another country for burial. It's expensive (e.g. €900 to €1,800 within Europe) to fly a body to another country for burial, although the cost may be covered by an international insurance policy which includes repatriation.

A body cannot be interred or cremated sooner than 24 hours after death. However, burial or cremation usually takes place within 48 hours of death and where there's no refrigeration it **must** take place within 72 hours. Refrigeration is, however, available in most areas and costs around €35 a day.

Although cemeteries in Spain are mostly Catholic, a person of any creed can be buried there. There are also foreign cemeteries in some cities and towns, e.g. there's a British cemetery in Malaga and an international cemetery in Benalmádena (Costa del Sol). Burials and cremations can be made only in official cemeteries. In most Spanish cemeteries, 'interment' is above ground and bodies are placed in niches set into walls, which are rented for a number of years, e.g. 5 to 50 (the rent is from €30 a year). The cheapest 'graves' are in municipal cemeteries, where typical rentals are around €300 for five years, then €30 per year up to 50 years.

After the rental period has expired, bodies are intered in a common burial ground within the consecrated cemetery grounds. After a number of years (e.g. 25), all graves are exhumed in some areas and the remains buried in a large communal tomb, although this occurs mostly on the islands where land is at a premium. **To avoid this you must buy a plot outright, which can cost €3,000 or more.** Note that cemeteries often have limited opening hours and aren't open to the public at all hours, as they are in most countries.

When a resident of Spain dies, all interested parties must be notified (see **Inheritance & Gift Tax** and **Wills** on pages 239 and 242). You need several copies of the death certificate, which are required by banks and other institutions.

Cost

Dying is an expensive business in Spain, where a burial must be arranged through an undertaker (*funeraria*), who takes care of everything, including death certificates. It may be necessary to engage a local funeral company, but undertakers' fees are roughly the same in most areas. Always check the cost of a funeral in advance and make sure that you aren't paying for anything you don't want. The cost of a full-service funeral is between around €1,200 to €2,500, depending on your choice of coffin, etc.; this includes five years' rent on a cemetery niche (*nicho*) but there may be extra costs for transportation and other services.

Always check exactly what's included and excluded. Embalming isn't common in Spain and is expensive, e.g. €1,200. The cost of cremation is from €300, although there aren't many crematoriums in Spain. A service may be held before a cremation (with the body present) or after it (with the urn containing the deceased's ashes). Most undertakers expect to be paid in cash. It's possible to take out an insurance policy (*seguro de decesos*) for funeral expenses with a Spanish or foreign insurance company, although it's very expensive.

MEDICAL TREATMENT ABROAD

If you're entitled to public health benefits in Spain or another EU country, you can take advantage of reciprocal healthcare agreements in most other European countries. Everyone insured under Spanish social security is covered for medical expenses while travelling abroad, provided certain steps are taken to ensure reimbursement. In some cases, you must obtain a European Health Insurance Card (EHIC/*tarjeta sanitaria europea* – see below) from your local social security office before leaving Spain. **This also applies to foreign residents of Spain planning to visit their home EU country.**

Full payment (possibly in cash) must usually be made in advance for treatment received abroad, although you will be reimbursed on your return to Spain. Note, however, that in the UK everyone receives free emergency treatment. You're also reimbursed for essential treatment in some other countries, although you must obtain detailed receipts.

Note that reimbursement is based on the cost of comparable treatment in Spain. In certain countries, e.g. Canada, Japan, Switzerland and the US, medical treatment is very expensive and you're advised to take out travel or holiday insurance when visiting these countries. **This is advisable wherever you're travelling, as it provides considerably wider medical cover than reciprocal healthcare agreements (and includes many other benefits, such as repatriation).** If you do a lot of travelling abroad, it's worthwhile having an international health insurance policy (see page 206).

Visitors to Spain

If you're an EU resident visiting Spain, you can take advantage of reciprocal healthcare agreements (see above). Some non-EU countries also have reciprocal agreements with Spain. EU residents should apply for a European Health Insurance Card/EHIC (previously an E-111) from their local social security office at least three weeks before travelling to Spain. The EHIC is available from social security offices in your home country or online (e.g. in the UK 🖳 www.ehic.org.uk and in Ireland 🖳 www.ehic.ie) and is valid for three to five years depending on the issuing country. However, you must continue to make social security contributions in the country where it was issued and if you become a resident in another country (e.g. in Spain) it becomes invalid. It covers emergency hospital treatment but doesn't include prescribed medicines, routine treatment, special examinations, X-rays, laboratory tests, physiotherapy, dental treatment or repatriation.

If you use the EHIC in Spain, you must present the card to the medical practitioner who is providing treatment and pay for treatment in cash. You must apply for reimbursement to your home country's social security department (instructions are provided with the card), which can take a number of months. If you travel to Spain or to another EU country **specifically** for medical treatment or maternity care in a public hospital, you need form E-112 and prior authorisation from your country's social security department (both difficult to obtain). Form E-112 authorises treatment in a Spanish or other EU public hospital without pre-payment.

Britons planning to visit or live in Spain can obtain information about reciprocal health treatment in Spain (and other countries) from The Pension Service, International Pension Centre, Newcastle-upon-Tyne NE98 1BA, UK (☎ 0191-218 7777, 💻 www.dwp.gov.uk).

Bermeo, Biscay

13.
INSURANCE

In all matters regarding insurance, you're responsible for ensuring that you and your family are legally insured. Spanish law is likely to differ from that in your home country or your previous country of residence, never assume that it's the same.

Spanish law provides for various obligatory state and employer insurance schemes. These cover sickness, maternity, work injuries, disability and unemployment and provide various pensions. However, the average Spaniard is more prone to taking risks than people of many other countries and carries less insurance than, for example, northern Europeans. On the other hand, Spanish employees have considerable protection under social security and are entitled to higher benefits than employees in many other EU countries (although in most cases you would be unwise to rely solely on social security to meet your needs).

There are a few compulsory insurances in Spain, including third-party car insurance (see page 155), third-party liability insurance for tenants and homeowners, and mortgage life insurance for mortgage holders. If you lease a car or buy one on credit, a lender may insist that you have comprehensive car insurance (see page 154). Voluntary insurance includes private pensions, disability, health, household, dental, travel, car breakdown and life insurance.

Most Spanish and European Union (EU) residents and their families receive health treatment under the Spanish social security (*seguridad social*) system. If you don't qualify, it's essential to take out private health insurance (see page 201), which is obligatory for most non-EU residents.

It's unnecessary to spend half your income insuring yourself against every eventuality from the common cold to being sued for your last cent, but it's important to insure against any event that could precipitate a major financial disaster, such as a serious accident or your house falling down. Regrettably, you cannot insure yourself against being uninsured or sue your insurance broker for giving you bad advice.

If you're moving to Spain, ensure your family has full health insurance during the interval between leaving your last country of residence and obtaining health insurance in Spain. One way is to take out a travel insurance policy. However, if possible, it's usually better to extend a private health insurance policy to cover you in Spain than to take out a new policy, particularly if you have an existing health problem that won't be covered by a new policy.

☑ SURVIVAL TIP

As with anything connected with finance, it's important to shop around when buying insurance. Just collecting a few brochures from insurance agents and making a few telephone calls could save you a lot of money.

Note that if you wish to make a claim on an insurance policy, you may be required to report an incident to the police within 24 hours (in some cases this may be a legal requirement). Obtain legal advice for anything other than a minor claim.

See also **Car Insurance** on page 154 and **Breakdown Insurance** on page 174.

INSURANCE COMPANIES & AGENTS

There are numerous Spanish and foreign insurance companies to choose from, providing a range of insurance services or specialising in certain fields only. Many of the British and other foreign insurance companies operating in Spain cater particularly for the needs of expatriates, major insurance companies having offices or agents throughout Spain (there are also insurers which can be contacted only by telephone or via the internet). Insurance agents, brokers (*corredor de seguros*) and companies are listed in the yellow pages under *Seguros* and many advertise in the expatriate press. Most insurance companies or brokers provide a free appraisal of your family's insurance needs.

There are many independent brokers in Spain, including many British and other foreign brokers in resort areas, who can offer you a choice of policies and should save you money. However, as in many countries, it's often difficult to obtain completely unbiased insurance advice, as brokers may be influenced by the commission offered for selling a particular policy. As with all financial matters in Spain, be careful who you choose as your broker and the company you insure with, as a number of companies have gone bust in recent years (particularly in the motor insurance sector) and insurance fraud isn't unknown.

When buying insurance, particularly car insurance (see page 154), shop around. Obtain recommendations from friends, colleagues and neighbours (but don't believe everything they tell you!). Compare not only the costs but also the terms and benefits provided by a number of companies before making a decision. Note that premiums (*premios*) are sometimes negotiable.

Spanish residents are free to insure their car, home or life with any insurance company registered in the EU, without the need for the insurer to be registered in Spain. The company must be registered in its home country and insurance cover must correspond to the minimum legal requirements. Note, however, that should a dispute arise over a claim, it will usually be dealt with in the country where the insurance company is registered.

If you take out insurance through a broker in Spain, it's important to check that your insurance premium has been paid to the insurance company concerned and that you receive your policy quickly. It isn't widespread, but there have been occurrences where a policy (e.g. health) has been cancelled when the premium paid to a broker wasn't passed to the insurance company (or was paid late).

If you have a complaint regarding an insurance policy, you should address it in the first instance to the company; large companies usually have a complaints department (*defensores del asegurado*). If you don't receive satisfaction, you can send a complaint to the Servicio de Reclamaciones, Dirección General de Seguros y Fondos de Pensiones (DGSFP), Paseo de la Castellana, 44, 28046 Madrid (☎ 913 397 000, 🖳 www.dgsfp. mineco.es – go to *Protección al Asegurado*). Note that the DGSFP concerns itself only with Spanish insurance companies and foreign companies with a registered office in Spain.

INSURANCE CONTRACTS

Read all insurance contracts before signing them. If you don't understand Spanish, have your legal adviser check a policy and don't sign it until you clearly understand the terms and the cover provided. Many foreign insurance companies operating in Spain provide policies and information in English and other foreign languages. Note, however, that an insurance policy issued in Spain is usually written under Spanish law and that the Spanish document is always the legal one. Like insurance companies everywhere, some will use any available legal loophole to avoid paying out in the event of a claim and therefore it pays to deal only with reputable companies. Policies often contain legal loopholes in the small print and if you don't understand them you should obtain independent professional legal advice before signing a contract.

If you believe that you have a valid claim you should persevere, despite any obstacles placed in your path. The wheels of justice grind very slowly in Spain and it may take you a number of years to gain satisfaction, but if you have a legitimate claim you will usually eventually receive compensation (plus interest from the date of the claim).

Always check the notice period required to cancel (*cancelar/anular*) a policy. In Spain most insurance policies are automatically extended for a further period (usually a year) if they aren't cancelled in writing by registered letter two or three months before the expiry date. You may cancel an insurance policy before the term has expired without penalty if the premium has increased, the terms are altered, an insured object is lost or stolen or if your circumstances have changed, e.g. a new job, redundancy, retirement, marriage or divorce. This must, however, still be done in writing and by registered post. You're usually entitled to a refund of any unused premiums paid.

☑ SURVIVAL TIP

If you wish to make a claim, you must usually inform your insurance company in writing by registered letter within two to five days of the incident (e.g. for accidents) or 24 hours in the case of theft. Thefts should also be reported to the local police station within 24 hours, as the police report (*denuncia*) constitutes evidence of your claim. Usually, an insurance company sends an adjuster to evaluate the extent of damage, e.g. to your home or car.

One of the advantages of taking out a policy with a foreign insurance company is that you have a policy you can understand (apart from all the legal jargon) and can make claims in your own language. This is usually a good option for the owner of a holiday home in Spain. However, bear in mind that insuring with a foreign insurance company may be more expensive than insuring with a Spanish company and in certain cases a policy may still need to be written under Spanish law.

SOCIAL SECURITY

Spain has a comprehensive social security (*seguridad social*) system covering over 90 per cent of the population. It provides healthcare (see **Chapter 12**), sickness and maternity benefits; compensation and pensions for industrial injuries; unemployment payments; old age pensions; invalidity and death benefits. Social security benefits in Spain are among the highest in the EU, as are social security contributions. The total contributions per employee are an average of around 30 per cent of gross pay, some 25 per cent of which is paid by employers. With the exception of sickness benefits, social security benefits aren't taxed.

Two-thirds of social security spending is on cash benefits such as pensions (old age, disability, orphans' and widows') and sickness and housing benefits, which are distributed through the Instituto Nacional de Seguridad Social (INSS). The Instituto Nacional de Empleo (INEM) distributes unemployment benefits. Less than a third of revenue is spent on healthcare, administered through the regional health services, and social services, which are the responsibility of the Instituto de Migraciones y Servicios Sociales (IMSERSO).

Spain has a separate social security system for members of the civil service and the armed forces, and special schemes for farm workers, seamen, the self-employed, domestic servants and other groups.

The Spanish social security system has been under severe financial strain (partly due to widespread fraud and non-payment of bills by town halls). An ageing population and increasing unemployment have contributed to a huge increase in spending on healthcare, pensions and unemployment benefits, although there have been cuts in government spending in recent years and the record number of social security contributions from employees (more than 19.4m, including 2.14m foreigners) means the outlook has improved somewhat. Nevertheless, most analysts agree that present levels of social security benefits (particularly pensions) are unsustainable and payments must be slashed if the system isn't to be bankrupted. Yet the government's priority is to increase the pension fund (by regular injections of 'cash') rather than reduce Spain's high social security contributions. In July 2008, the state pension fund had a balance of over €56bn, guaranteeing pensions until at least 2015, although it's still expected to run into problems after that.

For more information contact your local social security office or the Instituto Nacional de la Seguridad Social, Subdirección General de Relaciones Internacionales, Padre Damián, 4, Madrid 28036 (freephone ☎ 900 166 565, 🖳 www.seg-social.es).

Eligibility & Exemptions

Generally, if you're an employee in Spain, you will be insured under Spanish social security legislation and won't have any liability for social security contributions in your home country or country of domicile. However, social security agreements exist between Spain and over 40 countries, including all EU countries, Australia, Canada and the US, whereby expatriates who remain registered as employed in their home country may continue to be members of their home country's social security scheme for a limited period.

EU nationals transferred to Spain by an employer in their home country can continue to pay social security abroad for one year (form E-101 is required), which can be extended for another year in unforeseen circumstances (when form E-102 is needed). This also applies to the self-employed. However, after working in Spain for two years, EU nationals **must** contribute to the Spanish social security system.

If you're retired and living in Spain and receive a state pension from another EU country, or from a country with a social security agreement with Spain, you and your spouse are automatically entitled to health benefits under Spanish social security (if one spouse is aged 65 or over and is entitled to public health treatment, then the other aged under 65 may also be entitled to it). You must prove your entitlement to a pension by obtaining form E-121 from your home country's social security administration, which must be produced when registering with Spanish social security (see below). Form E-121 has indefinite validity and doesn't need to be renewed. If, however, you retire to Spain before reaching the Spanish retirement age, you must have private health insurance (see page 201).

If you qualify to pay social security contributions abroad, it may be worthwhile doing so, as contributions in some countries are lower than those in Spain. If you or your spouse work in Spain, but remain insured under the social security legislation of another EU country, you can claim social security benefits from that country. If the spouse and children of an EU national employed in Spain remain in their home country, they will continue to be covered by the social security system of that country.

If you're receiving an invalidity pension or other social security benefits on the grounds of ill-health, you should establish exactly how living in Spain will affect those benefits, as they may cease when you take up residence in Spain. In some countries, there are reciprocal rights regarding invalidity, but you must confirm that they apply in your case before going to live in Spain.

If you're working in Spain, in order to qualify for social security benefits you must have been employed in Spain for a certain period and have made certain minimum contributions, although if you've made contributions in another EU country, those contributions are usually taken into account when calculating your right to benefits. Note that your entitlement to non-Spanish social security benefits (apart from pensions), even those from another EU country, usually ends when you take up permanent residence in Spain.

If you're in receipt of a state pension in another EU country and move to Spain, you must take both copies of your form E-121 (see above) to the pension department at your local social security office in Spain. One copy is retained and the other stamped and returned to you. You must produce passports and (certified) birth certificates for all dependants and a marriage certificate (if applicable). You may also need to provide copies with official translations, but check first, as translations may be unnecessary. You also need proof of residence such as a property deed (*escritura*) or a rental contract.

After you've registered you receive a registration card (*tarjeta sanitaria*), similar to a credit card, usually by post around four to eight weeks later. A married couple with one partner working are covered by the same number, as are all dependants, but each receives a card. Dependants include your spouse (if he or she isn't personally insured); your children supported by you under the age of 16 (or under the age of 20 if they're students or unable to work through illness or invalidity) and ascendants, descendants and relatives by marriage supported by you and living in the same household. Separated, divorced and widowed people continue to receive benefits for at least one year after the 'event', or in the case of separated people, for as long as their spouse is employed provided they aren't eligible for benefits from other sources.

When applying for benefits or for social security reimbursements, you must contact the office listed on your social security card and quote your social security number or produce your card. Note that there's a compulsory contribution period (or 'waiting' period) before a new subscriber can claim certain social security benefits, which varies according to the benefit, e.g. you must have contributed for 180 days over the last five years to qualify for sick pay.

Citizens of an EU country who visit Spain as tourists can also use the Spanish public health system (see page 180).

In the UK, information regarding social security rights within the EU is provided in two booklets: *Your Social Security Rights When Moving within the European Community*, available from The Pension Service, International Pension Centre, Tyneview Park, Whitley Rd, Newcastle-upon-Tyne NE98 1BA, UK (☎ 0191-218 7777, 🖳 www.dwp.gov. uk) and *The Community Provisions on Social Security*, available online only from 🖳 http:// bookshop.eu.int.

Registration

If you're working in Spain, your employer will usually complete the necessary formalities to ensure that you're covered by social security. If he doesn't, you must obtain an attestation that you're employed in Spain and register at the nearest social security office to your home. Your local town hall will give you the address of your local office or you can find it under *Seguridad Social* in your local yellow pages.

Contributions

Social security contributions (*cuotas*) for employees are calculated as a percentage of their taxable income, although for certain contributions there's a maximum salary on which contributions are due. The minimum monthly salary on which you must usually pay social security contributions is the official minimum salary (€600 a month), of which 37.2 per cent is the monthly payment for social security. However, only a small proportion, 6.4 per cent, is deducted from the employee's salary and the remainder is paid by the employer.

The self-employed (*cuenta propia*) pay a minimum of around €245 a month (the maximum is around €820), which is subject to a 20 per cent surcharge if you don't pay it on time. Any self-employed person, even if he works only part-time, must contribute to social security. However, if you don't work for the whole of a calendar month (or more) you aren't required to pay social security during that period, e.g. if you operate a business in Spain and close for the month of January. Note that if you're self-employed and have a number of separate jobs, you require two sets of papers and must pay social security twice. Domestic workers (*empleados de hogar*) who are self-employed and work part time for a number of employers pay reduced social security contributions of €153.98 a month. However, if they're employed full-time by one employer, they must receive the minimum wage (€600 a month) and pay normal employee contributions.

Contributions start as soon as you start work in Spain and not when you obtain your residence permit (*residencia* – see page 54).

Benefits

Spanish social security includes benefits for health, sickness, maternity, work injury, housing, unemployment, retirement, invalidity and death. Social security benefits are paid as a percentage of your salary and are subject to minimum and maximum payments, as detailed below. Anyone living in Spain who is in receipt of a state pension in any EU country is entitled to the benefits of Spanish social security.

Health Benefits

Public health benefits include general and specialist care, hospitalisation, laboratory services, drugs and medicines, basic dental care, maternity care, appliances and emergency transportation. With the exception of pensioners and the disabled, members must pay a percentage of the cost (around 40 per cent) of certain treatment and medicine.

Sickness Benefits

When an employee is ill, he continues to receive all or part of his salary; this is paid by his employer for a certain period and thereafter by social security (see **Sick Leave** on page 45). A self-employed person can also receive 60 per cent of his monthly social security contributions (what is known as 'two-thirds of precious little') for the first 20 days and 75 per cent afterwards, provided he obtains a doctor's certificate stating that he's incapable of carrying out his usual occupation.

Unemployment Benefits

Unemployment in Spain is among the highest in western Europe and although membership of the state social security system is mandatory, only some 50 per cent of unemployed people qualify for benefit (young people who have never been employed don't, for example). There's no such thing as supplementary benefit (e.g. as in the UK) or supplemental security income (e.g. as in the US), although many regions pay a 'social wage' to the unemployed who don't qualify for unemployment benefits and there's a 'safety net' for agricultural workers, who can claim the minimum

unemployment benefit if they can prove that they've been employed for a minimum number of days a year.

The good news (for EU citizens, at least) is that social security payments made in another EU country are taken into account and credited to EU workers in Spain, so that they may be eligible for full unemployment benefit during a period of unemployment even if they haven't worked in Spain. If you're entitled to unemployment benefit in another EU country and have been claiming it for at least four weeks, you can continue to receive unemployment benefit (at your home country's rate) in Spain for up to three months while looking for work.

You must inform the unemployment office in your home country that you intend to seek work in Spain well in advance of your departure. If you qualify for a transfer of benefit to Spain, your home country's unemployment service provides a certificate of authorisation, which is necessary to register in Spain. You must register for work at your nearest regional unemployment office within seven days of leaving your home country, so that your eligibility for benefit isn't interrupted.

However, there may be a delay of up to three months before job-seekers actually start to receive benefit, so you must be able to finance yourself during your job search in Spain. During this period, you're entitled to healthcare in Spain, for which you require a certificate of entitlement (form E-119), although Spanish bureaucrats aren't very co-operative with this scheme and you must persevere to obtain your rights. If, after three months, you don't have a job you must leave Spain, as you're permitted to remain for only three months without a residence permit (see page 54). A residence permit won't be issued if you don't have a job or an adequate income.

Maternity & Paternity Benefits

Maternity benefit (*baja por maternidad*) is available to women who have made social security contributions for at least 180 days during the last five years. The equivalent of their full salary is paid to eligible women by social security for 16 weeks (18 weeks for multiple births), of which a minimum of six weeks must be taken after the birth. Under the Equality Law (*Ley de Igualdad*) introduced in 2006, a father is allowed to eight days' paternity benefit (*baja por paternidad*) on the birth or adoption of a child and the mother can transfer up to ten weeks of her maternity leave to the father. One parent is allowed up to two years' unpaid leave to look after the child, during which time the parent's social security contributions are paid by the state. Check with your local social security office for further information.

Old Age, Invalidity & Death Benefits

The Spanish state retirement (*jubilación*) pension is paid at 65 for men and women. Contributions are paid by employers and employees, and vary according to your income. Spanish state pensions are the highest in Europe after Swedish pensions. The current minimum pension (after 15 years' contributions) is €658.75 per month for a couple and €528.55 per month for a single person. The maximum monthly pension is €2,337.75. Spanish pensions are indexed to take account of rises in the cost of living and increase annually in accordance with the inflation rate of the previous year. Pensioners, like salaried employees, receive 14 payments a year instead of 12, with an extra payment in July and December.

A worker earning over around €2,800 per month can choose to pay the maximum contributions (around €820 per month for a self-employed person) in order to receive the maximum pension of €2,337.75 per month after 35 years' contributions.

Early or partial retirement is permitted under Spanish law and anyone with sufficient credits can choose to retire early. The widowed partner of a state pensioner is entitled to the full pension payable to his or her spouse, while dependent children are entitled to an additional 20 per cent. When there's no surviving parent, dependent children are also entitled to the widow's pension.

If you move to Spain after working in another EU country (or move to another EU country after working in Spain), your state pension contributions can be 'exported' to Spain (or from Spain to another country). Spanish state pensions are payable abroad and most countries pay state pensioners living in Spain the same pension that they would receive in their home country, with annual increases indexed to the cost of living.

Under EU regulations, the total contributions paid into different member states' insurance systems are taken into account when accessing an individual's rights to a state pension (this also applies to invalidity pensions). The number of years' contributions paid in different countries are added together and each country pays the percentage for which it's liable, e.g. if you worked for 20 years in the UK, 5 years in Germany and 15 years in Spain, the UK would pay 50 per cent, Germany 12.5 per cent and Spain 37.5 per cent of your state pension. Contact your home country's social security administration for more detailed information.

If you retire to Spain before your home country's state retirement age, it's advisable to continue to contribute to the state pension scheme; otherwise your state pension could be reduced.

Various organisations, such as the Fondo Nacional de Asistencia Social (FAS), provides old age pensions for those who don't qualify under other schemes.

As in all western European countries, state pensions are under pressure from governments that can no longer afford to pay them, due to the ever dwindling number of workers who are supporting a growing number of retirees. There are around 8m pensioners in Spain in 2007, and the figure is expected to reach 12m by the year 2040. Spain has particular problems, as state pensions remain far too generous (for the government – pensions are **never** too high for pensioners!), despite reductions in the last few years, and more people receive their income from the state than from the private sector. The Spanish government is trying to shift some of the burden onto private insurance companies, so far without much success.

SUPPLEMENTARY PENSIONS

Until recently, supplementary or private pensions (*planes de pensiones*) were unusual in Spain. However, with the long-term future of state pensions in doubt and government 'subsidies' of company and private pensions, many people are taking out supplementary pensions, which may be combined with a private health insurance scheme. In many cases, the combined state and supplementary pensions are equal to an employee's final salary.

It's important for anyone who doesn't qualify for a state pension or who will receive only the minimum state pension to contribute to a supplementary or private pension fund. (Note that you must contribute to Spanish social security for 15 years before you're entitled to a state pension – see above). There are a wide range of private pension funds in Spain (many provided by banks) and it's also possible to continue to contribute to a personal pension plan abroad or to an offshore fund. However, contributions to foreign pension schemes aren't tax deductible in Spain, although many major European private pension companies have offices or agencies in Spain.

Most experts advise that the best pension scheme for most people is one that doesn't require fixed monthly payments but allows you to pay irregular lump sums. In Spain, there's usually a small minimum monthly payment, possibly as low as €50 a month, and allowable lump sum contributions are usually from €600. A pension should be index linked to insure that it keeps pace with inflation. With an index-linked policy, capital is tax free after contributions have been made for 15 years, with an increasing scale of tax penalties for early surrender. With certain offshore pensions, there's no tax relief but all benefits are paid tax free. Where applicable, annual contributions to a company pension plan (up to certain limits) are tax-deductible for Spanish taxpayers.

Civil service pensions, which are taxable in your home country, don't usually need to be declared to the Spanish authorities. Note, however, that civil service pensions are usually taken into account when calculating your Spanish tax rate if you have other income which is taxable in Spain.

PRIVATE HEALTH INSURANCE

The vast majority of people in Spain are covered for health treatment under social security (see page 195 and **Chapter 12**). However, most people who can afford it take out private health insurance, which provides a wider choice of medical practitioners and hospitals, and more importantly, frees them from public health waiting lists. If you aren't covered by Spanish social security, it's important to have private health insurance, unless you have a **very** large bank balance.

Note that the US doesn't have a reciprocal health agreement with Spain and therefore American students and other Americans who aren't covered by social security **must** have private health insurance in Spain. Proof of insurance must usually be provided when applying for a visa or residence permit (see page 54).

Make sure you're fully covered in Spain before you receive a large bill. It's foolhardy for anyone living and working in Spain (or even visiting) not to have comprehensive health insurance. If you or members of your family aren't adequately insured, you could face some very high medical bills.

When changing employers or leaving Spain, you should ensure that you have continuous health insurance. If you're planning to change your health insurance company, you should ensure that no important benefits are lost.

The policies offered by Spanish and foreign companies differ considerably in the extent of cover, limitations and restrictions, premiums, and the choice of doctors, specialists and hospitals, as outlined below.

Spanish Companies

There are a large number of Spanish health insurance companies, some of which, such as Adeslas, Asisa, Sanitas (owned by the British company BUPA) and Vital Seguros, operate nationally while others are restricted to certain cities or provinces (although non-national policies have participating hospitals throughout Spain for emergency cases). Spanish insurance companies provide their members with a patient's membership card together with a list of contracted doctors, specialists and hospitals in their area that accept the company's cards. Some insurance companies also operate their own clinics. Usually, it's impossible to go to just any doctor, clinic or hospital, although some companies offer a free choice of doctors and hospitals for a higher premium.

The main disadvantage of the 'contract' system is that in some areas you may have to travel long distances to see a specialist or to be admitted to hospital.

If you're taken to a hospital in an emergency that isn't on your insurance company's list, you won't be covered under your policy.

Annual premiums for a family of four (say, two adults aged 40 and two children under 16) range from around €2,100; a man under 60 might pay from €500 (policies for women under 60 are up to twice as expensive). There may be an annual surcharge for those over 60, which increases with age, and supplements for pregnant women or for certain non-standard services, such as basic dental treatment. Some insurance companies offer group policies to expatriate clubs and organisations, which can work out much cheaper than individual policies. Major Spanish insurance companies pay 90 per cent of medical expenses and policy holders pay the remaining 10 per cent. When a policy allows a free choice of practitioners and hospitals, clients may be expected to pay the first 20 per cent of bills.

Foreign Companies

There are a number of foreign health insurance companies with agencies or offices in Spain, including AXA PPP Healthcare (⌨ www. axappphealthcare.co.uk), BUPA International (⌨ www.bupa-intl.com), Exeter Friendly Society (⌨ www.exeterfriendly.co.uk) and International Health Insurance (Denmark – ⌨ www.ihi.com).

Many foreign health insurance companies offer policies designed for expatriates, which usually include repatriation to your home country and international cover. However, if you need private health insurance to obtain a residence permit (see page 54), you must ensure that a foreign policy will be accepted by the Spanish authorities (those listed above are all accepted).

The inclusion of repatriation may be an important consideration if you need treatment which is unavailable in Spain, but available in your home (or another) country. International cover may be for certain areas only, e.g. Europe, worldwide excluding North America, and worldwide including North America. A policy may offer full cover anywhere within Europe and limited cover in North America and certain other countries (e.g. Japan). Some policies offer the same cover worldwide for a fixed premium, which may be an important consideration for globetrotters. Note that an international policy allows you to choose to have non-urgent medical treatment in another country.

Usually there's an excess (deductible), which may apply to each visit to a doctor or specialist, to each claim or to each illness. Obviously, a 'per illness' policy is best, as a single excess will apply, for example, to a visit to a family doctor, prescribed medicines, a consultation

with a specialist and hospitalisation, if they're all associated with the same illness.

Most companies offer different levels of cover; for example, AXA PPP Healthcare offer standard, comprehensive and prestige levels of cover. A basic policy doesn't usually include maternity cover and may offer no benefits or restricted benefits for outpatient treatment (which means that you must pay for visits to a family doctor) and may also exclude outpatient medicines, dressings, surgical/dental appliances, spectacles, contact lenses or hearing aids. Cover for dental treatment, spectacles and contact lenses may be available as an option, although there may be a hefty excess, which usually means that you're better off paying bills yourself. There may also be an annual limit for ambulance costs. Children (e.g. up to age 16) may be covered free on a parent's policy and children up to certain age (e.g. 26) may receive a 50 per cent premium reduction.

There's always an annual limit on total annual medical costs (which should be at least €350,000 to €400,000), and some companies also limit costs for specific treatment or types of treatment, such as specialists' fees, operations and hospital accommodation. Some policies include permanent disability cover, e.g. €150,000, for those in full-time employment.

A medical isn't usually required for most health policies, although existing health problems are excluded for a period, e.g. one or two years. Note, however, that it's impossible to obtain insurance with some companies if you're above a certain age, e.g. 75. Premiums are usually related to age, although some companies (such as the Exeter Friendly Society) don't relate premiums to age provided you join before a certain age, e.g. 60 or 65.

The cost of international health insurance varies considerably depending on your age and the extent of cover. Premiums can sometimes be paid monthly, quarterly or annually, although some companies insist on payment annually in advance. Annual premiums vary from around €1,000 to over €4,500 for the most extensive cover. Some companies have an excess of around €100 per claim (or €150 for dental treatment) and it may be possible to choose an increased voluntary excess of €300 to €1,000 and receive a discount (e.g. 10 or 20 per cent).

If you have existing private health insurance in another country, you may be able to extend it to include Spain. On the other hand, you may save a substantial amount by switching to another company without losing any benefits (you may even gain some). To compare policies, it's best to visit an insurance broker offering policies from a number of companies.

Choosing a Policy

When comparing the cost of Spanish health insurance with a foreign policy – in fact when comparing any policies – carefully compare the benefits and exactly what's included and excluded. All policies include limitations and restrictions, e.g. injuries as a result of participation in certain high-risk sports aren't usually covered, or dialysis treatment may be excluded or covered for only a limited number of days a year in hospital, e.g. 20 to 60. Certain services aren't provided during the first six months cover, e.g. medical check-ups and dental care, and some services may be included only for an extra premium and an excess payment. Most policies don't cover illnesses contracted within a certain period of taking out a policy or existing illnesses for a period, e.g. one or two years (irrespective of whether you were aware of the illness or not). Many Spanish policies additionally limit costs for a particular specialist or treatment in a calendar year. Steer clear of policies with severe restrictions (such as a maximum 20-day hospitalisation period) and always have the small print checked.

Note that some foreign insurance companies don't provide sufficient cover to satisfy Spanish regulations and you should check the minimum cover necessary with a Spanish consulate in your country of residence before taking out a policy.

On the other hand, Spanish health insurance policies are designed for those living permanently in Spain and most offer only emergency cover abroad. Emergency medical cover abroad is paid up to a limited amount only, e.g. €2,500 or €5,000, which is very little if you must be hospitalised (international travel policies typically include medical expenses equal to €300,000 or more). Spanish policies, not surprisingly, don't include repatriation to another country. The consensus among expatriates is that although Spanish health insurance may sometimes be cheaper, it doesn't offer wide cover and isn't good value for money compared with some foreign health insurance schemes. The main advantages of a foreign health insurance policy are that treatment is unrestricted and you can choose any doctor, specialist, clinic or hospital in Spain, and usually abroad.

Another important consideration for many foreigners is being able to choose an English-speaking medical practitioner or a hospital with English-speaking staff (or staff that speak another language). This is impossible with Spanish insurance unless a policy allows a free choice of practitioners and hospitals.

Spanish insurance companies can (and will) cancel a policy at the end of the insurance period if you have a serious illness with endless high expenses and some companies automatically cancel a policy when you reach the age of 65. You should avoid such a company at all costs, as to take out a new policy at the age of 65 at a reasonable premium is difficult or impossible. Some companies won't accept new clients aged over 60 while others accept new clients up to the age of 75.

In some countries, premium increases are limited by law, although this may apply only to residents in the country where the company is registered and not to overseas policy holders. On the other hand, many policies have clauses allowing annual increases bearing no relation to inflation or increases in the cost of living.

With health insurance, as with most other things in life, you generally get what you pay for and can tailor your premiums to your requirements. The most important questions to ask are does the policy provide the necessary cover and is it good value. If you're in good health and able to pay for your own out-patient treatment, such as visits to your family doctor and prescriptions, then the best value policy may be one covering only specialist and hospital treatment.

Claims are usually settled in major currencies and large claims are usually settled directly by insurance companies (although your choice of hospitals may be limited). Always check whether a company pays large medical bills directly. If you're required to pay bills and claim reimbursement from the insurance company, it may take you several months to receive your money (some companies are slow to pay). It isn't usually necessary to have bills translated into English or another language, although you should check a company's policy. Most companies provide 24-hour emergency telephone assistance.

DENTAL INSURANCE

It's unusual to have full dental insurance (*seguro de dentista*), as the cost is prohibitive. The cost of extractions is reimbursed the Spanish public health service (see **Dentists** on page 187), and some Spanish insurance companies include coupons for basic dental care such as check-ups, X-rays and cleaning in their standard premium, while others offer more comprehensive dental cover as an optional extra. Some foreign health policies include basic dental care and most offer optional (or additional) dental cover, although there are many restrictions and cosmetic treatment is excluded. The cost of dental insurance may be dependent on the condition of your teeth. Where applicable, the amount payable by a health insurance policy for a particular item of

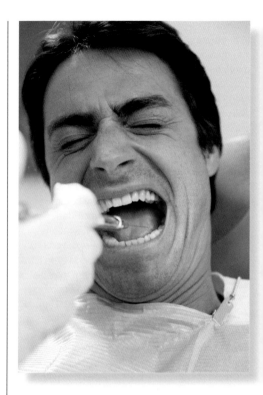

treatment is fixed. A detailed list of refunds is available from insurance companies.

HOUSEHOLD INSURANCE

Household insurance (*seguro de hogar*) generally includes the building, its contents and third-party liability, all of which are contained in a multi-risk household insurance policy. Policies are offered by Spanish and foreign insurance companies and premiums are similar, although foreign companies may provide more comprehensive cover.

Building Insurance

Although building (*continente*) insurance isn't compulsory, it's advisable for homeowners to take out insurance that covers damage to a building due to fire, smoke, lightning, water, explosion, storm, freezing, snow, theft, vandalism, malicious damage, acts of terrorism, impact, broken windows and natural catastrophes (such as falling trees). Policies vary in what they include and exclude and you should read the small print. Building insurance should include glass and cover all buildings on a property, aerials and satellite dishes, gardens and garden ornaments. Note, however, that if a claim is the result of a defect in a building or its design, e.g. the roof is too heavy and collapses, the insurance company won't pay up (another reason why it's advisable to have a survey before buying a home).

It's particularly important to have insurance for storm damage in Spain, which can be severe in some areas. If floods are one of your concerns, make sure that you're covered for water coming in at ground level, not just for water seeping in through the roof.

 Caution

If you own a home in an area that has been hit by a succession of natural disasters (such as floods), your household insurance may be cancelled. Always read the small print of contracts.

Building insurance is based on the cost of rebuilding your home and should be increased each year in line with inflation. Make sure that you insure your property for the true cost of rebuilding.

Contents Insurance

Contents (*contenido*) are usually insured for the same risks as a building (see above) and are insured for their replacement value (new for old), with a reduction for wear and tear for clothes and linen. Valuable objects are covered for their actual declared (and authenticated) value. Most policies include automatic indexation of the insured sum in line with inflation. A comprehensive contents insurance policy may also cover money, frozen food and property belonging to third parties stored in your home, and pay you for accidental damage to sanitary installations, theft, replacement of locks following damage or loss of keys, and alternative accommodation.

Some risks are usually subject to additional premiums, e.g. loss of credit cards, requirement for emergency assistance (plumber, glazier, electrician, etc.) or redecoration, loss of rent, and the need to travel to Spain to deal with damage or a claim

(e.g. for holiday homeowners). Many policies include personal third-party liability, e.g. up to €300,000, although this may be an option.

Items of high value must usually be itemised and photographs and documentation (e.g. a valuation) provided. Some companies even recommend or insist on a video film of belongings. When claiming for contents, you should produce the original bills if possible (always keep bills for expensive items) and bear in mind that replacing imported items in Spain may be more expensive than buying them abroad. Contents policies contain security clauses and if you don't adhere to them a claim won't be considered. For example, a building must usually have iron bars (*rejas*) on ground-floor windows and patio doors, shutters and secure locks. Most companies give a discount if properties have steel reinforced doors, high security locks and alarms (particularly alarms connected to a monitoring station).

An insurance company may send someone to inspect your property and advise on security measures. Note that policies only pay out for theft when there are signs of forced entry, and you aren't covered for thefts by a tenant (but may be covered for thefts by domestic personnel). if you're planning to let a property, you may be required to inform your insurer. Note that

All-risk policies offering a worldwide extension to a household policy for jewellery, cameras and other items aren't usually available from Spanish insurance companies, but are offered by foreign companies. See also **Crime** on page 312.

Community Properties

If you own a property that's part of a community development, the building is insured by the community (although you should ensure that it's comprehensively insured). You must, however, insure your own contents and be insured for third-party risks (*riesgo a terceros*) in the event that you cause damage to neighbouring properties, e.g. through flood or fire. Contents insurance policies usually include third-party liability up to a maximum amount, e.g. €300,000.

Rented Properties

Your landlord will usually insist that you have third-party liability insurance, and a lease normally requires you to insure against 'tenant's risks', including damage you may make to the rental property and to other properties if you live in an apartment, e.g. due to floods, fire or explosion. You can choose your own insurance company and aren't required to use one recommended by your landlord.

Premiums

Premiums are usually calculated on the constructed area in square metres (m^2) of a property, its age, the value of the contents and the security protection, e.g. window protection at ground level, the number of entrance doors and their construction. As a rough guide, building insurance costs around €18 a year per €5,000 of value insured, e.g. a property valued at €100,000 will cost €300 a year to insure. Contents insurance costs from around €25 a year per €5,000 of value insured (e.g. a premium of €40 for contents valued at €10,000) and may be higher for a detached villa than an apartment, e.g. up to €25 per €5,000 insured. In general, detached, older and more remote properties cost more to insure than apartments and new properties (particularly when they're located in towns), due to the higher risk of theft. Premiums are also higher in certain high-risk areas.

Holiday Homes

Premiums are generally higher for holiday homes, due to their vulnerability, particularly to burglary. Premiums are usually based on the number of days a year a property is inhabited and the interval between periods of occupancy. Cover for theft, storm, flood and malicious damage may be suspended when a property is left empty for an extended period. Note that you're required to turn off the water supply at the mains when vacating a building for more than 72 hours. It's possible to negotiate cover for periods of absence for a hefty surcharge, although valuable items are usually excluded (unless you have a safe).

If you're absent from your property for long periods, e.g. longer than 90 days a year, you may be required to pay an excess on a claim arising from an occurrence that takes place during your absence (and theft may be excluded). It's important to ensure that a policy specifies that it's for a holiday home and **not** a principal home.

In areas with a high risk of theft (e.g. major cities and most resort areas), an insurance company may insist on extra security measures. It's unwise to leave valuable or irreplaceable items in a holiday home or a property that will be vacant for long periods. Note that some insurance companies will do their utmost to find a loophole which makes you negligent and relieves them of liability.

Claims

If you wish to make a claim, you must usually inform your insurance company in writing (by registered letter) within two to seven days of an incident or 24 hours in the case of theft. Thefts should also be reported to the local police within 24 hours, as the police report (*denuncia*), of which you receive a copy for your insurance company, constitutes irrefutable evidence of your claim. Check whether you're covered for damage or thefts that occur while you're away from your property and are therefore unable to inform the insurance company immediately.

> ☑ **SURVIVAL TIP**
>
> Take care that you don't under-insure your home and its contents and that you periodically reassess their value and adjust your insurance premium accordingly. You can arrange to have your insurance cover automatically increased annually, by a fixed percentage or amount, by your insurance company.

If you make a claim and the assessor discovers that you're under-insured, the amount due will be reduced by the percentage by which you're under-insured. For example, if you're insured for €5,000 and you're found to be under-insured by 50 per cent, your claim for €1,500 will be reduced by 50 per cent to €750.

TRAVEL INSURANCE

Travel insurance (*seguro de viajes*), also known as holiday insurance, is recommended for all who don't wish to risk having their holiday or travel ruined by financial problems or to arrive home broke. As you probably know, anything can and often does go wrong with a holiday, sometimes before you even get started (particularly when you don't have insurance). The following information applies equally to residents and non-residents, whether they're travelling to or from Spain or within Spain.

Travel insurance is available from many sources, including travel agents, insurance companies and agents, banks, automobile clubs and transport companies (airline, rail and bus). Package holiday companies and tour operators also offer insurance policies, some of which are compulsory, too expensive and don't provide adequate cover. You can also buy 24-hour accident and flight insurance at major airports, although it's expensive and doesn't offer the best cover.

Before taking out travel insurance, carefully consider the range and level of cover you require and compare policies. Short-term holiday and travel insurance policies should include cover for holiday cancellation or interruption; missed flights; departure delay at the start **and** end of a holiday (a common occurrence); delayed, lost or damaged baggage; lost or stolen personal effects and money; medical expenses and accidents (including evacuation home); flight insurance; personal liability and legal expenses and default or bankruptcy insurance, e.g. against a tour operator or airline going broke.

14.
FINANCE

Spain is no longer one of the poorer countries in the European Union (EU); according to the *Economist* it had an estimated per capita gross domestic product (GDP) in 2007 of US$31,835, compared with France at US$33,626, Germany at US$33,991 and the UK at US$35,048 (Spanish government figures put Spain's 2007 GDP per capita at around $34,557). The country currently boasts the eighth largest economy in the world, as well as the fastest growth rate among the original 15 members of the EU (EU15). Unemployment has decreased significantly, although it still stands at around 9.5 per cent, and inflation was at 4.2 per cent in 2007.

In the last two decades, Spain has become a member of the 'real' world and its cost of living and taxes have increased accordingly. It's no longer a low-tax country as many people still believe – unless, of course, you come from Belgium, the Netherlands or Scandinavia, in which case almost anywhere else is a low tax country! The cost of living has increased (and personal debt has risen considerably), though it's still lower than in most other EU countries, and for many the quality of life:cost of living 'ratio' is better in Spain than almost anywhere else in the world.

Personal and family debt is an increasing problem in Spain and in 2008 accounted for 143 per cent of a family's disposable income, considerably higher than five years ago, but a similar proportion to the US and UK. Most debt is in the form of mortgages (Spaniards owe over ten times more on their homes than ten years ago) and the rises in mortgage interest rates during 2008 had serious effects on the average family's budget.

Like all developed countries, Spain has extremes of wealth and poverty and there's a vast difference in prosperity between the rich north and the poor south and west of the country (an imbalance which regional policies and vast injections of EU aid have done little to alleviate).

When you arrive in Spain to take up residence or employment, ensure that you have sufficient cash, travellers' cheques and/ or credit cards to last at least until your first pay day, which may be some time after your arrival. During this period you will find that an international credit card is useful; major credit cards, e.g. MasterCard and Visa, are widely accepted in Spain. Note, however, that compared to many other developed countries, particularly the UK and US, Spain isn't a credit economy and the Spanish prefer to pay (and be paid) in cash than with a credit card or cheque. Don't assume that a business accepts credit cards, but check in advance.

If you wish to borrow money to buy property or for a business venture in Spain, you should carefully consider where and in what currency it should be raised. Note that it's difficult for foreigners to obtain business loans in Spain, particularly for new ventures, and you shouldn't rely on it. On the other hand, if you earn your income in euros, this may affect your financial commitments abroad, particularly if these currencies are devalued. List all your probable and possible expenses and do your homework thoroughly **before** moving to Spain – afterwards it may be too late!

If you're planning to invest in property or a business in Spain that's financed with money earned or held in a currency other than euros, it's important to consider present and possible future exchange rates (don't be too optimistic!).

If you plan to live permanently in Spain, you should ensure that your income is and will remain sufficient to live on, bearing in mind currency devaluations, rises in the cost of living, unforeseen expenses, such as medical bills, and anything else that may reduce your income (including stock market crashes and recessions!). In 2007/8, many UK pensioners with a fixed income paid in sterling saw it fall dramatically, as the euro/sterling exchange rates worsened and the Spanish cost of living rose. See **Chapter 13** for information about social security and pensions.

Competition for your money (*dinero*) is considerable, and financial services are offered by clearing and commercial banks, savings banks, foreign banks, the post office, investment brokers and a range of other financial institutions.

FOREIGNER'S IDENTIFICATION NUMBER

All residents and non-resident foreigners with financial affairs in Spain must have a foreigner's identification number (*número de identificación de extranjero/NIE*). This is similar to the fiscal number (*numero de identificación fiscal/NIF*) all Spaniards have (and which is the same as their identity card and passport numbers). An *NIE* works as identification and, in effect, a tax number. Without an *NIE*, you won't be able to purchase property, open a bank account, arrange credit terms or use temporary employment agencies. When you buy a property, you must apply for an *NIE*, which is required when the property is registered in your name.

Your *NIE* must be used in all dealings with the Spanish tax authorities, when paying property taxes and in various other transactions. Anyone saving money or assets or receiving credits or loans in Spain must give his *NIE* to the relevant bank within 30 days of the operation. A bank cannot issue a cheque against a deposit without reporting your *NIE* and must report to the authorities any activity where an *NIE* hasn't been provided. Banks

and individuals can be heavily fined for non-compliance with the law regarding identification numbers.

The form for an *NIE* can be downloaded from the Ministry of Interior website (🖳 www.mir.es – go to *Información sobre Trámites*, then *Extranjeros* and then *Modelos de Solicitud*). Applications for an *NIE* can only be made in person, however, and you should go to a national police station (*comisaría*) with a foreigners' department (expect to queue for most of the morning). A representative can apply on your behalf only if you've given him a power of attorney made out abroad and translated into Spanish. However, once you've applied, anyone can collect the *NIE* on your behalf. If you have an employment contract or a letter from a Spanish employer or business stating why it requires you to have an *NIE*, you can obtain a number in around a week. Otherwise, you may have to wait up to three months.

SPANISH CURRENCY

Along with 14 other EU countries (Austria, Belgium, Cyprus, Finland, France, Germany, Greece, Ireland, Italy, Luxembourg, Malta, the Netherlands, Portugal and Slovenia), Spain uses the euro (€) as its currency. (These countries together are known as 'eurozone' countries.) Euro notes and coins became legal tender on 1st January 2002, replacing the peseta. The euro is divided into 100 cents (*céntimo*) and coins are minted in values of 1, 2, 5, 10, 20, 50 cents, €1 and €2. The 1, 2 and 5 cent coins are copper-coloured, the 10, 20 and 50 cent brass-coloured. The €1 coin is silver-coloured in the centre with a brass-coloured rim, and the €2 coin has a brass-coloured centre and silver-coloured rim.

The reverse ('tail' showing the value) of euro coins is the same in all eurozone countries, but the obverse ('head') is different in each country. Spanish coins carry the word '*España*', the date of minting, and one of three designs: the king's head on the €1 and €2 coins, a bust of Cervantes on the 10, 20 and 50 cent coins, and the cathedral in Santiago de Compostela on the 1, 2 and 5 cent coins. All euro coins can, of course, be used in all eurozone countries (although minute differences in weight

occasionally cause problems in cash machines, e.g. at motorway tolls!).

As in most other eurozone countries, many people in Spain still claim to have difficulty determining the value of items in euros and the vast majority of Spaniards still 'think' (and talk) in pesetas, particularly for large amounts. As yet, there are no slang terms for euros – there were several for pesetas.

Euro banknotes (*billetes*) are identical throughout the eurozone and depict a map of Europe and stylised designs of buildings (as the member countries couldn't agree which actual buildings should be shown!). Notes are printed in denominations of €5, €10, €20, €50, €100, €200 and €500 (worth over £390 or $785!). The size of notes increases with their value. Euro notes have been produced using all the latest anti-counterfeiting devices. Nevertheless, you should be wary of forgeries, especially of €200 and €500 notes. In printing and labelling, the euro symbol may appear before the amount (as in this book), after it (commonly used by the Spanish, e.g. 24,50€) or even between the euros and cents, e.g. 16€50. When writing figures (for example on cheques), a full stop (period) is used to separate units of millions, thousands and hundreds, and a comma to denote fractions.

It's advisable to obtain some euro coins and notes before arriving in Spain and to familiarise yourself and your family with them. You should have some euros in cash, e.g. €50 to €100 in small notes, when you arrive, but should avoid carrying a lot of cash. This saves you having to change money on arrival at a Spanish airport (where exchange rates are usually poor and there are often long queues). It's best to avoid €100 notes, if possible, as these sometimes aren't accepted, particularly for small purchases. Note also that shops and businesses don't generally accept €200 and €500 notes.

IMPORTING & EXPORTING MONEY

In theory, there are no restrictions on the import or export of funds by residents or non-residents, although you're required to declare amounts over €6,000 (see below). A Spanish resident is permitted to open a bank account in any country and to import (or export) funds in any currency. However, when a resident opens an overseas account, his Spanish bank must routinely inform the Bank of Spain (within 30 days) of account movements above €3,000. When importing funds for the purchase of a property (or any other major transaction) in Spain, non-residents must have the transfer of funds verified by a certificate from their bank (*certificado de inversiones*).

Declaration

Sums of €6,000 to €30,000 (per person and journey) must be declared to the customs authorities (on form B-1) when entering or leaving Spain. Non-EU nationals wishing to import or export sums above €6,000 must obtain authorisation from the Dirección General de Transacciones Exteriores (DGTE) by completing form B-2 at a bank. These regulations are designed to curb criminal activities, particularly drug trafficking, and also apply to travellers stopping in Spain for less than 24 hours. If you don't declare funds, they're subject to confiscation.

Residents receiving funds from non-residents or making payments to them of over €6,000 (or the equivalent in foreign currency) in cash or cheques must declare them within 30 days. A form must be completed (B-3), which includes the name, address and *NIE* of the resident, the name and address of the non-resident, and the reason for the payment.

International Bank Transfers

When transferring or sending money to or from Spain, you should be aware of the alternatives and shop around for the best deal.

♦ Personal cheque – It's possible to send a creditor a cheque drawn on a personal account and to pay cheques drawn on a foreign account into a Spanish bank account, although they can take weeks to clear and fees are high. Some people like to receive cheques (e.g. for foreign pensions) by post from their overseas banks, but not only must you wait for them to clear, you're also at the mercy of the notoriously unreliable Spanish post office (see Chapter 6).

♦ Bank draft (*cheque bancario*) – Another way to transfer money is via a bank draft, which should be sent by registered post. Note, however, that if it's lost or stolen it's impossible to cancel payment and you must wait six months before a new draft can be issued. Bank drafts aren't treated as cash and must be cleared like personal cheques.

♦ Bank transfer (*transferencia bancaria*) – A 'normal' transfer should take three to seven days, but in reality it usually takes much longer and an international bank transfer between non-affiliated banks can take weeks! (It's usually quicker and cheaper to transfer funds between branches of the same bank than between non-affiliated banks.) In fact, the larger the amount the longer it often takes (surprise, surprise!), which can be particularly awkward when you're transferring money to buy a property.

♦ SWIFT transfer – One of the safest and fastest methods of transferring money is via the SWIFT system. A SWIFT transfer should be completed in a few hours, funds being available within 24 hours, although even these can take five working days. Most banks are members of the SWIFT system.

♦ Telegraphic transfers – One of the quickest (it takes around ten minutes) and safest methods of transferring cash is via a telegraphic transfer, e.g. Moneygram (🖳 www.moneygram.com) or Western Union (🖳 www.westernunion.com), but it's also one of the most expensive, e.g. commission of 7 to 10 per cent of the amount sent! Western Union services are available at post offices (☎ 902 197 197, 🖳 www.correos.es) in Spain – a system known as 'Money in minutes' (*Dinero en minutos*). There are reduced rates for transfers to and from certain countries, such as Russia.

Money can be sent via overseas American Express offices by Amex card holders (using Amex's Moneygram service) to American Express offices in Spain in just 15 minutes.

The cost of transfers varies considerably, not only in exchange rates (through which banks extract their 'commission'), but also in transfer charges, e.g. for a SWIFT transfer. If you intend to send a large amount of money to Spain or abroad for a business transaction such as buying a property, you should ensure you receive the commercial rate of exchange rather than the tourist rate.

In spite of an EU directive limiting the costs banks can pass on to customers, Spanish banks charge what they like when making transfers abroad – up to 0.7 per cent of the amount transferred. This can amount to a lot of money if you've sold a property in Spain and are transferring the money abroad!

Some banks levy very high charges (as much as 4 per cent) on the transfer of funds to Spain to buy a home, which is the subject of numerous complaints, while others charge nothing if the transfer is made in euros. Always check charges and rates in advance and agree them with your bank (you may be able to negotiate a lower charge or a better exchange rate). If you have your pension paid into a bank in Spain from another EU country, you should have it transferred in euros, for which (under EU regulations) there should be no charge and money must be deposited in your account within five working days.

Spanish (and Portuguese) banks are reportedly the slowest in Europe to process bank transfers. It isn't unusual for transfers to and from Spain to get 'stuck' in the pipeline (usually somewhere in Madrid), which allows

the Spanish bank to use your money for a period interest free. For example, transfers between British and Spanish banks sometimes take from three to six weeks and the money can 'disappear' for months or even completely!

It may be cheaper and quicker to obtain a banker's draft and pay that into your foreign account, but check the fees first. Failing that, you can withdraw cash from your Spanish account free of charge, but the amount may be limited and it is, of course, risky to carry too much cash with you.

Obtaining Cash

One of the quickest methods of obtaining small amounts of cash (e.g. less than €1,000) in Spain is to draw on debit, credit or charge cards (if you bank with some UK banks, e.g. Nationwide or the Post Office, withdrawals are free). Many foreigners living in Spain (particularly retirees) keep the bulk of their money in a foreign account (perhaps in an offshore bank) and draw on it with a cash or debit card in Spain. This is an ideal solution for holidaymakers and holiday homeowners (although homeowners will still need a Spanish bank account to pay their bills). Most banks in major cities have foreign exchange windows (and there are banks with extended opening hours at international airports and main railway stations in major cities), where you can buy and sell foreign currencies, buy and cash travellers' cheques, and obtain a cash advance on credit and charge cards.

Note that most banks make a minimum charge of between €3 and €6, so it's expensive to change small amounts. However, some banks charge a flat fee of €3, irrespective of the amount, especially if you're a client of the bank.

There are numerous private *bureaux de change* (including most travel agents), many of which are open long hours, and some shops (such as El Corte Inglés department stores) have an in-house *bureau de change*. Note that banks at airports and railway stations often offer the worst exchange rates and charge the highest fees. There are automatic change machines at airports and in tourist areas in major cities accepting up to 15 currencies including US$, £ Sterling and Swiss francs. Most *bureaux de change* charge no commission (but always check –

and compare their exchange rates) and are also usually easier to deal with than banks. If you're changing a lot of money, you may be able to negotiate a better exchange rate. However, commercial *bureaux de change* don't usually offer the best exchange rates and you're usually better off changing money at a bank. (The posted exchange rates may apply only when changing high amounts, so ask before changing any money.) Note that 'no commission' usually means a poor exchange rate!

A euro exchange rate (*cambio*) for most European and major international currencies is listed in banks and daily newspapers, and announced on Spanish and expatriate radio and TV programmes – but don't expect to get this rate when changing money!

BANKS

Although Spanish banks aren't renowned for their efficiency, the service they offer has changed out of all recognition in the last few decades, during which the number of banks and branches has increased considerably (some have also gone bust!). Spanish banks have become highly automated and their cash dispensers (ATMs) are among the world's most advanced (the ServiCaixa system, part of the Servired network, is particularly good and offers a wide range of functions including tickets for concerts and theatres, mobile telephone top-ups and the facility to pay bills as well as cash withdrawal) and most ATMs have multi-language options.

On the other hand, where human involvement is concerned some Spanish banks remain Neanderthal. Fortunately, most banks also offer home banking services via telephone and/or the internet, and there are several internet/telephone-only banks: ING Direct (☎ 901 020 901, 🖳 www.ingdirect.es), Openbank (☎ 902 365 366, 🖳 www.openbank. es), owned by Banco Santander, and Uno-e (☎ 901 111 113, 🖳 www.uno-e.es), owned by BBVA. All three internet banks offer (relatively) high-interest current accounts with immediate access to your money, as well as the usual banking services.

> A strange idiosyncrasy of some Spanish banks is that they sell goods such as household appliances, bicycles and computers, and non-financial services (e.g. holidays and property).

There are two main types of bank in Spain: clearing banks (*bancos*) and savings banks (*cajas de ahorros*). The Spanish clearing banks with the largest branch networks are the two giants, Banco Santander (the fourth largest bank in Europe) and Banco Bilbao Vizcaya-Argentaria (BBVA), and the smaller Banco Popular, Banesto and Sabadell Atlántico. All banks in Spain are listed in yellow pages under *Bancos*.

Spain also has around 50 savings banks, which were originally charitable organisations granting loans for public interest and agricultural policies. Savings banks are similar to building societies in the UK and savings and loan banks in the US and hold around 45 per cent of deposits and make some 25 per cent of personal loans. The two largest Spanish savings banks are La Caixa (some 3,600 branches) and Caja Madrid (almost 1,900 branches). In general, savings banks offer a more personal, friendly service than clearing banks and are excellent for local business (many have limited regional branch networks). However, although they provide the same basic services as clearing banks, they aren't always best for international business.

There are also some 100 co-operative savings banks (*cooperativas de crédito*), whose members are agricultural co-operatives, although they play only a small part in Spain's banking system and hold just a few per cent of total bank assets.

There are around 50 foreign banks operating in Spain – fewer (and with an overall smaller market share) than in most other European countries. Most major foreign banks are represented in Madrid and Barcelona, but branches are rare in other cities. Among foreigners in Spain, the British

are best served by their national banks, in the major cities and resort areas. Barclays, Deutsche Bank and Lloyds TSB are the most prominent foreign banks in Spain. These banks are full members of the Spanish clearing and payment system and can provide cheque accounts, cash and credit cards, direct debits and standing orders, and loans and mortgages. The Royal Bank of Scotland also operates at some Banco Santander branches.

Foreign banks in Spain operate in the same way as Spanish banks, so you shouldn't expect, for example, a branch of Barclays in Spain to resemble a branch in the UK or any other country. Surprisingly, considering the size and spending power of foreign residents and tourists in Spain, most Spanish banks make few concessions to foreign clients, e.g. by providing general information and statements in foreign languages and multilingual staff. Exceptions to this include Bancaja (🖳 www.bancaja.es), Bankinter (🖳 www.bankinter.es), Cajamar (🖳 www.cajamar.es), Solbank (🖳 www.solbank.es) and Unicaja (🖳 www.unicaja.es).

Opening Hours

Normal bank opening hours are from between 8.15 and 9am until between 1.30 and 2pm, Mondays to Fridays, and from between 8.30 and 9.30am until 1pm on Saturdays, except in summer (banks are closed on Saturdays from April to September). Savings banks open all day on Thursdays (until 7pm) but are closed on Saturdays. Some branches in major cities remain open continually from the morning until 4 or 4.30pm from autumn to spring, although they may close earlier on Fridays.

Some banks are experimenting with longer hours at certain branches and opening from, for example, 8.15am until 8.30pm (or from around 8.15am to 2pm and again from around 4.30 until 7.45pm). Banks in shopping centres may open all day until late in the evening (some are open the same hours as hypermarkets, e.g. from 10am until 10pm). At major international airports and railway stations in major cities, there are also banks with extended opening hours, although they often have long queues.

Banks are closed on public holidays, including local holidays (banks in neighbouring towns may close on different days), and they may also close early during local *fiestas*.

Note that many *bureaux de change* have long opening hours and some are even open 24 hours in summer in some resort areas.

Opening an Account

 Caution

If you use an overseas account to pay your Spanish mortgage, utility services and council taxes, you may be required to produce a residence certificate or *Residencia* to prove your country of residence. Failure to produce the required documents could result in your bank account being frozen. This requirement is part of an EU initiative to crack down on tax dodgers.

You can open a bank account in Spain whether you're a resident or a non-residentm but it's better to open an account in person than by correspondence from abroad. Ask friends, neighbours or colleagues for their recommendations and just go along to the bank of your choice and introduce yourself. You must be aged at least 18 and provide proof of identity (e.g. a passport), your address in Spain and your passport number or *NIE*. If you wish to open an account with a Spanish bank while you're abroad, you must first obtain an application form, available from foreign branches of Spanish banks or direct from a Spanish bank in Spain. You must select a branch from the list provided, which should preferably be close to where you will be living in Spain. If you open an account by correspondence, you must provide a reference from your current bank.

All Spanish bank accounts have 20 digits: the first four are the bank code, the next four are the branch code followed by the sort code (two digits) and then your account number (ten digits).

Non-residents

If you're a non-resident, you're entitled to open a non-resident euro account (*cuenta de euros*

de no residente) or a foreign currency account only. An important point to note is that when importing funds for the purchase of a property (or any other major transaction), you must have the transfer of funds verified by a certificate from your bank (*certificado de inversiones*). Although it's possible for non-resident homeowners to do most of their banking via a foreign account using debit and credit cards, they need a Spanish bank account to pay Spanish utility and tax bills (which are best paid by direct debit). If you own a holiday home in Spain, you can have your correspondence (e.g. cheque books, statements, payment advices.) sent to an address abroad, although some banks no longer offer this service.

Residents

To open a resident's account you must usually have a residence permit (*permiso de residencia*), certificate of residence (*certificado de residencia*) or evidence that you have a job in Spain. Note that it isn't advisable to close your bank accounts abroad when you live in Spain, unless you're sure that you won't need them in the future. Even when you're resident in Spain, it's cheaper to keep money in local currency in an account in a country you visit regularly than to pay commission to convert euros. Many foreigners living in Spain maintain at least two cheque (current) accounts: a foreign account for international transactions and a local account with a Spanish bank for day-to-day business.

Cheque Accounts

The most common account in Spain is a cheque or current account (*cuenta de ahorro con talonario/cuenta corriente*), which are provided by all Spanish banks. However, many Spaniards don't trust cheques and prefer to deal in cash. Personal cheques cannot be guaranteed and aren't usually accepted for payment by local retailers, although banks can issue a book of certified cheques and some supermarket chains issue identity cards (which they sometimes misleadingly call 'credit' cards), allowing customers to pay with personal cheques. Cheque account holders are normally issued with cash or debit cards (see page 219), although you must usually ask for one.

The peculiarities of Spanish cheque accounts are outlined in the sections below.

Charges

Spanish banks levy some of the highest charges in Europe for day-to-day transactions such as cheque processing, standing orders, direct debits and credit card transactions. Always obtain a list of charges before opening an account and compare the charges levied by a number of banks. A number of transactions ('entries') per year (e.g. 30) are usually free, after which there's a charge per transaction (e.g. €0.25), although a bank manager can waive certain charges. If you arrange to have your salary or pension paid into a Spanish bank account (called *domiciliación de nómina*), you may qualify for a choice of gifts, entry in a grand draw to win a car or other prizes, and low or no-fee services such as a low-interest overdraft or a free credit card.

Interest

Spanish cheque accounts pay little interest on account balances, e.g. just 0.1 or 0.2 per cent on the average balance. Generally, a cheque account that pays a 'normal' rate of interest requires a minimum balance of around €1,500 and even then it may pay interest only on the balance above this amount. So there's little point in keeping a lot of money in a cheque account when you can put your money in a deposit or savings account (see below) and earn interest on the whole balance.

Writing Cheques

Spanish cheques (*cheques* or *talones*) may be different from those you're familiar with. Your account details (*código cuenta cliente/CCC* with 20 digits – see **Opening an Account** above) are printed at the top right of cheques and statements. This information is required when payments are to be made directly to or from your account, e.g. for direct debits. The payee's (*páguese a*) name should be written in the top left corner (it's usual to write *Sr. D.* in front of a man's name and *Sra. Da.* in front of a woman's). The amount in figures should be written in the top right corner. Many people put a hash (#) sign before and after the amount, e.g.

#4.500,25€#, so that it cannot be altered, although this isn't obligatory. The amount should also be written in words (*en letras*) on the line below the payee's name, e.g. for the above amount *cuatro mil quinientos euros con veinticinco céntimos*.

The date must be written in words under the amount (in words) and after the town where the bank is located. You should sign in the bottom right corner below the date. The amount and date in words must usually be written in Spanish, although some banks allow you to write it in English and other languages. Note that your bank isn't required to reimburse you for a falsified cheque if you've been negligent when writing it.

If a cheque is made out to the bearer, the words *al portador* must be added. When making a cheque out to a named person, you should write, for example, '*Páguese a John Smith por este cheque*'. To ensure that a cheque can be paid only into the account of the payee, you must add *y Cia* between diagonal lines on the front or add *a abonar en cuenta* before the name of the payee.

Note that, in order to pay a cheque into your bank account, you must sign the back.

Validity

Spanish cheques are valid indefinitely, although it isn't wise to keep a cheque for longer than six months before cashing it. All cheques, including post-dated cheques, are payable on presentation (if the funds are available). If you write a cheque without sufficient funds in your account, your bank must pay out whatever is in your account as part payment, although this isn't always done, and, if the cheque is issued and payable in Spain, send you a 'notarial protest' (*declaración substitativo de impago/ declaración equivalente*) within 15 days (they have 20 days if it's issued in another European country and 60 days if it's issued outside Europe). You're obliged to pay a penalty of 10 per cent of the unpaid amount of a cheque, e.g. if you write a cheque for €1,000 and have only €750 in your account, you must pay the €250 shortfall plus a €25 penalty. **It's illegal to overdraw a bank account without prior agreement and it can lead to many problems.**

⚠ Caution

Beware of accepting cheques from foreigners (even for small amounts), as they often bounce, resulting in a bank fee, e.g. €3, plus the loss of your money!

You cannot usually stop payment of a cheque unless the cheque or cheque book has been lost or stolen, when a police report (*denuncia*) must be produced. If your cheque book is lost or stolen, you must notify your bank by telephone immediately and confirm the loss in writing. Any cheques written after you've informed your bank of a loss aren't your responsibility.

Bills of Exchange

Cheques aren't usually used to pay instalments on credit purchases in Spain. Instalments payments are made via bills of exchange (*letra de cambio*), one of which is issued for each payment due. You're required to sign one for each payment to be made (e.g. 24 if you're paying monthly for an item over two years), and they're then presented to your bank for payment by your creditor each month. Make sure they're made out in the name of the company that sold the goods and not an individual. If funds aren't available to pay a bill of exchange, you will receive a 'bill of exchange protest' (*letra protestada*) from your bank asking you to pay the amount due plus extra costs. **You should never sign *letras* on behalf of a company or someone else,** **as you're held personally responsible for payment.**

Standing Orders & Direct Debits

You can have standing orders (*domiciliación de pagos*) and direct debits (*domiciliación bancaria*) paid by your Spanish bank by simply completing a form at your bank and giving them a copy of a bill. This is the best way to pay all regular bills, such as electricity, gas, water, telephone, local taxes and community charges. However, you should check your statements to ensure that payments have been made, as banks cannot always be relied upon.

Deposits

You can pay cheques drawn on a foreign bank into a Spanish account in all major currencies. Your bank may credit your account immediately, which means that you can draw on the money before the cheque has been cleared (which may take weeks). Many banks charge a flat fee per cheque (e.g. €3 or €5), so it pays to write cheques for large amounts, and you receive the exchange rate for cheques and travellers' cheques (which is higher than when changing cash).

Correspondence

All correspondence from Spanish banks is in Spanish and it's advisable to learn to interpret your statements and other correspondence you receive. The most common words used in statements are *fecha* (date), *debe* (debit), *haber* (credit), *fecha operación/valor* (date of operation/transaction), *saldo* (balance) and *concepto* (description). Account statements (*estados* or *comunicaciones de movimentos*) are sent to customers monthly or quarterly, although you can request one at any time by asking for an *extracto* or an *avance*. Most banks now provide the option of receiving all correspondence via your online account.

Security

Bogus emails claiming to be from your bank and asking for confidential information such as your account numbers and PIN are widespread in Spain. The emails look authentic, as they contain the bank's logo and the sender's email address includes the bank's domain. In many cases, unsuspecting recipients send personal details or click on a website link included in the email and the fraudsters access (and empty) their accounts. If you're in any doubt about the authenticity of an email, contact your bank immediately.

Debit Cards

All Spanish banks offer customers combined cash or debit cards (*tarjeta de débito*), which are widely used and accepted throughout Spain. Purchases and cash withdrawals are automatically debited from your cheque or savings account. You don't receive a monthly statement, although you can obtain account balances and mini-statements from cash machines (ATMs), and cannot overdraw your account with a debit card. A card allows you to withdraw up to €600 per day from ATMs operated by your own bank – less from those of other banks.

There are many thousands of ATMs in Spain, where the three main networks are *Red 6000*, *Servired* and *Telebanco 4B* (indicated by a blue and yellow striped logo with the inscription '4B'). Cash can also usually be obtained from a network other than the one your card belongs to, for which there's a fee (from €1.50 to €3). Most ATMs accept a bewildering number of Spanish and foreign cards, usually illustrated on machines, including credit and charge cards (see opposite). Note, however, that although foreign debit cards such as those belonging to the Visa network, can be used to obtain cash in Spain, they're usually treated as credit cards and a charge is made.

Most ATMs are located outside banks. In cases when they're located inside the bank or in a lobby, you may need to run your card through a card reader to gain access. The procedure for withdrawing money from an ATM is usually as follows:

1. If the machine is in working order, a message such as *Introduzca su tarjeta, por favor* (Insert your card, please) is displayed. If your card is rejected, try again; if it's rejected a second time, try another machine. If a machine is temporarily out of order, a message such as *Cajero temporalmente fuera de servicio* is displayed.

2. Most machines permit you to choose the language in which instructions are displayed. If this is the case, the first screen will show a selection of languages.

3. Next you're asked to enter your personal identification number (PIN) and press the green 'enter' (*anotación*) button. If you make a mistake, press the yellow 'erase' (*borrar*) button and re-enter your PIN. As a security measure, if you enter the wrong PIN three times, your card will be retained by the machine and you must contact your bank for its return.

4. Select the service required, e.g. balance enquiry (*saldo*), statement enquiry (*extracto de saldo*) or cash withdrawal (*sacar dinero*).

5. If you've chosen to withdraw cash, the screen will usually display a choice of amounts, e.g. €20, €50, €100, €150 and €200. Note however, that some machines only offer amounts payable in €20 and €50 notes. If the amount you wish to withdraw isn't displayed, you can press the 'other amounts' (*otras cantidades*) button and enter the amount required. If you make a mistake, press the yellow 'erase' (*borrar*) button and re-enter the correct amount. If you request more than your current credit limit (or account balance), you will be asked to request a smaller amount.

6. Remove your card, cash and receipt (machines may automatically issue a receipt or ask you if you require one – *¿Desea un recibo?*) when instructed.

The 'cancel' (*cancelar*) button can be used to terminate a transaction at any point and your card will be returned; you then can start again, if required.

☑ SURVIVAL TIP

Note that it's inadvisable to rely entirely on a debit (or credit) card to obtain cash in Spain, as your card may be 'swallowed' by an ATM and it may be some time before it's returned via your bank.

If you lose your cash card or it's stolen, you must report it to your bank as soon as possible or phone the appropriate number: *Red 6000*, ☎ 902 206 000; *Servired*, ☎ 902 192 100; or *Telebanco 4B*, ☎ 902 114 400.

Complaints

If you have a complaint regarding your bank, don't expect to receive a quick resolution (or any resolution at all). A complaint should be addressed to the ombudsman (whose title may be something like *defensor del cliente*) of your bank. The Bank of Spain (Banco de España, Servicio de Reclamaciones, Alcalá, 50, 28014 Madrid, ☎ 900 545 454, 🖵 www.bde.es – information available under '*Servicios al Público*') can provide further information on filing a complaint.

CREDIT & CHARGE CARDS

Credit and charge cards are usually referred to collectively as credit cards (*tarjeta de crédito*) in Spain, although not all cards allow you to repay the balance over a period of time. Visa and MasterCard are the most widely accepted credit cards and are issued by most Spanish banks. Charge cards such as American Express and Diners Club aren't as widely accepted in Spain as they are in the UK and US (the Spanish wisely prefer cash, which cannot be traced by the tax authorities!).

The annual fee for a credit card varies according to the issuing bank and is usually between €10 and €25 per year for a standard Visa or MasterCard and between €40 and €60 a year for a 'gold' card. Always check annual fees and interest charges, as they vary greatly. Some credit cards provide free travel insurance (e.g. Europ Assistance) or life insurance (in the event of an accident) when travel costs are paid for with the card, or operate a points system whereby you earn points every time you use a card. Before obtaining a credit or charge card, compare the costs **and** benefits.

In some countries (e.g. the UK), credit card users are protected against a purchase going 'wrong', such as a company going bust or goods being faulty (which also applies to goods purchased overseas).

It's advisable to retain your foreign credit cards when you live in Spain, at least for a period. One of the advantages of using a credit card issued abroad is that your bill is usually rendered or your account debited around six weeks later, thus giving you a period of interest-free credit, except when cards are used to obtain cash, when interest starts immediately. You may, however, find it more convenient and cheaper to be billed in euros than in a foreign currency, when payments can vary with exchange rate fluctuations.

Most ATMs in Spain accept credit and charge cards. Note, however, that there's a standard charge (e.g. 1.5 per cent) for using a foreign credit card to obtain cash in Spain and, if you use a Spanish credit card, a high interest rate is usually levied from the day of the withdrawal. In order to withdraw cash from an ATM with a credit card, you must obtain a PIN from the issuing bank. Cardholders can usually withdraw any amount up to their credit balance or personal limit.

Major department and chain stores issue their own free account cards, among them Alcampo, Carrefour, Cortefiel and El Corte Inglés. Some cards allow credit, where the account balance may be repaid over a period, although interest rates are usually high (the El Corte Inglés card allows three months' free credit on certain items).

Note that in rural and resort areas, many small businesses don't accept credit cards. Never assume that a particular business (such as a restaurant) accepts credit cards or you may discover to your embarrassment that it doesn't.

⚠ **Caution**

Spain has one of the highest incidences of credit card theft in the EU. If you lose a credit card or have it stolen, report it immediately by telephone to the issuing office (see below) or your bank and confirm the loss in writing by registered letter. Your liability is usually limited to around €150 until you report a loss, after which you have no liability. Numbers to call are as follows: American Express, ☎ 902 111 135; Diners Club, ☎ 901 101 011; MasterCard, ☎ 900 971 231; Visa or Visa Electron, ☎ 900 991 124.

Even if you don't like credit cards and shun any form of credit, they do have their uses, e.g. no-deposit car rentals, no prepayment of hotel bills, the convenience of shopping by phone or via the internet, safety and security and, above all, convenience (although you must be wary of bogus charges and scrutinise statements).

MORTGAGES

Mortgages, or home loans (*hipotecas*), are available from most Spanish banks (for residents and non-residents), foreign banks in Spain, and overseas and offshore banks. In recent years, Spanish and foreign lenders have tightened their lending criteria due to the repayment problems experienced by many borrowers in the early '90s and the recent 'sub-prime' crisis, although over the last few years a record number of mortgages have been taken out, the average amount borrowed being around €120,000.

The amount you can borrow depends on various factors, such as your income, your trade or profession, whether you're an employee or self-employed, whether you're married and, if so, whether your partner works. Lenders may also have a maximum lending limit based on a percentage of your income, but this isn't required by law in Spain.

Terms & Conditions

Mortgages are granted on a percentage of a property's valuation, which is usually below the market value. The maximum mortgage in Spain is usually 80 per cent of the valuation for a principal home (*vivienda habitual*) and 50 to 60 per cent for a second home (*segunda residencia*). The normal term is 10 to 15 years, although longer terms are common, e.g. 30 to 35 years, and the maximum repayment period is 50 years. This may be shorter for second homes. Repayment mortgages are the most common type in Spain, although endowment and pension-linked mortgages are also available. Payments can usually be made monthly or quarterly.

Some banks offer mortgages of up to 80 per cent of the value of a property (usually for new developments) without proof of income, although you must usually provide proof of your monthly income and outgoings such as mortgage payments, rent and other loans or commitments. If you want a Spanish mortgage to buy a property for commercial purposes, you must provide a detailed business plan in Spanish.

Some foreign lenders apply stricter rules than Spanish lenders regarding income, employment and the type of property on which they will lend. Foreign lenders, e.g. offshore banks, may also have strict rules regarding the nationality and domicile of borrowers (some won't lend to Spanish residents), and the percentage they will lend. They may also levy astronomical charges if you get into arrears. If you raise a mortgage outside Spain for a Spanish property, you should be aware of any impact this may have on your foreign or Spanish tax liabilities or allowances.

Note that a mortgage can be assumed by the new owner (called *subrogación*) when a

property is sold, which is common practice in Spain.

Rates

Spanish mortgages have recently been among the most competitive in Europe. Around 90 per cent of home loans in Spain have a variable (*interés variable*) instead of a fixed interest (*interés fijo*) rate and they've traditionally been set at 0.3 to 1 per cent above the European inter-bank rate (EURIBOR). In July 2008, rates for variable mortgages ranged from 4.95 to 5.5 per cent and those for fixed mortgages from 5.25 to 7 per cent. Note, however, that a low interest rate may be more than offset by increased commission charges. Always shop around for the best interest rate and ask the effective rate (*tasa anual equivalente/TAE*), including commissions and fees.

Lenders are required, on demand, to issue a list of conditions and interest rates (*hojas vinculantes*) that are binding on the lender for ten days. This enables you to compare rates among lenders.

Information on mortgage rates offered and fees charged by Spanish banks can be found on the Ausbanc (Banking Ombudsman) website (💻 www.ausbanc.com).

Charges

You must add expenses and fees, totalling around 10 per cent of the purchase price, to the cost of a property. In Spain, it's customary for a property to be held as security for a home loan, i.e. the lender takes a first charge on the property, which is recorded at the property registry office, and certain fees are payable to the notary (*notario*) for registering the charge against the property.

Most lenders levy an 'arrangement' fee (*comisión de apertura*) of 0.5 to 2.5 per cent of the purchase price. Although it's unusual to have a full survey carried out in Spain, most lenders insist on a 'valuation' (usually costing between €150 and €300) before they will grant a loan. Mortgages also usually have a cancellation fee of around 1 per cent. Note that, if you're a Spanish taxpayer, you can claim payments (capital and interest) on your Spanish mortgage against your tax liability (see **Income Tax** on page 226).

Spanish banks often insist that you take out home insurance cover with them together with the mortgage, although you aren't legally required to do so and should shop around before you take on insurance cover with a bank, as their rates are invariably higher than other insurers'.

Changing Lenders & Terms

It's quite easy to change your mortgage lender or re-negotiate mortgage terms with your existing lender. There are essentially two ways of doing so: by 'compulsory substitution' (*subrogación forzosa*), whereby a lender offering more favourable terms/interest rates takes over your existing mortgage, and by 'variation' (*novación modificativa*), whereby the existing lender offers a reduced interest rate or changes the repayment period. Banks may charge a maximum of 2.5 per cent when a lender wishes to cancel a mortgage with fixed interest and take one with variable interest (a common event when interest rates are falling). If you wish to re-negotiate your mortgage terms, it's a good idea to contact your branch manager to see what sort of deal your bank is prepared to offer you – most banks are keen to keep their mortgage customers. On the other hand, some lenders offer to pay all the associated expenses if you switch your mortgage to them!

If you're unable to meet your mortgage payments, lenders are usually willing to re-schedule your mortgage so that it extends over a longer period, thus allowing you to make lower payments. Some banks offer 'flexible' mortgage payments with the possibility of not paying two or three instalments a year. Note that you should make arrangements with your lender immediately you stop paying your mortgage, as lenders are quick to embargo a property and could eventually repossess it and sell it at auction, which can take just a few months.

Second Homes

If you have equity in an existing property, in Spain or abroad, it may be better to re-mortgage (or take out a second mortgage on) that property than to take out a new mortgage for a second home in Spain. It involves less paperwork (and therefore lower legal fees) and a plan can be tailored to your requirements. Depending on your equity in your existing property and the cost of your Spanish property, this may enable you to pay cash for a second

home. Note, however, that when a mortgage is taken out on a Spanish property it's based on that property and not the individual, which could be important if you get into repayment difficulties.

If you let a second home, you may be able to offset the interest (pro rata) on your mortgage against letting income. For example, if you let a Spanish property for three months of the year, you can offset a quarter of your annual mortgage interest against your letting income.

Foreign Currency Mortgages

It's possible to obtain a foreign currency mortgage (i.e. other than in euros) in Spain or abroad. In previous years, high Spanish interest rates meant that a foreign currency mortgage was a good bet for many foreigners, though this may no longer be true. In any case, you should be extremely wary about taking out a foreign currency mortgage, as interest rate gains can be wiped out overnight by currency swings and devaluations. It's generally recognised that you should take out a mortgage in the currency in which you're paid or in the currency of the country where the property in question is situated. When choosing between a euro loan and a foreign currency loan, make sure that you take into account all costs, fees, interest rates and possible currency fluctuations. If you have a foreign currency mortgage, you must usually pay commission charges each time you transfer foreign currency into euros or remit money to Spain.

TAXATION

Spain is no longer the tax haven it was in the '60s and '70s, when taxes were low and tax evasion was a way of life. Spain's taxes have increased dramatically during the last few decades, although allowances are generous and income tax and social security contributions combined remain among the lowest in the EU (Spain's fiscal burden is 37.1 per cent of GDP compared with an average of 39.6 per cent in the EU). Although income tax rates have been reduced over the last three years, indirect taxes (e.g. on fuel) have recently been increased. Before you decide to settle in Spain permanently, you should obtain expert advice regarding Spanish taxes. This will (hopefully) ensure that you take maximum advantage of your current tax status and that you don't make any mistakes that you will regret later.

⚠ **Caution**

Today it's difficult to avoid paying taxes in Spain and penalties for doing so are severe. Nevertheless, tax evasion is still widespread; many non-resident homeowners and foreign residents think that they should be exempt from Spanish taxes and are among the worst offenders.

As you would expect in a country with millions of bureaucrats, the Spanish tax system is inordinately complicated and most Spaniards don't understand it. In fact, even the experts have difficulty agreeing with the tax authorities (Agencia Estatal de Administración Tributaria/ AEAT), and different tax advisers often giving different advice. It's difficult to obtain accurate information from the tax authorities and, just when you think you have it cracked (ho! ho!) the authorities change the rules or hit you with a new tax.

Taxes are levied by three tiers of government in Spain: central government, regional governments and municipalities. Government taxes are administered by the Ministry of Economy and Taxation (Ministerio de Económica y Hacienda), which has its headquarters in Madrid and assessment and tax collection centres in provincial capital towns. Although the level of taxes in Spain isn't excessively burdensome, the number of taxes can be bewildering. At the last count there were around 15, including the following:

◆ **Business tax** (*impuesto sobre actividades económicas/IAE*) – payable by all businesses with an annual turnover of more than €600,000, including the self-employed. Note, however, that all businesses and the self-employed must register with the tax authorities irrespective of annual turnover.

◆ **Capital gains tax** (*impuesto sobre incremento de patrimonio de la venta de un bien inmueble*) – payable by residents and non-residents on the profits made on the sale of certain property and other assets located in Spain;

◆ **Company or corporation tax** (*impuesto sobre sociedades*) – payable at the rate of 30 per cent on the profits made by partnerships and registered companies such as a *Sociedad Anónima* (*SA*) or *Sociedad Limitada* (*SL*). Small and medium-size enterprises with an annual turnover below €8m pay 25 per cent company tax on profits. The Canary Islands, particularly Gran Canaria and Tenerife, are something of a company tax haven, with 1 to 5 per cent rates, depending on a number of factors, including type of activity and creation of employment.

◆ **Income tax** (*impuesto sobre la renta de las personas físicas/IRPF*) – payable by residents on worldwide income and by non-residents on income arising in Spain. Non-residents must also pay an imputed 'letting' or deemed property income tax based on property values (see page 228).

◆ **Inheritance & gift tax** (*impuesto sobre sucesiones y donaciones*) – payable by residents on the transfer of worldwide assets and by non-residents on Spanish assets;

◆ **Offshore company tax** (*impuesto especial*) – payable by offshore companies that don't declare the individual owner of property in Spain or the source of investment.

◆ **Property tax** (*impuesto sobre bienes inmeubles urbanos/IBIU*, formerly called *contribución urbana*) – payable by all property owners, whether resident or non-resident;

◆ **Social security** (*seguridad social*) – not strictly a tax, but payable by employees and the self-employed (see page 195);

◆ **Value added tax/VAT** (*impuesto sobre el valor añadido/IVA*) – payable on a wide range of goods and services at varying rates (see page 225);

◆ **Vehicle registration tax** (*impuesto sobre circulación de vehículos*) – payable by all those owning a Spanish-registered vehicle (see **Taxes** on page 146);

- **Waste/drainage tax** (*basura y alcantarillado*) – payable by most property owners, whether resident or non-resident;

- **Wealth tax** (*impuesto sobre el patrimonio*) – abolished in 2008 for all taxpayers, but non-residents owning high-value capital assets, including property, in Spain are still required to pay wealth tax for the year 2008 (see page 234).

There are other taxes relating to the construction and purchase of property in Spain, which include transfer tax (*impuesto de transmisiones patrimoniales/ITP*) and a local 'value increase' tax (*plus valía*), which is levied by councils (at various rates) when properties are sold (in addition to capital gains tax). If you purchase property in an urbanisation without the proper infrastructure, you may need to pay an exceptional municipal tax (*impuestos especiales municipales*) to bring the infrastructure up to the required standard. In addition to VAT, taxes are levied on cars, alcohol, petrol and tobacco products.

Most taxes in Spain are based on self-assessment, meaning that individual taxpayers are liable to report and calculate any tax due within the time limits established by law. Tax forms must be purchased by taxpayers and are usually obtainable from a tobacconist's (*estanco*), although some are available only from tax offices (*agencia tributaria*). Penalties and interest are levied for late payment or non-compliance, although there's a five-year statute of limitations (*prescripción*) on the collection of back taxes in Spain, i.e. if no action has been taken during this period to collect unpaid tax, it cannot be collected.

Fiscal Representation

The term fiscal representative (*representante fiscal*) refers to any person or agent who provides tax and other financial services; this may be a professional, such as an accountant (*contable*) or tax adviser (*asesor fiscal*), or it may be a non-professional who merely deals with your financial affairs on your behalf. (All accountants and tax advisers in Spain act as fiscal representatives for their clients.) It isn't necessary (but is recommended) for non-resident owners of a single dwelling in Spain to have a fiscal representative; if you have more than one asset in Spain, e.g. separate title deeds for a property and a garage or garden, or you own a commercial property, you **must** have a fiscal representative. A foreign company owning a property in Spain must have a fiscal representative, and a foreigner receiving income from a business in Spain may need one.

If you fail to appoint a representative when you're required to have one, you can be fined up to €6,000.

Even if they don't have a professional fiscal representative, non-residents should appoint someone in Spain to look after their financial affairs and declare and pay their taxes. The Spanish tax authorities will communicate with this person, and he can also receive your bank statements and ensure that your bank is paying your regular bills (such as electricity, water and telephone) by standing order and that you have sufficient funds in your account to pay them. Your representative (professional or not) can also apply for an identification number (*número de identificación de entranjero/NIE*) on your behalf.

Your representative can be a Spaniard or a foreign resident in Spain, an individual or a

company (such as a bank). The local provincial office of the Ministry of Finance must be notified of the appointment of a representative within two months by letter and the representative must expressly communicate his acceptance of the appointment to the office where your taxes are to be paid. Before employing a representative, you should obtain recommendations from friends, colleagues and acquaintances. However, bear in mind that, if you consult a number of 'experts', you're liable to receive conflicting advice.

Note also that some representatives fail to pay tax bills on time (or at all), thereby incurring their clients a fine equal to 20 per cent of the amount due. You should therefore check with the town hall and tax authorities that your bills have actually been paid!

Professional fiscal representation usually costs at least €150 per year for a single person and €300 for a couple, depending on the services provided, although many representatives charge only 50 per cent more for a couple than for a single person. There may be additional charges for tax administration and completing tax returns, the cost depending on the complexity of your tax affairs. For the relatively small cost involved, most people (residents and non-residents) are usually better off employing a professional representative to handle their Spanish tax and other financial affairs than doing it themselves, particularly as the regulations change frequently; you can often save more than the representative's fee in avoided tax.

VALUE ADDED TAX

Value added tax or VAT (*impuesto sobre el valor añadido/IVA*) is levied on most goods and services in Spain. Most prices in shops are quoted inclusive of value added tax (*IVA incluido*); where they're exclusive (e.g. the prices of office equipment) they will be marked *más IVA*.

Certain goods and services are exempt from VAT, including healthcare (e.g. doctors' and dentists' services), educational services, insurance, banking and certain financial services, social security services, sports and cultural activities, postal services, state lotteries, land and second-hand property, the letting of residential property, the transfer of a business (provided the buyer continues the existing business), and certain transactions that are subject to other taxes. Exports are also exempt from VAT.

VAT applies to the mainland and the Balearic Islands but isn't levied in the Canary Islands, Ceuta and Melilla. Instead, the Canary Islands have an indirect general tax (*impuesto general indirecto Canario/IGIC*), which is levied on goods and services at the rate of 4.5 per cent, and Ceuta and Melilla levy various sales taxes on imports, services and production. Spain has the following rates of VAT (it's the declared aim of the EU to have just one rate of VAT for all members, although this will take some time to accomplish, particularly as only Denmark currently has one rate and all other members have at least two!):

VAT Rates	
Rate	Applicability
4% (super reduced rate)	Basic foodstuffs such as bread, flour, milk, cheese, eggs, fruit & vegetables; books, newspapers & magazines; certain pharmaceutical products; disabled vehicles & prostheses; subsidised housing
7% (reduced rate)	Food; drink (other than alcohol & soft drinks); fuel; water; communications; medicines; feminine hygiene products; transport; hotels; restaurants (excluding five-fork rated restaurants); theatres & cinemas; certain sports services; new dwellings
16% (standard rate)	All other goods & services, including utility bills, car hire and five-fork rated restaurants

VAT is payable on goods purchased outside the EU and, unless it has already been paid, on goods purchased in an EU country; you may be asked to produce a VAT receipt. People who are resident outside the EU can obtain exemption from VAT on purchases of individual items in Spain costing over €100. Retailers can provide information and the necessary forms. You must show your passport and complete a form and the shop posts the refund to your home address.

INCOME TAX

Spanish income tax (*impuesto sobre la renta de las personas físicas/IRPF*) is payable on earned and unearned income. Taxable income includes salaries, pensions, capital gains, property and investment income (dividends and interest), and income from professional, artistic, business or agricultural activities. It also includes employee benefits and perks such as overseas and cost of living allowances, contributions to profit sharing schemes, bonuses (annual, performance, etc.), storage and relocation allowances, payments in kind (such as free accommodation or meals), stock options, and the cost or value of language lessons provided for a spouse, a company car for personal use, home leave or holidays (paid by your employer) and children's private education. If you're a non-resident or own more than one property in Spain, your 'income' also includes 2 per cent of its fiscal value (*valor catastral*) – see **Tax on Deemed Letting Income** on page 229.

Major tax reforms introduced in recent years are designed to make taxation simpler for the taxpayer and the authorities and to reduce tax fraud, which is still widespread.

☑ SURVIVAL TIP

If you're able to choose the country where you're taxed, it can be to your advantage to pay Spanish income tax, as rates are low and there are more allowances than there are in some other countries; you should obtain advice from an international tax expert.

Moving to Spain (or another country) often provides opportunities for legal 'favourable tax planning'. To make the most of your situation, it's advisable to obtain advice before moving to Spain, as there are usually a number of things you can do in advance to reduce your tax liability, in Spain and abroad. Be sure to consult a tax adviser who is familiar with the Spanish tax system and that of your present country of residence. For example, you may be able to avoid paying tax on a business abroad if you establish residence and domicile in Spain before you sell it. On the other hand, if you sell a foreign home after establishing your principal residence in Spain, it becomes a second home and you may then be liable to capital gains tax abroad (this is a complicated subject and you should obtain expert advice). You should notify the tax authorities in your former country of residence that you're going to live permanently in Spain.

Employees' income tax is deducted at source by Spanish employers, i.e. pay-as-you-earn (*retenciones*), and individuals aren't responsible for paying tax on their salary as, for example, in France, although they must still make a tax declaration and, of course, pay tax on any income other than salary. Self-employed people must pay their income tax quarterly (*pago fraccionado*). Non-residents who receive an income from a Spanish source and non-resident property owners should instruct their fiscal representative to file an income tax declaration on their behalf (or do it themselves).

Tax evasion is illegal and a criminal offence in Spain, and offenders can be heavily fined or even imprisoned. Although Spanish tax inspectors make few inspections, they target them at those among whom tax fraud is most prevalent, such as the self-employed. Note also that new legislation has been introduced to tackle fraud, and 'fiscal nomads' will find it more difficult to avoid Spanish taxation in future. On the other hand, tax avoidance (i.e. legally paying as little tax as possible, if necessary by finding and exploiting loopholes in the tax laws) is highly recommended! Residents have a number of opportunities to legally reduce their taxes, although non-residents have very few or none at all.

You can obtain free tax advice from the information section (*servicio de información* or

79.53
426.60
&11.01
|89.65
&50.22

oficina de información al contribuyente) at your provincial tax office in Spain, where staff will answer queries and advise you on completing your tax declaration (unfortunately, they won't complete it for you!). Some offices, particularly those in resort areas, have staff who speak English and other foreign languages. The tax office provides a central telephone information service (☎ 901 335 533), available from 9am to 9pm Mondays to Fridays from 1st April to 30th June and from 9am to 7pm Mondays to Fridays the rest of the year. If you require information about income tax and value added tax (VAT) refunds or need to order tax labels, the tax office runs an automatic telephone service, which is open 24 hours a day, seven days a week (☎ 901 121 224). There's also a useful website (🖥 www.aeat.es), although your Spanish needs to be fluent to understand most of it; there are few pages in English.

Liability

Your liability for income tax in Spain depends on whether you're officially resident there. Under Spanish law you become a fiscal resident in Spain if you spend 183 days there during a calendar year **or** your main centre of economic interest, e.g. investments or business, is in Spain. Temporary absences are included in the calculation of the period spent in Spain (or Spanish territories). If your spouse and dependent minor children normally reside in Spain and have residence permits (and you aren't legally separated), you're considered to be a tax resident in Spain (unless you can prove otherwise). Note that similar rules apply to other EU countries; for example, the UK limits visits by non-residents to 182 days in any one year or an average of 91 days per tax year over a four-year period.

If you're tax resident in two countries simultaneously, your 'tax home' may be determined under international treaty rules. Under such treaties you're considered to be resident in the country where you have a permanent home; if you have a permanent home in both countries, you're deemed to be resident in the country where your personal and economic ties are closer. If your residence cannot be determined under this rule, you're deemed to be resident in the country where you have a habitual abode. If you have a habitual abode in both or in neither country, you're deemed to be resident in the country of which you're a citizen. Finally, if you're a citizen of both or neither country, the authorities of the countries concerned will decide your tax residence between them!

Spanish residents are taxed on their worldwide income, whereas non-residents are taxed in Spain only on income arising in Spain, which is exempt from tax in their home countries (see **Double-taxation** below).

If you plan to live permanently in Spain, you should notify the tax authorities in your previous country of residence. If you move to Spain to take up a job or start a business, you must register with the local tax authorities soon after your arrival.

If your gross earned annual income from work (one source or one employer only) in Spain is less than €22,000, you're exempt from making a tax declaration, as your salary will have been correctly taxed at source. If your gross income from more than one source (e.g. from a pension and investments) is less than €10,000, you aren't required to make a tax declaration or pay Spanish income tax. However, if you're entitled to deductions for pension plans or housing, you must make a tax declaration irrespective of your earnings.

Double-taxation

Spain has double-taxation treaties with around 50 countries, including all European Economic Area (EEA) countries (except Cyprus), Argentina, Australia, Bolivia, Brazil,

Canada, Chile, China, Cuba, Ecuador, India, Indonesia, Israel, Japan, Mexico, Morocco, the Philippines, Russia, South Korea, Switzerland, Thailand, Tunisia, Turkey, the US and Venezuela. Treaties are designed to ensure that income that has already been taxed in one treaty country isn't taxed again in another treaty country. Treaties establish a tax credit or exemption on certain kinds of income, in your country of residence or the country where the income was earned. Where applicable, a double-taxation treaty prevails over domestic law.

Citizens of most countries are exempt from paying taxes in their home country when they spend a minimum period abroad, e.g. a year. The US is one of the few exceptions. US citizens can obtain a copy of a brochure, *Tax Guide for US Citizens and Resident Aliens Abroad*, from American consulates or from 🖥 www.irs.gov/publications – go to publication 54.

However, even if there's no double-taxation agreement between Spain and another country, you can still obtain relief from double taxation through a direct deduction of any foreign tax paid or through a 'foreign compensation' (*compensación extranjera*) formula.

Note that taxpayers entitled to double-taxation relief must still make a tax declaration in Spain and, if their tax liability in another country is lower than that in Spain, they must pay the Spanish tax authorities the difference. If you're in doubt about your tax liability in your home country, contact your nearest embassy or consulate in Spain.

Expatriate Workers

Tax breaks for foreign workers were introduced in 2004 as an incentive for foreign companies to establish their headquarters or a permanent office in Spain and to encourage executives and employees to work there. Under the scheme, foreign employees living in Spain can choose to be taxed at a flat rate of 25 per cent during the year of their arrival and for the following five years. Under this tax regime, you don't qualify for any allowances or deductions and must meet the following requirements:

◆ You must be a first-time resident of Spain or have been non-resident during the ten years before you move to Spain.

◆ You must have a work contract for a job, which must be carried out in Spain.

◆ Your employer must be a company with a permanent establishment in Spain.

Property Owners

The liability for income tax of property owners depends on whether they're resident or non-resident in Spain. Non-resident property owners and resident owners of more than one property must also pay a so-called tax on deemed letting income (see below).

Residents: Property income earned by residents is included in their annual income tax declaration and tax is payable at the standard income tax rates (see page 231). You're eligible for deductions such as repairs and maintenance, security, cleaning costs, mortgage repayments (Spanish loans only), management and letting expenses (e.g. advertising), local taxes, and insurance, plus an amortisation deduction of 3 per cent per year of the value of the property. You should seek professional advice to ensure that you're claiming everything you're entitled to.

Non-residents: Non-resident property owners are liable for income tax at a flat rate of 24 per cent on any income arising in Spain, including income from letting a property. Income must be declared on Form 210 (*Impuestos Sobre la Renta de las Personas Físicas y Sobre Sociedades*) and paid quarterly to the tax authorities. There's a 10 per cent surcharge for late payment. For any part of

the year when you don't have rental income, e.g. the winter, you must still make a tax declaration, e.g. for tax on deemed letting income, using Form 214 (*impuesto sobre el patrimonio y sobre la renta de no residentes*), which is obtainable only from a tax office.

Non-residents owning a single property in Spain can declare their income tax at any time during the year, e.g. the declaration for 2008 could be made any time up to 31st December 2009, using Form 214. (A wealth tax declaration must also be made, but for 2008 only – see page 234 – and this can be done on the same form.)

Form 214 is a simple form and homeowners with a knowledge of Spanish should be able to complete it themselves (instructions in Spanish are printed on the reverse). When a husband and wife own a property jointly, they should complete separate forms, although it's possible for a couple to make their declaration on one form (check with your fiscal representative). When a property is used partly for letting and partly for habitation, an apportionment is made between the amount of time used for each purpose. This tax may be offset against taxes paid in other countries.

Non-residents must pay property income tax at a bank in cash or by debit from a Spanish bank account.

Taxable Income

Deemed Letting Income

The tax that causes most confusion (and resentment), particularly among non-resident property owners, is the tax on deemed or notional letting income (*rendimientos del capital inmobiliario*, usually referred to simply as *renta*). All non-resident property owners and all residents owning more than one property in Spain are deemed to receive an income of 2 per cent of the fiscal value (*valor catastral*) of their property (1.1 per cent if the fiscal value has been revised since 1st January 1994). Non-residents pay tax at a flat rate tax of 24 per cent on this income (for example, if you own a property valued at €100,000, 2 per cent of this is €2,000, on which the 24 per cent 'income' tax is €480); there are no deductions. Residents must add the deemed

letting income to other income for income tax purposes. Principal residences are exempt from this tax.

Pensions

The taxation of pensioners changed in 1992, and since then pensions have been taxed according to the source of the income, as detailed below. Taxation of investment capital and insurance-based pensions can be very complicated and you should obtain expert professional advice from an accountant or tax adviser **before** deciding where and how to receive your pension. See also **Supplementary Pensions** on page 200.

Employment-based pensions: Employment-based pensions are taxed in the same way as salary income (see above). You're entitled to the same allowances and deductions, and the same tax rates apply. However, the situation isn't as straightforward if your pension is paid from a savings scheme such as a pension fund established through an employment relationship with tax advantages in your home country.

Investment capital pensions: Investment capital pensions, whereby you pay a sum of money or transfer assets such as property to another party in return for annuity payments (or a monthly income) for a fixed period or until death, may give rise to capital gains and interest income, each of which is taxed differently in Spain.

Insurance-based pensions: Insurance schemes that permit you to choose between taking the whole amount accrued in a lump sum and having it paid in the form of annuities may be taxed as capital gains (see page 237) or as ordinary income.

Civil service pensions: Foreign civil service pensions are usually tax free in Spain may not need to be declared to the Spanish authorities if they're your only source of income, although this depends on the country paying your pension and whether it has a double-taxation treaty with Spain (see page 227); you may need to provide the tax office with proof that your pension is taxed at source. Civil service pensions don't include United Nations pensions, as the UN cannot tax its former employees (unlike individual countries). Note, however, that if you have other income that's taxable in Spain, your civil service pension is usually taken into account when calculating your Spanish tax rate and it must usually be declared. If you pay tax in error on a pension that wasn't in fact taxable, you can claim a refund only for the previous five years, which is Spain's statute of limitations (if they aren't collected, taxes also usually lapse after five years).

Non-resident pensions: Non-resident pensions received from a Spanish source are subject to special tax rates depending on the amount, as follows:

Amount	Tax Rate	Cumulative Tax
Up to €12,000	8%	€960
€12,000 to €18,700	30%	€2,970
Over €18,700	40%	

Allowances

Before calculating your income tax liability, you can deduct certain costs from your gross income (allowances). The resultant figure is your taxable income. The following allowances apply to the fiscal year 2007, i.e. tax declarations made in 2008. Note that there are numerous regional variations and additional allowances to which not everyone is entitled.

♦ any withholding tax paid during the previous year;

♦ all social security payments (see **Chapter 13**);

♦ a 'personal minimum' (*mínimo personal*) allowance, which is currently €5,050. If you're over 65, this amount is increased by €900. If you're over 75, it's increased by €1,100.

♦ **one** of the following deductions from your income (these deductions also apply if you were unemployed and accepted a job in a different locality to where you live):

– €4,000 if your annual salary (i.e. earned from paid employment) is less than €9,000;

– €4,000 minus 22.91 per cent of the difference between your salary and €9,000 if your annual salary is between €9,000 and €13,000; e.g. if your salary is €12,000, the deduction would be €4,000 - (€3,000 x 0.2291 = €687.30) = €3,312.70;

– €2,600 if your annual salary is over €13,000 or the income is from other sources, e.g. investments;

♦ **one** of the following deductions if you're disabled (these allowances may also be claimed by a disabled person's dependants and parents):

– €2,270 if your disability is between 33 and 65 per cent, plus deductions of €2,800 from income and €2,000 for care if you have mobility problems;

– €6,900 if your disability is above 65 per cent, plus deductions of €6,200 from income and €2,000 for care if you have mobility problems;

♦ the following deductions for dependants:

– €1,800 for a first child;

– €2,000 for a second child;

– €3,600 for a third child;

– €4,100 for a fourth and each additional child;

– €1,400 for each child under three (for childcare fees);

– an additional €1,400 maternity/ paternity allowance for each child under three (the parent must be contributing to social security); note that the parent can opt for this allowance to be deducted from his gross income or choose to receive a monthly payment of €100.

– €1,000 if you have someone aged over 75 living with you and their annual income is below €8,000;

♦ professional and trade union fees;

♦ Spanish company pension contributions up to a maximum of €10,000 if you're aged between 50 and 52. If you're between 52 and 65, you can contribute a maximum of 50 per cent of your income.

♦ a percentage of an annuity (life or fixed-period), depending on your age;

♦ if you're a divorced parent, child-support payments made as a result of a court decision (maintenance payments may be taxable subject to provisions made under court orders).

Calculation

Income tax rates for individuals (*personas físicas*) start at 24 per cent on taxable income (i.e. once the above allowances have been deducted) up to €17,707.20 and rise to 43 per cent on income above €53,407.20. Tax is divided between the Spanish state (60 per cent of the total), known as the 'general scale', and the autonomous regions (40 per cent), as shown in the two tables below, although some regions (e.g. the Basque Country, Catalonia and La Rioja) offer deductions from tax due. You must add the two rates to obtain the total tax payable (see *table 1* below).

The table below (*table 2*) shows the total income tax payable (the above general and autonomous region scales combined).

Table 1

Income Tax Rates – General Scale

Taxable Income	Tax Rate	Cumulative Tax
Up to €17,707	15.66%	€2,772.90
€17,707 to €33,007	18.27%	€5,568.20
€33,007 to €53,407	24.14%	€10,494.76
Over €53,407	27.13%	

Income Tax Rates – Autonomous Region Scale

Taxable Income	Tax Rate	Cumulative Tax
Up to €17,707	8.34%	€1,476.76
€17,707 to €33,007	9.73%	€2,965.45
€33,007 to €53,407	12.86%	€5,588.89
Over €53,407	15.87%	

Table 2

Income Tax Rates – Combined

Taxable Income	Tax Rate	Cumulative Tax
Up to €17,707	24%	€4,249.73
€17,707 to €33,007	28%	€8,533.73
€33,007 to €53,407	37%	€16,081.73
Over €53,407	43%	

Credits

Before arriving at your final tax bill, you can make certain deductions from the tax due (referred to here as 'credits' to avoid confusion with the deductions from salary that count as tax allowances – see above), including the following:

♦ 75 per cent of any *plus valía* tax paid as a result of a property sale;

♦ 15 per cent of the cost of the purchase or renovation of your principal residence up to €9,015 (excluding additions such as a garage or swimming pool and normal maintenance and repairs);

♦ mortgage payments (capital plus interest) up to €9,015;

♦ 15 per cent of the amount invested in a 'housing savings' account (*cuenta vivienda*) up to €9,015.

Any personal income tax paid in another country is also deducted from your tax due. However, if you pay higher tax abroad than you would have paid in Spain, you won't receive a rebate from the Spanish tax authorities!

Declaration

An annual income tax declaration (*declaración sobre la renta de personas físicas*) for the year ending 31st December must be lodged between 1st May and 20th June of the following year by residents and non-residents with income in Spain (other than income from property letting). This deadline also applies to declarations for property tax and wealth tax for residents, although if you're entitled to a refund (*devolución*) it's extended until 30th June.

If your gross earned income is below €10,000 (for an individual declaration), it isn't necessary to complete an income tax declaration. Note that, if you're a Spanish resident, this limit applies to your worldwide family income if it's taxed in Spain but doesn't include income taxed in another country. If you're resident in Spain, however, the authorities will ask to see your income tax declaration when you renew your residence permit (*residencia*). It's therefore advisable to make a declaration in any case, simply ticking the box marked *declaración negativa* to indicate that your income is blow the threshold.

Unless your tax affairs are simple, it's advisable to employ an accountant or tax adviser (*asesor fiscal*) to complete your tax return and ensure that you're correctly assessed. There are 'foreign' tax assessors (*asesores de extranjero*) who specialise in filing returns for foreigners, particularly non-residents. The fees charged for filing tax returns vary and for residents are around €60 for a simple return and €100 for an ordinary return. The fee for filing a tax return for a non-resident is usually around €50. Make sure that you have your tax return stamped as proof of payment by your adviser.

There are four kinds of tax declaration form in Spain, as detailed below.

Draft Declaration

The draft declaration (*borrador*) can be used by any taxpayer and is the simplest method of declaring your income. Instead of your having to purchase, complete and return a tax form, a draft declaration is sent to you by the tax authorities, with figures and calculations based on your income the previous year. Taxpayers who request a draft declaration in their previous year's declaration (via the tick box *petición de borrador/datos*) receive the draft by post during March and April; anyone else can request one before 15th June.

Once you receive the draft, you must confirm or contest the figures. If the figures are correct, you can confirm this with the tax office by one of the following methods:

♦ at a tax office or participating bank;

♦ by phone, Mondays to Fridays, 9am to 9pm (☎ 901 200 345);

♦ online (🖳 www.aeat.es);

♦ by SMS (☎ 5025) – Write the word 'RENTA' followed by a space, then enter your draft reference number, followed by another space and then your *NIE*.

♦ at a cash machine following the instructions under the Renta section.

According to tax office statistics, the majority of taxpayers whose draft declaration is correct and are entitled to a tax refund receive this at the beginning of May – considerably earlier than those using other types of declaration. If the draft isn't correct, you must contact a tax office, explaining the changes to be made.

Abbreviated Declaration

The *declaración abreviada* (Form 103) consists of two pages. It's used by taxpayers whose income derives entirely from earnings or from pensions and investments that have already been subject to Spanish withholding tax. If your income consists of a pension that has had deductions made in another country and which you intend to subtract from your Spanish declaration, you cannot use this form, but must use a simple declaration (see below).

Simple Declaration

The *declaración simplificada* consists of five pages and is for those with the same sources of income (usually below €600,000) as for the abbreviated declaration (see above) plus income from letting, certain business and agricultural income, and capital gains from the sale of a permanent home where the total gain will be invested in a new home in Spain. Form 101 is used for the declaration and payment of the first stage of income tax (and for claiming

refunds), while Form 102 is used for the second payment.

Ordinary Declaration

The *declaración ordinaria* (Form 100) consists of 13 pages and is for those with incomes from all sources other than those mentioned above, e.g. business or professional activities (this includes the self-employed) and capital gains.

Procedure

With the exception of a draft declaration, tax returns aren't sent out by the tax office and must be purchased each year from a tobacconist's (*estanco*) or from tax offices for around €1.50 to €2 each. If you're unable to obtain a tax return from a tobacconist's, you can obtain one from a tax adviser or your local tax office. An instruction booklet is provided with returns, and the tax office publishes a booklet, *Manual Práctico – Renta* (costing €1.50), containing examples of how to complete tax forms and an interpretation of the current Finance Act. You can also use computerised tax returns included in the computer programme *Programa PADRE* (downloadable from 🖳 www.aeat.es or available on a CD-ROM from tax offices). The advantage of using the *Programa PADRE* is that all calculations are done for you, although you need to have a good command of Spanish to use it.

If you can use the abbreviated or simple declaration, you should be able to complete your own tax form, perhaps with a little help from the tax office. You can contact the information section (*servicio de información*) of your local tax office, which may have multilingual staff. However, tax offices won't help you complete an *ordinaria* tax form over the telephone and you must make an appointment (☎ 901 223 344). When you go to the tax office for an appointment, you should take along the following:

♦ your end-of-year bank statements (*estado de cuenta*) showing any interest received and your average balance (*saldo medio*);

♦ any papers relating to stocks, shares, bonds, deposit certificates or any other property owned, in Spain or abroad;

- declarations and receipts for any taxes paid in another country (if you're seeking to offset payment against your Spanish taxes);
- your passport, residence permit and *NIE*.

However, most people require professional help to complete the *simplificada* and *ordinaria* tax forms.

If tax is due, you can submit your return to the district tax office where you're resident for tax purposes or at a designated bank in the province. If no payment is due, you must file it at the tax office. If you delay filing your tax return by even a day, you must pay a surcharge on the tax due (see below), although it's possible to request a payment deferral.

You can also submit your return online, for which you need to obtain an 'electronic or digital signature certificate' (*certificado de firma electrónica/digital*), which allows secure identification via the internet. The procedure for obtaining a certificate is relatively simple and can be found on several official websites, including AEAT (💻 www.aeat.es), FNMT (💻 www.cert. fnmt.es) and Social Security (💻 www.seg-social. es). First you register online and are allocated a reference code, which you must take in person to an authorised office, which include tax offices, social security offices, some council offices (e.g. Madrid and Valencia city councils) and Spanish consulates abroad. For an updated list of authorised offices, consult one of the above websites.

At the office, you quote your reference code, show identification (e.g. passport or residence permit) and sign a digital signature form. You then obtain your digital signature certificate when you re-visit the website where you obtained the reference code, and the signature is stored on your computer. Note that you must use the same computer and the same user section to receive the digital signature certificate, which can then be 'exported' to other computers.

> ☑ **SURVIVAL TIP**
>
> You should retain copies of your tax returns for at least five years, which is the maximum period that returns are liable for audit by the Spanish tax authorities.

Payment

Unless deducted at source, your income tax in Spain must be paid in full or in part at the same time as your tax declaration is made. You can pay the whole amount when the form is filed or 60 per cent with your declaration and the balance by the following 5th November. Payment must be made in cash; if you're filing at a bank where you hold an account, they will make an electronic transfer to the tax authorities.

Late payment of any tax bill usually incurs a surcharge of 20 per cent. Large fines can be imposed for breaches of tax law and in certain cases forfeiture of the right to tax benefits or subsidies for a period of up to five years. The fraudulent evasion of €30,000 or more in tax is punishable by fines of up to six times the amount defrauded and/or imprisonment, although it's rare for anyone to be prosecuted for tax evasion in Spain.

Leaving Spain

The tax year in Spain is the calendar year and runs from 1st January to 31st December. If you leave Spain during the tax year (i.e. on any day other than 31st December!), you may be entitled to a tax refund (*devolución*), which usually requires the completion of a tax return including your income and deductions from 1st January of the departure year up to the date of departure. The authorities may require evidence that you're leaving the country, e.g. proof that you have a job in Spain or have bought or rented a property there. Before leaving Spain permanently, you should pay any tax due for the previous year and the year of departure and obtain a tax clearance statement to show to the tax authorities in your new country of residence, although this isn't obligatory.

WEALTH TAX

After the 2008 fiscal year (effective from tax declarations made in 2009), Spain will no longer levy a wealth tax (*impuesto sobre el patrimonio*). It's calculated that around 1m residents (most residents didn't 'qualify' for wealth tax) will benefit from the exemption and thousands of non-resident property owners. The information below is for those required to make a tax declaration in 2009.

The value of your assets is taxed on a sliding scale from 0.2 per cent on assets valued up to €167,129 to 2.5 per cent on assets valued over €10.7m. For example, a non-resident with a property valued at €500,000 would be liable for a wealth tax bill (for the 2008 tax year only) of €1,665.

Assets include property, vehicles, boats, aircraft, businesses, cash (e.g. in bank accounts), life insurance, gold bars, jewellery, stocks, shares and bonds. The value of property is whichever is the highest among the purchase price, its fiscal value (*valor catastral*) and its value as assessed by the authorities.

If you're a non-resident and your country of residence has a double-taxation treaty with Spain, bank balances and interest are taxable only in your country of residence. Deductions can be made for mortgages (for residents and non-residents), business and other debts, and any 'wealth' tax paid in another country, but there's no tax 'allowance' and non-residents must pay wealth tax on all their assets in Spain (though for most non-resident property owners these consist only of the property itself).

Non-residents owning a single property in Spain can make their declarations for tax on deemed letting income and wealth tax on a single form at any time during 2009 (for the 2008 tax year). This is Form 214 (*impuesto sobre el patrimonio y sobre la renta de no residente*). Non-residents can have a financial representative in Spain make the declaration and arrange for payment on their behalf.

PROPERTY TAX

Property tax (*impuesto sobre bienes inmuebles urbana/rústica* or *IBI*) is payable by resident and non-resident property owners in Spain and goes towards local council administration, education, sanitary services, social assistance, community substructure, and cultural and sports amenities. Before buying a property, check with the local town hall that there aren't any outstanding property taxes for the past five years. As with all property-related taxes and debts, if the previous year's taxes are unpaid, the new owner becomes liable (you can, however, reclaim the tax from the previous owner – if you can find him!), and the town hall has five years in which to bill you or take legal action to recover unpaid taxes. It's now obligatory for the vendor to produce his last *IBI* receipt when completing a sale in front of a notary, but it's preferable to uncover any debts before you reach this stage in a purchase!

When you buy a property in Spain, you must register your ownership with the local town hall so that property tax can be applied.

Registration must be done within two months of signing the deed and there are fines of up to €1,000 for non-registration.

Many local authorities also levy fees (*tasas*) for services such as rubbish collection, street and beach cleaning, issuing documents, local parking restrictions and fire-fighting services. These vary greatly from one authority to another (e.g. the charge for rubbish collection, which in some cases also includes sewerage, can be as little as €50 or as much as €400 per year).

Assessment

Property tax is based on the fiscal or rateable value (*valor catastral*) of a property, which has traditionally been around 70 per cent of a property's market value. However, due to the huge increase in property prices in most parts of Spain over the last five years, fiscal values are often far lower than the market price – often less than half. As a result, many municipalities are now reviewing fiscal values in their areas and increases of up to 50 per cent can be expected, with corresponding rises in property taxes. If you receive an official communication (usually in the form of a registered letter) that the fiscal value of your property is about to increase greatly, you should check that it has been correctly calculated.

Property values are calculated according to a variety of measurements and evaluations, including the area (in square metres) of the property (the built, terraced and land areas), building and zoning restrictions in the area, the quality of the building (e.g. whether it's classified as luxury, normal or basic), the date of construction, and the proximity of services and roads. To check that a property is correctly specified, go to the town hall or the *urbanismo* (the office that deals with building regulations), ask to see its dossier (*expediente*)

and obtain a *certificación catastral*, which is the property description used to determine the *valor catastral*, sometimes accompanied by plans and photographs. Check that the data recorded is correct, as errors are fairly common.

You can appeal against the valuation of your property or an increase in valuation if you believe it's too high – particularly if it's higher than that of similar properties in the same area, although you have only 15 days in which to lodge an appeal (yet another good reason for non-residents to have a local financial representative). Note that, if an error has been made in your assessment, it can take years to have it corrected, although it's important to persevere.

It's important that the fiscal value of your property is correct, as a number of taxes are linked to this value, including deemed letting income tax and wealth tax, as well as property tax.

Tax Rates

Property tax rates depend on the population of the municipality and the level of public services provided and can vary considerably for similar properties in different areas. Rates tend to be higher in resort and coastal areas than in inland areas. Some municipalities have invested huge sums in recent years in improving civic amenities, e.g. building indoor sports complexes (with swimming pools, gymnasiums, etc.) and cultural centres, and have increased property taxes to pay for them.

Major revisions are permitted only once every eight years, but rates can be adjusted annually in accordance with coefficients set by the state government in its budget.

The basic property tax rates are 0.3 per cent for agricultural properties (*rústicas*) and 0.5 per cent for urban properties (*urbana*). However, provincial capitals, towns with over 5,000 inhabitants and towns providing 'special services' can increase the rate to up to 1.7 per cent. To calculate your property tax, simply multiply the fiscal value of your property by the tax rate, e.g. if the fiscal value of your property is €100,000 and the tax rate is 1 per cent, your annual bill will be €1,000.

Payment

Payment dates of property taxes vary with the municipality but are usually between 1st September and 31st October. **Note that few town halls send out bills; it's your responsibility to find out how much you must pay and when.** Payment can usually be made in cash or by guaranteed bank cheque at the tax collection office or by postal giro at certain banks, and some municipalities accept payment by recognised credit card, e.g. MasterCard and Visa. Non-resident property owners should pay their *IBI* (and other local taxes) by direct debit from a Spanish bank account.

If the tax isn't paid on time, a surcharge (*recargo*) of 10 to 20 per cent is levied in addition to interest (plus possible collection costs), depending on how late your payment is. If you're unable to pay your property tax, you should talk to your local tax office. They will be pleased that you haven't absconded and will usually agree to a deferred payment schedule.

Some town halls offer discounts for early payment to encourage residents to pay their bills early and thus spread the municipality's income throughout the year.

Non-payment

In the past, many people have been able to avoid paying property taxes, owing to a *laissez-faire* attitude towards tax collection on the part of municipalities, who considered they were doing well if around 65 per cent of taxes were collected! However, in recent years, local municipal tax authorities have made strenuous efforts to collect unpaid property taxes. If you owe back taxes and refuse to pay them, your property can be seized and sold at auction, perhaps for as little as 10 per cent of its value. Local authorities also have the power to seize vehicles and block bank accounts. If you don't pay your property taxes, your name will also be listed in your province's 'official bulletin' (*Boletín Oficial de la Provincia/BOP*), so that everyone knows!

You will usually be given plenty of warning before this happens, but if you're due to be absent from your property for an extended period, you should make sure that your property taxes are being paid; there have been many cases of foreigners arriving in Spain after a long absence to find that their homes have been sold to pay taxes!

CAPITAL GAINS TAX

Capital gains tax (*impuesto sobre incremento de patrimonio*) is payable on the profit from the sale of certain assets in Spain, including antiques, art and jewellery, stocks and shares, property and businesses. Capital gains (*incremento de patrimonio*) revealed as a result of the death of a taxpayer, gifts to government entities and donations of certain assets in lieu of tax payments are exempt from capital gains tax (CGT). Capital losses (*disminución de patrimonio*) can be offset against capital gains, but not against ordinary income. Capital losses in excess of gains can be carried forward to offset against future gains for a five-year period.

Exemptions

Residents over 65 are exempt from CGT on the profit made from the sale of their principal home, irrespective of how long they've owned it. Note, however, that the Spanish Tax Office defines a 'principal home' as the place where you've lived permanently for **at least three years**.

Residents below 65 are exempt from CGT on the profit made from the sale of their principal home, provided that all the profit is invested in the purchase of another principal home in Spain within two years of the sale. Any profit that isn't reinvested is subject to CGT at the residents' tax rate (see below).

CGT Rates

Residents and EU non-residents are taxed at a flat rate of 18 per cent (although counted as 'income', capital gains aren't taxed at the usual income tax rates!). Non-EU non-residents are taxed at a flat rate of 35 per cent.

CGT on Property

Capital gains tax on property (*impuesto sobre el incremento de patrimonio de la venta de un bien inmeuble*) is based on the difference between the purchase price (as stated in the title deed) and the sale price of a property, less buying and selling costs (and costs of improvements), subject to a complex calculation, which depends on the date of purchase – whether before or after 31st December 1996 – as detailed below.

Each calculation involves an adjustment for inflation according to a coefficient or inflation index (*coeficiente de actualización*), which is applied when you sell to allow for inflation and the loss of value of the amount originally invested. The coefficients for the years up to 2008 are shown below – new figures are published annually, usually in January:

Purchase Date	Coefficient or Inflation Index for 2008 Sale
1994 & earlier	1.241
1995	1.311
1996	1.267
1997	1.241
1998	1.217
1999	1.195
2000	1.172
2001	1.149
2002	1.126
2003	1.104
2004	1.082
2005	1.061
2006	1.040
2007	1.020
2008	1.000

Property Purchased before 31st December 1996

Capital gains on assets purchased before 31st December 1996 are calculated on a sliding scale according to how long they've been owned and are also subject to an inflation index (see above). After the first two years of ownership (when CGT is applied to 100 per cent of the value), there's an annual deduction of 11.11 per cent on the profit. This means that gains on property are free of tax after 11 years (i.e. purchases made before 31st December 1986), as shown in the table below:

Year Purchased	Deduction on Profit
1996	0%
1995	0%
1994	11.11%
1993	22.22%
1992	33.33%
1991	44.44%
1990	55.55%
1989	66.66%
1988	77.77%
1987	88.88%
1986	99.99%

Example: a second home purchased in 1992 for €100,000 with deductible costs totalling €10,000 (the purchase price was therefore effectively €110,000) and sold in 2008 for €250,000 with deductible selling costs of €15,000 (the effective selling price is therefore €235,000):

1. Apply inflation coefficient of 1.241 to purchase price (see table above): €110,000 x 1.241 = €136,510.

2. Deduct adjusted purchase price from effective selling price: €235,000 - €136,510 = €98,490.

3. Apply deduction on profit (see above table): €98,490 x 33.33 per cent = €32,502.

4. Apply CGT rate to net figure:

   - CGT for non-EU non-resident: €32,502 x 35 per cent = €11,376.

   - CGT for resident and EU non-resident: €32,502 x 18 per cent = €5,850.

Property Purchased after 31st December 1996

Gains arising from property purchased after 31st December 1996 are calculated 'simply' by using the coefficient or inflation index (see table above).

Example: a second home purchased in 2001 for €200,000 with deductible costs totalling €10,000 (the effective purchase price was therefore €210,000) and sold in 2008 for €350,000 with deductible selling costs of €20,000 (the effective selling price is therefore €320,000):

1. Apply inflation coefficient of 1.149 to purchase price (see table above): €210,000 x 1.149 = €241,290.

2. Deduct adjusted purchase price from effective selling price: €320,000 - €241,290 = €78,710.

3. Apply CGT rate to net figure:

   - CGT for non-EU non-resident: €78,710 x 35 per cent = €27,549.

   - CGT for resident and EU non-resident: €78,710 x 18 per cent = €14,168.

Non-resident Sellers

If you're a non-resident and are selling your home in Spain, the buyer (whether he's resident or non-resident) is obliged to subtract 5 per cent from the purchase price and pay it to the Spanish Ministry of Finance within 30 days of the transaction. You must then apply (on Form 212) for a return of the difference between his 5 per cent payment and your CGT liability within three months of the payment. If you don't, the tax office will keep the money. If a representative or agent obtains the refund for you, you should request copies of the above forms and a statement showing the tax paid and the agent's fees.

If you're buying from a resident, ask him to provide a resident's fiscal certificate (*certificado de residencia fiscal*) issued by the tax office (*AEAT*) to prove it. A notary accepts a residence card or even registration with the town hall as proof of residence, but the tax authorities accept only a fiscal certificate as proof of residence in Spain. If the tax authorities aren't satisfied that the seller is resident, the buyer has to pay the 5 per cent retention and a fine.

INHERITANCE & GIFT TAX

As in most countries, dying doesn't free you (or, more correctly, your beneficiaries) from the clutches of the tax man; nor does giving your money away before you die. Spain imposes a tax on assets or money received as an inheritance or gift (*impuesto sobre sucesiones y donaciones*). The estates of residents and non-residents are subject to Spanish inheritance and gift tax if they own property or have other assets in Spain. Inheritance and gift tax is paid by the beneficiaries, e.g. a surviving spouse, and not by the deceased's estate.

The country in which beneficiaries must pay inheritance tax is usually decided by their domicile. If they're domiciled in Spain, Spanish inheritance tax is payable on an inheritance, whether the inheritance is located (or received) in Spain or abroad. There are currently numerous proposals for inheritance and gift tax reform, including the abolition of all inheritance tax or a substantial reduction on lower amounts. Several regions have already introduced substantial inheritance tax reductions (see below).

Inheritance tax is currently in a state of change in Spain and you should take expert legal advice on the latest regulations before making any decisions regarding the disposal of assets in Spain.

Tax is payable by beneficiaries within six months of a death if this occurred in Spain, although it's possible to obtain a six-month extension (to one year), and within 30 days of the transfer of a lifetime gift. If a death occurs abroad, the inheritance tax declaration and the payment of inheritance tax duties must be made within 16 months.

Tax is assessed on the net amount received and accrues from the date of death or the date of a gift. Some people have managed to avoid inheritance tax by failing to inform the Spanish authorities of a death (after five years and six months the tax can no longer be collected), although this is illegal.

Exemptions

Those who have been Spanish residents for at least three years receive an exemption of 95 per cent of inheritance tax when their principal residence or family business (in Spain) is bequeathed to a spouse, parent or child who has been living with them for at least two years before their death. The principal residence must be valued at less than €122,606 (there's no limit for a business) or the inheritance mustn't exceed €122,606 per heir, above which normal inheritance tax rates apply.

For example, if the residence is worth €150,000, you pay tax at only 5 per cent on the first €122,606 and tax at the full rate on the balance of €27,394. The inheritor must retain ownership of the property for a minimum of ten years, although if he dies within the ten-year period no further tax is payable. If the property or business is sold during this period, tax may be levied at the discretion of the relevant authorities, e.g. the regional government.

Several regions have abolished inheritance tax for residents including the Balearics, the Basque Country, Cantabria, Castile-La Mancha, Madrid, Navarra and Valencia, which effectively means that around 40 per cent of the Spanish population will not be liable for inheritance tax when they inherit.

Liability

Inheritance and gift tax liability depends on your relationship to the donor, the amount inherited and your wealth before receipt of the gift or inheritance.

Relationship

Direct descendants and close relatives of the deceased receive an allowance before they become liable for inheritance tax, as shown below.

Inheritance Tax Relationship		
Group	Includes	Allowance
1	Direct descendants under 21	€15,956.87 plus €3,990.72 for each year under 21 up to a maximum of €48,000
2	Direct descendants over 21, direct ascendants (parents and up), spouse or partner*	€15,956.87
3	Relatives to third degree (and ascendants by affinity) including brother, sister, uncle, aunt, niece or nephew	€7,993.46
4	Unrelated people and more remote relatives (including common-law partners*)	None

* Note that most regions recognise common-law partners as spouses for inheritance tax purposes if they're registered as such in the region.

Inheritance Tax Liability

Value above Allowance	Tax Liability Rate	Cumulative Tax Liability
Up to €7,993	7.65%	€611
€7,994 to €15,980	8.50%	€1,290
€15,981 to €23,968	9.35%	€2,037
€23,969 to €31,955	10.20%	€2,852
€31,956 to €39,943	11.05%	€3,735
€39,944 to €47,930	11.90%	€4,685
€47,931 to €55,918	12.75%	€5,703
€55,919 to €63,905	13.60%	€6,790
€63,906 to €71,893	14.45%	€7,944
€71,894 to €79,880	15.30%	€9,166
€79,881 to €119,757	16.15%	€15,606
€119,758 to €159,634	18.70%	€23,063
€159,635 to €239,389	21.25%	€40,011
€239,390 to €398,777	25.50%	€80,655
€398,778 to €797,555	29.75%	€199,291
Over €797,555	34.00%	

Amount Inherited

Your inheritance tax liability is calculated as a percentage of the amount inherited (in excess of any allowance), as shown above. Note that Catalonia has a different inheritance tax scale.

A recent consumer survey found that Castilla La Mancha, Castile León and Madrid are the regions with the most favourable inheritance tax allowances, while Andalusia, Catalonia and Extremadura have the least.

Inheritance/Gift Tax Rates

Current Wealth	Relationship Group		
	1/2	3	4
Up to €402,678	100%	158.82%	200%
€402,678 to €2,007,380	105%	166.76%	210%
€2,007,380 to €4,020,770	110%	174.71%	220%
Over €4,020,770	120%	190.59%	240%

Current Wealth

Your current wealth is the value of all your assets **before** the inheritance transfer.

Calculation

Once you've worked out your relationship group and calculated your inheritance tax liability, use the table above to calculate the inheritance or gift tax payable based on your current wealth by multiplying your inheritance tax liability (shown in the table) by the percentage shown under the relevant relationship group.

For example, if you're in relationship group 3 (giving you a tax allowance of €7,993.46) and you've inherited €79,886.46, you must pay tax on €71,893, so your tax liability is €7,944; if you earn between €402,678 and €2,007,380 (lucky you!), you must pay tax at 166.76 per cent, which amounts to €13,247.41.

WILLS

It's an unfortunate fact of life that you're unable to take your hard-earned money with you when you make your final exit. All adults should make a will (*testamento*), irrespective of how large or small their assets (each spouse should make a separate will). If a foreigner dies without a will (intestate) in Spain, his estate may be automatically disposed of under Spanish law and the law regarding obligatory heirs (see below) applied.

A foreigner resident in Spain is usually permitted to dispose of his Spanish assets according to the law of his home country, provided his will is valid under the law of that country. If you've lived in Spain for a long time, it may be necessary for you to create a legal domicile in your home country for the purpose of making a will.

A will made by a foreigner regarding Spanish assets isn't invalidated if it doesn't bequeath property in accordance with Spanish law, as Spanish law isn't usually applied to foreigners and the disposal of property (buildings or land) in Spain is governed by the law of the deceased's home country unless there's a dispute among the beneficiaries, in which case Spanish law is applied.

Law of Obligatory Heirs

Under Spanish law, a surviving spouse retains all assets acquired before marriage, half the assets acquired during the marriage, and all personal gifts or inheritances which have come directly to the spouse. The remaining assets must be disposed of under the law of 'obligatory heirs' (*herederos forzosos*), which is as follows.

When a person dies leaving children, his estate is divided into three equal parts. One third must be left to the surviving children in equal parts. Another third must also be left to the children, but the testator decides how it's to be divided. A surviving spouse has a life interest in this second third and the children who inherit it cannot dispose of it freely until the surviving parent dies. The final third can be freely disposed of. If a child has died leaving children of his own, they automatically inherit his share. If the deceased has no children, his surviving parents have a statutory right to one-third of his estate if he has a surviving spouse or half of his estate if he doesn't.

This law normally applies only to Spanish nationals, but if a foreigner dies intestate, it may also apply to him.

Types of Will

There are three kinds of Spanish will, each of which is described below. Note that, where applicable, the rules relating to witnesses are strict and, if not followed precisely can render a will null and void.

Although it isn't necessary to have a Spanish will for Spanish property, it's advisable to have a separate will for **any** country in which you own property; in that way, when a person dies, assets can be dealt with immediately under local law without having to wait for the granting of probate in another country (and the administration of the estate is also cheaper). Having a Spanish will for your Spanish assets speeds up the will's execution and saves the long and complicated process of having a foreign will executed in Spain. **Note that, if you have two or more wills, you must ensure that they don't contradict or invalidate one another.** You should periodically review your will to ensure

that it reflects your current financial and personal circumstances.

Open Will

An open will (*testamento abierto*) is the normal and most suitable kind of will for most people. It's unnecessary to employ a lawyer to prepare an open will, although it's usually advisable. It must, however, be prepared by a notary, who is responsible for ensuring that it's legal and properly drawn up. Its contents must be known to the notary and to three witnesses, who can be of any nationality; each of them must sign the will. The notary will give you a copy (*copia simple* or *copia autorizada*) and send a copy to the general registry of wills (*Registro General de Actos de Ultima Voluntad*) in Madrid. The original remains at the notary's office. If you don't understand Spanish, you need an official translation into a language that you speak fluently.

Closed Will

A closed will (*testamento cerrado*), whose contents remain secret, must be drawn up by a Spanish lawyer to ensure that it complies with Spanish law. You must take the will to a notary, who seals the envelope and signs it, as must two witnesses, and then files and records it as for an open will.

Holographic Will

A holographic will (*testamento ológrafo*) is a will made in your own handwriting or orally. If written, it must be signed and dated and must be clearly drafted in order to ensure that your wishes are absolutely clear. No witnesses or other formalities are required. It can be voluntarily registered with the registry of wills. On the death of the testator it must be authenticated before a judge, which delays the will's execution. An oral will must be made in the presence of five witnesses, who must then testify to a notary the wishes of the deceased. The notary then prepares a written will and certifies it. For anyone with a modest Spanish estate, e.g. a small holiday home in Spain, a holographic will (but preferably a written one) is sufficient.

Cost & Procedure

The cost of preparing a simple open or closed will is around €150 plus the notary's fee (around €60). Spanish wills can be drawn up by Spanish lawyers and notaries abroad, although it's cheaper to do it in Spain.

Executors aren't normal in Spain and, if you appoint one, it may increase the inheritance tax payable. However, if you appoint an executor, you should inform your heirs so that they will know who to notify in the event of your death. It isn't advisable to name a lawyer who doesn't speak Spanish as your executor, as he will have to instruct a Spanish lawyer (*abogado*), whose fees will be impossible to control. If you appoint a lawyer as your executor, he is permitted to charge a maximum of 5 per cent of the estate's value.

Your beneficiaries in Spain must produce an original death certificate or an authorised copy. If you die outside Spain, a foreign death certificate must be legally translated and notarised for it to be valid in Spain. The inheritance tax declaration and the payment of inheritance tax duties must be made within six months of your death if you die in Spain and within 16 months if you die elsewhere (otherwise, a surcharge may result). Inheritance tax must be paid in advance of the release of the assets to be inherited in Spain, and beneficiaries may therefore need to borrow funds to pay the tax before they receive their inheritance. Note that the winding-up of an estate can take a long time in Spain.

> ☑ **SURVIVAL TIP**
>
> Keep a copy of your will(s) in a safe place and another copy with your lawyer or the executor of your estate. Don't leave them in a bank safe deposit box, which in the event of your death is sealed for a period under Spanish law. You should keep information regarding bank accounts and insurance policies with your will(s), but don't forget to tell someone where they are!

Note that in Spain, marriage doesn't automatically revoke a will as in some other countries.

Spanish inheritance law is a complicated subject and it's important to obtain professional legal advice when writing or altering your will(s).

COST OF LIVING

No doubt you would like to try to estimate how far your euros will stretch and how much money (if any) you will have left after paying your bills. Spain is no longer the El Dorado it once was and the cost of living has risen considerably in recent years. Inflation is no longer low (over 5 per cent in June 2008), and many Spaniards have seen a drop in their standard of living in recent years, particularly as salaries have only risen in line with inflation and interest rates and oil prices (not directly included in inflation calculations) have increased dramatically.

In July 2008, government officials calculated that the rise in consumer prices such as petrol, basic food stuffs and utilities, and in mortgage repayments costs the average Spanish family around €100 extra a month. Consumer groups consider the cost to be much higher, particularly among families who recently took out large mortgages (the group most affected by rises in mortgage interest rates).

There's a huge variation between average incomes in different regions of the country, e.g. GDP is an average of just €15,000 per year in Extremadura, compared with the national average of €22,152 and Madrid's average of €28,850 (2007 government statistics). The charity Cáritas claims that some 20 per cent of the population (around 8m people) live in 'poverty', defined as earning less than half the average income (currently around €1,250 per month). Around 5 per cent of the population live in 'extreme poverty', with an income below €120 per month.

In the last few decades, inflation has brought the price of many goods and services in line with that of most other European countries. Among the more expensive items in Spain are quality clothes and many consumer goods.

On the other hand, many things remain cheaper than in northern European countries, including property (provided you avoid the hot spots), cars, rents, food (which costs around the same as in the US), alcohol, hotels, restaurant meals and general entertainment. A recent Eurostat survey found that food and drink in Spain is 24 per cent cheaper than the EU average. Around €200 will feed two adults for a month, including (inexpensive) wine, but excluding fillet steak, caviar and expensive imported foods.

A couple owning their home can 'survive' on a net income of as little as €400 per month (many pensioners live on less) and most can live comfortably on an income of €800 per month (excluding rent or mortgage payments). In fact, many northern Europeans (particularly Scandinavians) who live modestly in Spain without overdoing the luxuries find that their cost of living is up to 50 per cent less than in their home country. Shopping for expensive consumer goods such as hi-fi equipment, electronic goods, computers and photographic equipment in other European countries or North America or via the internet can yield further savings.

15.
LEISURE

I f you want guaranteed sunshine, miles of sandy beaches, good food and wine, an abundant choice of entertainment and a wide variety of accommodation – and you don't want to pay the earth – then Spain is the place for you. As the Spanish National Tourist Office's slogan says, 'Don't just imagine it. Live it.' Although the vast majority of holidaymakers (and residents) come to Spain to recline on a beach, there's much (much) more to the country than the *costas* and a few islands. Spain offers infinite variety with something for everyone, including magnificent beaches; spectacular unspoilt countryside; a wealth of mountains and waterways; vibrant nightlife; bustling, sophisticated cities; superb wine and cuisine; a surfeit of art, culture and serious music; numerous festivals and *fiestas* and above all tranquillity. Spain is a nation of bon viveurs with an insatiable thirst for fun and pleasure – nobody can throw a better party than the Spanish.

Tourism took off in Spain in the early '60s. The number of visitors grew steadily over the next few decades and currently stands at over 58.5m a year (the UK and Germany account for over 45 per cent of the market). In 2007, Spain was the second most popular tourist destination in the world after France, and tourism accounts for some 12 per cent of gross domestic product (GDP) and employment; the most popular regions are Catalonia, the Balearics and the Canaries. As well as catering for the package-holiday market, Spain appeals to holidaymakers in search of golf, spas, culture and scenery.

Outside its beach resorts, Spain's main attractions are its lively cities, particularly Madrid and Barcelona, which have an intense rivalry. Barcelona is Spain's most international and European city, elegant and compact, while Madrid is a sprawling metropolis and one of the world's most friendly and free-wheeling cities. Madrid has a wealth of world-class museums and art galleries, and is blessed with magnificent parks and gardens, whereas Barcelona is an architectural masterpiece and one of the world's most handsome cities. Both offer superb cuisine and a bustling, vibrant nightlife, and are just

warming up when most other European cities are going to bed.

Naturally, there's much more to Spain than Madrid and Barcelona, and the country has a wealth of other beautiful historic cities, including Avila, Burgos, Cáceres, Cadiz, Cordoba, Cuenca, Gerona, Granada, Malaga, Mérida, Palma de Mallorca, Pamplona, San Sebastian, Salamanca, Santander, Santiago de Compostela, Segovia, Seville, Toledo and Valencia, to name just a handful.

Spain has an unusually colourful history; over the centuries it has been home to Phoenicians, Iberians, Romans, Visigoths and Moors, all of whom have left their mark and added to the country's rich heritage and culture. It's a land steeped in tradition with a wealth of artistic, cultural and historical treasures scattered the length and breadth of the country. There are a surfeit of excellent art galleries and museums throughout Spain, and traditional *fiestas* and music festivals are held in all regions and major towns throughout the year.

One of the foremost attractions of Spain is its outstanding countryside, sadly enjoyed by few visitors. Spain's rugged beauty is almost unparalleled in Europe; it harbours a wealth of unique flora, fauna and wildlife, and contains more (and larger) unspoilt areas than any other European country, many preserved as national parks and nature reserves.

Information regarding local events and entertainment is available from tourist offices and is published in local English-language newspapers and magazines. In most cities, there are magazines and newspapers dedicated to entertainment, and free weekly or monthly programmes (e.g. *Guía del Ocio*) are published by tourist organisations in major cities and tourist resorts. Many towns produce a monthly cultural programme and some foreigners' departments also produce newsletters listing local cultural events. Many newspapers publish weekly magazines or supplements containing a detailed programme of local events and entertainment, and numerous websites provide information on events, e.g. 🖥 www.guiadelocio.com and 🖥 www.lanetro.com. There are also many excellent guidebooks to Spain (see **Appendix B**).

ACCOMMODATION

Many types of accommodation are available in Spain, catering to all tastes and pockets, from sumptuous, *gran lujo* hotels to humble hostels. If you want to rub shoulders with the real Spanish, start at the bottom rather than the top of the accommodation chain. Note, however, that it can be difficult to find good (or any) hotels in small villages and towns or on main roads in many areas, and Spain doesn't have the tradition of 'charming' country hotels that you can find throughout the UK and France, although this is changing.

Hotels (and other accommodation in Spain) are regulated by the government and all legally registered establishments must display a blue plaque showing their category and class in white letters, as listed below.

Several of the above categories of accommodation, including hostels, pensions, guesthouses and inns are described in more detail under **Budget Accommodation** below. Residential hotels are generally cheaper than standard hotels and offer fewer services and public lounges. Residential hotels and hostels don't provide a restaurant service but may offer breakfast or a cafeteria service. Hostels often provide better accommodation (and better value) than inexpensive hotels (a three-star hostel is roughly equivalent to a one-star hotel).

Budget Accommodation

There's a variety of budget accommodation in Spain, including the following:

♦ **Casas de Huéspedes** – a kind of guesthouse that offers basic accommodation. Food isn't usually served. Long-stay guests (*huéspedes permanentes*) are usually preferred.

♦ **Casas rurales, casas rústicas & casas de labranza** – see below;

♦ **Colegios mayores & residencies** – see below;

Hotel Ratings

Category	Description
*H (*hotel*)	Standard hotels as described on the following pages
*HR (*hotel residencia*)	Residential hotels without a restaurant
*HA (*hotel apartamento*)	Self-contained apartments or chalets with kitchenettes, offering reasonable weekly or monthly rates, but little service
*RA (*residencia apartamento*)	Similar to ordinary apartments except that they're mainly let for short periods to tourists and may provide breakfast
*M (*motel*)	Roadside lodgings for short stays, located on or close to motorways and other main roads

- **Fondas** – generally a village inn with basic facilities and rooms, usually located over the bar. Food may be served (some may not offer rooms without full board), although this isn't always the case.

- **Hospedajes** – basic accommodation consisting of rooms/lodgings, not very different from the two types of guesthouse (see above). Long-stay guests are usually preferred.

- **Hostals** – hostels offering similar accommodation to hotels. They're the most upmarket type of budget accommodation with wash basins in all rooms, but they don't usually offer full board.

- **Pensiones** – a kind of guesthouse that offers basic accommodation. Food may be served (some may not offer rooms without full board), although this isn't always the case. Long-stay guests (*huéspedes permanentes*) are usually preferred.

Spain doesn't have bed-and-breakfast accommodation to the same extent as, for example, the UK or France, although some private homes (*casas particulares*) offer bed and breakfast off the beaten tourist track, and there are 'bed and breakfast' organisations in cities and large towns. Beds (*camas*) and rooms (*habitaciones*) are advertised in the windows of private houses, and above bars and roadside restaurants such as *ventas*, perhaps with the phrase *camas y comidas* (beds and meals). They often provide the cheapest of all accommodation and are usually spotlessly clean.

When booking budget accommodation you should enquire about the exact location and the facilities provided, as standards vary from clean and homely abodes to 'fleapits' unfit for human habitation – even within the same category of accommodation. Note that budget accommodation is often basic, usually lacks heating and guests are often subject to curfews. A list of budget accommodation can usually be obtained from local tourist offices and rooms to let can also be found by asking at local bars and restaurants.

When staying in budget accommodation, it's advantageous if you speak some Spanish, as your hosts may not speak any foreign languages.

Rural Cottages

In country areas, there are cottages and farmhouses (*casas rurales*, *casas rústicas* and *casas de labranza*), officially referred to as *turismo rural*, providing the opportunity to experience the Spanish country way of life and possibly make contact with Spanish families. Rural tourism is currently experiencing a boom in Spain, with Spaniards and foreign visitors, and you can rent a room in a house (meals are usually provided) or rent the whole house with self-catering facilities. Accommodation is usually in traditional houses, some of which may be centuries old.

Several annual guides are published on rural tourism, e.g. *Guía de Alojamiento de Turismo Rural* (Anaya Touring) or *Anuario de Turismo Rural* (Susaeta) and there are numerous websites (e.g. 🖳 www.azrural.com and 🖳 www.toprural.com), which usually allow you to book accommodation online. The most popular areas in 2007 were Castile León, Catalonia, Castilla La Mancha and Cantabria. Book early for the summer months, particularly in coastal areas and in the north of Spain.

University Dormitories & Monasteries

Rooms are often available in university dormitories (*colegios mayores* and *residencias*) during the summer holidays and in monasteries all the year round. Working monasteries offer basic lodgings. Prayer, silence and seclusion are the order of the day (plus superb architecture and perhaps some Gregorian chant). They may accept guests of both sexes or men only and payment is often in the form of a 'donation' (e.g. €15 or €20 per night) rather than a fixed fee. There are set meal times and reservations must usually be made in advance. Many monasteries have hospices or guest quarters (*hospederías*).

If you're a fan of Gregorian chant, you may wish to visit the monastery of Santo Domingo de Silos (Burgos), although you must book years in advance since the astounding success of their recordings.

Cost

The cost of budget accommodation varies considerably. The cheapest is around €20 per person, per day for full board (*pensión completa*) consisting of breakfast, lunch and dinner. Half board (*pensión media*) may also be offered at a slightly reduced rate. Rates at rural cottages and farmhouses usually range from €15 to €30 for a single or double room. Hostels charge from €15 to €25 for singles and €20 to €30 for doubles, plus an extra €4 or so for a room with a bath or shower. The cheapest accommodation is generally found in *casas de huéspedes* and *hospedajes*.

If a room doesn't have a private bathroom, which usually contains a shower rather than a bath, you may be charged an additional fee to use a communal bathroom. As with most accommodation in Spain, large discounts are usually offered for long stays during winter. Budget establishments seldom accept credit cards and 7 per cent value added tax (VAT) is added to all bills.

Self-catering

There's a wealth of self-catering accommodation in Spain, and it's is extremely popular, particularly with Spanish families. It includes apartments, townhouses, villas, farmhouses and country houses (*fincas*). Note that standards vary considerably, from dilapidated, ill-equipped apartments to luxury villas with every modern convenience. You don't always get what you pay for and some properties bear little resemblance to their descriptions. Unless a company or property has been highly recommended, it's best to book through a reputable organisation such as Interhome (🖳 www.interhome.com) or a tourist agency. Tourist apartments (*apartamentos turísticos*) in Spain are graded by one to four keys as shown below:

- **Luxury** (four keys) – a top-quality building in a good location with air-conditioning, heating, 24-hour hot water, parking, a reception and information desk, private telephone, bar and restaurant or cafeteria. Lifts are provided if the building is higher than two floors.

- **First class** (three keys) – a quality building with heating and hot water, reception and information desk, telephone to reception, and lifts if the building is higher than three floors;

- **Second class** (two keys) – a well built structure with heating, hot water, a telephone at the reception desk and on each floor, and lifts if the building is higher than three floors;

♦ **Third class** (one key) – hot water, at least a shower in all apartments and a lift if the building is higher than three floors.

Most accommodation is let for a minimum of seven nights (except for public holiday weekends such as Easter). The cost per night usually ranges from €30 for a studio (sleeping two people) in low season, to €60 per night in high season (July-August). A two-bedroom apartment or townhouse (sleeping four to six) costs from around €60 per night in low season to €100 per night in high season, although rates depend on the location and the quality of the accommodation.

Rates usually include linen, gas and electricity, although heating in winter, e.g. gas or electric heaters, is usually charged extra. (It's illegal to install electricity coin meters in rental accommodation in Spain.) Beware of gas heaters with faulty ventilation ducts, as they've been responsible for a number of deaths in self-catering accommodation due to gas poisoning. Extra beds and cots (e.g. €6 per night or €20 per week) can usually be rented.

In Madrid and other cities, there are luxury serviced apartments costing around €50 to €150 per night (€300 to €900 a week) for a studio or one-bedroom apartment sleeping two and €150 to €250 per night (€900 to €1,500 a week) for a two- or three-bedroom apartment sleeping four to six. VAT at 7 per cent is added to bills and may be included in quoted rates. During the low season, which may extend from October to May, rates may drop to as little as €300 to €450 a month for a two-bedroom apartment, although there's usually a minimum let of two months. Naturally, you can rent a wide variety of villas and luxury properties throughout Spain, the cost of which can be astronomical.

☑ SURVIVAL TIP

Pets are usually prohibited in self-catering accommodation.

Properties in resort areas always have a swimming pool (shared in the case of apartments and townhouses), in use from around May to October, and most are close to a beach. Some properties have an heated indoor swimming pool and other facilities such as tennis courts. Most holiday apartments are fairly basic, often with tiny kitchens and bathrooms (there may only be a shower), and have a combined lounge/dining room, a patio or balcony. If you need non-standard items, such as a cot or high chair, you should mention them when booking.

Properties are generally well stocked with cooking utensils, crockery and cutlery, although you should check (before your first shopping trip). Some things that may come in handy are a sharp knife, a teapot, egg cups, a pepper mill, a filter coffee machine and a few of your favourite foods, such as tea, instant coffee, and relishes and condiments. Most people take a few essential foods and supplies with them and buy fresh food on arrival, although many self-catering properties provide a 'welcome pack' with essentials for when you first arrive.

It's essential to book for the high season or a holiday weekend (e.g. at Easter). There's usually a 25 per cent deposit, with the balance payable on arrival. Normally, you must arrive by 5pm on your first day and vacate the property by noon on your day of departure. Outside the high season of July and August, self-catering accommodation can usually be found on the spot by asking around in bars and restaurants or by obtaining a list from the local tourist office.

CAMPING & CARAVANNING

Spain has over 800 campsites (*campings* or *campamentos*), two-thirds of which are on the coast, with a total capacity of over 400,000 pitches. Many campsites accommodate only 300 to 400 people and some cater exclusively for naturists. Campsites are inspected and approved by the Spanish tourist authority and classified under four categories according to their amenities: L (luxury/*lujo*), first class (*primera clase/1a*), second class (*segunda clase/2a*) and third class (*tercera clase/3a*).

Even the most basic camp grounds must have 24-hour surveillance; a fenced area;

unlimited drinking water; first aid and fire prevention facilities; toilets and showers (there may be a fee for hot showers); washing and washing-up facilities and rubbish collection. Most camps also provide a range of other services and facilities which may include a post office, playground, currency exchange, cable TV, telephones, safes, launderette, bottled gas, electricity/water hook-ups for caravans and motor caravans, swimming pool(s), tennis courts and other sports facilities, shops, supermarket, hairdresser, disco, restaurants and bars.

All campsites post their daily fees (usually from noon until noon the following day, calculated per car or caravan, per person and per tent) at the entrance. Fees are from €4 per person, per day plus from €4 for a car and around the same for a caravan or camping space (although fees can be as high as €15 a day at a deluxe site). There are reductions of around 20 per cent for children, e.g. under ten. Motor caravans are charged between €5 and €10 a day and electricity hook-ups cost an additional €2 to €5 a day. VAT at 7 per cent must be added to all fees. Some sites charge extra for hot showers, sports (such as tennis courts) and the use of ironing facilities or a freezer.

Most campsites offer reduced rates outside the high season of June to August, although many are open only during the 'summer', e.g. April or May to September. It's advisable to book for the high season, particularly for campsites situated in coastal areas in July and August. Note that many campsites don't accept dogs.

An international camping carnet isn't necessary in Spain when camping at registered sites, although it's required when camping 'wild'. However, it's advisable to have one, as it's accepted as proof of identification by campsites. Before camping in open country you should check that wild camping is permitted and obtain permission from the owner of private land. Wild camping is often prohibited during the dry season due to the danger of fires or when there's an official campsite in the immediate vicinity (you aren't permitted to camp within one kilometre of an official campsite).

> **⚠ Caution**
>
> Camping is forbidden on beaches, river banks and in mountains, and you can be fined for camping illegally.

The Spanish Federation of Camping Sites (Federación Española de Empresarios de Camping, C/Valderribas, 48, 3, 1ºC, 28007 Madrid, ☎ 914 481 234, www.fedcamping.com) publishes an annual guide (*Guía de Campings*) listing sites (by region), with illustrations and plans. Another useful guide (published annually) is the *Guía Ibérica de Campings* (RACE-Península), which includes campsites in Portugal. Bookings can be made directly with campsites and through the Spanish Federation of Camping Sites.

TurEspaña publishes a free camping map (*Mapa de Campings*) showing all official campsites, and free regional and provincial maps are available from local tourist offices, as well as an annual official guide *Guía Oficial de Campings*. If you're a newcomer to camping and caravanning, it's advantageous to join a camping or caravan club, from which you can obtain useful information (including guides to campsites), caravan and travel insurance, participation in rallies, priority booking and a range of other services and benefits.

BULLFIGHTING

A book about Spain wouldn't be complete without a 'few' words about bullfighting (*la lidia*), commonly referred to as the *fiesta nacional*. Foreigners love or loathe bullfighting and it provokes controversy even among Spaniards. To many it's a barbaric and sadistic blood sport with no merit whatsoever and should be banned. It's claimed by those opposed to bullfighting that over 80 per cent of Spaniards are against it, although it remains highly popular with over 40m paying spectators a year and top fights are shown live on television. It is, however, banned in the Canary Islands and in a few areas in mainland Spain, including Barcelona, which joined the anti-bullfighting league in 2004, much to the surprise of many in Spain.

Plaza de Toros de las Ventas, Madrid

If you're opposed to bullfighting on moral and ethical grounds, it's best not to go, as you certainly won't enjoy it and may well be distressed. If you feel you ought to watch it at least once, it's advisable to watch a bullfight (*corrida*) on TV before deciding whether to see one in the flesh. If you decide to go to a fight, you should **never** cheer for the bull, particularly if it has gored the bullfighter (*matador* or *toreros*), which is considered bad form.

Bullfighting isn't considered a sport in Spain, but an art (the art of *tauromachy*), and is reported in the arts and culture sections of newspapers. It's certainly not a contest, as there can be only one 'winner', although bullfighters can and do get killed every year (in addition to some 8,000 bulls) and even some spectators (*espontáneos*) who jump into the ring to try their hand. Aficionados hail it as a spectacle encompassing tradition, excitement, pageantry, beauty, danger, bravery, skill and drama. Whatever you may think of it, bullfighting is an essential part of Spain's heritage and culture and has had a profound influence on Spanish consciousness. Children aren't admitted to bullfights.

Scores of books about bullfighting are published each year and magazines and newspapers devote many pages to it. Among the many books written about bullfighting are *Death in the Afternoon* by Ernest Hemingway (Grafton), *Or I'll Dress You in Mourning* by Larry Collins (Weidenfeld & N) and *Blood*

Sport: A Social History of Spanish Bullfighting by Timothy Mitchell (University of Pennsylvania Press).

History

Andalusia is the birthplace of bullfighting, where Ronda is regarded as the cradle of modern bullfighting, and many of Spain's top bullfighters are Andalusian. Pedro Romero (immortalised by Goya in his painting *Tauromaquia*), who developed the classical style used today, is considered the father of modern bullfighting and ended his career in the 1820s at the aged of 72, having killed over 5,500 bulls without once being gored. Other famous bullfighters of the last two centuries include Juan Belmonte, Manuel Benítez (*El Cordobés*), Espartero, Rafael Gómez (*El Gallo*), Joselito and Manuel Rodríquez Sánchez (*Manolete*).

There have also been a few American and English bullfighters, and even women are beginning to make their mark in the ring. However, women find it hard to gain acceptance in what is the world's most macho (*machista*) 'profession', and some of Spain's top male bullfighters refused to share a bill with Cristina Sánchez, Spain's leading female bullfighter (now retired).

Spain's most famous bullfighter is currently José Tomás, whose reappearance in the ring in 2008 after several years' retirement brought widespread acclaim from aficionados, particularly at the San Isidro fair in Madrid, when he was carried out through the main door (the highest honour in bullfighting).

Top bullfighters are huge stars, feted like pop stars or star footballers, and can command fees of anywhere between €20,000 and €200,000 per fight.

Bullrings

There are some 500 permanent bullrings (usually exactly circular) in Spain. The most famous are Madrid's *Las Ventas* (the biggest in Spain, seating 25,000), Seville's *La Maestranza* and Pamplona's, followed by Bilbao's and Valencia's. There are also rings in many smaller towns, including the resort towns of Benidorm, Marbella and Torremolinos.

Towns holding over ten bullfights per year include Madrid, Malaga, Seville, Valencia and Zaragossa.

Season & Times

The official season runs from 19th March until 12th October. The most popular day is Sunday, but bullfights are also held on public holidays and during festivals. The most famous bullfighting fiestas are staged during Valencia's *fallas* festival (March); the April Fair in Seville; the San Isidro festival in Madrid (May), with 23 consecutive days of fighting; Granada's Corpus Christi celebrations (June); Pamplona's San Fermín festival (July); Bilbao's *Semana Grande* (August); and Zaragossa's *Feria de Pilar* (October).

A bullfight is held at 4 or 5pm, depending on the heat and time of the year, and is one of the few things in Spain that starts on time. It lasts two hours. Sometimes two fights are held on the same day. Bullfights are announced by posters stating whether it's a full bullfight with senior bullfighters and mature bulls, or a novice bullfight with younger bulls and junior bullfighters (a *novillada, gran novillada* or *corrida de novillos*). Matadors are listed on posters in order of seniority. Note that posters sold outside bullrings as souvenirs rarely advertise current fights and most feature famous dead or retired bullfighters.

Live bullfights are shown on Spanish TV almost daily throughout the season and recorded fights are screened twice weekly in the off-season.

Tickets

The price of tickets (*billetes*) varies considerably with the bullring, the bullfighters and the occasion. Tickets for even a 'small' bullfight usually range from €10 to €100 and can start as €35 in tourist areas, although locals usually pay nothing like the prices charged to tourists. Seats are usually designated as being in the shade (*sombra*) or the sun (*sol*), shaded seats not surprisingly being more expensive. Sun and shade

(*sol y sombra*) seats are those that become shaded or sunny as the fight progresses. Also, the closer you are to the action, the more expensive the seat, ringside barrier (*barrera*) seats in the shade therefore costing an arm and a leg – so to speak.

The seats behind the ringside seats are called *tendidos* and may be divided into high (*alto*) and low (*bajo*) areas. The cheapest seats in the highest rows at the back are *gradas* or simply *filas*, costing around €12 in a large ring. Cushions (*almohadillas*) can be rented for around €1 and are essential, as the 'seats' are usually stone or concrete.

Tickets show the section name and number (e.g. *tendido* 10), the row (*fila*) and the seat (*asiento*) number. It's best to purchase tickets from the box office (*taquilla*) at the bullring or at an official ticket office. Tickets sold by agents usually have a high surcharge. You should avoid buying tickets from touts.

CINEMA

Spain has over 2,000 cinemas (*cines*) nationwide and around 1,300 cinema clubs. Although it has lost a lot of its former popularity to television and many cinemas have closed in the last few decades, cinema remains reasonably popular in Spain, where over 10 per cent of adults see a film each week. In major cities, most cinemas have three or four performances (*sesiones*) a day, at two- or three-hour intervals, e.g. 4.30pm, 6.30pm, 8.30pm and 10.30pm (some have an extra

performance on Saturdays and public holidays (*festivos*), shown in listings as *S y F*).

Ticket prices are among the lowest in Europe and are generally around €5 (sometimes less in smaller towns). On certain days, e.g. Wednesdays in Madrid (designated the *día del espectador* or 'spectator's day'), tickets are reduced to €4 for all performances. Other discounts are available for students, pensioners and children under 13. Some cinemas also have a 'couple's day' (*día de la pareja*), usually midweek, when couples pay half-price.

Most cinemas are fairly small, although multi-screen cinemas (e.g. with 15 screens) have sprung up all over the country, particularly in shopping centres. There are outdoor and drive-in cinemas in the summer in many areas, some free, e.g. in the Parque del Retiro in Madrid.

Most foreign films are dubbed into Spanish, usually indicated by the letters *VE* (*versión española*). However, a number of private theatres in the major cities and resort towns specialise in screening original soundtrack films, indicated by the letters *VO* (*versión original*), with Spanish subtitles (*subtitulada*). Restricted films that aren't recommended for children less than a certain age (e.g. 13 or 18) are listed as *no recomendada para menores de 13/18 años*, while a film with no age restrictions is classified as *todos los públicos*. Cinema programmes are published in daily newspapers and entertainment guides.

There has been a revival of Spanish films since censorship ended and some 20 per cent of films shown in Spain are now Spanish-made. Spain stages some 40 film festivals each year, notably in Barcelona, Gijón, Madrid, San Sebastian and Vallodolid. However, US-made films dominate most cinemas, particularly those owned by US companies! In order to protect its indigenous film industry, the Spanish government introduced a highly unpopular quota system in 1994, forcing cinemas to show European films at least one day in three, and in June 2004, the government introduced a new ruling that all television companies must invest a certain amount of their profit in film-making in Spain.

Pedro Almodóvar is Spain's most famous film director and his numerous films, depicting complex relationships in often surrealist and *kitsch* settings, are known the world over. In 2000 his film *All About My Mother* (*Todo sobre mi madre*) won the Oscar for the best foreign film and in 2006 Penélope Cruz, the star of his latest film, *Return* (*Volver*), won the Best Actress award at the Cannes Film Festival.

FESTIVALS

Fairs and *fiestas* are an important part of cultural and social life in Spain, where over 3,000 are celebrated each year. The Spanish are inveterate revellers and almost every village and town has its annual fair (*feria*), lasting from a few days to a few weeks. They're usually held on the local saint's day (*patrón* or *patrona*), marked in red on Spanish calendars, when an effigy of the saint is paraded around the town in a procession. Village fairs often include a pilgrimage (*romería*) to a local shrine on horseback and in horse-drawn wagons, where a grand celebration is held.

There are also numerous local *fiestas* in celebration of the harvest, deliverance from the Moors, safe return from the sea and a variety of obscure events (the Spanish use any excuse to have a party!).

The first national festival of the year is *Martes de Carnaval* (Spain's Mardi Gras), held in February and best experienced in Cadiz or Tenerife. Holy Week (*Semana Santa*) is a major tourist attraction in many cities and towns, particularly in Seville and the rest of Andalusia. The main attractions are huge religious processions with ornate floats depicting scenes from the Passion and masked men decked out in ghostly costumes with pointed hats (imitated by the Ku Klux Klan in the US). Other major festivals include Corpus Christi in May or June; the feast day of Spain's patron saint, Santiago, on 25th July; and the Assumption of the Virgin (*la Asunción*) on 15th August.

Dates for most festivals are fluid and when they fall on a Tuesday or Thursday the day is usually 'bridged' with the preceding or following weekend to create a four-day holiday. Check exact dates with TurEspaña and local tourist offices in Spain.

Essential ingredients for a fair, festival or *fiesta* include costumes, processions, music, dancing and feasting. Processions often include huge papier-mâché statues called giants or bigheads (*gigantones* or *cabezudos*), which take many months to create and may be ritually burnt during the festival (the most famous is the *fallas fiesta* held in Valencia in March). The largest festivals include bullfights, flamenco music and dancing, funfairs, circuses, fireworks, plays, concerts, music recitals and competitions.

In Extremadura, the Basque Country and Navarre, summer *fiestas* often feature an *encierro de vaquillas*, bulls, cows or calves stampeding through the streets. The most famous of these is the *Fiesta de San Fermín* in Pamplona (although there are many others), when the slow of foot and foolhardy (usually foreigners) are often injured and occasionally killed. Another tradition, called the *toro del aguardiente*, is to set a table with a bottle of brandy and glasses in the middle of a bullring; those wishing to enjoy a glass must risk being tossed by a small bull (some people will do anything for a free drink!).

Foreigners are usually welcome to join in, although you may need an invitation to take part in some religious festivals. There's rarely any violence or serious crime at Spanish festivals, which are a great occasion for all the family (children often stay up all night), and any drunkenness or hooliganism is likely to be among foreigners. Pickpockets and bag snatchers are, however, fairly common at major festivals, which tend to attract thieves in droves.

FLAMENCO

Flamenco consists of a flamboyant dance and colourful music accompanying a song (*cante*). (Castanets, although symbols of Spain to many foreigners, are rarely used by the best dancers.) It has been referred to as the soul of Spain and, like bullfighting, is an essential part of the country's culture and traditions. The history of flamenco, in particular the origin of the name (literally 'Flemish'), is obscure,

although it's believed to have originated in the 18th century with the gypsies of Andalusia. Its songs of oppression and doomed romance were taken up by the peasants of Andalusia and spread throughout Spain in the 20th century as they migrated in search of jobs.

Flamenco consists of two main groups of songs, the small song (*cante chico*), which is lively and cheerful, and the big or deep song (*cante jondo*), lamenting lost love, sadness, death, hardship and the struggle for life. The 'classical' flamenco repertoire consists of some 60 songs and dances. The best flamenco singers tend to live tormented lives and many die of alcohol and drug abuse, including the revered Camarón de la Isla, who died in 1992 (fans are still mourning his loss). Antonio Ruiz Soler, Spain's most famous flamenco dancer, died in 1996 aged 74. In the last few years flamenco has increasingly been blended with music from other cultures such as the salsa, rumba and blues, which is known as the 'new flamenco' (*nuevo flamenco*) or 'flamenco fusion' (one

of the most famous and controversial 'fusion' dancers is Joaquín Cortes).

Flamenco has been shamelessly exploited by the Spanish tourist industry and it's commonly performed in shows advertised as 'genuine flamenco *fiestas*', which although enjoyable are a pale imitation of the real thing. Generally, the more commercially orientated the performance, the less authentic it's likely to be. In fact, the idea of a staged performance is alien to the whole concept of flamenco, which is traditionally informal and spontaneous.

In 'real' flamenco, performers should be possessed of a spirit or demon (*duende*) with a primitive, ecstatic allure that seduces listeners.

Real flamenco can be experienced in specialist bars and small members-only clubs (*peñas*) in Andalusia and other regions of Spain, to which foreigners are rarely admitted. The best chance most foreigners have of experiencing more or less authentic flamenco is at one of the big summer festivals held in Cadiz, Jerez, Granada, Malaga and Seville or during festivals and *fiestas* in small villages off the tourist track.

Many books have been written about flamenco, including *Songs of the Outcasts: an Introduction to Flamenco* by Robin Totton (Amadeus Press), *In Search of the Firedance* by James Woodall (Sinclair Stevenson), *Flamenco!* by Gwynne Edwards (Thames & Hudson) and *Duende: a Journey in Search of Flamenco* by Jason Webster (Black Swan).

GAMBLING

The Spanish are a nation of gamblers and bet a higher proportion of their income than almost any other nation. It's estimated that the Spanish gamble well over €1.9bn a year – equal to around €480 per head or some 15 per cent of the average net household income. They bet on almost anything, including lotteries, football and horse racing (illegal betting shops, where punters bet on foreign horse and greyhound racing, are common in resort areas), bingo, slot machines, casino games, and the big *jai-alai* games in the Basque Country and Madrid. Prizes can run into hundreds of thousands of euros – but not many people win them.

The most popular form of gambling is the state national lottery (*Lotería Nacional*) run in aid of charities and the Catholic Church. Lottery tickets are sold at lottery offices at face value (€20) or can be purchased from street vendors (10 per cent commission is added) and through ONCE (the Spanish organisation for the blind) kiosks manned by the blind or those with impaired sight. ONCE also sells tickets for its own daily draw (Friday's has the largest prize) and scratch cards (known as *Rasca y Gana*). ONCE takes some €60 a year from every Spaniard – a turnover that many international companies would be proud of.

Spain's (and the world's) biggest lottery, known as 'the fat one' (*El Gordo*), is held at Christmas and consists of 108 series of 66,000 tickets, each costing €200 – a total 'wager' of around €1.4bn, some 70 per cent of which is paid in prizes. The top prize for each series is around €2m, the second just under €1m and the third €500,000. Not surprisingly, €200 is too much for most people and it's possible to buy tenth shares (*décimos*) in a ticket, costing €20 each. Many clubs and charities buy a *décimo* and offer shares in those (called *partcipaciones*) for a couple of euros, usually adding a small surcharge.

'The fat one' has its own website (💻 www.elgordo.com) and there are several villages in Spain that regularly sell winning tickets for *El Gordo*, such as the tiny village of Sort (meaning 'luck' in Catalan), in the Pyrenees where coachloads of hopeful lottery ticket buyers flock every autumn!

Tickets are usually sold out long before the draw on 22nd December, which is televised live (it takes three hours) and traditionally made by the children of the San Ildefonso school in Madrid. Winning numbers are published in newspapers on 23rd December and the list is posted in lottery offices for three months following the draw. Winners must claim their prizes, as they aren't sent to them automatically (unclaimed winnings go back to the state). If you win a big prize, you can take your ticket to a Spanish bank, which gives you a receipt and collects your winnings on your behalf. Lottery prizes are free of all taxes.

Spain's second-largest lottery is called the kid (*El Niño*), after the baby Jesus, and takes place on 5th January.

Spain has some 20 casinos, and there's also one in Gibraltar. The most common casino games are American and French roulette, black jack, *punto y banca* and *chemin de fer*, plus the ubiquitous slot machines. There's usually an entry fee, e.g. €6, and visitors must show their passports (to identify professional gamblers). Most casinos are open from late afternoon until the early hours of the morning, e.g. 5pm until 4 or 5am. Dress code is smart casual (no jeans, sandals or T-shirts).

MUSEUMS & GALLERIES

Spain has over 800 museums (*museos*) and many important collections, particularly in Madrid and Barcelona, and there has been an explosion in the number of art galleries (*galerías de arte*) in the last decade throughout the country, particularly for contemporary art. Spain has a distinguished history in the field of art and has produced many of the world's greatest artists, including Goya, El Greco, Velázquez, Murillo, Picasso, Dalí, Miró and Juan Gris. Modern art is a passion with the Spanish and the annual Contemporary Art Fair (ARCO) held in February in Madrid is one of the world's largest modern art exhibitions.

Madrid

Spain's premier art gallery is the Museo Nacional del Prado (called simply the Prado, 🖳 www.museoprado.es) in Madrid, housing one of the world's richest art collections. It contains over 5,000 paintings, including an unrivalled collection of Spanish masters. The museum has recently doubled its floor space to allow many more of its works to be displayed, as well as creating space for temporary exhibitions, theatres and cafés.

The capital boasts many other celebrated art collections, including the Museo Lazaro Galdiano (🖳 www.flg.es),

the Museo Thyssen-Bornemisza (🖳 www.museothyssen.org) and the Museo Nacional Centro de Arte, Reina Sofía (🖳 www.museoreinasofia.es) – one of Europe's top contemporary art galleries, housed in a modernised 18th-century hospital, with a monumental 78,000m^2 (836,160ft^2) of exhibition space. The Prado, Thyssen-Bornemisza and Reina Sofía museums are known as Madrid's 'Art Triangle' and the Paseo de Prado, connecting the three (and due to be semi-pedestrianised), as the 'Art Walk'. A Museum Card (called the *Paseo del Arte*) allows access to all three museums and costs €14.40.

Barcelona

Although it isn't so richly endowed with museums as Madrid, Barcelona boasts a number of important collections, including the Museu Picasso (🖳 www.museupicasso.bcn.es), the Museu d'Art de Catalunya (🖳 www.mnac.es), the Fundació Joan Miró (🖳 www.bcn.fjmiro.es), the Museu d'Art Modern and the Barcelona Museum of Contemporary Art/MACBA (🖳 www.macba.es).

Modernism is particularly strong in Barcelona, which is the Spanish 'capital' of modernist architecture. (One of its major attractions is the Parc Güell, designed by Spain's greatest architect Antoni Gaudí and housing the Casa-Museu Gaudí.

Also not to be missed are Gaudí's Casa Milà apartment building and his most famous work, the remarkable unfinished Temple Expiatori de la Sagrada Familia.) The Barcelona *Articket* (⬜ www.articketbcn.org), allowing you to visit seven major art museums in the city for €20 and valid for six months, is available from art museums and tourist offices in Barcelona.

Other Locations

The Museu Dalí (Dalí Theatre-Museum – ⬜ www.salvador-dali.org) in Figueras (the birthplace of the artist) on the Costa Brava, is itself a surrealist work of art and is the second most visited museum in Spain after the Prado. A futuristic art gallery funded by the Guggenheim Foundation (⬜ www.guggenheim-bilbao.es) was opened in Bilbao in 1999 and is one of Europe's most beautiful galleries as well as an architectural masterpiece. Malaga (Picasso's birthplace) has the Picasso Museum (⬜ www.museopicassomalaga.org), housing the largest collection of his works in the world. Valencia boasts an excellent museum of modern art, the Institut Valencià d'Art Modern (⬜ www.ivam.es), and León Spain's latest contemporary art museum (the MUSAC), housed in a spectacular stained-glass cube (⬜ www.musac.org.es).

Opening Times

Most major museums open from 9am to 7pm, Tuesdays to Sundays. Smaller museums may open only between 9 and 10am until 2 or 3pm, although some re-open after the *siesta* from 4 to 7pm. Some museums have extended opening hours in the summer. Opening times vary considerably and are subject to frequent change, so check in advance (they're usually listed in guide books). Many smaller museums open erratically. **Most museums (including the Prado) are closed on Mondays.**

Charges

Entrance fees to Spain's museums, galleries and other sites are usually between €1.50 and €3. Many museums provide free entrance to students, some have reduced fees for students and senior citizens, and a few provide free entry on one day a week (including the Prado), usually Sundays. A pensioner's card (*tarjeta de pensionista*) allows free entry to state museums and monuments (operated by the Patrimonio Nacional) and discounts elsewhere. An annual museum card (€36) is also available allowing free entry to all state-owned museums in Spain.

The city of Madrid offers tourists the *Madrid Card* system, allowing free entry to museums and monuments, unlimited free travel on public transport and discounts in shops and theatres. The card is valid for one, two or three days, priced at €42, €55 and €68 respectively (discounts are available for online purchases), and can be purchased by telephone (☎ 902 088 908) or online (⬜ www.madridcard.com) and in tourist offices and travel agents in Madrid. The €6 entrance fee for the Prado and Reina Sofía museums is a bargain and entrance is free to students with an international student card, pensioners over 65, those under 18 and the unemployed.

In Barcelona, the *Barcelona Card* (⬜ www.barcelonacard.com) allows discounted entrance to museums, shows and attractions, unlimited free travel on public transport and discounts in shops and restaurants. The card is valid for two, three, four or five days, priced at €24 to €36, and can be purchased at tourist offices and attractions in the city.

Most cathedrals, monasteries and famous churches, many of which house great works of art, charge admission fees to non-worshippers. Student admission is usually half price or less and children under 14 may be admitted free.

It's possible in Spain to visit numerous businesses, particularly those connected with the food and drink industry such as vineyards, distilleries, breweries, mineral water springs, farms and dairies. Spain has numerous zoos, the best of which are Barcelona, Madrid and Fuengirola (Malaga), whose innovative zoo was acclaimed by *National Geographic* as the best in Spain.

MUSIC

Music is extremely popular in Spain and an essential ingredient of any festival or *fiesta*. Top international soloists, bands and orchestras give concerts throughout the country at all times of year. Spain has a wealth of traditional folk music and dance, particularly flamenco and classical guitar, which are popular throughout the country. It's renowned worldwide for its classical guitar, popularised by Andrés Segovia and Narciso Yepes and featuring memorably in the music of Albéniz, Granados, de Falla and Rodrigo. An international festival of the guitar is held in Córdoba in July.

Rock and pop music is, of course, popular with young Spaniards and there are many excellent home-grown bands, although the most widely played music is American and British. Among the most popular forms of Spanish pop music are root-rock (*rock-con-raíces*), a sort of rock version of flamenco singing, and rave music (*bacalao/baKalao*). Madrid has the most lively and varied music scene, although the Catalans are recognised as Spain's most 'serious' music lovers, particularly with regard to opera, jazz and Catalan song. Jazz has a large following in Spain and jazz festivals are staged in many cities in summer, including Barcelona, San Sebastian, Santander and Sitges.

Spain's most popular singer is crooner Julio Iglesias, who has sold more records in more languages than any other musical artist in history (over 160m albums, some 200 of which have gone 'gold' or 'platinum'). In contrast, one of Spain's biggest national and international hits in recent years was surprisingly the Benedictine monks of Santo Domingo de Silos (Burgos), whose album of Gregorian chant (*Las Mejores Obras del Canto Gregoriano*) topped music charts around the world, selling over 5m copies.

The Spanish pop music industry, in common with that in most countries, has suffered badly at the hands of 'pirates', who sell illegally copied compact discs (CDs) for around €3, largely on the streets through immigrant 'workers'. Since 2000, one out of every four CDs sold has been an illegal copy. Despite spectacular police raids and arrests of the copiers and sellers, piracy is a major problem facing the future of the Spanish music industry.

Madrid, Barcelona and Valencia all stage classical music concerts. Major concerts in Madrid are held at the magnificent Auditorio Nacional de Música (⌨ www.auditorionacional.mcu.es), home of the Spanish national orchestra (*Orquesta Nacional de España/ONE*), where tickets for most concerts cost between €15 and €70. Annual concert cycles are also performed by the National Orchestra and Choir of Spain, and Spanish Radio and Television at the Teatro Real in Madrid. Free open-air concerts are held in summer by the city brass band (*banda municipal*) in the Templete del Retiro in Retiro Park. One of the most popular forms of music in Madrid is *zarzuela*, a form of light opera or operetta, performed in the Teatro de Zarzuela. In Barcelona, major concerts are held at the eccentric art nouveau Palau de la Música. One of the world's most spectacular auditoriums is El Palau de les Arts in Valencia.

Spain also stages a wealth of excellent music festivals, including a festival of religious music (*Semanas de Música Religiosa*) in Cuenca at the end of March; the international festival of music and dance (*Festival Internacional de Música y Danza*) in Granada in June/July (Spain's most important musical event); the Santander international festival (*Festival Internacional de Santander*) of music, dance and drama in July/August; the international music festival (*Festival Internacional de Música*) in Barcelona in September/October and the autumn festival in Madrid from mid-September until the beginning of October (it also includes drama and ballet performances).

NIGHTLIFE

Spain is famous for its vibrant nightlife, which extends until dawn and beyond in major cities such as Madrid and Barcelona (not for nothing are Madrid's party-goers known as 'the cats' or *los gatos*). In major cities and resort areas, there's a wide choice of nightlife for all ages, cabarets, discos, sex shows, flamenco, jazz and other music clubs, bars, nightclubs, music halls, and restaurants with floor shows (*tablaos*). Karaoke is popular in many pubs and clubs in resort areas.

Plaza Mayor, Madrid

For many Spaniards the 'day' doesn't begin until nightfall and most clubs and discotheques don't start to warm up until after midnight. At weekends, many young Spaniards literally rock around the clock and in the major cities and resorts some discotheques **open** at daybreak, while others are in business non-stop from Friday night until Monday afternoon. Not surprisingly, Spaniards reportedly sleep less than other Europeans.

Ibiza is the spiritual home of the 'Euroraver' and is **the** place to be in summer, when it boasts Europe's most vibrant nightlife and biggest and boldest dance clubs.

The authorities in Madrid and Barcelona have been forced to restrict Spain's incessant day and nightlife in some cities, in an attempt to reduce drug use (particularly amphetamines and ecstasy) and the resulting high number of fatal car accidents. Bars in these cities must now close at 2.30am and discos at 4.30am, although most owners ignore the new regulations unless forced to close by the police. Some towns are also cracking down on discos making excessive noise.

Discos are found in the smallest of towns, although they may be no more than a bar with music and a dance floor. The entrance fee, which often includes a drink, is usually around €6 but can be as high as €30, though women are often given free entry or are charged less than men. Some discos have no entrance fee but **very** expensive drinks, e.g. between €5 and €20. Some discos have early evening sessions for teenagers with an entrance fee of around €3. Live music is common in bars, many of which have a small dance floor and offer free entrance or charge a small fee, e.g. €2.

It's important to be fashionably dressed to gain access to the most exclusive discos, but in general any casual dress is acceptable, including jeans and T-shirts. There's usually a 'bouncer' on the door checking that guests are suitably attired and haven't had too much to drink.

Discos, nightclubs, music bars and clubs, dinner/dancing venues and cabarets are listed in English-language publications and in Spanish newspapers under *Salas de fiestas* and *Espectáculos*.

BARS & CAFES

One of the delights of living in Spain is the many excellent pavement cafés and bars – and in particular their delicious coffee and low prices. Few countries can match Spain for the number, variety, quality and economy of its watering holes. An aperitif at midday or in the evening is a ritual in Spain, though drinking habits vary considerably from region to region and the information below is necessarily of a general nature.

Bars

Spain's cities and resort areas contain a wealth of bars and pubs; there are over 8,000 in Madrid alone (reportedly more than in the whole of Norway). They include cocktail bars, piano bars, disco bars, jazz, rock or flamenco bars, bar-cafeterias, bar-restaurants, cabaret bars, casino bars, beach bars, wine bars (*bodegas*), taverns (*tabernas*), *mesones* (a bar specialising in serving wine and *tapas*), *cervecerías* (a bar specialising in beer, usually with a wide selection of imported beers on tap), gay bars, roof-top bars, pool-side bars, youth bars, topless bars, and a huge variety of foreign bars and pubs. 'Pubs' tend to be flashy bars, often with live music, satellite television, expensive drinks and no food.

For homesick Britons there are numerous pseudo-British bars in resort areas, usually equipped with satellite television systems showing English football, cricket and other sporting events. Television can be even more obtrusive in Spanish bars, where customers are fed a constant diet of soccer, bullfights, game shows and dubbed foreign films. Don't expect to have a quiet conversation in a bar with a TV.

☑ SURVIVAL TIP

It's cheaper to drink while standing at a bar; sitting at a table may cost you 50 per cent more and a table on a pavement or terrace (*terraza*) can be double the bar price. You may not be permitted to buy a drink at the bar and take it to a seat outside. Eating is also more expensive at a table than at the bar.

Bars are usually open from noon to 4pm and from 8pm until midnight or later, although some are open all day and others only open in the evenings. In resort areas, many bars (and restaurants) are closed outside the high season. There are no national licensing laws in Spain, where closing time is usually when the owner decides to shut up shop or when the last customer goes home, which is usually in the early hours of the morning. However, some town halls fix bar closing times, e.g. 2am.

Cafés

Traditional café life can still be found in Spain, where a café is rarely simply somewhere to grab a cup of coffee and a pastry. Its myriad roles include library (you can borrow and read a newspaper); public telephone 'box'; public toilet (there's a the dearth of 'proper' public toilets in Spain); lounge; business or social meeting place; study; academic or debating arena; and refuge (from the sun or rain). Cafés often have a billiard room and some even a live orchestra or chamber music. Around 5pm is the hour of *tertulia*, the café get-together that's a national institution.

It's customary to buy a drink when you use the toilet in a bar or café, although owners don't usually mind non-customers using their facilities.

To attract the attention of a waiter (*camarero*) or waitress (*camarera*) in a busy bar or café, it's customary to call out 'attention, please' (*¡oiga, por favor!*) or simply to shout your order at the waiter. In small family bars and cafés, you're usually served by the landlord or landlady (*dueño/dueña*), who won't normally accept tips (*propinas*). Tipping is, however, common in bars, although tips are usually small and often consist of the small change from your payment, left in a saucer. Tips are often put in a communal tin or box (*bote*) and shared among the staff, although this practice isn't common in restaurants, where waiters tend to keep their own tips.

Drinking

The legal age for drinking in Spain is 18, although it isn't always enforced. Under 18s are permitted on licensed premises with an adult but cannot consume alcohol. Although Spaniards are heavy drinkers by most standards, you rarely see them intoxicated. Drunkenness is associated with a loss of dignity and anyone who cannot hold his drink is scorned. Nevertheless, alcoholism is a serious problem in Spain, particularly among expatriates, many of whom are unable to control their drinking. Newcomers should be particularly wary of drinking too much, which is all too easy with Spain's low prices and generous measures. A surfeit of sun and alcohol can be deadly. See also **Wine** on page 265.

Coffee

Spain is a Mecca for coffee lovers and Spanish coffee is among the best value in Europe. It's

served in ice-cream parlours (*heladerías*) and restaurants as well as in cafés and bars, and is freshly made with 'real' coffee beans. A 'normal' coffee is an espresso, which is served black (*café solo*), while a coffee made with half milk is a *café con leche*, usually drunk by Spaniards for breakfast (often accompanied by a brandy!). Coffee with a dash of milk is a *café cortado*. If you want a large black coffee, ask for a *doble* or a *grande*. Should you wish to drink weak, milky coffee, ask for a *manchada*, which means 'stained milk'.

Decaffeinated coffee (*descafeinado*) is widely available; it may be fresh, although many bars just empty a sachet of instant coffee into a cup of hot milk. Iced coffee (*café con hielo*) is also available and is usually served black. It's often served spiked with brandy, whisky or anisette, when it's called a *carajillo*, which may be served with a small slice of lemon and a coffee bean floating on top. In some areas, a coffee is routinely accompanied by a glass of cold water.

A coffee usually costs from €1, although in tourist haunts and fashionable *terrazas* it can be as much as €3.

Tea

Tea (*té*) is available in most bars and cafés and is usually drunk black or served with a slice of lemon (*té con limón*). If you want tea with milk, it's best to ask for *té con un poquito de leche fría* (tea with a little cold milk), because if you ask for simply *té con leche* you're likely to get tea made with half water and half hot milk! However, it's best not to drink 'English' tea in bars and cafés at all, as it's invariably awful. Herbal teas such as camomile (*manzanilla*) and mint (*mentapoleo*) are also widely available. There are tea rooms (*salones de té*) in the major cities and afternoon tea is often served in luxury hotels, sometimes to a background of live classical music.

Cocktails & Spirits

Cocktails and spirits are much cheaper in Spain than in most other countries and are served in larger measures (the Spanish don't use official measures when pouring drinks, in defiance of European Union regulations). Most spirits are ordered by brand name, as there are Spanish (*nacional*) equivalents for most foreign tipples. (If you as for 'a brandy', you'll generally be served Spanish brandy.) Most people notice little difference between Spanish gin, vodka and rum, and more expensive imports when they're used in cocktails. However, Spanish whisky drunk on its own is terrible in comparison with scotch, Irish whiskey or bourbon. (Some bars and discotheques reportedly buy inexpensive spirits in bulk to refill well known brand bottles and charge higher price, though whisky is less likely to be substituted, as it's difficult to reproduce the flavour of a particular whisky and it's less likely to be drunk in a cocktail.) *Pacharán*, made from sloes, is a popular after-dinner drink.

Cocktails and spirits are usually served with lots of ice (*hielo*), which those with sensitive stomachs may wish to avoid (depending on the water source).

Soft Drinks

A wide variety of non-alcoholic ('soft') drinks (*refrescos*) are available in Spain, including ubiquitous international brands such as Pepsi, Coca Cola and Fanta. Other common drinks include sweetened fruit juice (*zumo* or *jugo*), fresh juice (*zumo natural*), including orange (*naranja*) and lemon (*limón*), iced fruit juices made from fruit syrups or coffee (*granizados*), tonic (*tónica*) and bitter (*kas*). Mineral water is sold in sparkling (*con gas*) and still (*sin gas*) versions.

A popular thirst-quenching drink is a *horchata de chufa*, a concoction made from the tuberous root of the *chufa* (known in English as 'earth almond') and served with crushed-ice; there are even dedicated *chufa* cafés called *horchaterías*. Other popular soft drinks include a black and white (*negro y blanco*), a combination of ice cream (*helado*) and coffee, and creamy milk shakes (*batidos*). Bars also serve non-alcoholic beer, oddly called *sin* (literally 'without').

Beer

Beer (*cerveza*) is extremely popular in Spain and, somewhat surprisingly, most Spaniards prefer it to wine. In general, a bar serves one brand of local draught beer and possibly a few bottled beers. A *cervecería* is a bar that specialises in beer and usually has several brands on tap and a wide range of bottled beers, including imported brands. Spanish beers come in light (*dorada*) and dark (*negra*) varieties, the most famous brands including San Miguel, Cruzcampo, Dorada, Aguila, Estrella and Mahou.

A small bottle of beer (300ml) is a *botellín*, while a small glass of draught beer is called a *caña*. A *caña doble* is twice as large as a *caña* (and is often served when you don't specify a size) and a large beer is a *tubo* (tube) or *jarra* (mug or jar), although this can also mean a jug or pitcher. In tourist resorts, customers who ask for '*una cerveza*' are often served a *tubo*. Draught beer is generally cheaper than bottled beer and costs around €1 to €1.50 for a small glass (*caña*). For something lighter try *clara*, a refreshing shandy made with beer and sweetened seltzer (*gaseosa*).

Spanish beer is quite strong – usually around 5 per cent alcohol.

Other Drinks

Wine (*vino*) is sold by the glass (*copa*) in bars and cafés and is ordered by simply asking for a glass of red, white or rosé (*una copa de tinto/*

blanco/rosado). If you don't specify the colour, you're usually served red wine. It's inexpensive by northern European standards, costing as little as €1 for a glass of house wine (*vino de la casa* or *vino del lugar*) often served from a barrel or a carafe.

If you fancy trying your hand at drinking from a wineskin (*odre/bota de vino*) or *porrón* (a glass carafe with a pouring funnel), don't wear your best clothes.

Table wine (*vino corriente* or *vino de mesa*) is often drunk mixed with sparkling mineral water, soda or lemonade – called a *tinto de verano* (literally 'summer red') when made with red wine. *Sangría* is a punch made with peaches, oranges, seltzer, sugar, red wine and a dash of brandy. It's available everywhere and can be surprisingly strong, although it isn't usually well made in bars. A similar drink is *zurra* made with white wine, brandy, vermouth and sugar, garnished with orange and lemon segments and diluted with water and ice. Sherry (*jerez*) is popular, particularly in the south, and 'apple wine', i.e. cider (*sidra*), is a common drink in the north of Spain.

Food

Bars and cafés in Spain aren't just somewhere to get a drink, and many serve snacks and meals from morning until late at night. In addition to *tapas* (see below), bars (and cafés) normally serve sandwiches and rolls (*bocadillos*), toasted sandwiches (*tostadas*) and various egg dishes, including fried eggs (*huevos fritos*) and cold Spanish omelette (*tortilla de patata*). In village bars, there's often no menu and you just ask the patron what he has to offer. There's invariably something, if only what the family is eating, such as stew, grilled seafood or salad.

You can also find a wide selection of appetising snacks in food shops such as *panaderías* and *croissanterías*.

Tapas

Tapas (meaning 'lids', as they were originally little saucers of snacks served on top of a drink) are the world's greatest snack food. They're a way of life throughout Spain, although more common in the north and the major cities, where it's customary to drop into a bar after work to have a drink accompanied by *tapas*. They consist of small dishes of olives, mushrooms, pickled vegetables, kebabs (*pinchos morunos*), ham, seafood (baby eels, tuna, squid, octopus, clams, mussels, lobster, prawns, anchovies), garlic potatoes, pieces of omelette (*tortilla*), meatballs, tripe, huge potato crisps, peanuts, Russian salad, cheese, salami, nuts, pickled carrots, sausage, snails, stewed pimento, cubes of pork in sauce, pig's ear or pickled artichoke hearts (to name but a few).

In southern Andalusia, a favourite *tapa* is *huevos revueltos* – not 'revolting eggs' but softly scrambled eggs with a variety of flavourings, including wild asparagus, shrimps, ham, beans and mushrooms. *Tapas variadas* is a selection of *tapas* and an excellent introduction for the uninitiated. Most *tapas* can also be ordered as sandwiches in French bread.

Tapas are usually eaten at the counter in a bar, accompanied by draft beer, wine or sherry, although they may also be eaten as an *entrée* before a meal. Among the best places to eat *tapas* is a traditional *mesón* or *tasca* (many of which are also restaurants), where there's a counter full of hot and cold appetisers. If you don't speak Spanish, it's best to choose a bar where the dishes are displayed along the bar, rather than one where they're simply listed on a blackboard.

> *Tapas* are served in various sizes: a standard *tapa* is an appetiser-like serving, a *pincho* or a *porción* a slightly larger serving, and a *ración* is the same size as a starter. Always state the size of serving you want.

Some bars automatically serve free *tapas* with every drink, midday and evening, although this custom isn't so widespread nowadays. However, it's still possible to find places where you can get a small glass of wine (*chato*) and a *tapa* for €1. *Tapa* etiquette dictates that you don't usually have a choice of free *tapas*. When not served free, *tapas* cost around €1 to €3 for a serving.

Paying

In a bar or café, it's usual to 'run a tab' and pay for your drinks when you leave, although you may be asked to pay when you're served in a busy establishment or a tourist spot such as a beach bar. Your account may be chalked on the counter itself or written on a pad kept behind the bar. If your waiter is going off duty, he will ask you to pay. Service and tax is included in the price and it's unnecessary to tip, although most people leave their small change (e.g. €0.20) and a group may leave €1 after an evening's drinking.

When Spaniards have a drink together, the one who made the invitation or suggestion usually pays (although they may argue about it). If you're invited for a drink by a Spaniard, he will invariably insist on paying, even if he is of modest means. The foreign habit of trying to work out who has drunk what and splitting the bill accordingly is alien to the Spanish.

RESTAURANTS

Like most Latins, Spaniards live to eat (and drink), and one of the greatest attractions of Spain is its abundance and variety of inexpensive eating places. In fact, anyone who loves good food and wine is guaranteed a happy life in Spain, which boasts one of the healthiest diets in Europe. Dining out is a popular social occasion and it's common for Spaniards to entertain their friends at a restaurant rather than at home. You will often see large family groups, encompassing three or four generations and including children of all ages (children are welcome in all but the most exclusive restaurants in Spain). However, the restaurant trade has been hard hit by live TV coverage of football matches, which are screened six nights a week in Spain (the most extensive coverage in Europe).

Spain offers a wealth of eating places from luxury international restaurants (with matching prices) to humble *bodegas* and *cantinas* serving homely fare at bargain prices. Traditional eating and drinking places include *mesónes* in urban areas, *ventas* in the countryside, and *merenderos*, *chiringuitos* and *chamboas* (specialising in seafood) at the beach. A *marisquería* is an up-market fish restaurant, *cocederos* and *freidurías de pescado* are basic places to enjoy fresh fried fish, while an *asador* specialises in roast meat, poultry or fish. It's also possible to 'dine out at home' in many towns, where restaurants and caterers provide gourmet take-away meals complete with simple cooking instructions, or a chef and waitress will cook and serve dinner in your home for a moderate charge.

Spaniards don't drink a lot of alcohol with their meals and many prefer mineral water (*agua mineral*) or lemonade. If you want tap water ask for *agua del grifo* or *agua corriente*.

Spanish Cuisine

Anyone who says Spanish food is boring, unimaginative or always swimming in garlic and olive oil hasn't ventured far off the tourist trail. Spanish cuisine is among the most varied and sophisticated in Europe and is greatly influenced by other Mediterranean countries and Arab cooking. Each region has its specialities (*platos típicos*) based on local produce, meats and fish, and every province and most large towns boast one or more local culinary delights, even if it's just a sausage or cheese. Spanish cooking largely consists of simple, wholesome fare and is noted for its high-quality fresh ingredients. Spices, particularly hot spices, are used sparingly and the best Spanish cooking is a subtle combination of flavourings and sauces intended to enhance (rather than smother) the flavour of the main ingredients.

Generally, the further north you go in Spain, the better the food, the majority of *haute cuisine* restaurants being situated in the Basque Country, Madrid and Barcelona. Basque cuisine (heavily influenced by French) is possibly the finest in Spain, San Sebastian being the region's gastronomic capital, with some half a dozen Michelin-starred restaurants. San Sebastian is also famous for its all-male gastronomic societies (*sociedades populares/cofradías*), where members do the cooking in turn. Asturias,

Catalonia and Galicia are also noted for the excellence of their cuisine.

Spain's most famous dishes include *gazpacho* (cold tomato, cucumber and onion soup in Andalusia, the recipe varying with the region), *paella* (a seafood and rice dish originally from Valencia), and *tortilla española* (Spanish omelette from Castile), all of which are found on tourist menus throughout Spain. However, there's much more to Spanish cooking than these stereotypes, and the country boasts many other delicacies, including roast suckling pig (*cochinillo asado*) and lamb (*cordero asado*); casseroles and stews such as *cocido madrileño* made from salt pork, beef and stewing hen; 'exotic' dishes such as bull's tail (*rabo de toro estofado*) cooked in a sauce of onions and tomatoes; and game such as partridge braised with ham, tomatoes, wine and anchovies (*perdices al torero*). Spain also has a wide variety of desserts (*postres*), although in budget establishments dessert may consist of fresh fruit or Spanish 'flan' (*crème caramel* or *crema catalana*) only.

The Arab habit of adding fruit and nuts to meat and fish dishes is common in Spain, as are unusual combinations of meat, fish and fowl. Meat is usually excellent throughout Spain, particularly pork and chicken (often free-range). When ordering steak you should specify how you want it cooked, i.e. **very** rare (*vuelta y vuelta*, literally 'turned'), rare (*poco hecho*), medium (*hecho*) or well done (*muy hecho*).

Spain is noted for the quality and variety of its fish (*pescados*) and shellfish (*mariscos*), and fish lovers will think they've died and gone to heaven.

The quality and variety of Spanish seafood is unrivalled and includes sea bream, grouper, trout, tuna, salmon, swordfish, turbot, angler fish, sea bass, hake, eels, cod, squid, king crabs, spider crabs, jumbo shrimp, scallops, mussels, lobster, cockles, oysters, prawns, crayfish, octopus, cuttlefish, clams and the most prized of all shellfish, *percebes* (goose barnacles), costing up to €200 a kilo.

Seafood is excellent throughout Spain, even in Madrid and other inland cities, although it's best in the north (particularly Galicia) and south-western Andalusia. However, fish and seafood is rarely cheap and in up-market restaurants can be very expensive (it's usually priced per 100g rather than per 'dish'). In coastal areas, there are numerous seafood restaurants (*marisquerías*), serving nothing else, and open-air, beach restaurants such as *merenderos*, *chiringuitos* and *chamboas*, most of which are unpretentious and serve inexpensive fried fish and chips (although some are sophisticated and expensive). Good fish restaurants often keep a variety of live fish and shellfish in tanks from which you can choose your meal.

The most common seafood dish is *paella*, usually eaten by Spaniards only at lunchtime and best (i.e. most authentic) in Valencia, where it originated.

Foreign Cuisine

Spain isn't noted for non-Spanish cuisine (why should it be?), although there's an abundance of good foreign restaurants in Spanish cities and resort areas. There's also a plethora of fast food outlets such as hamburger bars (*hamburgueserías*) and British-style 'restaurants' that serve 'full English breakfasts all day', although you're unlikely to find any of these (thankfully) in rural areas. Foreign restaurants cater mostly to foreigners (with menus in English or German), as the Spanish generally prefer to stick to their own cuisine.

Although Spanish food can sometimes be terrible, particularly in some tourist establishments on the *costas*, it usually offers better value (and often better quality) than foreign cuisine. In general, it's best to follow the locals' example. In resorts, restaurants that open all year round may offer better service and value than seasonal and beachside restaurants catering primarily to tourists.

Menus

A Spanish menu (*el menú* or *la carta*) is usually written in two or three languages in resorts and

some cities, e.g. Spanish plus English and/ or German, although in Barcelona they may be only in Catalan, particularly in high-class establishments.

Set Menus

All restaurants must offer a set menu of the day or house menu (*menú del día*, *cubierto* or *menú de la casa*) at lunchtime at 80 per cent of the price each course would cost separately. The set menu is usually written on a blackboard outside and may not be included in the printed menu inside. It usually consists of three courses (e.g. starter, main course with vegetables and a sweet) and may include a glass or small carafe of house wine and bread, although these are usually charged extra. In resort areas and major cities, many establishments offer 'tourist menus' (*menú turístico*), which may include a quarter to half a litre of wine or a beer, service and other charges. Many restaurants serve a selection of *tapas* before the first course as part of a set menu.

Set menus usually cost from €8 in small restaurants, *bodegas* and bars, up to €40 or more in high-class restaurants. Many restaurants have several set menus, e.g. at €15 and €30. Note that prices, quality and the choice of dishes on a set menu vary enormously.

Many restaurants, particularly those catering to foreign residents and tourists in resort areas, provide special menus at Christmas and New Year.

Wine

Wine (*vino*) is inexpensive in Spanish restaurants by northern European standards. A house wine (*vino de la casa* or or *vino del lugar*) costs from just €3 per bottle (*botella*) or carafe (*garafa*) in a modest establishment. However, the price increases rapidly as you go up market, although a good bottle can be purchased in most quality restaurants for from €10 (the mark up on wines in Spain is usually around 100 per cent of the supermarket price and can be as low as 50 per cent). Be wary of ordering a bottle of wine in a tourist area unless you've checked the price on the wine list, as rip-offs on wine (and food) are common in some places.

Wine is sometimes included in set menus, when two people may receive a bottle between them and one person a half bottle (*media botella*) or a quarter to half a litre. In an inexpensive rural establishment, there may be no choice of wine and you're served whatever comes out of the barrel. Most house whites and rosés are drinkable and may be produced locally. However, the quality of house red wine varies considerably – from good to terrible.

If you just order *vino* it's understood to mean red wine, which is often served chilled and drunk with everything from red meat to fish.

Buying wine by the glass instead of a bottle can work out expensive at between €1 and €2 a glass, especially considering it's usually 'plonk' which costs €1 to €2 a bottle (or carton) in a supermarket. If you drink more than a single glass you're better off ordering a bottle.

Ratings & Prices

Spanish restaurants are officially rated on a scale of forks, from one to five (five denoting the top grade), although a high fork-rating isn't necessarily a sign of quality cooking, as the criteria also include facilities, décor, length of menu and price. Prices per head range from €6 in the cheapest bar-restaurants to around €15 in a two- or three-fork restaurant, where two people can dine well for around €20 to €30, including a bottle of good wine. The best value is often found in inexpensive, unpretentious restaurants, particularly the 'dining rooms' (*comedores*) of bars, *pensiones* and *fondas*, many of which may serve food only at lunchtime.

There are also budget *cafeterías* (often self-service) in major cities and resort areas; these are graded from one to three cups depending on their facilities. The emphasis is usually on bland 'international' fare, although many serve

traditional Spanish dishes and they provide unbeatable value, e.g. €5 for all you can eat. *Cafeterías* also offer set meals called *platos combinados* (literally 'combination plates'), which are also available in many bars and inexpensive restaurants, consisting of one-course meals such as egg and chips, steak and/or fish with chips, and squid (*calamares*) and salad. *Platos combinados* usually include bread and possibly a drink and cost from €3 to €6. There are many excellent pizza places in resort areas, where 'real' pizzas are made in wood-burning ovens and usually cost around €5 to €12.

THEATRE, OPERA & BALLET

The vast majority of theatres in Spain are in Madrid and Barcelona, although there has been a huge theatre-building programme throughout the country in the last decade and many smaller towns now have municipal-sponsored theatres (*teatros municipales*) housed in cultural centres. The main theatres in Madrid include the Teatro de Zarzuela, Teatro Español, Teatro de la Comedia, Centro Dramático Nacional, Teatro María Guerrero and Centro de Nueva Tendencias Escénicas, a number of which are sponsored by the state or city. Spain has a long tradition of drama and a number of prolific playwrights such as Lope de Vega (who wrote or co-wrote almost 2,000 plays) and Tirso de Molina (who first dramatised the story of *Don Juan*). Classical and contemporary Spanish and foreign plays are performed throughout Spain and experimental theatre is particularly popular in Catalonia.

Theatre tickets usually range from €5 to €40, but prices are often reduced on certain days, e.g. Wednesdays or Thursdays. Some theatres offer student discounts. There are often two performances on one evening – at 7 or 7.30pm and 10 or 10.30pm – and 'matinee' (afternoon) performances on Saturdays, Sundays and public holidays, starting around 4.30pm. In summer, outdoor plays are performed in many cities, sometimes free. There are a number of amateur drama groups in the major cities and resort towns, performing in English in local theatres and restaurants (the latter performances known as 'supper theatre').

Opera is popular in Spain, which has produced some of the world's leading singers, including Victoria de los Angeles, Teresa Berganza, Montserrat Caballé, José Carreras, Plácido Domingo and Alfredo Kraus. Regular performances are held in Madrid, Barcelona, Oviedo, Bilbao and other cities, although only Barcelona has a 'proper' opera house, the Gran Teatro del Liceu (1847), whose season runs from September to July. Madrid's Teatro Real was reopened as the Teatro de la Opera in 1992 and stages opera, orchestral music, ballet and *zarzuela* (a form of light opera or operetta). Seville's 1,800-seat Teatro de la Maestranza stages opera as well as other classical music performances.

The National Ballet of Spain performs at the Teatro Monumental and the Teatro de la Zarzuela in Madrid, the latter staging opera from January to July and ballet from December to January.

TOURIST OFFICES

Tourism is promoted at four levels in Spain: by the national Ministry of Industry, Tourism and Commerce (Ministerio de Industria, Turismo y Comercio), which operates overseas through Spanish National Tourist Offices/SNTO (Oficinas Nacionales de España de Turismo) known as TurEspaña (⌨ www.spain.info); by regional and provincial governments; and by local municipalities. TurEspaña maintains offices in Argentina, Austria, Australia, Belgium, Brazil, Canada, China, Denmark, Finland, France, Germany, Italy, Japan, Mexico, the Netherlands, Norway, Portugal, Russia, Singapore, Sweden, Switzerland, the UK and the US.

There are tourist offices (*oficinas de turismo*) in all major cities and resort towns in Spain, which are operated by TurEspaña in major cities and by provincial governments and local municipalities in other cities and towns. In cities, there's usually a variety of tourist information outlets, including tourist offices at airports and railway stations, and even street tourist guides during the peak season in some cities.

The quality of information dispensed by local tourist offices varies enormously, as do office opening hours. Offices in resort towns are usually open from 9am to around 1pm and from 4 to around 7.30pm from Mondays to Fridays, and 9am to 1pm on Saturdays. In major cities, offices are open continuously, e.g. from 9am to around 7.30pm, Mondays to Fridays. Offices are usually closed on Sundays. Business hours are usually reduced in winter (except in ski resorts).

National, regional and local authorities publish a wealth of free brochures, pamphlets and detailed maps in many languages, available from TurEspaña offices worldwide and local tourist offices in Spain. TurEspaña publishes a free map (*mapa de comunicacions*) of Spain and regional tourist authorities produce a local calendar of events. When writing requesting information, you should include an international reply coupon and shouldn't expect a personal reply in English, although most office staff will understand a letter written in English. Many tourist offices have email facilities.

It's often advisable to collect information before arriving in Spain, as local tourist offices often run out, and local and regional tourist offices don't provide information about places outside their area.

Staff at tourist offices in major towns and resorts speak English and there are qualified multi-lingual guides at places of interest. Note that Spanish tourist offices don't usually make hotel bookings, although there are hotel reservation offices at international airports and main railway stations in major cities.

16.
SPORTS

Sports facilities in Spain vary considerably depending on the town or area and are usually excellent in major cities and resort areas, although sparse in rural areas. Many towns have municipal, all-weather sports complexes (*polideportivos*) and there's a wealth of private country clubs, sports centres and gymnasiums in cities and resort areas, most of which allow guests to use their facilities. All community developments in resort areas have swimming pools and many also have communal tennis courts and other sports facilities.

The cost of participation in most sports in Spain is reasonable and less than in most other European Union (EU) countries, with annual membership of a sports or country club usually between €300 and €600 a year. Most towns have sports centres and organise a wealth of sports activities and courses at all levels during the summer and other school holidays. Fees are low and are usually between €2 and €4 a session or €10 to €20 a month (or you can pay annually).

Sports facilities in Spain have been greatly improved in the last decade and now rival most other European countries. Many improvements have been tourist-driven, particularly regarding golf, skiing and watersports. Most Spaniards aren't great sports participants and are more at home watching a football or basketball match on television (TV) in a bar than working up a sweat. In general, Spaniards are more laid-back in their attitude towards sports and pastimes and they don't work as fervently as northern Europeans and North Americans to enjoy themselves.

Spain's athletes are prominent in many world sports, including football, basketball, tennis, golf, cycling and athletics. Other popular sports include swimming, handball, fishing, hiking, horse riding, *jai-alai*, *boules*, hunting, motor sports, volleyball and squash. Spain is a Mecca for watersports enthusiasts and sailing, waterskiing and windsurfing have a large following, as do aerial sports. However, football is the national sport and top teams such as Real Madrid and Barcelona enjoy a vast following throughout the world.

General information about sports facilities and events can be obtained from TurEspaña, while local information is available from regional, provincial and local tourist offices, all of which publish information regarding sports events and local sports venues. Many towns also publish an annual or monthly sports programme (*programa de actividades deportivas*). Numerous newspapers and magazines devoted to sport are published in Spain, including three daily sports newspapers in Barcelona alone, although they tend to concentrate mostly on football.

Information about particular sports can be obtained from the Spanish Sports Council (*Consejo Superior de Deportes*), Avda Martín Fierro s/n, 28040 Madrid (☎ 915 896 700, 🖳 www.csd.mec.es).

A player's licence (which covers all sporting accidents) is necessary to participate in competitive sports in Spain.

AERIAL SPORTS

Spain is an outstanding country for all aerial sports, including light-aircraft flying, gliding, hang-gliding, paragliding, parachuting, sky-diving, ballooning and microlighting. Spain's many mountain ranges, particularly the Pyrenees, are excellent venues for hang-gliding and paragliding, due to the strong air currents that allow pilots to stay aloft for hours. Paragliding, which entails jumping off a steep mountain slope with a parachute, is technically easier than hang-gliding. Participants must complete an approved course of instruction, after which they receive a proficiency certificate and are permitted to go solo. Competitions are held throughout the country, often with cash prizes. If you employ an instructor for any aerial sport, ensure that they're qualified.

A flight in a balloon is a marvellous experience, although there's no guarantee of distance or duration and trips are dependent on wind conditions and the skill of your pilot. A flight usually costs around €150 (often including food and champagne) and is made at dawn or in the evening when the air is more stable. There are balloon meetings and competitions throughout Spain, particularly in summer. It is, however, an expensive sport and participation is generally limited to the wealthy. A list of ballooning clubs is available from TurEspaña and local tourist offices.

There are flying clubs at most airfields in Spain, where light aircraft and gliders can be rented. Parachuting and free-fall parachuting (sky-diving) flights can also be made from many private airfields. The south of Spain is an excellent place to learn to fly, as it's rarely interrupted by bad weather. The latest craze to have taken off in Spain is microlight (or ultralight) flying, which is a low-flying go-cart with a hang glider on top and a motorised tricycle below, and one of the cheapest and most enjoyable ways to experience real flying.

For information about aerial sports contact the Real Federación Aeronáutica Española, Carretera de la Fortuna s/n, 28044 Madrid (☎ 915 082 950, 🖳 www.rfae.org), whose website has numerous links to aerial associations in Spain. A useful publication about aerial and other so-called 'active' sports is *Guía de Turismo Activo de España* (El País Aguilar), which includes listings of activities and companies around Spain. The Aventure Tourism website is also a useful source of information (🖳 www.turismoaventura.com).

> **⚠ Caution**
>
> Every year several people are killed and numerous injured in Spain as a consequence of taking part in a dangerous sport without adequate training or safety measures. Before taking up any dangerous sport, you're advised to make sure that you have adequate health, accident and life insurance and that your affairs are in order. You should also check the credentials of the company whose services you use.

CYCLING

Spain is one of the foremost cycling countries in Europe, where cycling is a serious sport and a relaxing pastime. Bicycles (*bicicletas*) are inexpensive in Spain, where you can buy a men's 21-speed mountain bicycle (*bicicleta de montaña*) for as little as €250 from a supermarket. Bicycles should ideally be fitted with an anti-theft device such as a steel cable or chain with a lock. If your bicycle is stolen, report it to the local police. Bicycles can be rented in major cities and most resorts by the hour or day (e.g. €5 to €10). Not surprisingly in a country with so many hills, mountain biking is a popular sport and bikes can be rented in many mountain resorts and can even be taken on specially-adapted chair lifts to the tops of mountains.

Cycling in Madrid and other cities can be dangerous and isn't recommended (if you cycle in cities, you should wear a smog mask, a crash helmet and a crucifix). In addition to the hazards of traffic and pollution in towns and cities, cyclists must contend with the often debilitating heat, interminable hills and poor roads in many areas. However, cycling is usually pleasant in coastal areas and the flatlands outside high summer. Cyclists must use cycle lanes where provided (although there are few in Spain) and mustn't cycle in bus lanes or on footpaths. Spanish motorists usually give cyclists a wide berth when overtaking (but don't count on it), although tourists aren't always so generous, particularly those towing caravans.

It isn't necessary to wear expensive sports clothing when cycling, although a bike helmet is advisable for all riders. Head injuries are the main cause of death in bicycle accidents, most of which don't involve accidents with automobiles, but are a result of colliding with fixed objects or falls. **Always buy a quality helmet that has been approved and subjected to rigorous testing.** Reflective clothing is also advisable. Take **particular** care on busy roads and don't allow children onto public roads until they're competent riders.

Cycling is a popular competitive sport in Spain where over 5,000 annual cycling races and events are staged at all levels throughout the country. These include many professional races such as the tour of Spain (*Vuelta de España* – 🖳 www.lavuelta.com – in English, French and Spanish), the third most important world cycle race after the tours of France and Italy, is in its 63rd year and is held over three weeks in September/October. Other national races include the tour of Andalusia and the tour of the Basque Lands. Spain has a number of top cycling teams and top cyclists in Spain include Pedro Delgado, winner of the Tour de France in 1988, Miguel Indurain, Spain's greatest cyclist, who won the Tour de France from 1991 to 1995, Alberto Contador, winner

of the Giro di Italia 2008 and Tour de France in 2007, Oscar Pereiro and Carlos Sastre, second and fourth respectively in the Tour de France in 2006.

Madrid (as well as most other large towns and cities) has an annual bicycle *fiesta* in May when the roads are closed to vehicles and taken over by some 300,000 to 400,000 cyclists of all ages. There are road and track cycling clubs throughout Spain, although aspiring champions should bear in mind that they must be extremely fit to join organised trips over mountain routes. For information about clubs and competitions contact the Spanish Cycling Federation (Federación Española de Ciclismo), C/de Ferraz, 16-5º, 28008 Madrid (☎ 915 400 841, 🖳 www.rfec.com). Many companies organise cycling holidays in Spain, including TurEspaña, Spain's national tourist board.

Useful books describing many beautiful cycle routes in Spain are *España en Bici* by Paco Tortosa and María del Mar Fornés (RBA), *Cycle Touring in Spain* by Harry Dowdell (Cicerone Press) and *The Trailrider Guide: Spain: Single Track Mountain Biking* by Nathan James and Linsey Stroud (Revolution Publishing).

FISHING

Spain is a paradise for fishermen with its 2,000km (1,250mi) of coastline and over 75,000km (46,000mi) of rivers and thousands of lakes and reservoirs. The most common freshwater fish include various types of barbel, black bass, bogue, bream, carp, mullet, perch, pike, sturgeon, tench and trout. Salmon are found in streams and rivers in the Cantabrian range and in Galicia, and trout are common in the upper reaches of rivers throughout Spain. Sea fishing is very popular, particularly among locals, and you can sea fish without a licence from the shore (although local restrictions mean that fishing isn't allowed from many beaches) or rent a boat and go out to sea, but deep-sea fishermen need a licence from the provincial Comandancias de Marina. Boat rental, perhaps with a local fisherman as a guide, and deep-sea fishing trips can be arranged throughout Spain. Generally, sea fishing is prohibited from one hour after sunset until one hour before dawn.

Common saltwater fish include grouper, sea bream, mackerel, cod, tuna, mullet, bonito, swordfish and various species of shark, although sea fishing is declining in popularity, as Spanish waters are largely 'fished out' (particularly the Mediterranean). The Canaries are in the great fishing grounds of the Atlantic, where some of deep-sea fishermen's largest catches, e.g. marlins, tuna and sharks, are found in abundance. Deep-sea fishing trips are also available and organised from most mainland Spanish ports, and competitions are held regularly.

Freshwater fishing requires a licence (*licencia de pesca*), valid for one, three or five years and issued by regional governments. Licences are available from various organisations such as town halls, savings banks and regional offices, and some regional governments issue them online. You need to present proof of identity and evidence of civil liability insurance (in some regions only, e.g. Andalusia) and pay the fee, which varies from €4 to €12 for one year. In many regions, fishing licences are free for the over 65s. The website *Su Licencia* (🖳 www.sulicencia. com) processes licence applications online for most regions in Spain for a fee of around €20. **Penalties for fishing without a licence are high and if you're caught you will probably also have your rods confiscated.**

The fishing season varies according to the particular species of fish, e.g. the trout season starts in March and the salmon season commences on the first Sunday in March. The salmon season closes on the second Sunday in July and the trout season at the end of August or September. On most rivers there are restrictions on the number of licences issued each day and on the size of fish (and often the number) that may be caught, and the bait and technique that can be employed. Information about local fishing areas and fishing permits is available from local town halls and tourist offices. Tourist offices may also provide a fishing map (*Mapa de Pesca Fluvial*) showing where to fish and what you may catch, plus details of seasons and licences.

There are numerous regional and local fishing clubs throughout Spain. Two useful books in English for fishermen are *The Essential Guide to Coarse Fishing in Spain* by Phil Pembroke (Santana Books) and *Flyfishing in Spain* by Phil Pembroke (Philip Pembroke).

FOOTBALL

Football (*fútbol*) or soccer, is Spain's national sport and easily the country's most important participant and spectator sport. Spanish football fans are among the most dedicated and fervent in Europe and are matched in their fanaticism only by the Italians. Every town in Spain has a football pitch and team, and indoor football (*fútbol sala*) is also played in sports centres throughout the country. Spanish children learn to play football almost as soon as they can walk, with the most promising players being snapped up by the major clubs and coached from an early age in football schools.

Not surprisingly, Spain has many sports newspapers devoted almost exclusively to football, where every aspect of the players' public and private lives are analysed and debated. Countless TV minutes are dedicated to analysing every other move or even word uttered by a football player or manager. All news bulletins include an item on football and the 'sports section' in most news is merely a euphemism for football. Only when Spain achieves prowess in a sport other than football (such as when a Spanish driver wins a Formula 1 motor race) does football take a back seat!

The Spanish league is one of the most competitive in Europe and Spanish teams enjoy considerable success in European competitions – Barcelona won the Champions' League in 2006 and Sevilla won the UEFA cup. Spain has never been able to repeat its clubs' successes at international level and the Spanish national team is a constant source of disappointment – between 1984 and 2008, Spain had failed to get beyond the quarter-finals in any international competition. However, Spain's success in the 2008 European Cup where the team were champions restored the nation's faith in its football team.

The Spanish league is divided into three main divisions, two of which are sub-divided into regional competitions. Division 1 (with 22 teams) and division 2a are national leagues. Division 2b is divided into four regional leagues (I central, II north, III east and IV south) and division 3 consists of local groups regionalised for financial reasons. Spanish clubs also compete in the Spanish Cup (*Copa del Rey*) and the European Cup (UEFA). The Spanish football season runs from September to June, with a break from Christmas eve until the end of January.

Matches are usually played on Sundays (occasionally Saturdays), starting at 5pm, and evening matches (many televised) are also held most weeks starting as late as 9.30pm. Generally, you must queue to buy tickets on match days, although tickets for major games are sold in advance at ticket agencies in El Corte Inglés shops around the country. Tickets for the top matches start at around €10 (standing) and go up to €100 or more for seats.

Hooliganism and violence are rare at Spanish football grounds and families can usually safely take their children to matches, although incidents of violence do occasionally occur, particularly at 'high-risk' matches, e.g. between Real Madrid and Barcelona.

There's a huge gulf between the top Spanish clubs and the rest regarding every aspect of the game, not least their stadiums. Real Madrid and Barcelona (Barça) in particular stand head and shoulders above the rest and have a huge international following (both clubs' websites have Japanese-language options!). Real Madrid play at the imposing 130,000-seat Santiago Bernabeu stadium, while Barcelona's home is the equally impressive 120,000-seat Nou Camp stadium. Outside the top handful of clubs, attendances at many first division matches are low.

A number of division one matches are shown live on TV each week, invariably involving either (or both) Real Madrid or Barcelona,

and are screened in bars throughout Spain. Gambling on football is also popular and is organised through a tote system called the *Quiniela*. Spanish football is dominated by arch rivals Real Madrid (league winners in 2006/7 and 2007/8) and Barcelona, with few other teams getting a look in. Other top teams include Valencia, Deportivo A Coruña and Real Sociedad.

In the early '90s, Spanish football went through one of the worst periods in its history. However, like British premiership and Italian clubs (although without the corruption!), many clubs have been rescued financially by the vast revenue from televised football matches, although many clubs are still deep in debt. Top clubs demand instant success and tend to swap their coaches almost as often as their players change their shirts. Real Madrid has had around ten coaches in the last decade, which looks like secure employment when compared with Atlético Madrid's almost 30 coaches in the same period! Barcelona has also had its fair share of managers in the last few decades.

Spanish football is renowned for its gifted players and fluent attacking style, although there are a surprising number of sterile one-sided games, lacking in excitement and passion, when teams appear paralysed by the fear of losing. Spanish football is equally noted for its cynical 'gamesmanship' (i.e. cheating) which includes every underhand trick in the book, e.g. obstruction, body-checking, shirt-pulling, elbowing, diving, 'accidental' tripping and collisions, and faked injuries, all of which Spanish players have perfected. Players often do their utmost to get opposing players booked or sent off. However, as is obvious during many international matches, these practices are universal!

GOLF

Golf is one of the fastest growing sports in Spain (over 200,000 golfers are registered with the national federation) and is becoming increasingly popular with the Spanish, although it's still regarded by many as an elite game for rich businessmen, foreign tourists (foreigners comprise around 75 per cent of players on the Costa del Sol) and the elderly in many parts of

Spain. Spain has over 250 courses with many more planned. Most courses are concentrated in the main tourist areas and islands, and include Europe's biggest concentration of golf courses – along the western Costa del Sol from Malaga to Cadiz, dubbed the 'Costa del Golf', where there are over 45 courses.

With the exception of a few months in the summer when it's too hot, southern Spain has the perfect climate for golf, particularly during the winter, although Spain's water shortage is affecting existing and planned courses, which are supposed to be watered with desalinated or recycled water.

The Costa del Sol boasts a floodlit golf course for insomniacs (the *Dama de Noche*) open 24-hours a day (a minimum of ten golfers are needed to book the course at night).

Spanish golf courses are invariably excellent and beautifully maintained. Most courses are located in picturesque settings (sea, mountain and forest), many designed by famous designers such as Robert Trent Jones, Jack Nicolas and Severiano Ballesteros and linked with property development. Properties on or near golf clubs (often including 'free' life membership) are popular with foreigners seeking a permanent or second home in Spain, and are among the cheapest golf properties in Europe. Some golf clubs offer golf shares for around €10,000 or €20,000, usually providing members with a number of free rounds or even free golf for life. Many golf clubs are combined with country or sports clubs and offer a wide range of sports and social facilities, including swimming pools, tennis, squash, gymnasium, snooker/pool, and a bar and restaurant.

Spain has courses to suit all standards, although there are few inexpensive public courses and it's an expensive sport. Golf used to be relatively inexpensive, but has become much dearer in recent years, although fees remain lower than in many other European countries. Most courses are owned by syndicates and have annual membership fees of from around €1,500 for a single person (couples €2,000 to €3,000) and seasonal and daily fees for non-members. Most clubs don't have a waiting list for new members or strict handicap requirements for non-members, although they usually insist on golfers wearing suitable attire.

Green fees vary depending on the club and the season, and on the Costa del Sol are usually from around €80 in winter and from €50 in summer for 18 holes. In the north of Spain, fees may be cheaper in winter than in the summer or remain the same all year round. Fees at an exclusive club such as Valderrama (Cadiz) are as high as €300 a round and you may be restricted to teeing off only at certain times, e.g. between noon and 2pm. Green fees are often reduced early in the morning, e.g. for rounds starting within one hour of opening or anytime before noon, and late in the afternoon, e.g. between 3 and 5pm. Many clubs offer reductions to couples, senior citizens and groups and have weekly rates. Note, however, that many clubs restrict non-members to off-peak times and it's often difficult for non-members to get a game at weekends and during school holidays. Playing with a member usually entitles guests to a reduction on green fees.

Third party accident insurance is obligatory and costs around €2 a day.

You can rent golf clubs (from around €15), golf trolleys/carts (from around €5 per round or €15 for an electric trolley) and electric golf buggies (€25 to €50 per round) at all clubs. The golf cart has virtually made the caddie extinct and some courses are built in difficult terrain where it's almost mandatory to use a buggy. Some clubs include the price of a buggy in the green fees. Most clubs have a pro shop

with a club professional, driving ranges, practice putting and pitching greens, and offer individual and group instruction and a full programme of competitions. Clubs and a growing number of golf schools hold regular courses for all standards from beginner to expert.

Clubs are usually members of the Royal Spanish Golf Federation (Real Federación Española de Golf), C/Provisional Arroyo del Fresno Dos, 5, 28035 Madrid (☎ 915 552 682, 🖳 www.golfspainfederacion.com), who produce a detailed map of Spanish golf courses listing their vital statistics and an annual competition calendar (*Calendario Oficial de Competiciones*).

Spain hosts more regular PGA European Tour events than any other country, mostly at the beginning and end of the season when the weather in northern Europe is unreliable. Valderrama hosts the Volvo Masters Tournament in autumn, the richest event in Europe, and El Saler (south of Valencia) hosts the Spanish Open. Spain is the second strongest European golfing country after the UK, although it has had to beat off a strong challenge from Sweden. In the last few decades, it has produced many top male professional golfers, including Severiano Ballesteros, José María Olazábel, Miguel Angel Jiménez, Manuel Piñero, José María Cañizares, Miguel Angel Martín, Ignacio Garrido, Diego Borrego, José Rivero and Sergio García, plus a number of top female golfers.

Golf holidays are popular in Spain and a major source of revenue for clubs, most of which welcome visitors and often offer special rates. Some hotels cater almost exclusively for golfers and offer golf holiday packages inclusive of green fees (or reduced green fees). Many regions and provinces publish golf guides (*Golf Guía Práctica*) with maps. A number of free and subscription golf magazines are published in Spain, most with articles printed in Spanish and English, including *Andalucía Golf*, *Costa del Sol Golf News* and *Sun Golf*. There are numerous websites dedicated to golf in Spain, including Golf in Spain (in English, German and Spanish) which specialises in golf holidays and where you can reserve golf rounds online (🖳 www.golfinspain.com). TurEspaña publishes a brochure including all golf course details and their location on a map of Spain (downloadable in pdf from 🖳 www.spain.info).

HIKING

Spain has some of the finest hiking (*excursiones*) areas in Europe and few countries can offer its combination of good weather and spectacular, unspoilt countryside. Spain is unrivalled in Europe for its diversity of landscape, profusion of flora and fauna, and its variety of native animals and birds, many unique. Serious hikers can enjoy mountain walking in some of the most spectacular scenery in Europe. Spring and autumn are the best seasons for hiking in most of Spain, when the weather generally isn't too hot or too cold, although winter is the best time in the south of Spain.

** Caution**

Some hiking paths can be extremely dangerous in winter and are only safe in summer.

Hiking isn't a popular sport among the Spanish, although Spain is a favourite destination for foreign hikers. It has a wealth of hiking areas, including the Basque Country, Cantabria and Asturias in the north (an area often described as 'Switzerland by the sea' containing the *Picos de Europa*), the Basque mountains and the Cantabrian Cordillera – all areas of outstanding beauty. The Pyrenees and the Ebro region are Spain's most popular and accessible hiking regions, assisted by the abundance of winter sports resorts and ski-lifts that whisk you to the mountain tops.

The north of Spain has many outstanding hiking routes, the most famous of which is the old 'pilgrim's way' from Le Puy in France to Santiago de Compostela in Galicia, designated a *Grande Randonnée* (GR65) by the French. It offers some of the most beautiful scenery in Spain and takes two or more months to complete the whole route, although most hikers complete a small section at a time. Several other pilgrims' ways run through Spain to Santiago including the *Camino de la Plata*, which starts in Seville.

Spain's longest circular route, known as the *Sulayr*, has recently been opened and runs 340km (212mi) around the base of the Sierra

Nevada range and takes 19 days to complete. Really serious walkers may be interested in the European hiking route (GR7) running from Tarifa (Cadiz) through natural areas in Andalusia, Murcia and Valencia on its way to Greece some 2,100km (1,300mi) away. Easier, but no less beautiful, walks can be found on Spain's 'Greenways' (*Vías Verdes*), all of which follow disused railway lines through spectacular countryside (see 🖥 www.viasverdes.com).

In central Spain, outstanding hiking areas include the Gredos and Guadarrama Sierras, the Alcarria region, the Sierra of southern Salamanca, the Las Hurdes of northern Extremadura, El Bierzo of western León and the Sierra Morena in the south. Andalusia also has an abundance of spectacular hiking areas, including the Alpujarras and the Sierra Nevada in Granada, the Sierra de Grazalema running from Cadiz to Malaga, and the Serranía de Ronda. Spain has nine national parks (four in the Canary Islands), including the Coto de Doñana near Cadiz, Europe's largest nature reserve, and numerous other areas designated as natural parks. For information contact the Ministry of the Environment (Ministerio de Medio Ambiente, ☎ 915 976 000, 🖥 www.mma.es).

There are tens of thousands of kilometres of official footpaths throughout Spain, most of which are marked with parallel red and white stripes painted on rocks and trees, and accompanied by arrows when the direction changes. The sign of two crossed lines indicates that you should **not** go in that direction. Where paths cross they're shown by different colours, e.g. green and yellow instead of red and white. The best hiking maps are published by the Instituto Geográfico Nacional (IGN) and the Servicio Geográfico del Ejército (SGE) in scales of 1:200,000, 1:100,000, 1:50,000 and occasionally 1:25,000. The SGE series are generally considered to be more accurate and up to date than those published by the IGN, although neither is up to the standards of the best American and British maps.

Editorial Alpina produces 1:40,000 and 1:25,000 map booklets for the most popular mountain and foothill areas of Spain and the Mapa Topográfico Nacional de España produce a series of 1:50,000 scale maps covering the whole of Spain and showing most footpaths and tracks. Hiking booklets containing suggested walks are

published by some regional tourist organisations and maps showing city walks are available in many cities.

In mountain areas, there are over 200 refuge huts (*refugios*) for climbers and hikers, equipped with bunks and a basic kitchen, where overnight accommodation costs as little as €1.50. Some are staffed in spring and summer and provide food, although most are unstaffed and you must therefore carry your own food, sleeping bags, cooking utensils and other essentials. Many huts are kept locked and enquiries should be made in advance about where to obtain the key. For information contact the Spanish Mountain Sports Federation (Federación Española de Deportes de Montaña y Escalada/FEDME), C/ Floridablanca, 84, 08015 Barcelona (☎ 934 264 267, 🖥 www.fedme.es).

A number of books about hiking in Spain are published in English, including *Trekking in Spain* by Marc Dubin (Lonely Planet) and *Trekking and Climbing in Northern Spain* by Iija Schreder and Jim Thompson (New Holland Publishers), and there are many books dedicated to walking in particular regions, such as those published by Cicerone. Hiking tours and holidays are organised for hikers of all ages and fitness levels throughout Spain, and there are expatriate groups of ramblers in resort areas throughout the country. For more information contact the Spanish Mountain

Sports Federation (Federación Española de Deportes de Montaña y Escalada/FEDME), C/Floridablanca, 84, 08015 Barcelona (☎ 934 264 267, 💻 www.fedme.es). See also **Camping & Caravanning** on page 251.

MOUNTAINEERING & ROCK-CLIMBING

Those who find hiking a bit tame may like to try mountaineering, rock-climbing or caving (subterranean mountaineering), all of which are popular in Spain. Sport climbing, where climbs are previously 'equipped' with bolts, is predominant in Spain and is the safest form. Spain is a great country for amateur rock-climbers and mountaineers, and provides a wealth of challenges and some of the best areas in Europe outside the Alps. Around 10,000 caves have been discovered in Spain, many with prehistoric rock paintings and stalactites. Some caves are long and dangerous and should be explored only with an experienced guide.

If you're an inexperienced climber, it's advisable to join a club and 'learn the ropes' before heading for the mountains. There are over 750 climbing clubs in Spain, many maintaining their own mountain huts and refuges. Information can be obtained from the Spanish Mountain Sports Federation (Federación Española de Deportes de Montaña y Escalada/FEDME), C/Floridablanca, 84, 08015 Barcelona (☎ 934 264 267, 💻 www.fedme.es). The FEDME also produce 1:50,000 scale maps for mountain areas (see also **Hiking** on page 277 for information regarding maps and refuges). A number of climbing books are published for the most popular regions of Spain. Comprehensive information about all aspects of mountaineering is included on the website 💻 www.spainmountains.com.

It's important to hire a qualified and experienced guide when climbing in an unfamiliar area, who are available through climbing clubs and schools throughout Spain (if you find a guide other than through a recognised club or school, ensure that they're qualified). It's important to note that Spain doesn't have the sophisticated mountain rescue services provided in Alpine countries and if you get into trouble you may need to rely on your own resources and those of your companions. Many climbers lose their lives each year, usually through their inexperience and recklessness.

 Caution

Needless to say, it's extremely foolish, not to mention highly dangerous, to venture into the mountains without proper preparation, excellent physical condition, adequate training, the appropriate equipment and an experienced guide.

PELOTA

Pelota (or *jai alai*) was invented by the Basques, who comprise many of the best players in north America and whose national sport it is. Every town of any size in the Basque Country (on both sides of the border with France) and many in the neighbouring provinces of Navarra and La Rioja has a three-sided court (*frontón*), on which *pelota* is played (it's also played in other parts of Spain). It's played by two or five players who throw a ball against the end wall usually with a woven basket (*chistera*) strapped to an arm, although a leather glove or even bare hands are also used (there are over 20 versions played in some 25 countries).

The *chistera* combines the functions of glove and catapult, in which the ball is caught and hurled back against the wall at speeds of up to 200kmh (124mph). *Pelota* is the fastest ball game in the world and players sometimes wear crash helmets to protect themselves from being struck on the head by the ball. However, the real purpose of *pelota* is a vehicle for gambling and huge sums are wagered on top games. For information contact the Federación Española de Pelota, C/Los Madrazos, 11-5º, 28014 Madrid (☎ 915 214 299, 💻 www.fepelota.com).

RACKET SPORTS

Racket sports are popular in Spain, particularly tennis. Tennis' popularity has grown tremendously in the last few decades and there are now thousands of courts at tennis and country clubs, hotels, urbanisations, and municipal and private sports centres. Courts (many floodlit) have a variety of surfaces, including tennis-quick (fast cement court), clay (*arcilla*), cement (*hormigón*), artificial grass and plexipave. There are also indoor courts in the north of Spain, although these are rare in the south and the islands, where the weather permits outdoor tennis to be played all year round. Many tennis clubs offer a variety of other sports facilities, including swimming pools and a gymnasium or fitness centre.

Most private clubs and hotels allow guests to use their courts, with fees ranging from around €5 an hour at a hotel to €35 for daily use of tennis courts and other facilities at a private tennis club, perhaps with a lesson and a 'free' meal included. Courts at private clubs cost from around €4 an hour (€6 floodlit) to around €10 an hour (€15 floodlit) for members and up to double for non-members. Most clubs open from early morning until as late as 11pm or midnight. Many urbanisations have private tennis courts which can be used free of charge by residents (they're maintained through community fees), although floodlighting must usually be paid for via a coin meter. Courts are usually available on a first come, first served basis, although there may be a booking system in the summer season when demand is high.

Annual membership of a private club usually costs from €350 to €700 a year in a resort area, although fees can be astronomical at exclusive clubs in major cities. Weekly, monthly and six-monthly membership may also be available. Most clubs have special rates for families, children (e.g. under 18) and possibly senior citizens. Many clubs provide saunas, whirlpools, solariums and swimming pools, and most have a bar and restaurant. All clubs organise regular tournaments and provide professional coaching (individual and group lessons), and many clubs and hotels offer resident tennis schools throughout the year. Individual lessons cost from around €25 an hour. Information regarding competitions and tennis clubs can be obtained from the Royal Spanish Tennis Federation (Real Federación Española de Tenis), Avda Diagonal, 618 –2ºB, 08021 Barcelona (☎ 932 005 355, 🖳 www.rfet.es).

Tennis was long regarded as an elite sport in Spain and although it remains so in some private clubs, it's now a sport of the people and one of Spain's most popular participant sports. In the last few years, Spain has become one of the world's strongest tennis countries – Spain is currently sixth in the Davis Cup rankings and was the 2004 champion. Its many top male tennis players include Albert Costa, Carlos Moya, Alex Corretja, Juan Carlos Ferrero, Feliciano López and current world no.2 Rafael Nadal, four-times winner of the French Open 2005 to 2008), and Wimbledon champion in 2008, the first Spaniard to win the tournament since Manolo Santana in 1962. Among the best female players are Anabel Medina, Virginia Ruano (winners of the women's doubles at the French Open 2008) and Magüi Serna. Spain's top female player, Arantxa Sánchez Vicario, retired in 2002. The majority of top players come from Catalonia, the powerhouse of Spanish tennis.

Squash is gaining popularity in Spain with an increasing number of courts in many areas. There are now squash clubs in most large towns and many tennis clubs and sports centres have a number of squash courts. However, the standard is relatively low due to the lack of experienced coaches and top class competition, although it's continually improving. Rackets and balls can be rented from most squash clubs for the American version of squash, called racket ball, which is played in Spain on a squash court.

Badminton isn't widely played and facilities are rare, although some sports centres have badminton

courts and there are badminton clubs in some areas.

SKIING

Skiing (*esquí*) is a popular sport in Spain, where it's growing faster than in any other European country. Spain is the second most mountainous country in Europe after Switzerland and has over 30 ski resorts in 14 provinces, where the season extends from December to April or May. The most popular form of skiing is naturally downhill (*esquí de descenso*), although cross-country (*esquí nórdico*) skiers are also catered for in many resorts. With Andorra, Spain offers the cheapest skiing holidays in Western Europe and is becoming increasingly popular with beginners and intermediate skiers wishing to avoid the high cost of skiing in the Alps.

Most of Spain's resorts aren't sophisticated or developed and most don't offer sufficient challenges to satisfy the demands of advanced skiers, particularly regarding off-piste skiing.

The majority of Spain's resorts are located in the Pyrenees in the provinces of Gerona (Nuria and La Molina), Huesca (Astún, El Cadanchú, Cerler, Formigal and Panticosa), and Lérida with Baqueira-Beret (Spain's most fashionable resort, popular with the Spanish royal family, and Europe's most extensive ski resort outside the Alps), and Boí-Taüll, Masella, La Molina and Supert-Espot. Other skiing regions include the Cordillera Cantábrica region (with the resorts of Alto Campoo, San Isidro, Valdezcaray and Valgrande Pajares), the Guadarrama and Gredos mountains north of Madrid (includes La Pinilla, Navacerrada, Puerto de Navacerrada, Valcotos and Valdesquí), Galicia (Cabeza de la Manzaneda), the Sierra de Gúdar (Teruel) and the Sierra Nevada (Granada).

Although encompassing a relatively small area, the Sierra Nevada (also called 'Sol y Nieve') near Granada is Spain's most famous resort. The Sierra Nevada is Europe's most southerly winter sports resort and a common boast is that you can ski there in the morning and swim in the Mediterranean in the afternoon. The resort is centred around the village of Paradollano at 2,100m (6,890ft), with undercover parking for 2,800 vehicles. It has 19 lifts with a capacity of over 32,000 passengers an hour, around 84km (52mi) of pistes and 30 runs, and skiing up to a height of 3,400m (11,155ft). Snow is generally guaranteed, as the resort has an extensive network (over 250) of snow-making machines covering many pistes. For reservations and snow and weather conditions contact ☎ 902 708 090 or visit 🖥 www. sierranevadaski.com (information is given in English and Spanish).

Although cheaper in Spain than many other countries, downhill skiing is an expensive sport, particularly for families. The cost of equipping a family of four is around €1,000 for equipment and clothing. If you're a beginner it's better to rent ski equipment (skis, poles, boots) or buy second-hand equipment until you're addicted, which, if it doesn't frighten you to death, can happen on your first day on the pistes. Most sports shops in Spain have pre-season and end of season sales of ski equipment.

Most resorts have a range of ski lifts, including cable cars, gondolas, chair-lifts and drag-lifts. Pistes in Spain are rated as green (very easy – *muy fácil*), blue (easy – *fácil*), red (difficult – *difícil*) or black (very difficult – *muy difícil*). Adult ski passes cost between €30 and €60 per day or €100 to €150 for five days, depending on the number of lifts provided, with passes for children costing around one-third less. Ski rental costs around €20 a day or €70 for six days and boots around half this (the smaller the resort, generally the lower the cost of ski and boot rental). Most resorts have ski schools and the larger resorts such as Sierra Nevada have Spanish and international ski schools.

Most resorts offer a variety of accommodation, including hotels, self-catering apartments and chalets. Accommodation is more expensive during holiday periods (Christmas, New Year and Easter), when ski-lift queues are interminable and pistes are often overcrowded. These periods (and school holidays in February) are best avoided, particularly as the chance of collisions is greatly enhanced when pistes are overcrowded. Outside these periods and particularly on weekdays, resorts are generally free of crowds and queues.

Mono-skiing and snow-boarding are particularly popular (and generally unrestricted) in Spain and are taught in most resorts. Other activities may include paragliding, parasailing, hang-gliding, ice-skating, snow-shoe walking, sleigh rides, climbing, snow scooters and snowmobiles. Heli-skiing, where helicopters drop skiers off at the top of inaccessible mountains, is possible in Spain. There's also night skiing on floodlit runs in some resorts.

Many winter resorts also provide a variety of mostly indoor activities, including tennis, squash, curling, heated indoor swimming pools, gymnasiums, saunas and solariums.

You can find excellent food in the Pyrenees which is influenced by Basque and French cuisine, and skiers are amply provided with mountain restaurants in most resorts. There's also an excellent choice of restaurants and bars resorts, which have the most lively and cheapest (with Andorra) nightlife of any country in Europe. Spaniards aren't such fanatical skiers as other Europeans and many tend to rave all night and ski only in the afternoons, rather than ski from dawn to dusk.

For further information about skiing and other winter sports in Spain contact the Asociación Turística de Estaciones de Esquí y Montaña (ATUDEM), C/Padre Damián, 43 –1ª, Oficina 11, 28036 Madrid (☎ 913 591 557, 🖳 www. atudem.org) or the Federación Española de Deportes de Invierno (🖳 www.rfedi.es).

The latest weather and snow conditions are broadcast on Spanish television (usually on Thursday or Friday evenings) and radio, published in daily newspapers, and are available direct from resorts (which provide recorded telephone information). TurEspaña (see page 269) publishes a comprehensive brochure, *Ski Resorts*, which includes a map showing the location of all resorts plus a guide to each resort (downloadable in pdf from 🖳 www.spain.info).

SWIMMING

Not surprisingly, swimming (*natación*) is a favourite sport and pastime in Spain, with its glorious weather, 2,000km (1,240mi) of beaches (*playas*), and a profusion of swimming pools (*piscinas*). The beach season in Spain lasts from around Easter to October, although many people sunbathe on beaches all year round in the south of Spain, and the Canaries offer year round beach weather. Most people find the Mediterranean too cold for swimming outside June to September and the Atlantic is generally warm enough only in July and August (in northern and southern Spain).

Spanish beaches, almost all of which are public, vary considerably in size, composition and amenities. Surfaces include white, grey, black (in the Canaries) and even red (fine and coarse) sand, shingles, pebbles and stones. Beaches are generally kept clean all year round, particularly in popular resorts, although in some areas they're covered in rubbish and large stones and look more like waste areas than public beaches.

It's difficult to find a totally unspoilt beach, as pollution and high-rise buildings blight most Spanish beaches, although there are a few in remote areas of the mainland and the islands. The best beaches are to be found on the Atlantic coast, on the smaller islands in the Balearics (e.g. Formentera and Menorca) and in the Canaries (e.g. Fuerteventura), where it's even possible to find a deserted beach outside the main tourist season.

Most beaches are extremely crowded in summer and during school holidays, when bodies are packed in like sardines. Beaches away from the main resorts are less crowded and if you have a boat you can visit small coves that are inaccessible from the land. Most beaches have municipal guards, first-aid stations, toilets, showers, bars and restaurants, and some have special paths for those in wheelchairs. Deck chairs, beach-beds and umbrellas can be rented on most beaches, and a wide range of facilities are usually available in summer, including volleyball, pedalos and boats for rent, plus most watersports. Dogs and camping are forbidden on most beaches.

Many resorts have made a huge effort to clean up their beaches in recent years and the number of resorts awarded the coveted EU 'blue flag' (*bandera azul*) has risen in all areas. 455 blue flags were awarded to Spanish beaches in 2008 (Catalonia and the Comunidad Valenciana have the most), which is around a fifth of the total for the whole of Europe. A list of blue flag beaches and marinas can be found on 🖳 www. blueflag.org. However, some beaches are still dangerously polluted by untreated sewage and industrial waste, and bathing in some areas (particularly close to industrial towns and cities)

There are stinging jellyfish in parts of the Mediterranean and they swim near the beaches – 2007 was a particularly prolific year when warm currents swept thousands near beaches in Andalusia and Murcia.

A comprehensive description and a rating out of 100 of all Spanish mainland and island beaches can be found on ⌨ www.esplaya.com.

Most Spanish towns have a municipal swimming pool (*piscina municipal*), including heated indoor pools (*piscina cubierta*) and outdoor pools (*piscinas al aire libre*). The entrance fee to a pool varies considerably (e.g. €2 to €5 for adults) depending on whether it's an outdoor or indoor pool and its facilities and location. Many pools offer reduced-price, multiple-ticket options. Opening hours may vary day-to-day and most municipal pools don't open during the evenings. Heated indoor pools are open all year round and most outdoor pools are open only during the summer, e.g. from June to September. Public pools in cities are usually overcrowded, particularly at weekends and during school holidays, while pools in hotels and private clubs are less crowded, although more expensive. For further information contact the Spanish Swimming Federation (Federación Española de Natación), C/Juan Esplandiú, 1, 28007 Madrid (☎ 915 572 006, ⌨ www.rfen.es).

There are strict safety regulations at all public and community swimming pools. Regulations usually depend on the depth of a pool, its size (surface area in square metres) and the number of properties it serves, and are established and enforced by local municipalities. They usually include such matters as water quality and treatment, and the provision of showers, non-slip pathways, life belts, first-aid kits and lifeguards. It's usually compulsory to wear a swimming hat in a public or community pool. Usually a lifeguard must be on duty whenever a public or community pool is open (very large pools may require two lifeguards). Note, however, that many hotels and communities have pools without lifeguards. It's important to ensure that young children don't have access to swimming pools, and private pools should be fenced to prevent accidents (also take extra care around rivers and lakes).

isn't advisable. The pollution count (which cannot always be believed) must be displayed at the local town hall: blue = good quality water, green = average, yellow = likely to be temporarily polluted, and red = badly polluted.

Topless and nude bathing is widespread and there are a number of official nudist beaches (*playas naturale/playas de nudistas*) in Spain such as the Costa Natura village situated near Estepona (Malaga) on the Costa del Sol and Almanat near Almayate (Vélez-Malaga), while on the Balearic island of Formentera it's almost standard practice. Topless bathing is permitted on all Spanish beaches, some of which have a section for nude sunbathing. Note, however, that it's possible to get arrested for nude sunbathing on some beaches. Topless bathing is less acceptable at swimming pools, although there are naturist pools in some cities and resorts.

Swimming can be dangerous at times, particularly on the Atlantic coast where some beaches have lethal currents, but even the Mediterranean can be dangerous and several swimmers drown every year. **Swimmers should observe all beach warning signs and flags.** During the summer months most beaches are supervised by lifeguards who operate a flag system to indicate when swimming is safe; a green flag means that it's safe (calm sea), yellow indicates possible hazardous conditions (take care) and red (danger) means bathing is prohibited. The Red Cross (*Cruz Roja/Puesto de Socorro*) operate first-aid posts on most beaches during the summer season.

Most swimming pools and clubs provide swimming lessons and run life-saving courses. Spain also has many water parks (*parque acuático*) and watersports centres where facilities include indoor and outdoor pools, water slides, flumes, wave machines, river rapids, whirlpools and waterfalls, sun-beds, saunas, solariums, Jacuzzis, hot baths and a children's area. Most water parks are open only during the summer season, e.g. from June to September.

It's important to protect yourself against the sun to prevent sunburn and heat-stroke, which includes using a high protection sun cream (factor 20 minimum, factor 30 in summer), a sun block on sensitive areas (e.g. lips, moles and nipples), and drink plenty of water. Even if you think you're used to Spain's fierce sun, you should limit your exposure and avoid it altogether during the hottest part of the day in summer (noon till 5pm), wear protective clothing (including a hat) and use a sun block.

WATERSPORTS

Spain is a Mecca for watersports enthusiasts, which is hardly surprising considering its immense coastline (7,880km/4,896mi), many islands, numerous lakes and reservoirs, and thousands of kilometres of rivers and canals. Popular watersports include sailing, windsurfing, waterskiing, jet-skiing, rowing, canoeing, kayaking, surfing, rafting and sub-aquatic sports. In addition to the Atlantic and Mediterranean, many reservoirs and lakes are also popular venues for sailing, waterskiing and windsurfing. Coastal resorts often have designated areas for windsurfing, waterskiing and jet-skiing, and it's forbidden to operate outside these areas. Wet suits are recommended for windsurfing, waterskiing and sub-aquatic sports, even during the summer.

Rowing and canoeing is possible on many lakes and rivers, where canoes and kayaks can usually be rented. Spain's premier canoeing event is the 22km (14mi) Descenso del Sella down the Sella river in Asturias (from Arriondas to Ribadasella), which takes place on the first Saturday in August. Surfing is popular along the Atlantic coast of the Basque Country and Cantabria: however, Lanzarote in the Canaries is the Hawaii of the Atlantic to surfers and Fuerteventura is also good. Spain also has

Europe's foremost windsurfing and kitesurfing area at Tarifa (see below). There are clubs for most watersports in all major resorts and towns throughout Spain and instruction is usually available.

Scuba-diving is a popular sport in Spain, where there are many diving clubs offering instruction and equipment and boat rental. Scuba-diving can be dangerous and safety is of paramount importance. For this reason, many experts don't recommend learning to dive while on holiday. Holiday divers should, in any case, dive only with a reputable club, and, due to the dangers of decompression, stop diving 24 hours before taking the flight home. A diving permit (costing around €10) is required to dive in Spanish waters and is obtainable from clubs and schools. Among the best areas for scuba divers are the seas around the Balearic and Canary islands. For information contact the Spanish Subaquatic Federation (Federación Española de Actividades Subacuáticas), C/ Santaló, 15 –3º, 08021 Barcelona (☎ 932 009 200, ⌨ www.fedas.es).

Spain has some of the world's best windsurfing areas, including Fuerteventura in the Canaries, El Mádano in south Tenerife, and Tarifa at the southernmost tip of Spain on the Strait of Gibraltar. Tarifa is a kitesurfers' paradise and Europe's windiest place, where winter winds from the south-west or north-east can reach up to 120kph (75mph) and the average wind speed is 34kph (21mph). There

are numerous websites for windsurfers, which usually include weather reports and news of competitions (e.g. 💻 www.surferos.net and 💻 www.windtarifa.com – this site includes seven-day wind predictions). The monthly magazine, *Surf A Vela*, is a must for all windsurfing fans in Spain.

A popular sport is canyoning, a combination of abseiling and white-water rafting consisting of descending gushing rivers, waterfalls and canyons with the aid of ropes. It can be dangerous and only 'lunatics' need apply. The best white-water area in Spain is the Pyrenees.

Be sure to observe all warning signs on lakes and rivers. Take particular care when canoeing, as some rivers have 'white water' patches that can be dangerous for the inexperienced. It's sensible to wear a life-jacket when canoeing, irrespective of whether you're a strong swimmer. All watersports equipment can be rented, although you're usually required to leave a large deposit and should take out insurance against damage or loss.

Spain has a wealth of marinas and harbours, many with over 1,000 berths (including Benalmádena and Puerto Banús on the Costa del Sol), which are scattered liberally along Spain's coasts. Puerto Banús near Marbella is Spain's answer to St Tropez, where the rich go to sea (and to be seen) – full of vast ostentatious yachts, flashy cars and beautiful people. There are also numerous sailing clubs (*club náutico*) based at marinas and sports harbours, all of which offer tuition and courses. Crewed and uncrewed yachts can be rented in resorts, although you need a skipper's certificate or a helmsman's overseas certificate to rent an uncrewed yacht.

Despite the large number of marinas, berths can be difficult to find in summer in some areas, although temporary berths can usually be found on public jetties and harbours. Moorings can be expensive, particularly in the most fashionable resorts such as Marbella. The cost of keeping a yacht on the Atlantic coast is cheaper than on the Mediterranean or in the islands, although even here it needn't be too expensive providing you steer clear of the most fashionable berths (e.g. from as little as €15 a day for an 8 x 3 metre berth in low season to €50 a day for a 20 x 5 metre berth in high season).

Races take place in many classes (such as dinghies) all year round, while yacht racing is generally restricted to between April and October, during which there are big regattas in the Balearics (where the most prestigious event is the Copa del Rey which takes place off Palma de Mallorca in August) and the Bay of Cadiz. Boating holidays are popular in Spain, where boats of all shapes and sizes can be rented in harbours and coastal resorts. For information about marinas and competitions contact the Spanish Sailing Federation (Federación Española de Vela), C/Luís de Salazar, 9, 28002 Madrid (☎ 915 195 008, 💻 www.rfev.es).

Spain is a good place to buy a yacht, as prices are very competitive. However, a 'wandering yacht' cannot escape value added tax (VAT), as it must be levied on all yachts purchased in EU countries by EU citizens at the time of sale. Note that VAT is paid in the country of registration or destination and therefore you should compare Spain's 16 per cent VAT (*IVA*) with the country of purchase. EU residents aren't permitted to register their vessels abroad simply to avoid paying VAT, and any vessel registered outside the EU must be located there and is liable for import duties if berthed in an EU port. All vessels kept permanently in Spain must be registered there. Buyers from non-EU countries remain exempt from VAT, providing they export their yachts to non-EU waters. However, a foreign-registered boat can be kept in Spain and used there for six months a year by a non-resident, but must be sealed (*precintado*) when it isn't being used. Boats can be operated on Spanish tourist flag registration to avoid paying Spanish taxes.

Valencia was the venue for the world's oldest yachting competition, the America's Cup in 2007 and is also due to host the next America's Cup in 2009 (the holders are Switzerland, which doesn't have a lot of coastline). The summer breezes in the Mediterranean around the city are deemed to be perfect for the race. Further information is available from the official website (💻 www.americascup.com). Alicante hosts the start of the Volvo Ocean Race in 2008.

17.
SHOPPING

Spain isn't one of Europe's great shopping countries, for quality or bargains, although the choice and quality of goods on offer has improved considerably since Spain joined the European Union (EU). Prices of many consumer goods such as television (TV) and stereo systems, computers, cameras, electrical apparatus and household appliances have fallen dramatically in recent years and are now similar to most other EU countries.

Small family-run shops (*tiendas*) still constitute the bulk of Spanish retailers, although the shopping scene has been transformed in the last decade with the opening of numerous shopping centres (many beautifully designed) and hypermarkets. Following the trend in most European countries there has been a drift away from town centres by retailers to out-of-town shopping centres (malls) and hypermarket complexes, which has left some 'high streets' run down and abandoned. The biggest drawback to shopping in cities and towns is parking, which can be a nightmare, although many Spanish cities have improved parking facilities and pedestrianised central streets in an attempt to lure shoppers back to city centres.

With the exception of markets, where haggling over the price is part of the enjoyment (except when buying food), retail prices are fixed in Spain and shown as *Precio de Venta al Público (PVP)*. It's important to shop around and compare prices, as they can vary considerably, not only between small shops and hypermarkets, but also among supermarkets and hypermarkets in the same town. Note, however, that price differences often reflect different quality, so make sure you're comparing similar products.

The best time to have a shopping spree is during the winter and summer sales (*rebajas*) in January-February and July-August respectively, when bargains (*gangas*) can be found everywhere and prices are often slashed by 50 per cent or more (the best bargains are usually clothes).

Among the best buys in Spain are the diverse handicrafts which include antiques, cultured pearls, shawls, pottery, ceramics, damascene, embroidery, fans, glassware, hats, ironwork, jewellery, knives, lace, suede and leather, paintings, porcelain (e.g. Lladró from Valencia), rugs, trinkets and carved woodwork.

Shopping 'etiquette' in Spain may differ considerably from what you're used to, particularly in market places and small shops. The Spanish (and many tourists) don't believe in queuing and people often push and shove their way to the front. Don't expect shop assistants to serve customers in order; you must usually speak up when it's your turn to be served or take a numbered ticket from a dispenser. You also shouldn't expect service with a smile, except perhaps when you're being served by the owner. Shop assistants may sometimes be surly and unhelpful, and some staff give the impression they couldn't care less about your custom, although customer service has improved greatly in recent years. On the other hand, in small shops where you're a regular customer, you will be warmly received and many shopkeepers will even allow you to pay another day if you don't have enough money with you.

In major cities and tourist areas, you must be wary of pickpockets and bag-snatchers, particularly in markets and other crowded places. Never tempt fate with an exposed wallet or purse or by flashing your money around. The Spanish generally pay cash when shopping, although credit and debit cards are widely accepted. However, personal cheques (even local ones) aren't usually accepted.

For those who aren't used to buying articles with metric measures and in continental sizes, a list of comparative weights and measures are included in **Appendix D**. For information about chemists (pharmacies) see **Medicines** on page 183.

SHOPPING HOURS

Shopping hours in Spain vary considerably depending on the region, city or town and the type of shop. There are no statutory closing days or hours for retail outlets, except in Catalonia where shops must close by 9pm. Large shops must open on a minimum of eight Sundays and public holidays (*festivos*) a year, but the actual number depends on the region. Most regions have opted to open on eight *festivos* only except for Murcia where shops open on 12 Sundays and public holidays a year and Madrid with a record 20 *festivos* annually. Shops located in zones of 'great tourist influence' (beach resorts and historic towns) can apply to open all year round, not just during the summer months.

> As in other European countries, small shopkeepers (who close for *siestas* and at weekends) are having increasing difficulty competing with hypermarkets and department stores.

A big surprise for many foreigners is the long afternoon *siesta*, when most small shops close from 1.30 or 2pm until around 5pm. Apart from department stores and many large supermarkets, there's no such thing as afternoon shopping in Spain. The *siesta* makes good sense in the summer when it's often too hot to do anything in the afternoon, but it isn't so practical in winter when evening shopping must be done in the dark. However, foreigners

are often divided over Spain's shopping hours, some seeing them as an inconvenience, others a bonus. Many people actually find they prefer to shop in the evening when they get used to it.

Most small shops open from between 8.30 and 9.30am until between 1 and 2pm and from around 5pm until between 7.30 and 9pm, Mondays to Fridays, and from 9.30am until 2pm on Saturdays. Note, however, that in some areas most shops are closed on Monday mornings. Department stores, hypermarkets and many supermarkets are open continually from around 9.30 or 10am, until between 8 and 10pm from Mondays to Saturdays. Department stores and hypermarkets may also open on Sundays (e.g. 10am to 3pm or noon to 8pm) and public holidays (e.g. 10am to 10pm).

During the summer, shops in resort areas (particularly food shops and tobacconists) often remain open until 10 or 11pm (except in Catalonia). Shops in resort areas may also remain open longer on Saturdays and open on Sunday mornings in the summer. The OpenCor chain (part of El Corte Inglés giant) with branches all over the country opens 24-hours a day every day of the year and in major cities such as Madrid and Barcelona and some resort towns there are 24-hour, American-style, drugstores comprising a supermarket, cafeteria, tobacconist and restaurant.

In general, shops close for one whole day and one half day each week, usually on Saturday afternoon and Sunday (some shops also close on Mondays or Monday mornings). In Madrid and other cities, some shops close for the whole of August, when most people are on holiday.

FOOD

The hallmark of Spanish cooking is the use of fresh local produce and not surprisingly, shopping for food (and eating) is a labour of love in Spain, where the range and quality of fresh food is unsurpassed. Many Spanish housewives shop daily, not because it's necessary, but out of enjoyment and the opportunity to socialise. The Spanish housewife has traditionally preferred to shop in small specialist food shops and markets, rather than in large soulless supermarkets and hypermarkets, although this is changing. Some

70 per cent of food in Spain is now purchased in self-serve supermarkets and hypermarkets and the days of the family-run shop are numbered. Those that remain survive by offering a friendly and personal service (advice, tastings, etc.), stocking local fare and providing better quality than supermarkets.

If you wish to save money on your weekly food bill, it isn't only what you buy, but where you shop that's important. In general, it's best to shop at markets and small stores where the Spanish shop. It takes more time, but is better value than shopping at supermarkets and the quality is also usually better. It helps if you speak some Spanish, although it's easy to point and say *un kilo* or *medio kilo* (half a kilo). In some areas, foreign food shops operate clubs allowing members to buy food at wholesale prices.

The Spanish haven't developed a taste for foreign foods and are parochial in their food tastes. Consequently, Spain doesn't import a lot of foreign foods, although there are specialist imported food shops in major cities and resorts with many foreign residents. Most supermarkets offer a selection of foreign foods, but don't expect to find shelves packed with imported meat, cheese or wine. If you insist on buying expensive imported foods, your food bill will skyrocket.

Meat

Pork (*carne de cerdo*) is the most widely consumed meat in Spain (see below) and, with chicken, the cheapest. Veal (*carne de ternera*) is also fairly common, although expensive. Beef (*carne de vaca*) and lamb (*carne de cordero*) are expensive, but usually tasty and free of BSE (although there have been isolated outbreaks). Suckling pig (*cochinillo*) and baby lamb (*cordero*) are favourite dishes in central Spain, where they're roasted in a wood or clay oven. Game is plentiful outside summer and fresh rabbit is available throughout the year. Kebab meat for barbecues is sold cubed and marinated.

Many villages and all towns have a butcher's shop (*carnicería*) selling all kinds of meat, although generally speaking, pork is the preserve of the *charcutería* (see below). Chicken (*pollo*) and eggs (*huevos*) are sold in specialist shops called *pollerías*; eggs are also sold in a *huevería* (egg shop). A *casquería* sells offal such as a bull's testicles (*cojones* – considered a delicacy in Spain) and also the meat of bulls killed during bullfights (*toro/carne de lidia*), which isn't sold in an ordinary butcher's shop (but is available in some supermarkets).

Meat is cut differently in Spain than in many other countries and is seldom pre-cut and packaged in a butcher's shop (as it is in supermarkets). Meat is usually purchased 'on the bone' or minced. Cold meat is sold by weight or by the slice (*rodaja*). Like most foods in Spain, the range of meat varies with the region, and butchers are happy to give advice on its preparation and cooking.

Pork

Pork can be purchased from a specialist pork butcher (*charcutería*), who also sells cold meats (*fiambres*) and cheese (*queso*). Spanish raw ham is renowned and among the best in the world, although the best types are expensive. The finest Spanish ham is named after the town where it's produced, e.g. *jamón Serrano* and *jamón de Jabugo*. It's similar to Parma ham and is widely used in Spanish recipes. Cured processed ham (*jamón de York*) is also good and much cheaper than raw ham. You can buy smoked ham or bacon (*beicon*) in Spain, although it's usually of the streaky variety. Spain is also famous for its sausages, such as *chorizo* (spicy paprika) and *morcilla* (blood, sometimes with nuts). The large *chorizo* sausage is similar to salami and is intended for slicing and eating raw; a red string indicates hot and a white string mild.

Fish

The Spanish are great fish eaters and generally eat fish around three times a week. It's usually bought from a fishmonger (*pescadería*), although shellfish is also sold at seafood restaurants (*marisquería*), which sell cooked and uncooked seafood, as well as *tapas*.

Fish is surprisingly expensive in Spain due to poor local catches and restrictive EU quotas, which mean that it must be caught in remote fishing grounds. Shellfish is reasonably priced. Fish is invariably excellent throughout Spain, even in Madrid, where fresh fish is delivered daily from the coasts.

The most common fish include bass, dorado, hake, grouper, monkfish, mullet, sea bream, salmon, sardines and trout, although they vary with the region. Note that the same fish may have different names in different parts of Spain or the same name may be used for different kinds of fish. The best areas for price and variety are Galicia and the Basque Country, where most of Spain's fish is landed. Fish is cut (*cortado*), cleaned (*limpiado*), gutted (*destripado*) and scaled (*descamado*) on request. Larger fish, such as swordfish and tuna, are usually sold in fillets (*filetes*) or slices (*rodajas*). In inland towns and villages, fish is commonly sold frozen. Canned fish is also popular, particularly tuna, of which there are numerous varieties.

Bread & Cakes

Bread (*pan*) is sold in a bakery (*panadería*) in Spain and is usually baked on the premises, even by supermarkets. A wide variety is available, although there are two main types; country bread (*pan chapata*), which is heavy and round and lasts several days, and *pan de barra*, which is a long, thin, crusty loaf similar to a French *baguette* that stays fresh for only a few hours. Among the many other types of bread available are wholemeal (*pan cateto* or *integral*), round peasant bread (*hogaza*), round bread (*gallegos*) and German bread (*pan alemán*), which is an extremely tasty dark wholegrain bread often sold in supermarkets.

There are also many regional styles of loaves, usually referred to simply as *pan*.

Sliced bread (*pan de molde*) isn't sold in a bakery, although most slice bread free on request. Bread is sold by weight and prices are similar throughout Spain. Many supermarkets have a bread counter where bread is often baked on the premises. Bakers also sell French-style croissants, cakes and tarts. A *bollería* sells bread and rolls (*bollos*). Traditionally, bread and pastries weren't sold in the same shop in Spain, although bakeries nowadays sell a wide range of cakes and biscuits. If you want pastries, you must usually go to a pastry or cake shop (*pastelería* or *confitería*), which sells sweet breakfast rolls, cakes, gateaux, fruit tarts, pastries, biscuits and sweets. The best cakes and pastries are found in Catalonia and Majorca, although in general, Spanish cakes aren't up to the standards of northern European countries. The larger pastry shops often incorporate a bar or tea room (*salón de té*).

A unique Spanish treat is fried doughnuts or long fluted shapes of lightly fried dough or fritters called *churros*, usually sold at a *churrería* and costing around €0.75 a serving. They're traditionally eaten with a cup of thick, sweet, hot chocolate in which it's 'obligatory' to dip your *churros*. They're an essential part of Spanish life, particularly on Sunday mornings in winter and in the small hours of the morning after a night on the town!

Fruit & Vegetables

Fruit and vegetables are best purchased from a market or a fruit and vegetable shop (*frutería*), rather than from supermarkets, where produce is often under-ripe or past its best. The variety and value of locally-grown fruit and vegetables in Spain is second to none, and most are available throughout the year (vegetarians can live cheaply in Spain). However, don't be influenced by the low prices and buy more than you can eat within a few days, as fruit and vegetables go off quickly in hot weather (unless stored in a refrigerator). It's easy to buy too much, particularly when prices are low, e.g. oranges at €0.75 a kilo, strawberries €1.50 a kilo, apples €1.20 a kilo, tomatoes €0.75 a kilo and lettuces for €0.40 each. Note that in small shops you shouldn't handle the produce unless invited to do so, although you can usually serve yourself.

Olive Oil

Olive oil (aceite de oliva) is part of the staple diet of Spaniards and merits a special mention. Spaniards consume around ten litres of olive oil per head each year (compared with around a third of a litre in many northern European countries) and have one of Europe's lowest number of deaths from heart disease (along with France, Italy and Portugal – all large consumers of olive oil). The finest quality is classified as virgen and is made by a single cold pressing. There are two grades of virgen oil, extra and fino, both green in colour. Extra has the least acidity and is the most expensive. Among the best olive oils are Sierra de Segura from Jaén and Borjas Blancas from Lérida, although most people have their own particular favourites. The finest oil is classified as pure olive oil (aceite puro de oliva). Refined (refinado) oil is blended with virgen oil and is light yellow in colour. Puro is a mixture of virgen and refined oil.

There are four controlled areas of production (denominación de origen) in Spain, although fine olive oil is also produced in other areas, and some 60 varieties. Olive oil can be purchased direct from producers, when you will usually be treated to a tasting as if you were buying wine. Olive oil has varying acidity (acidez), e.g. 0.3°, 0.4° or 0.5°, which are tasteless in salads and odourless in cooking (generally the lower the acidity, the better the olive oil). If you want more flavour, choose an acidity of 1°.

Apart from its use in cooking and as a salad dressing, olive oil is also used in rolls instead of butter, which goes off quickly in hot weather, and eaten on bread sprinkled with salt.

Cheese

There are some 300 varieties of cheese (queso) in Spain, although most are produced in tiny quantities and many are unknown outside Spain or the area of production. Despite the fact that cheese has been produced in Spain for over 3,500 years, the Spanish have the lowest consumption of cheese in Europe and over the years many varieties have simply vanished. Spanish cheese is mainly hard and Cheddar-like and most are an acquired taste. The hard salty manchego and similar cheeses are the most common (often served as a tapa) and can be old and ripened (añejo), cured (curado), milder and younger (semi curado) or very young (tierno). Other common cheeses are El Cigarral, similar to mild English Cheddar, Cabrales, a delicious blue sheep's cheese from Asturias, and Idiazábel from Navarra.

Although cow's cheese (queso de vaca) is the most common, Spain is renowned for its sheep (queso de oveja) and goats' (queso de cabra) cheeses, which are widely available. Many cheeses are often a mixture of cow and sheep's milk. Soft fresh cheeses are also made in many areas, although they aren't often seen in shops. A wide range of foreign cheeses is available in supermarkets, including Brie, Camembert, Cheddar, Danish Blue and Edam, plus numerous processed cheeses. Dairy products are generally more expensive in Spain than in other European countries.

Organic Food

Spain produces a vast amount of organic food, including fruit and vegetables, dairy products and meat, and an ever-growing number of farmers are switching their methods to organic farming. However, most of the organic food produced in Spain is for export (mostly to the UK and Germany) and only a small percentage of what's produced actually reaches the home market. As a consequence, organic food isn't only expensive, sometimes three times its non-organic price, but also difficult to obtain.

a delicatessen selling dairy foods, wines and liqueurs (often combined with a bar). Remote areas are served by mobile shops (*venta ambulante*), which travel around the countryside selling fresh bread, meat, fish, fruit and vegetables, in addition to preserved foods.

ALCOHOL

Drinking is an integral part of everyday life in Spain, where most people have a daily tipple. Low taxes mean that Spain has the cheapest alcohol in the EU – even cheaper than buying it duty-free. Whatever your poison, you will find something to suit your taste among the many excellent wines, beers, spirits and liqueurs produced in Spain or the numerous imported beverages. Spain is, however, most famous for its wine, particularly its sherry.

Sherry

Sherry (*jerez*) is world famous and Spain's most celebrated export, which has been produced for hundreds of years (dominated by the English since the 16th century). Sherry takes it name from Jerez de la Frontera in Andalusia where it's produced and where three-quarters of the population is employed in its production in some way or another. It's produced mainly from the Palomino grape, which is also the only vine that the chalky soil in the south-west region of Spain will support. Sherry is matured in oak barrels and produced from a variety of vintages, using the unique *solera* method of production of progressively blending young and old wines.

There are various types of sherry to suit most tastes and occasions. Dry (*fino* or *seco*) and the medium dry (*amontillado*) are usually drunk chilled as an aperitif, while the sweet *oloroso* and *dulce* (brown, cream or amoroso) are drunk at room temperature as after dinner drinks. There's also a dry (*seco*) variety of *oloroso*. The very dry *manzanilla* has a slightly salty after taste, attributed to the salty soil of the coastal area in Sanlúcar de Barrameda where it's produced. Sherry lovers can tour the wineries (*bodegas*) in Jerez for a few euros and enjoy tastings.

In large cities, there are some specialist shops and large supermarket chains such as Alcampo and Hipercor stock a limited number of products. Organic eggs and chicken are relatively easy to buy and most supermarkets stock them. If you don't live near an organic food outlet, try local markets, particularly in small villages or buy direct from small farms after ensuring their produce really is organic.

Miscellaneous Food Shops

A general store (*alimentación* or *ultramarino*) sells dairy foods, hams and other cured meats, wine, canned and packaged goods, and sometimes fresh produce and meat. In towns, many general stores have become small self-service supermarkets. A *bombonería* is a sweet shop or candy store selling a delicious assortment of hand-made chocolates, truffles and candies, all guaranteed to wreck your diet and your teeth. A *heladería* is an ice cream parlour, usually selling homemade ice cream and often combined with a café or bar. They're popular and ubiquitous in resort areas.

A *herbario* is a herb and spice shop, a *lechería* a dairy shop and a *mantequería*

Wine

Spain has a 2,000-year history of wine production and has more acres (around 20m) of vineyards than any country in the world, although it rates third after France and Italy in wine production. An extraordinary diversity of wines is produced in Spain, due to the country's different climatic and soil conditions, matched by few other nations. While most aren't as famous as the wines of France and some other countries, the best Spanish wines compare favourably with many classic foreign wines. Although Spain still produces oceans of mediocre 'plonk' and Spanish wine has a generally poor international reputation, it also makes some of the best value-for-money wines in Europe, including many great wines.

The quality of Spanish wine has improved enormously in the last few decades, during which modern methods of production and the introduction of new grape varieties (such as chardonnay and cabernet sauvignon) have transformed wine production. However, some cheaper red wines are unreliable and it isn't unusual to find bad (e.g. corked) bottles.

Classification

Spain has some 70 wine-producing regions, 65 of which are officially designated areas with a *Denominación de Origen (DO)* classification, indicated by a small map on the back label (labels also contain official seals, such as Rioja's 'stamp'). Regulations relating to *DO* regions include the type of grapes that can be used, yield per hectare, minimum alcohol strength, permissible amount of natural sugar, maturity process and period, bottling and labelling. Wine from another region cannot be mixed with a *DO* wine. There's also a further quality classification, *Denominación de Origen Calificada (DOC)*, which has so far been awarded only to Rioja.

The designation *vino de mesa* applies to blended wine or wine made from grapes grown in unclassified vineyards, while *vino de la tierra* is local wine from a defined area that doesn't qualify for a *DO*. Note, however, that there are many excellent Spanish wine producers who choose not to belong to a *Denominación de Origen* or who produce wines that contain grape varieties which aren't permitted under *DO* regulations.

Production Areas

Nearly every region produces wine, from sweet dessert whites to dry reds, modest table wines to fine vintages. Spanish wine regions fall into three main areas: the north, where the best wines are produced, containing the regions of Rioja, Penedés, Tarragona, Ribera del Duero and Galicia; the central zone, including La Mancha, Valdepeñas, and the coastal region of the Levante, containing half of Spain's total vineyards and producing some 35 per cent of its wine and the dry southern zone which produces (almost exclusively) aperitif and dessert wines, including sherry.

Rioja

The most famous Spanish red (*tinto*) wine is Rioja, a strong wine high in tannin, often with a distinctive 'oaky' flavour (from the oak barrels). Some 40 per cent of Rioja is aged in barrels, the rest being drunk within one or two years of bottling. Few Spanish wines can match Rioja for price and quality and many connoisseurs believe that vintage Riojan wines can hold their own with the best France has to offer and account for nearly 40 per cent of Spanish wine sales. You usually cannot go wrong with Rioja and even the cheapest young wines are highly palatable. Good white (*blanco*) wines are also produced in Rioja, which is subdivided into three geographical areas (or sub-regions) of production: Alavesa, Alta and Baja.

Like the best French wine-producing regions, Rioja declares an annual vintage, classified as follows: poor (*mediana*), normal, good (*buena*), very good (*muy buena*) and excellent (*excelente*).

Riojas are generally released at their optimum drinking time and don't need to be kept for years before they can be enjoyed, although some good quality (aged) wines will continue to improve for 7 to 20 years. Riojan red wines are divided into four categories depending on the amount of aging they've undergone. The best Riojan wines are labelled *reservas* or *gran reservas* and they can reach high prices for exceptional years. *Gran reservas* (which account for just 3 per cent of total production) spend a minimum of two years maturing in oak barrels and four more in the *bodega* before being sold. A *reserva* spends at least a year in the barrel and three in the *bodega* and a *crianza*, at least a year in the barrel and another in the bottle. A *sin crianza* or *conjunto de varias cosechas* (*CVC*) wine isn't aged (it spends no time in oak and is fermented in stainless steel vats) and is made from a combination of vintages.

There's a huge number and variety of Riojan red and white wines, most of which are excellent quality and value for money – part of the enjoyment is experimenting and finding those that best suit your palate and pocket!

For those wanting more information, there's a Rioja Wine website (🖳 www.riojawine.com), available in Spanish, English, French and German.

Sparkling Wines

Spanish sparkling wine made by the *méthode champenoise* or *método tradicional* is called *cava* and is often as good as French champagne and at around €5 a bottle it's much cheaper. *Cava* was actually marketed as champagne (*champán* or *méthode champenoise*) for many years, although this was prohibited after complaints from the French. It isn't, however, an inferior Spanish 'champagne', but a quality sparkling wine in its own right (it's also made with different grapes from champagne). It's usually less than a few years old and vintage *cava* is rare.

Among the best-known producers are Castellblanch, Codorníu and Freixenet (Carta Nevada and Cordón Negro are top brands). *Cava* is classified by its sweetness, which includes very dry (*brut de brut*, *brut nature*, *brut reserva*, *vintage*), dry (*brut*), fairly dry (*seco*), semi-dry (*semiseco*), semi-sweet (*semidulce*) and sweet (*dulce*). *Rosado* or *Rose*

denotes a pink wine. All *cava* wines come under the same *DO*, irrespective of where they're produced. Spain also produces lesser sparkling wines (*vinos gasificados*), which are carbonated white and rosé wines (not highly rated).

Other Wines

Other regions worthy of special mention include Penedés, where two-thirds of Catalonia's wine is produced. Penedés is renowned for its white wines, although it also produces good reds and much of Spain's premier sparkling wine (see above). The most famous producer in Penedés is Torres, who produce celebrated red (including Sangre de Torre and Gran Coronas) and white wines (e.g. Gran Viña Sol). The main difference between the wine produced in Rioja and Penedés is that vintage Riojan wines are aged in oak and Penedés wines in the bottle. However, Spain's most exclusive and expensive wines are produced by Vega Sicilia in the Ribera del Duero wine district. They cannot be purchased in shops and are allocated by the producer.

Priorato is also known for its excellent red wines. Navarra is famous for producing the best rosé wines in Spain (and is also becoming known for its reds), while Albariños of the Rías Baixas district in Galicia produces what many consider to be the best white wines in Spain. Rueda and Somontano are also noted for their white wines. Tarragona makes excellent dessert wines (*vinos generosos*) and the world's strongest red wine (up to 18 per cent proof).

Buying Wine

Most people buy their wine from supermarkets and hypermarkets, although the quality and range of wines on offer isn't usually outstanding. An off-licence (confusingly also called a *bodega*) usually has a larger selection of wines and other drinks than a supermarket, and the prices are usually comparable. Shops often have special offers, particularly around Christmas and New Year, when prices are reduced across the board. However, you should